Experience the California Coast

Beaches and Parks in Southern California

COUNTIES INCLUDED

LOS ANGELES · ORANGE · SAN DIEGO

Dedicated to Alan G. Sieroty, member of the California State Assembly (1967–1977) and State Senate (1977–1982), whose legislative achievements on behalf of California's coast reflect wisdom, inspiration, and unequaled foresight.

Experience the California Coast

Beaches and Parks in Southern California

COUNTIES INCLUDED

LOS ANGELES · ORANGE · SAN DIEGO

State of California

Arnold Schwarzenegger, *Governor*

California Coastal Commission

Peter Douglas, *Executive Director*   Susan Hansch, *Chief Deputy Director*

Steve Scholl
Editor and Principal Writer

Erin Caughman
Designer and Co-Editor

Jonathan Van Coops
Mapping and GIS Program Manager

Gregory M. Benoit
Principal Cartographer

Gabriel Buhr   Sylvie B. Lee
John Dixon, Ph.D.   Diana Lilly
Jonna Engel, Ph.D.   Ellen Lirley
Lesley Ewing, P.E.   Laurinda Owens
Jack Gregg, Ph.D.   Christiane Parry
Mark Johnsson, Ph.D.   Andrew Willis
Contributing Writers

Jo Ginsberg
Consulting Editor

Woodcuts by Tom Killion

Linda Locklin
Coastal Access Program Manager

University of California Press

Berkeley   Los Angeles   London

University of California Press, one of the most distinguished
university presses in the United States, enriches lives around the
world by advancing scholarship in the humanities, social sciences,
and natural sciences. Its activities are supported by the UC Press
Foundation and by philanthropic contributions from individuals and
institutions. For more information, visit www.ucpress.edu.

University of California Press
Berkeley and Los Angeles, California

University of California Press, Ltd.
London, England

Library of Congress Cataloging-in-Publication Data

Beaches and parks in Southern California : counties included, Los Angeles,
Orange, San Diego / Steve Scholl, editor and principal writer ... [et al.].
    p. cm. — (Experience the California coast guides ; 3)
"California Coastal Commission."
 Includes bibliographical references and index.
 ISBN 978-0-520-25852-5 (paper : alk. paper)
1. California, Southern—Guidebooks. 2. Pacific Coast
(Calif.)—Guidebooks. 3. Beaches—California, Southern—Guidebooks.
4. Beaches—California—Pacific Coast—Guidebooks. 5. Parks—California,
Southern—Guidebooks. 6. Parks—California—Pacific Coast—Guidebooks.
I. Scholl, Steve. II. California Coastal Commission.

  F867.B343 2009

  917.94'90454—dc22

                        2008043128

Printed in China.

18 17 16 15 14 13 12 11 10 09

10 9 8 7 6 5 4 3 2 1

The paper in this publication meets the minimum requirements of
ANSI/NISO Z39.48-1992 (R 1997) (Permanence of Paper).

Contents

San Diego County
211–331

Features

Santa Monica, Palisades Park

© Tom Killion

Introduction

SOUTHERN CALIFORNIA'S coast has more to see and do than even its greatest fans may realize. Besides the well-known beaches of soft sand, warmed by the sun and lapped by surf, the coast has hidden pocket beaches, historic lighthouses, rocky shore and tidepools, world-class aquariums, and much more.

Since urban development of southern California began in the 19th century, major ports have been built where originally there were no harbors, and wide, sandy beaches have been created in some spots through placement of sand along stretches of once-narrow shore. Facilities for boating, swimming, and water-skiing have been created, drawing visitors, but often displacing highly productive wetlands. At the beginning of the 21st century, a hopeful trend in some locales involves the restoration of lost or damaged natural resources, some only lately recognized for their value to the environment and to our quality of life. Restoration and enhancement efforts are on-going at coastal wetlands such as Ballona in Los Angeles County, Bolsa Chica in Orange County, and the coastal lagoons of San Diego County.

This guidebook tells you what coastal resources are at each location and what you might do there. The book is meant to encourage all coastal visitors, whether equipped with beach blanket, binoculars, or bodyboard, to explore the richness and diversity of the California coast.

The state of California owns all tidelands, submerged lands, and the beds of inland navigable waters, holding them for "public trust" uses that include fishing, navigation, commerce, nature preserves, swimming, boating, and walking. Tidelands consist of the area on a beach or rocky coastline that is between the mean high tide line and the mean low tide line. The California Constitution guarantees the public's access to tidelands, although the state or other land manager may place restrictions on the time, place, and manner of use of tidelands.

Private property exists along parts of the California coast, inland of the tidelands. The public generally does not have a right to cross private property without permission to get to tidelands, although easements and other legal provisions allow public use of some private shoreline properties; see entries that follow for more information. This guidebook lists over 450 beaches and coastal accessways, all that are known to be publicly owned or otherwise open to the public along the coast of Los Angeles, Orange, and San Diego Counties. Not included here are a few commonly used trails over which the public lacks a legal right of access. In addition to all public coastal accessways, this book includes many wildlife reserves, marinas, maritime museums, and public parks near the shore.

All along the three counties described in this book, air temperatures are very mild. At Santa Monica, average high temperatures range from 69 degrees Fahrenheit in January to 79 degrees in July; at San Diego, average highs range from 64 degrees in January to 76 degrees in July. Rainfall on the southern California coast occurs generally in very modest amounts and usually only between December and March. Ocean water temperatures at most southern California beaches range in the summer from the mid-60s to about 70 degrees Fahrenheit.

Dogs also enjoy coastal outings, but their inquisitive nature can create hazards for coastal wildlife. In state parks, dogs must be kept on leashes that are no more than six feet long and in a tent or enclosed vehicle at night. Except for guide dogs, pets are not allowed in state park buildings, on trails, or on most beaches. Although allowed in some city and county beach parks, dogs may be subject to leash requirements. Please observe posted signs regarding dogs on trails and beaches and in parks. For more information on beaches and other attractions that allow dogs, check the index for "beaches and parks, dog-friendly." Glass containers and alcoholic beverages are prohibited on most urban beaches, and some communities prohibit smoking on the beach; check individual entries for more information.

The California Coastal Commission, along with the State Coastal Conservancy, the Department of Parks and Recreation, and the Department of Fish and Game, is charged with conserving, enhancing, and making available to the public the beaches, accessways, and resources of the coast. The Coastal Commission's responsibilities under the law known as the California Coastal Act include providing the public with a guide to coastal resources and maintaining an inventory of paths, trails, and other shoreline accessways available to the public. This book furthers those purposes, as do the first two books in the California Coastal Commission's new guidebook series, *Experience the California Coast, A Guide to Beaches and Parks in Northern California* and *Beaches and Parks from Monterey to Ventura*, as well as the previously published *California Coastal Resource Guide* and *California Coastal Access Guide*. The California Coastal Commission, the State Coastal Conservancy, and local governments in the three-county region addressed by this book continue to press for increased opportunities for legal, safe access to the beach.

Many commercial outfitters sell or rent surfboards, kayaks, bicycles, and other recreational gear. These facilities are too numerous to include by name here; check local yellow pages or Internet search services to find what you need. The editors welcome suggestions for future editions (see p. 333).

For an economical overnight stay, this guide lists hostels, state and local campgrounds, and, as space permits, private campground facilities. Campsites in public or private parks include family camps, group camps, sites with RV hookups, walk-in environmental campsites, hike or bike sites, and enroute (overflow) spaces. Many can be reserved in advance. Visitors are encouraged to check with clearinghouses such as the local visitor bureaus for additional campground listings; see the introduction for each county. Information about market-rate hotels, inns, eating establishments, and other visitor destinations is available from numerous other guidebooks and websites.

Enjoy your visits to California's spectacular coast. Keep safe by observing posted restrictions along hazardous stretches of shoreline. Remember that "sleeper" waves, meaning rogue waves of unexpected size, are a factor on the California coast. When possible,

For general information on state parks, including a list of camping and day-use fees and campgrounds available without a reservation, see: www.parks.ca.gov.

For state park camping reservations, call: 1-800-445-7275 (available 24 hours), or see: www.reserveamerica.com.

For other camping opportunities, see individual entries that follow.

For information on Hostelling International's facilities, see: www.hiayh.org.

swim near a lifeguard. When strolling the beach or checking out tidepools, make it a general rule not to turn your back on the ocean. Remember that large waves may wash over what look like safe spots on rocks and bluffs. Although lifeguard towers in many locations are staffed only during the summer months or on warm weekends, lifeguards patrol many parts of the southern California coast on a daily basis, year-round.

Natural conditions along the California coast are always changing, and the width of beaches and shape of bluffs can be altered by the seasonal movement of sand or by erosion. Coastal access and recreation facilities can be damaged by these forces, and trails, stairways, parking areas, and other facilities may be closed for repairs. When planning any trip to the coast, check ahead of time to make sure that your destination is currently accessible. Some facilities, such as park visitor centers, are run by volunteers and are open only limited hours; call ahead to check open times. Driving to the coast at peak periods can entail traffic and parking challenges; consider using public transit alternatives, which have increased in many locations in recent years; check with local transit providers for details.

This guide's purpose is to contribute to a better understanding of the importance of coastal resources, both to the quality of life for people and to the maintenance of a healthy and productive natural environment. This book is offered with the knowledge that a wide appreciation for the coast among Californians plays an important role in the protection and restoration of coastal resources.

Exploring tidepools at Crystal Cove State Park, Orange County

Using This Guide

Each group of sites is accompanied by a map and a chart of key facilities and characteristics. The "Facilities for Disabled" chart category includes wheelchair-accessible restrooms, trails, campsites, or visitor centers; text descriptions note where restrooms are *not* wheelchair accessible. The "Fee" category refers to a charge for entry, parking, or camping. Check the index for surfing spots, beaches with lifeguard service, and other recreational highlights. Most parks and recreational outfitters maintain websites, but URL addresses may change and space in the book is limited; use any Internet search engine to look for more information on facilities listed in this guide.

Brief introductions to coastal environments such as beaches, rocky shore, and coastal lagoons are included, along with highlights of plants, animals, and other resources that you may see there. For more information about the California coast, consult the Bibliography and Suggestions for Further Reading found on p. 341.

Sandy Beach / Rocky Shore / Trail / Visitor Center / Campground / Wildlife Viewing / Fishing or Boating / Facilities for Disabled / Food and Drink / Restrooms / Parking / Fee

Marine biologist doing owl limpet survey at Point Loma, San Diego County

Caring for the Coast

CAN YOU IMAGINE California without the coast? Our state is in many ways defined by its coastline, which provides us with endless enjoyment, beauty, solace, and adventure. It is easy to take this for granted. But what have you done for the coast lately? You can contribute to its good health by developing an awareness of how it is affected by your everyday actions, and striving to act in ways that will have beneficial results. Here are some tips. For more ideas and to take the Coastal Stewardship Pledge, visit www.coastforyou.org or call 1-800-COAST-4U.

Stash Your Trash

Each year, thousands of marine animals die after becoming entangled in or ingesting debris. Plastic is particularly harmful because it does not biodegrade. When exposed to the elements, plastic breaks up into smaller and smaller pieces, but these particles persist. Researchers have found alarming quantities of small plastic pieces in the open ocean, where they circulate continuously unless and until consumed by a bird, fish, or marine mammal.

Most of this debris comes from land and was carried to the ocean by rain, tides, or wind. Avoid contributing to this problem by always disposing of trash properly and by practicing the three "Rs"—reduce the waste you generate, buy reusable items, and recycle trash when possible. When going to the beach or out on a boat, bring a bag and pick up the debris you come across. Each piece you collect is one less hazard for a marine animal. Another way to help is to volunteer for a beach cleanup activity, such as Coastal Cleanup Day or the Adopt-A-Beach Program.

Teacher and student volunteers participating in a beach cleanup

Watch Your Step!

Certain types of coastal habitats and the wildlife that live there are especially sensitive to human encounters. To minimize your disturbance to these ecologically important places, please observe the guidelines that follow.

Coastal Wetlands

In southern California, population growth and associated coastal development have destroyed or degraded most of our coastal wetlands—a loss of greater than 90 percent, by some estimates. The remaining wetlands provide critical wildlife habitat and are a tremendous public resource. Wetlands can serve as a refuge for wildlife and for human visitors, too—a place to go for a respite from urban life, where you can experience nature and observe wildlife. This book describes many of these wetlands and the recreational opportunities available there. Take care when visiting wetlands; they are susceptible to damage if vegetation is disturbed by foot traffic, and sensitive wildlife species are vulnerable to disturbance by humans, dogs, and horses. When visiting wetlands, stay on prescribed pathways and boardwalks, and pay close attention to rules imposed by land managers. Where dogs are allowed, keep them leashed.

Upper Newport Bay

Tidepools exposed at low tide at Crystal Cove State Park

Tidepool Etiquette

Southern California tidepools offer the opportunity to see fascinating marine creatures at close range. However, given the high population density in southern California and the sensitivity of tidepool plants and animals to human contact, there is a real danger of these remarkable ecosystems being quite literally loved to death. It is critical that all visitors learn proper "tidepool etiquette." Please follow these rules when visiting tidepools, and help to educate other visitors as well.

• Watch where you step. Step only on bare rock or sand.

• Don't touch any living organisms. A coating of slime protects most tidepool animals, and touching the animals can damage them.

• Don't prod or poke tidepool animals with a stick. Don't attempt to pry animals off of rocks.

• Leave everything as you found it. Collecting tidepool organisms is illegal in most locations and will kill them. Cutting eelgrass, surfgrass, and sea palm is prohibited.

Watching Wildlife

Observing wild animals in their natural environment is a rare treat. To ensure that the encounter results in no harm to either the animal or the human observer, keep your distance and watch quietly. Stay clear of mothers with young, and never surround an animal, or trap an animal between a vessel and shore. Leave pets at home, or keep them on a leash and away from wildlife. Never feed wild animals. If a marine mammal appears sick, resist the temptation to "save" it. Instead, seek help from a professional. In Los Angeles County, call: 310-548-5677; in Orange County, call: 949-494-3050; in San Diego County, call: 1-800-541-7325.

Sensible Seafood Choices

Increasing consumer demand for seafood has led to overfishing. Some fishing practices destroy habitat and harm non-target fish and animals. Use your purchasing power to support healthy oceans by selecting seafood that is harvested in a sustainable and environmentally responsible manner. For a pocket guide to sensible seafood choices, visit www.montereybayaquarium.org/cr/seafoodwatch.asp.

Non-point Source Pollution

Another way that people affect the health of the coast is through non-point source pollution, which gets flushed into the ocean by stormwater runoff. Minimize your contribution to this problem by taking simple actions; for example, use least-toxic gardening products, maintain your car to prevent oil leaks, and pick up after your dog.

Whale Tail License Plate

California drivers can help the coast by purchasing a Whale Tail License Plate. The plate funds coastal access trails, beach cleanups, habitat restoration projects, and coastal and marine education programs throughout California, including grants to local groups. For information, call: 1-800-COAST-4U, or visit www.ecoplates.com.

Original plate shown—new whale tail design expected in 2010

Map Legend

TRANSPORTATION

———————— Major Road
———————— Minor Road
———(1)——— California State Highway
———(101)——— United States Highway
———(580)——— Interstate
·—·—·—·—·—·—· Railroad

SHORELINE AND HYDROGRAPHY

———————— Shoreline
———————— Rivers and Streams

Pacific Ocean, Bays
Lakes, and Ponds

TRAILS AND BIKE WAYS

Hiking Trail
Hiking Trail Along State Highway
Hiking Trail Along Road

Pacific Coast Bicentennial
Bike Route
Bike Route Along State Highway
Bike Route Along Road

TOPOGRAPHY AND BATHYMETRY

0   500 1000 2000 4000 8000 11000 14500 Feet
0   150 300 600   1200 2400 3350 4400 Meters
Elevations approximate

Bathymetry
200 meter interval

-16000   -12000   -8000   -4000   0   Feet
-4800   -3600   -2400   -1200   0   Meters
Depths approximate

BOUNDARIES

═ ═ ═ ═ ═ ═ ═ County
═══════════ State
═══════════ International

Crystal Cove SP   Public Land

Marine Corp Base Camp Pendleton   Military Land

NORTH ARROW AND BAR SCALE

N

0   100   200 Miles
0   100   200 Kilometers

MARINE PROTECTED AREAS

At publication, the status of Marine Protected Areas located offshore along the southern
California coast, including offshore islands, is under review by the California Department
of Fish and Game. For information, see: www.dfg.ca.gov/mlpa or call: 916-654-1885.

DATA AND INFORMATION SOURCES

California Coastal Commission
California Department of Fish and Game
California Spatial Information Library
U.S. Geological Survey

Protected open space data provided by
the Southern California Open Space
Council and GreenInfo Network, 2007

Page opposite: Malibu Pier, Los Angeles County

Los Angeles County

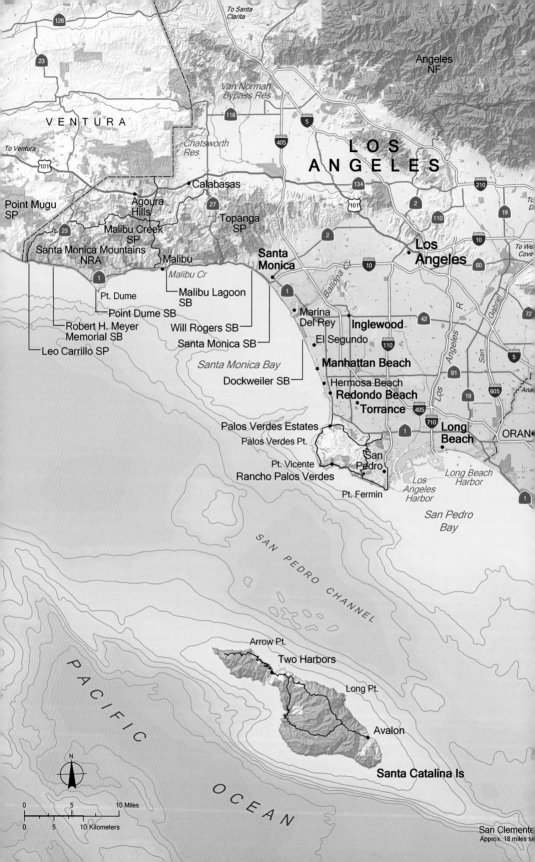

Los Angeles County

LOS ANGELES County, which includes 75 miles of mainland coast as well as Santa Catalina and San Clemente Islands, is America's most populous county. Over ten million residents, more than one out of four Californians, reside in Los Angeles County. Although the metropolitan area's rate of population growth has slowed since the great boom decade of the 1920s, when the city of Los Angeles more than doubled in population (from 577,000 to 1.2 million), Los Angeles has continued to grow. The county's residents are highly mobile: from 1995 to 2000, the number of those who moved their residence within the county or moved to the county from elsewhere was nearly as large as the number of those who stayed put.

The northwest coast of Los Angeles County consists of the rugged, largely undeveloped Santa Monica Mountains, which descend to a narrow ribbon of rocky and sandy shoreline. The adjacent coastline of Ventura County, which includes Point Mugu State Park, is similarly mountainous. To the east lies the intensely urbanized Los Angeles Basin, a broad, flat coastal plain formed by the Los Angeles, San Gabriel, and Santa Ana Rivers and Ballona Creek. The hills of the Palos Verdes Peninsula mark the southern end of Santa Monica Bay. East of Palos Verdes is San Pedro Bay, which once contained extensive wetlands at the mouths of the Los Angeles and San Gabriel Rivers. The bay is now the site of the ports of Los Angeles and Long Beach. Several miles of broad, sandy beach stretch from Long Beach southeast to Alamitos Bay. The coast of Los Angeles County has been dramatically altered in many places as a result of tremendous population growth and economic development.

As a recreation capital Los Angeles is known all over the world. Visitors to the area will find beautiful beaches, fishing piers, beach towns, famous surf breaks, and many other coastal attractions. As well-known as it is, the coast of Los Angeles still holds the unexpected. A lighthouse on a rocky shore, pocket beaches that are rarely crowded, and a century-old streetcar line running past mammoth ocean-going freighters can be found described in these pages. Up-to-date weather, surf, and tide reports for all Los Angeles County beaches are available at www.watchthewater.org.

Walk-in visitor centers are located in Hollywood at 6801 Hollywood Blvd. (323-467-6412) and in downtown Los Angeles at 685 S. Figueroa St. (213-689-8822), offering sight-seeing information and tickets to events.

The Port of Los Angeles has a visitor center at Berth 93, Pacific Cruise Ship Terminal, San Pedro (310-514-9484).

The Los Angeles County Metropolitan Transportation Authority offers an on-line trip planner at www.metro.net, or call: 1-800-266-6883.

Santa Monica Big Blue Bus; for information, call: 310-451-5444.

Beach Cities Transit (serving El Segundo, Manhattan Beach, Hermosa Beach, Redondo Beach, and Torrance); for information, call: 310-937-6660.

Long Beach Transit, 562-591-2301. From Dock 4 in Rainbow Harbor, Long Beach Transit provides Aqua Bus water taxi service to the *Queen Mary* and other destinations around Queensway Bay, and Aqua Link catamaran service to Alamitos Bay Landing.

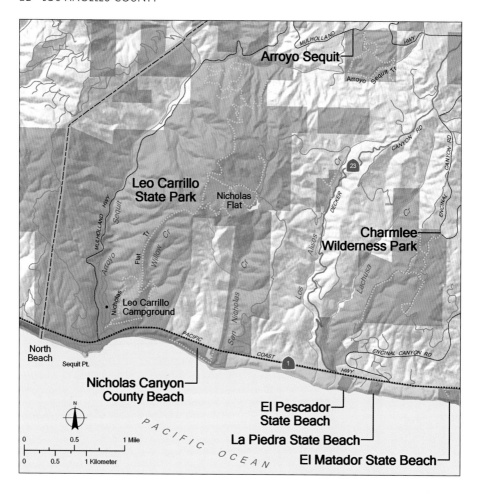

Leo Carrillo State Park

Leo Carrillo State Park to Meyer Memorial Beaches

	Sandy Beach	Rocky Shore	Trail	Visitor Center	Campground	Wildlife Viewing	Fishing or Boating	Facilities for Disabled	Food and Drink	Restrooms	Parking	Fee
Leo Carrillo State Park	•	•	•	•	•	•	•	•	•	•	•	•
Arroyo Sequit			•						•	•		
Nicholas Canyon County Beach	•						•	•	•	•	•	•
Charmlee Wilderness Park			•	•		•		•		•	•	•
El Pescador State Beach	•						•	•		•	•	•
La Piedra State Beach	•						•	•		•	•	•
El Matador State Beach	•		•				•	•		•	•	•

LEO CARRILLO STATE PARK: *36000 Pacific Coast Hwy., Malibu.* This well-equipped park offers a full range of recreational activities. There are two long sandy beaches, one on either side of Sequit Point, and smaller pocket beaches at the point. The beaches are popular for surfing, windsurfing, swimming, and diving. Lifeguards are on duty year-round; ask a lifeguard to borrow a beach wheelchair. At North Beach, on the upcoast side of Sequit Point, a volunteer-staffed visitor center is open on weekends from 10 AM to 3 PM.

At Sequit Point are sea caves and a natural tunnel, and near the point, tidepools support sea anemones, turban snails, limpets, crabs, and many species of algae. Naturalists give tidepool walks and other nature walks on selected weekends and offer special walks for school groups; for information, call: 805-488-1827. Beds of giant kelp grow offshore, providing habitat for fish including opaleye, kelp rockfish, olive rockfish, halfmoon, and cabezon, as well as a variety of invertebrates. Clear, turquoise waters make Leo Carrillo State Park an excellent diving and snorkeling area. The beaches are also popular with anglers. Commonly caught are calico bass and rockfish, which dwell on nearby reefs. Perch and croaker species and halibut are frequent shoreline catches. Fishing license required for those over 16 years of age. Gray whales migrate close to shore between November and May, and other marine mammals including pilot whales, orcas, dolphins, harbor seals, and sea lions also inhabit the ocean waters.

Inland of the beach, the stream known as Arroyo Sequit has been known to support spawning runs of steelhead trout. Casting their shade over Arroyo Sequit and Willow Creek are California bay, willow, black walnut, and western sycamore trees. Sunny

North Beach, Leo Carrillo State Park

Leo Carrillo State Park

slopes in the canyons hold chaparral and coastal sage scrub plants such as California sagebrush, laurel sumac, chamise, and mountain mahogany. Trails lead from the park entrance inland along Willow Creek to the Nicholas Flat Natural Preserve, where visitors may see acorn woodpeckers, quail, and red-tailed hawks. Hikers should bring plenty of water.

The park campground is set among shady trees. Facilities include 135 family campsites with tables and fire rings, hike-and-bike campsites, and a group campground; campsite 17 is wheelchair accessible. Ten family cabins are planned by 2009. Coin-operated hot showers are available. Campfire programs and a junior ranger program are offered during the summer months. A camp store is open year-round; hours are variable. Leashed dogs are allowed in the campground and on the beach, except between lifeguard towers 1 and 3. For park information, call: 818-880-0350. For camping reservations, call 1-800-444-7275.

ARROYO SEQUIT: *34138 Mulholland Hwy., Malibu.* Part of the Santa Monica Mountains National Recreation Area, this lovely park was acquired for public use by the Santa Monica Mountains Conservancy and transferred to the National Park Service. In spring there are meadows of wildflowers, and the stream known as Arroyo Sequit flows

all year. A mile-and-a-half-long loop trail is open to hikers and leashed dogs. Restrooms and picnic tables available. The park entrance is located on Mulholland Hwy. six miles from Pacific Coast Hwy. For information, call: 818-597-9192.

NICHOLAS CANYON COUNTY BEACH: *33850 Pacific Coast Hwy., Malibu.* A 23-acre sandy beach lies at the base of the bluff below Pacific Coast Hwy. Swimming, picnicking, and fishing are popular, as is surfing; locals know the beach as Point Zero. A fee parking lot with over 150 spaces is on the bluff, along with chemical toilets and a small paved observation area. A food truck is on site during the summer. A stairway and a wheelchair-accessible path lead down to the beach, which is also accessible from Leo Carrillo State Beach located upcoast. Lifeguard on duty during daylight hours. No alcohol, pets, or fires; park open 7 AM to 10 PM. For park information, call: 310-305-9546. For recorded diving and surf report, call: 310-457-9701.

CHARMLEE WILDERNESS PARK: *2577 S. Encinal Canyon Rd., Malibu.* Charmlee Wilderness Park, located high on the slopes of the Santa Monica Mountains, features a panoramic view of the coast and the Channel Islands. Picnic tables are placed to take advantage of the view. Hiking and equestrian loop trails, from less than a mile to about three miles in length, start at the parking area and continue through meadows and oak woodlands. The Nature Center houses interpretive displays, and there is a garden of labeled California native plants. Among the programs offered are wildflower hikes, monthly full moon hikes, and twilight marshmallow hikes. Reservations are required for programs; call: 310-317-1364.

Dogs on leash are allowed; no smoking, barbecues, or open flames. The sloping site is wheelchair accessible with assistance. Park is open 8 am to dusk; the Nature Center is open Saturday and Sunday, 9 AM to dusk. Fee for parking. Formerly a county park, this property is now managed by the City of Malibu; for information, call: 310-457-7247.

EL PESCADOR STATE BEACH: *32900 Pacific Coast Hwy., Malibu.* El Pescador, La Piedra, and El Matador State Beaches together make up the Robert H. Meyer Memorial State Beach. At El Pescador, picnic tables, a small fee parking lot, and restroom are on the bluff; a pedestrian trail, not wheelchair accessible, leads down the bluff to the sandy pocket beach, out of sight and sound of the highway. Open 8 AM to sunset. Dogs are not allowed on the beach. Call: 818-880-0350.

LA PIEDRA STATE BEACH: *32700 Pacific Coast Hwy., Malibu.* A nine-acre sandy beach lies at the base of the bluff, off Pacific Coast Hwy. A parking lot, picnic tables, and restrooms are on the bluff, and a non-wheelchair-accessible trail leads down the slope. Gulls, plovers, willets, and sanderlings feed along the shore.

EL MATADOR STATE BEACH: *32350 Pacific Coast Hwy., Malibu.* This is the largest of the three beaches that make up Robert H. Meyer Memorial State Beach. Like the other two, this park unit has a small parking lot, picnic tables, and restrooms on the bluff, and a non-wheelchair-accessible path leading down to the beach. The rocky bottom offshore supports beds of giant kelp and provides habitat for invertebrates such as gorgonian coral, anemones, keyhole limpets, and rock scallops. Kelp bass, senorita fish, and California sheephead also inhabit the nearshore waters. This long stretch of beach provides opportunities to fish for surf perch, corbina, and occasional inshore sharks and rays.

Elephant Rock, El Matador State Beach

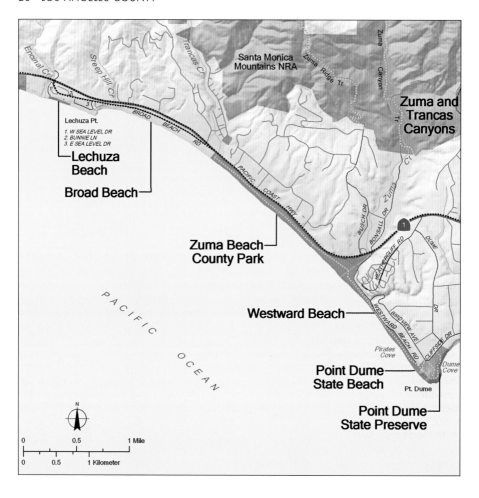

Dume Cove viewed from Point Dume

Point Dume

	Sandy Beach	Rocky Shore	Trail	Visitor Center	Campground	Wildlife Viewing	Fishing or Boating	Facilities for Disabled	Food and Drink	Restrooms	Parking	Fee
Lechuza Beach	•	•										
Broad Beach	•											
Zuma Beach County Park	•					•	•	•	•	•	•	•
Zuma and Trancas Canyons			•			•				•		
Westward Beach	•					•	•		•	•	•	
Point Dume State Beach	•	•	•			•	•		•	•	•	•
Point Dume State Preserve	•		•			•	•			•		

LECHUZA BEACH: *Broad Beach Rd. at West and East Sea Level Drives, Malibu.* This half-mile-long sandy beach, acquired on behalf of the public by the State Coastal Conservancy in 2000, is located seaward of a residential area, out of sight from Broad Beach Rd. There are three pedestrian beach access gates leading to Lechuza Beach. Gates are unlocked from dawn to dusk; push to open. One gate is located on West Sea Level Dr., a private street resembling a driveway that angles off Broad Beach Rd., 50 yards from Pacific Coast Hwy. The beach access gate is on the left-hand side of the lane. The second gate is on Broad Beach Rd., opposite Bunnie Ln. The third pedestrian gate is on Broad Beach Rd. adjacent to East Sea Level Dr., a private street. Street parking only; no facilities. Lechuza Beach is managed by the Mountains Recreation and Conservation Authority; call: 310-456-7049.

BROAD BEACH: *31344 and 31200 Broad Beach Rd., Malibu.* A long arc of sandy beach stretches from Lechuza Point to Point Dume. The County Dept. of Beaches and Harbors maintains two public stairways, located between residences, at the north end

Point Dume

of this long curving beach, known as Broad Beach. The accessways are located at 31344 and 31200 Broad Beach Rd., and they lead to the beach and ocean. Beach access gates are open from dawn to dusk. Respect private property. Street parking only; no facilities.

ZUMA BEACH COUNTY PARK: *30000 Pacific Coast Hwy., Malibu.* The largest and perhaps best-equipped beach park in Malibu, Zuma Beach County Park draws sunbathers, joggers, swimmers, and surfers in large numbers. Shore fishing, diving, and beach volleyball are also popular. From mid-March to late August, grunion spawn at the water's edge for several nights following a new or full moon. Anglers catch California corbina, opaleye, and barred and shiner surfperch.

Several beach cafés operate in the park. Facilities include restrooms, beach showers, and children's play equipment. Swimmers and surfers should be cautious of the rough waters and hazardous rip currents. Lifeguards are on duty during daylight hours, year-round. Recorded information on surfing and diving conditions is updated regularly; call: 310-457-9701. No alcohol, pets, or fires are allowed on the beach. Park hours are 7 AM to 10 PM. The fee parking lot has more than 2,000 spaces, including disabled parking spaces; beach wheelchair available at headquarters. Limited shoulder parking is also available on Pacific Coast Hwy. where not prohibited by signs.

ZUMA AND TRANCAS CANYONS: *Ends of Busch Dr. and Bonsall Dr., Malibu.* From the end of Busch Dr., the Zuma Ridge Trail leads some five miles inland to the Backbone Trail, near Encinal Canyon Rd. Parcels of private property are located within the canyons; note private property signs. Other trails, accessible from the ends of Busch Dr. and Bonsall Dr., lead into Zuma Canyon and to the Kanan-Edison and Zuma-Edison Roads, making a loop with the Zuma Ridge Trail. Another entry point to the canyons is at a signed parking area on the west side of Kanan Dume Rd., four and one-half miles from Pacific Coast Hwy., where the Backbone Trail crosses Kanan Dume Rd. Hikers should bring plenty of water. Dogs allowed on leash; all leashes, including retractable ones, must be six feet or less in length. For information, call: 818-597-9192.

WESTWARD BEACH: *Along Westward Beach Rd., Malibu.* Also known as "Free Zuma," this quarter-mile-long stretch of wide sandy beach can be reached from adjacent Westward Beach Rd., where limited parking is available along the road shoulder. The beach is managed by the County of Los Angeles. Restrooms and vending machines are located at the upcoast end of the beach near Westward Beach Rd.

POINT DUME STATE BEACH: *End of Westward Beach Rd., Malibu.* This wide sandy beach is managed by Los Angeles County

The state of California owns all tidelands, submerged lands, and the beds of inland navigable waters, holding them for "public trust" uses. Tidelands consist of the area on a beach or rocky coastline that is between the mean high tide line and the mean low tide line. The public has the right to use all lands seaward of the mean high tide line. In addition, portions of the privately owned dry sandy beach are available for some public uses, because of legal public access easements and deed restrictions.

For example, to view a detailed exhibit showing public use areas at Broad Beach or Carbon Beach, both in Malibu, follow the link to the Coastal Access Program on the California Coastal Commission's website at www.coastal.ca.gov; the website is occasionally updated. Members of the public using tidelands should exercise caution when there is a potential for encroaching on private land, just as private land owners should be cautious in questioning the public's right to be on areas of the beach covered by public rights.

Westward Beach

Dept. of Beaches and Harbors. Restrooms with outdoor showers and vending machines are located next to the parking lot; lifeguards on duty during daylight hours. Fee for parking.

POINT DUME STATE PRESERVE: *Cliffside Dr., Malibu.* This state park unit has limited facilities, but great views, beautiful native plants, and access to the beach at Dume Cove. The top of the promontory at Point Dume is a splendid location to look for whales, watch kayakers near the point, or enjoy vistas of beaches and shoreline up and down the coast. Extensive kelp beds grow on the rocky reef offshore, providing habitat for kelp bass, halfmoon, and mackerel.

A gravel path leads from Cliffside Dr. up a gentle slope to the top of the hill. Another path leads to the edge of the bluff overlooking Dume Cove, and a stair and trail provide access down the bluff to this somewhat remote, east-facing beach. Giant coreopsis, a peculiar native plant, is widespread at Point Dume. Much of the year, the plants look like little more than brittle, thick brown stumps, but in springtime they blossom forth with masses of brilliant yellow daisy-like flowers.

There are ten time-limited parking spaces on the shoulder of Cliffside Dr. adjacent to Point Dume State Preserve, including a disabled parking space; roadside parking is not permitted on surrounding streets. Visitors may do better to park at Point Dume State Beach and hike the trail that winds up the bluff from the south end of the parking lot to Cliffside Dr., a distance of less than one-quarter mile. Another option is to utilize the city of Malibu's free shuttle service that links the Point Dume State Beach parking lot with the Point Dume State Preserve. The shuttle operates daily from Memorial Day to Labor Day, 11 AM to 7 PM, and on weekends and holidays (except Thanksgiving, Christmas, and New Year's Day) during the remainder of the year, 11 AM to about 5 PM. The shuttle is a bright yellow taxi van. On Westward Beach Rd., the van driver picks up passengers opposite the foot of Birdview Ave. and departs on the hour and the half-hour. Wave to flag the driver down.

The Ocean

S OUTHERN CALIFORNIA owes its mild climate to the moderating effects of the Pacific Ocean, the largest body of water on our planet. Off southern California, the often-placid Pacific Ocean earns its name. Beneath the nearshore ocean is a complex seafloor known as a "continental borderland," which features islands, banks, troughs, seamounts, submarine canyons, shelves, and basins as deep as 8,000 feet below sea level. The ocean waters above the Southern California borderland extending from Point Conception in Santa Barbara County some 357 miles to Cabo Colnett in Baja California are called the Southern Californa Bight. The California Current, which flows southeasterly, roughly parallel to the coast and along the outer edge of the continental borderland, marks the outer boundary of the Southern California Bight.

Consider existence in a three-dimensional world of water that abounds with living organisms. Because visibility rarely exceeds 100 feet, partly because of the huge numbers of tiny plants and animals suspended in the water, ocean organisms rely for survival more on sound detection than on their sense of sight. Highly developed hearing and sound detection organs help an organism to detect predators or prey, navigate, stun and catch prey, find mates, socialize, and communicate. Ocean water is some 3,500 times denser than air, and sound travels five times faster in the ocean than in the air. Portions of the water column bounded by abrupt temperature and pressure changes serve as sound-fixing and ranging channels, which concentrate sound and enable it to travel long distances while losing little energy. Whales utilize these channels to communicate across miles of ocean. Due to the high density of water, many of the ocean's animals lack structural support, because the water serves that purpose. Some have skeletons, which provide a place for muscles to attach or help protect against predators.

The offshore ecological realm that includes the entire ocean water column is known as the pelagic zone. Pelagic life is found throughout the water column, although the numbers of individuals and species decrease with depth. The pelagic zone is broken for study purposes into sub-zones, primarily based upon light penetration. The epipelagic (or photic) zone, where the most light penetrates, extends from the surface to approximately 600 feet below the surface. This is where photosynthesis takes place and where

El Porto Beach

plants and animals are concentrated. Plankton, pinnipeds, whales, dolphins, and many species of fish, including tuna and swordfish, can all be found in the epipelagic zone.

The mesopelagic (or twilight) zone which extends from approximately 600 to 3,000 feet deep, supports the lanternfish, viper or dragonfish, hatchet fish, snipe eel, squid, and krill. The bathypelagic (or deep) zone, which is almost entirely dark, reaches from 3,000 to 12,000 feet below the sea's surface, and is inhabited by the anglerfish, fangtooth fish, vampire squid, giant squid, and slime stars. Biodiversity drops precipitously with greater depth, from the mesopelagic into the bathypelagic zone, where unique adaptations for high-pressure living in darkness are required. Even though these deep zones appear to support lower diversity than the photic zone, deep sea explorations continue to discover new and remarkable creatures.

Pelagic organisms exhibit many interesting adaptations for life in the ocean. Floating and drifting is one such adaptation. "Planktonic" organisms move at the mercy of ocean currents, thus saving themselves a lot of energy. Most plankton are microscopic, but larger organisms, such as jellyfish and salps (also known as pelagic tunicates), are included in this group; individual salps may reach six inches in length, and a chain of salps may be up to 100 feet long.

Like a spider weaving a web, some plankton capture prey by secreting a net of mucus, which, when full, is slurped back into the animal's mouth for digestion. Bioluminescence is another adaptation found in many organisms in the open ocean, especially those that live in deep water. Bioluminescence occurs when light is chemically created within special organs. The light serves several functions, including to illuminate or attract prey, recognize and attract mates, startle or distract predators, or camouflage an organism by enabling it to blend in with filtered light from above.

Counter-current heat exchange is an adaptation that enables the "cold-blooded" tuna to warm its own circulatory system and to swim at great speed, with a muscle system that is more like that of a warm-blooded animal. Counter-shading, characteristic of many ocean creatures, consists of a dark dorsal, or upper, body surface combined with a light ventral, or under, surface. Counter-shading serves as camouflage, for when a potential predator looks down, a dark surface is hard to see, and when it looks up, a light surface is hard to see.

While much of the open sea contains limited nutrients, the ocean abutting the southern California coast is often high in nutrients moved there by wind and wave action and by coastal upwelling. As a result, the nearshore ocean is a biologically rich area with a diverse food web. Bacteria and phytoplankton are primary producers that use sunlight to synthesize sugars and oxygen; these creatures, along with viruses, form the base of the ocean food chain. They are preyed upon by zooplankton, which in turn are fed upon by a huge variety of animals, including other zooplankton, squid, fishes, turtles, whales, and seabirds. Pinnipeds, dolphins, and many whales rely primarily on squid and fish as their prey. It is one of the wonders of the sea that some of the largest animals on earth, including the blue, fin, humpback, and gray whale, survive by eating zooplankton, including krill, which are some of the smallest animals on earth.

Southern California is indebted to the Pacific Ocean for more than its climate. Both commercial and recreational fishing are big industries in southern California. The ocean is a source of oxygen; over 50 percent of the world's oxygen comes from phytoplankton in the ocean. The ocean provides nearly endless recreational opportunities for the public.

Short-beaked common dolphin

The **short-beaked common dolphin** (*Delphinus delphis*) is the most abundant dolphin species, inhabiting tropical and temperate seas across the planet. This species has an elaborate color pattern consisting of a dark gray dorsal surface with a light gray flank and yellowish tan front that form an hourglass pattern along the dolphin's side. Common dolphins reach eight feet in length and live over 35 years. This is a very social species, often found in groups numbering over 1,000 individuals. Prey includes squid and small pelagic fish. Common dolphins are fast and active and are often seen "surfing" the bow wakes created by boats.

Blue shark

The **blue shark** (*Prionace glauca*) is the most abundant species of pelagic shark found off California. This shark has wide-ranging migration patterns and can be found from the Gulf of Alaska to the Chilean coast. It reaches a length of 12 feet and can live over 20 years. Blue sharks exhibit a counter-shading coloration pattern with a dark blue dorsal surface and a white ventral coloration. Female blue sharks give birth to broods varying from four to well over a hundred pups. Blue sharks are viviparous, meaning the young develop in the mother's body, rather than in eggs. Blue shark pups are 18 inches long at birth and emerge as completely developed, independent sharks. Common food sources for blue sharks include fishes and squids, as well as marine mammal carrion when available.

White seabass

The **white seabass** (*Atractoscion nobilis*), which can grow to five feet in length and more than 70 pounds in weight, is the largest member of the croaker family found on the Pacific Coast. The fish is neither white nor a true bass, and its common name likely arose because of the firm white flesh that is renowned as excellent table fare. Prior to and during spawning a male emits a loud croaking noise to signal the female of his intentions. The croaking is produced by a special sonic muscle that creates sound by massaging the air-filled swim bladder of the male fish. Because the white seabass is slow-growing and reaches maturity only after a prolonged period, the species is susceptible to overfishing. Take restrictions, prohibition of nearshore gill nets, and stock enhancement have helped the population of white seabass to show signs of recovery.

The **California flying fish** (*Cypselurus californicus*) is a member of the Exocoetidae family. It exhibits the ability to "fly," a trait unique to this family of fishes. The small, elongate fish are silvery blue in color and reach a maximum length of 15 inches. They have evolved long, wing-like pectoral and pelvic fins that assist in the escape behavior exhibited by this species. When startled, the flying fish rapidly vibrates its caudal, or tail, fin until it breaks the surface of the water; once airborne, the fish then utilizes its two pairs of "wings" to glide for distances over 200 yards. Flying fish are often attracted to bright lights after dark, and since the early 1920s tour boats out of Avalon on Santa Catalina Island have been taking tourists to observe the unusual flying fish of the California coast.

California flying fish

The **moon jelly** (*Aurelia aurita*) derives its name from the circular bell that resembles a full moon and constitutes the main body of this organism. The perimeter of the bell is lined by a fringe of short cilia that aid in the capture of food particles. Moon jellies reach a maximum size of 15 inches in diameter. They feed on various members of the plankton community, which are concentrated in the surface waters of the ocean. The moon jelly propels itself vertically in the water column with pulses of its bell that force water out from underneath the umbrella-shaped structure. Moon jellies, however, do not provide enough propulsion to swim against the ocean's currents and therefore drift passively throughout the ocean.

Moon jelly

The **sea gooseberry** (*Pleurobrachia* spp.) is a small, gelatinous, planktonic animal that resembles a jellyfish but is actually quite different—it is in the group of animals known as Ctenophores, meaning comb-bearing, or comb jellies. Comb jellies get their name from their eight pulsating rows of cilia, called "comb rows" that aid in locomotion. Sea gooseberries swim upward in a spiral, using tentacles to capture food. These unique and beautiful creatures, when viewed in an aquarium, appear opalescent as light reflects off their beating cilia. Sea gooseberries are egg-shaped and attain lengths of up to three-quarters of an inch. They have a broad distribution from Alaskan to Mexican waters and are found near the surface of the open ocean.

Sea gooseberry

Escondido Beach

Paradise Cove to Corral Canyon

	Sandy Beach	Rocky Shore	Trail	Visitor Center	Campground	Wildlife Viewing	Fishing or Boating	Facilities for Disabled	Food and Drink	Restrooms	Parking	Fee
Paradise Cove	•					•			•	•	•	•
Escondido Canyon Park			•							•		
Escondido Beach	•									•		
Latigo Point	•	•										
Solstice Canyon			•						•	•		
Malibu Beach RV Park					•		•		•	•	•	•
Dan Blocker County Beach	•	•								•		
Corral Canyon Park			•			•	•		•	•	•	

PARADISE COVE: *28128 Pacific Coast Hwy., Malibu.* A private sandy beach and fishing pier are located in a scenic cove, along with a full-service restaurant. Open daily, 8 AM to 10 PM on weekdays and 7 AM to 10 PM on Saturday and Sunday. Fee for parking and walk-ins; parking validation for restaurant diners. Surfboards, dogs, and boat launching not allowed. Lifeguards on duty during the summer. Call: 310-457-2503.

ESCONDIDO CANYON PARK: *Off Winding Way, Malibu.* This natural area features a waterfall, reached by a pleasant trail that follows the stream corridor of Escondido Canyon Creek. *Escondido* means "hidden" in Spanish. At trail's end, the water of the creek cascades down a rock face into a fern-fringed lower pool surrounded by western sycamore trees. A higher pool, largely out of sight from the lower one, receives the flow from a 150-foot-high waterfall.

A two-part hike is required to reach the falls. Park in the lot at the intersection of Winding Way and Pacific Coast Hwy. and then walk one mile uphill along the shoulder of private, residential Winding Way to the park entrance, where no vehicle parking is allowed. Walk through the park another mile under shady trees, crossing and recrossing Escondido Creek, to reach the falls. The trail is open to hikers and equestrians; dogs on leash are permitted. A picnic table is located near the park entrance; no other facilities. For information, call: 310-456-7049.

ESCONDIDO BEACH: *27400 block and 27150 Pacific Coast Hwy., Malibu.* A two-mile stretch of sandy Escondido Beach can be reached by two public accessways, both located adjacent to residential buildings. In the 27400 block of Pacific Coast Hwy., walk up a few steps from the road shoulder to a gate marked "Escondido Beach Access." Follow a level, narrow path to a steel stair structure, which leads down to the shore. The

Escondido Beach steel stair structure

View from Latigo Point

entrance gate is unlocked between dawn and dusk; visitors can exit at any time. On Pacific Coast Hwy. are two public parking spots reserved for beachgoers and accessible to eastbound vehicles only; park parallel. Additional shoulder parking is available farther west. Use caution when pulling into and out of roadside parking along busy Pacific Coast Hwy. Accessway maintained by the Mountains Recreation and Conservation Authority; no facilities. For information, call: 310-456-7049.

A second stair to the beach is located at 27150 Pacific Coast Hwy. on the east side of Escondido Creek. Limited roadside parking. Stairway gate is opened at dawn and locked at dusk by Los Angeles County Dept. of Beaches and Harbors; however, visitors can exit at any time. No facilities.

LATIGO POINT: *Latigo Shore Dr. and Pacific Coast Hwy., Malibu.* A long sandy beach and rocky Latigo Point can be reached from a stairway at the east end of a condominium complex on Latigo Shore Dr. The beach extends in both directions from the stairway. Walk east along the beach to Dan Blocker County Beach, and walk west from the stairway to a rocky intertidal area at Latigo Point, a popular surfing spot. At low tide, beachgoers can continue along the sandy beach west of Latigo Point.

The beach access stairway is maintained by the homeowners' association; the gate is open between dawn and dusk. Limited shoulder parking available on Pacific Coast Hwy.; dead-end Latigo Shore Dr. is a remnant of the old coastal highway and is usable by the public, although marked private. No facilities.

SOLSTICE CANYON: *3700 Solstice Canyon Rd., off Corral Canyon Rd., Malibu.* A unit of the Santa Monica Mountains National Recreation Area, this inland park contains picnic areas and hiking and equestrian loop trails leading into Solstice Canyon. Two parking areas are located off Corral Canyon Rd. Dogs on leash are allowed on trails. For information, call: 805-370-2301.

At the head of Solstice Canyon, with sweeping views, is the Castro Crest unit of the Santa Monica Mountains National Recreation Area. Take Corral Canyon Rd. to the end, where there is parking, a picnic area, and hiking and equestrian trails. The Backbone Trail links Castro Crest to Zuma and Trancas Canyons to the west and to Malibu Creek State Park to the east. Leashed dogs are allowed on trails.

MALIBU BEACH RV PARK: *25801 Pacific Coast Hwy., Malibu.* Campsites include 150 RV sites with full or partial hookups and 35 tent sites at this privately run facility inland of Dan Blocker County Beach. Campsites have views of the sea or mountains. Coin-operated laundry facilities, propane, picnic tables, showers, video game room, spa, and restrooms; barbecue grills are also available, but no wood fires are allowed. Overnight fee. Trails lead inland to Solstice Canyon and Corral Canyon parklands. For reservations, call: 310-456-6052.

DAN BLOCKER COUNTY BEACH: *26000 Pacific Coast Hwy., Malibu.* This narrow beach, nearly three-quarters of a mile long, is near the mouth of Corral Canyon. The beach, mostly of sand but partly cobble, is used by swimmers, surfers, anglers, and divers. Facilities are currently limited to shoulder parking and chemical toilets; lifeguard towers are staffed during daylight hours. For regularly updated recorded information on surfing and diving conditions, call: 310-457-9701. For information about beaches managed by Los Angeles County Dept. of Beaches and Harbors, call: 310-305-9503.

CORRAL CANYON PARK: *25623 Pacific Coast Hwy., Malibu.* Located on the inland side of Pacific Coast Hwy., this park offers visitors a view into an undeveloped watershed of the Santa Monica Mountains, as well as distant vistas of the ocean. The fee parking lot is located west of Corral Creek, next to the Malibu Seafood restaurant. Picnic tables, drinking water, and restrooms are next to the parking area. An equestrian loading and parking zone accommodates one horse trailer at a time. A loop trail, two-and-a-half miles long, winds up the canyon slopes through coastal sage scrub and native grassland habitats. Look for hawks overhead, searching for prey. A short segment of the trail follows Corral Creek, bordered by alder, coast live oak, western sycamore, and willow trees. In summer, there is pedestrian access to the beach under Pacific Coast Hwy., via a low-clearance underpass alongside Corral Creek. Call: 310-456-7049

Dan Blocker County Beach

Malibu is famous for its 26 miles of beaches, but at times you might wonder just where those beaches are. Many of them are tucked away behind a miles-long line of homes, out of sight and hearing from Pacific Coast Hwy. In addition to several large, well-equipped beach parks in Malibu, there are a dozen short pathways scattered along the Malibu shoreline that provide visitor access to beaches, including some that are typically uncrowded. To find these accessways, check the maps in this book and then look for the road signs erected by the County of Los Angeles, the Mountains Recreation and Conservation Authority, and the nonprofit group, Access for All, marking the entrances. On Pacific Coast Hwy., look for the Coastal Commission logo, a brown highway sign with a "foot and wave" symbol. Note that these pathway access points do not include off-street parking, restrooms, or any other amenities. Smoking, alcohol, and dogs are not permitted on beaches in Malibu, and fires are prohibited except at designated locations in Robert H. Meyer State Beach.

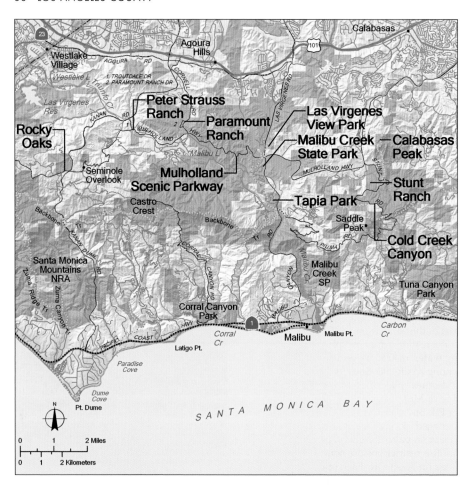

Malibu Creek Canyon

Santa Monica Mountains

	Sandy Beach	Rocky Shore	Trail	Visitor Center	Campground	Wildlife Viewing	Fishing or Boating	Facilities for Disabled	Food and Drink	Restrooms	Parking	Fee
Rocky Oaks			•			•	•		•	•		
Peter Strauss Ranch			•			•	•		•	•		
Paramount Ranch			•			•			•	•		
Mulholland Scenic Parkway										•		
Las Virgenes View Park			•							•		
Malibu Creek State Park			•	•	•				•	•		•
Tapia Park			•						•	•	•	
Calabasas Peak			•			•						
Cold Creek Canyon			•			•			•	•		

ROCKY OAKS: *Mulholland Hwy. and Kanan Rd., Santa Monica Mts.* This 200-acre park, part of the Santa Monica Mountains National Recreation Area, has picnic areas, drinking water, restrooms, and several loop trails among shady oak trees for hikers, bicyclists, and equestrians. The entrance is on the north side of Mulholland Hwy., just west of Kanan Rd. Smoking is prohibited on properties managed by the National Recreation Area, except on paved or gravel parking lots; special fire restrictions are sometimes in effect. Dogs on leash OK. Park open from 8 AM to sunset; for information, call: 805-370-2301.

PETER STRAUSS RANCH: *30000 Mulholland Hwy. at Troutdale Dr., Santa Monica Mts.* The park entrance is on the south side of Mulholland Hwy., and the parking lot is 100 yards to the east, across Triunfo Creek. There are picnic facilities on a lawn shaded by tall trees, an outdoor amphitheater for concerts and plays, and a historic building that now houses conference space, classrooms, and an art gallery. The Peter Strauss Trail makes a loop less than one mile long through vegetation that includes scrub oak, coast live oak, coffeeberry, and poison oak. Triunfo Creek is a perennial stream that provides habitat for aquatic insects, bullfrogs, birds, and a riparian flora of ferns, alder, and sycamore. Park open from 8 AM to sunset. Dogs on leash allowed on trails; only service dogs allowed in the buildings. Rangers and docents lead walks on selected dates. Call: 805-370-2301.

PARAMOUNT RANCH: *Cornell Rd., .4 mi. N. of Mulholland Hwy., Santa Monica Mts.* The park includes a movie ranch, where filming occurs regularly. There are also trails that wind through the 336-acre property, although there is no trail access to other units of the Santa Monica Mountains National Recreation Area. Facilities at Paramount Ranch include picnic areas, drinking water, restrooms, a five-kilometer running path, a large parking area, and a ranger station. Park open from 8 AM to sunset. Dogs on leash allowed on trails. Call: 805-370-2301.

MULHOLLAND SCENIC PARKWAY: *Through the Santa Monica Mts. from Leo Carrillo State Park to Hollywood Hills.* Mulholland Hwy. snakes some 30 miles through the Santa Monica Mountains from Leo Carrillo State Park to Calabasas. Mulholland Dr., unpaved in spots and subject to closure, continues east to the Hollywood Hills. Together, the roads make up the Mulholland Scenic Parkway. The route offers plenty of twists and turns, along with vistas of mountains, canyons, and the sea. Developed overlooks include the Seminole Overlook, one-half mile east of Kanan Rd., where interpretive panels explain volcanic formations on view from the site.

Malibu Creek State Park

LAS VIRGENES VIEW PARK: *N.E. corner, Las Virgenes Rd. and Mulholland Hwy., Calabasas.* Las Virgenes View Park offers more than a square mile of open space. The two-and-a-half-mile-long Las Virgenes View Trail leads to a high point with 360-degree views of peaks and the valley of Malibu Creek. Native grasslands include purple needlegrass and blue-eyed grass. The park is a joint project of the city of Calabasas, the Las Virgenes Municipal Water District, and the Santa Monica Mountains Conservancy. Open from sunrise to sunset. Hiking, equestrian, and bicycle use allowed; leashed dogs OK. Call: 310-456-7049.

MALIBU CREEK STATE PARK: *Along Las Virgenes Rd., 4 mi. S. of Hwy. 101, Calabasas.* This very large park, encompassing 8,000 acres, includes both day-use and camping facilities set in the scenic Santa Monica Mountains. The Chumash people once inhabited the area. In the mid-19th century, homesteaders settled in the valley of Malibu Creek. Maps, books, and information about local resources are available at the visitor center, open weekends and located three-quarters of a mile from the main parking area. There are 15 miles of hiking and equestrian trails and a self-guided trail for visu-ally impaired visitors. The park entrance is south of Mulholland Hwy., on the west side of Las Virgenes Rd.

Malibu Creek State Park offers 63 family campsites for tents and RVs and a group campground. Pay showers. For RVs, no hookups are available, and the maximum length is 30 feet; RV dump station available. For camping reservations, call: 1-800-444-7275; for park information, call: 818-880-0367. Leashed dogs are allowed in the day-use areas and campgrounds, but not on trails. Campfires allowed only in metal fire rings; additional restrictions apply during periods of high fire risk. Day use and camping fees apply.

TAPIA PARK: *Las Virgenes Rd., 5 mi. S. of Hwy. 101, Calabasas.* Tapia Park is a day-use unit of Malibu Creek State Park. The entrance is on the west side of Las Virgenes Rd., south of the main state park entrance. Malibu Creek flows through the park, which is studded with large oak trees. Facilities include shady picnic areas with barbecue grills, a sports field, and hiking and equestrian trails; a segment of the Backbone Trail winds through the park, past spring wildflowers that may include red fuchsia-flowering gooseberry.

In the heart of Malibu Creek State Park is 100-foot-high Rindge Dam. The dam was built in 1926 by May Knight Rindge, owner at the time of the Malibu Rancho, also called the Rindge Ranch. In less than 25 years the reservoir filled with sediment from Malibu Creek, and today the dam is entirely non-functional. A waterfall flows over the top of the dam in wet years into a year-round pool at the base. Drought years reduce the size of the pool considerably.

Since the aging dam is no longer functional, environmentalists and government officials have called for the dam's removal and restoration of Malibu Creek's historic steelhead trout fishery. Many streams in southern California were once populated by the southern steelhead, the southernmost steelhead trout species in the world. Today, the steelhead is threatened with extinction, since nearly all of the streams in southern California that used to provide steelhead spawning habitat have either been dammed, channelized, or polluted to the extent that steelhead habitat is no longer viable. Where the once plentiful fish used to swim wild and unrestricted in Malibu Creek, Rindge Dam has blocked the steelhead's upstream migration at a point three miles from the ocean, thus eliminating eight miles of former habitat above the dam. Studies of possible removal of the dam have included estimating how much sediment is located behind the dam (from 800,000 to 1,600,000 cubic yards) and considering the best way to remove the sediment from the canyon, without damaging wildlife resources. Options include gradual removal of the dam, allowing natural stream flow to carry sediment downstream, or removal of sediment by truck, perhaps for beach nourishment.

Leashed dogs are allowed in day-use areas, but not on trails. Fee for parking. For information, call: 818-880-0367.

CALABASAS PEAK: *Stunt Rd., off Mulholland Hwy., Calabasas.* One mile from Mulholland Hwy. a multi-use trail on the north side of Stunt Rd. leads steeply uphill. The route to 2,163-foot-high Calabasas Peak is a mile and a half long. No facilities. Call: 818-591-1701.

COLD CREEK CANYON: *Stunt Rd., S. of Mulholland Hwy., Calabasas.* Amid steep, thickly vegetated slopes flows Cold Creek, a perennial stream. A trail follows portions of the stream, and other trails climb the sides of the north-facing canyon. From Mulholland Hwy., take Stunt Rd. one mile to a pull-out and the Lower Stunt High Trail, which leads through a lush riparian zone that includes ceanothus and mugwort. A chemical toilet is located near the parking area; no other facilities. Visitors can explore the Cold Creek Valley Preserve or head uphill on the Lower Stunt High Trail; note that connecting trails into the adjoining UCLA Stunt Ranch Reserve are closed to the general public. Farther up Stunt Rd. is the Cold Creek Canyon Preserve, where public trail access is allowed by permit. For information and reservations, call the Mountains Restoration Trust: 818-591-1701. Habitat restoration days and docent-led walks in Cold Creek Canyon are offered by the Trust.

Cold Creek Canyon from Upper Stunt High Trail

Santa Monica Mountains from Palisades Park, *detail of print sized 11.5 x 18 inches*

© Tom Killion

Santa Monica Mountains National Recreation Area

VIRTUALLY next door to the West's largest city is a great, wild park. In dramatic contrast to intensely urban Los Angeles and the San Fernando Valley is the rugged landscape of the Santa Monica Mountains National Recreation Area. This unit of the national park system includes over 150,000 acres of mountainous land and coastline. Nearly 70,000 acres are protected park lands, interspersed with private lands. Management of the National Recreation Area is shared by the National Park Service and its main partners, the California Department of Parks and Recreation (the largest landowner in the recreation area, with eight state park units that encompass 35,000 acres); the Santa Monica Mountains Conservancy; and the Mountains Recreation and Conservation Authority; along with local governments and nonprofit entities. The park's component units stretch 46 miles from Point Mugu in Ventura County to the Hollywood Bowl in Hollywood.

Most of the National Recreation Area is in Los Angeles County. In adjacent Ventura County are Point Mugu State Park and Circle X Ranch, key facilities that offer overnight camping opportunities that are otherwise scarce in the Santa Monica Mountains. Trail corridors crisscross the National Recreation Area. The Backbone Trail runs east and west along the mountains, linking many park units. The Santa Monica Mountains National Recreation Area draws 33 million visitors annually to its beaches and inland sites, but it plays an important part in the lives of even those residents of the Los Angeles Basin who do not visit regularly. The park's open space serves as a reservoir of fresh air adjacent to urbanized Los Angeles, much of it located in the path of prevailing winds from the Santa Monica Mountains.

The plants and wildlife of the Santa Monica Mountains National Recreation Area are adapted to warm, dry summers, followed by short, rainy winters. The Mediterranean climate type, as this regime is known, is rare; only five locations around the world have such a climate, including the Mediterranean itself, western South Africa, central Chile, southwest Australia, and California. Each location is situated at about the same latitude as southern California, generally on a west-facing coast. The Santa Monica Mountains are significant not only as a conservation area in one of the world's rare climatic regions, but also for the role that the mountains play in California's ecosystems. The National Recreation Area affords protection to nearly 400 species of birds and more than 20 threatened or endangered species of plants or animals.

Cultural resources are protected too; over 1,000 archaeological or historical sites, including pictographs created by the Native American Chumash people, are located within the boundaries of the National Recreation Area. The Santa Monica Mountains are the ancestral home of both the Chumash people and the Tongva, called by the Spanish missionaries "Gabrielino" after San Gabriel Mission. The Satwiwa Native American Indian Culture Center in the Ventura County portion of the National Recreation Area recalls a Chumash village, Satwiwa, one of many sites inhabited by Native Americans among the rugged terrain of the Santa Monica Mountains.

The Santa Monica Mountains are part of the Transverse Range physiographic province. Mountains in this province trend roughly east-west, at almost right angles to most of California's other mountain ranges, which generally trend from northwest to southeast. The orientation of the Transverse Ranges, together with other geologic evidence, points to a massive rotation of the block of crust comprising these mountains. Most of the rocks making up this block of the Earth's crust were deposited over the past 80 million years in shallow marine or river settings. Several cycles of marine sedimentation, followed by folding, uplift, and erosion, produced alternating marine and terrestrial deposits. A period when the region's crust pulled apart and thinned, from 19 to 5 million years ago, allowed the intrusion of magma and the eruption of volcanoes throughout the region. Although the volcanoes have been eroded away, the conduits that fed them can be seen as "tabular dikes," or veins cutting across the sedimentary rocks throughout the range. Beginning about three million years ago, the latest period of uplift began, giving rise to the mountains we see today. This uplift warped the rocks into a broad arch, at many places cut by faults dipping at shallow angles to the north. This uplift continues today, most of it taking place episodically as movement along these faults, producing earthquakes such as the 1994 Northridge Earthquake.

———————— • • • ————————

Among the National Recreational Area's attractions is Paramount Ranch, which you may have seen before you ever visit. Beginning in 1927, movies set in the Old West were filmed here, along with stories set in ancient China, on the grasslands of Africa, and even on a South Seas island. Shot here were classic films starring Gary Cooper, including *A Farewell to Arms* (1932) and *Beau Geste* (1939), as well as *Blonde Venus* (1932) starring Marlene Dietrich, *Munster, Go Home* (1966), and *The Flintstones in Viva Rock Vegas* (2000). Famed director Cecil B. DeMille worked here, as did movie stars Bob Hope, Claudette Colbert, and others. A permanent western town was built on the property, serving as the set for numerous television shows, including *Dr. Quinn, Medicine Woman*. The National Park Service has revitalized the old movie ranch, and it is still used for filming. Elsewhere in the National Recreation Area, at Malibu Creek State Park, Twentieth Century Fox Studios once owned over 2,000 acres of rugged mountains and steep-sided canyons that were used in the filming of numerous movies and television shows, including *Tarzan Escapes* (1936), *Planet of the Apes* (1968), and *The Towering Inferno* (1974). The state of California acquired the land in 1974 for park use.

Paramount Ranch

Peter Strauss Ranch

The Peter Strauss Ranch unit of the National Recreation Area was originally a private home built in the 1920s by automobile designer Harry Miller, who created a retreat with an aviary, fruit trees, and a zoo. In the late 1930s, other owners converted the property to a weekend resort that featured what was then one of the largest outdoor swimming pools west of the Rockies. Triunfo Creek was dammed, and the resort became known as "Lake Enchanto." Actor Peter Strauss acquired the property after filming the TV miniseries *Rich Man, Poor Man* in the Santa Monica Mountains in 1976.

In 2005, the old King Gillette Ranch was added to the Santa Monica Mountains National Recreation Area. The property, located in the heart of the mountains at Las Virgenes Rd. and Mulholland Hwy., was acquired for the public by a partnership of agencies, including the Santa Monica Mountains Conservancy, the Mountains Recreation and Conservation Authority, the National Park Service, and California State Parks, relying on a mix of public funds and private donations. After making his fortune in razor blades, King Gillette purchased the property in 1926. Gillette hired Wallace Neff, a leading architect of the day, who designed a gracious, Spanish Colonial-style mansion, still standing on the property. There are also grand landscape features, such as formal rows of tall eucalyptus trees, a pond, and spacious lawns. Since Gillette's time, the ranch has had many owners, including Hollywood film director Clarence Brown, who hosted parties attended by Clark Gable and Greta Garbo.

The King Gillette Ranch is open for picnicking, hiking, and photography. By 2009, the site is planned to be the location of a new visitor center for the Santa Monica Mountains National Recreation Area. Until then, visit the old visitor center location at 401 W. Hillcrest Dr. in Thousand Oaks for maps, books, and information about the Santa Monica Mountains. The visitor center is open from 9 AM to 5 PM daily, except federal holidays. Call: 805-370-2301, or see: www.nps.gov/samo.

Backbone Tr

Malibu Creek
SP

PIUMA

RD

Carbon Cr

MALIBU CANYON RD

Piuma
Ridge
Park

Malibu

Cr

Malibu Creek
SP

Marie Cr

Papa Jack's
Skate Park

CROSS CREEK RD

Malibu Lagoon
Museum

Corral
Canyon
Park

Pepperdine
University

CANYON RD

Adamson House

Puerco Cr

MALIBU

PACIFIC   COAST   HWY

CIVIC CENTER
WAY

1

Carbon Beach

MALIBU

RD

Malibu
Lagoon

Malibu Pier

La Costa
Beach

Malibu
Colony

Malibu Pt.

Surfrider Beach

Malibu Bluffs
Park

Malibu Lagoon
State Beach

Puerco Beach

SANTA MONICA BAY

N

0   0.5   1 Mile

0   0.5   1 Kilometer

Malibu Lagoon State Beach

Puerco Beach to Carbon Beach

	Sandy Beach	Rocky Shore	Trail	Visitor Center	Campground	Wildlife Viewing	Fishing or Boating	Facilities for Disabled	Food and Drink	Restrooms	Parking	Fee
Puerco Beach	•											
Malibu Bluffs Park			•							•	•	
Papa Jack's Skate Park										•	•	•
Malibu Lagoon State Beach	•		•			•	•			•	•	•
Adamson House				•		•				•		•
Surfrider Beach	•						•		•	•	•	•
Malibu Pier						•	•	•	•	•		
Carbon Beach	•	•					•					

PUERCO BEACH: *25118, 24714, 24602, 24434, and 24318 Malibu Rd., Malibu.* A narrow sandy beach, lined with houses, can be reached by public access stairs located on Malibu Rd. Gates to the five stairways are opened at dawn and locked at dusk daily by the Los Angeles County Dept. of Beaches and Harbors; however, visitors may exit at any time. A small sign and litter receptacle mark each gate. Do not trespass on private property. A sixth publicly owned beachfront site on Malibu Rd., located between Nos. 24034 and 24056 but unmarked, provides views of the ocean, but no access down the steep bank; the State Coastal Conservancy plans future access improvements.

MALIBU BLUFFS PARK: *Malibu Canyon Rd. and Pacific Coast Hwy., Malibu.* The California Department of Parks and Recreation has leased a 30-acre blufftop portion of Malibu Lagoon State Beach to the city of Malibu for use as a community park. Facilities include ball fields, picnic tables, and an overlook for whale watching. For information, call: 310-317-1364. Several trails lead from the seaward edge of the ballfields down to Malibu Rd., over chaparral-covered slopes that remain part of Malibu Lagoon State Beach.

PAPA JACK'S SKATE PARK: *23415 Civic Center Way, W. of Cross Creek Rd., Malibu.* The city of Malibu operates this 10,000-square-foot skate facility. Open from 2:30 to 6:00 PM, Monday through Thursday, and 12:30 to 6:00 PM, Friday to Sunday. Skaters must wear protective gear; fee required. For information, call: 310-456-1441.

MALIBU LAGOON STATE BEACH: *23200 block of Pacific Coast Hwy., Malibu.* A world-famous surf break exists at Malibu Point, especially during summer when strong southwest swells refract around a rock reef and break over a gently sloping sandy bottom. Swimming, fishing, nature walks, and wildlife viewing are also popular at this park. Trails lead from the parking lot to lagoon overlooks and to the sandy beach. When the mouth of Malibu Creek is open to the sea, the creek separates the beach from Surfrider Beach to the east. Picnic tables and restrooms available; fee for parking. For information, call: 818-880-0350.

Malibu Lagoon State Beach

From the late 1800s until 1938, the entire 27-mile-long, 13,000-acre Malibu Rancho, one of the original Spanish land grants, belonged to the Rindge family, wealthy millionaires from Cambridge, Massachusetts. The Rindges zealously protected their privacy with fences, gates, and armed guards on horseback. After a long court battle between the Rindge family and the County of Los Angeles, eventually resolved by the U.S. Supreme Court, the State of California was granted the right to build a new highway along the Malibu coast.

The completion in 1929 of the Roosevelt Highway, now known as Pacific Coast Highway, opened up public access between Santa Monica and Oxnard through the previously inaccessible Rindge Ranch. It also opened up Malibu to development, and the area was immediately discovered by the rich and famous, including Hollywood movie stars and other personalities from the entertainment world. As early as 1929, the 30-foot-wide oceanfront lots in the Malibu Colony, located upcoast of the mouth of Malibu Creek, were leased by the Rindges at the rate of one dollar per oceanfront foot per month. In 1938 the lots were offered for sale, and they were quickly snatched up by Hollywood celebrities. Small beach cottages intended as weekend retreats were built initially, at an average cost of $2,600. Early residents included Barbara Stanwyck, Clara Bow, Gary Cooper, Gloria Swanson, and Ronald Colman. Many of the original beach cottages remained until the 1990s, but practically all of them have been demolished since then and replaced by much larger and more luxurious homes. The Colony's architectural style can best be described as eclectic. Homes and even vacant lots are now valued in the millions of dollars, and many of them are still used as second homes or vacation retreats.

Along with celebrity status and wealth often comes the desire for privacy. Today, the Malibu Colony is a gated community, and public access through the Colony's private streets is not permitted. But public access along the beach seaward of the mean high tide line is guaranteed by the California constitution, and public access also is available across some private properties where access easements have been granted to the public. Pedestrian access to the beach is available from Malibu Lagoon State Beach, downcoast of the Colony.

Roosevelt Hwy. (now PCH) and site of Malibu Colony, vista from 1929

Malibu Lagoon is a shallow, brackish lagoon at the mouth of Malibu Creek, which drains a large watershed in the Santa Monica Mountains. The original area of mudflats and saltmarsh was reduced by construction of Pacific Coast Hwy. and other structures, but the lagoon is still a valuable habitat; migratory birds rest and feed here, and fish in the lagoon include California killifish, mosquito fish, and topsmelt. To improve the lagoon's water quality and habitat values for birds and fish, restoration measures commenced in 2008. The parking lot has been relocated to a site farther from the lagoon, to minimize runoff from autos, and trails will be rebuilt, to minimize human impact on the lagoon's fauna. Small bird "islands" are also planned, to provide a refuge for California least terns, western snowy plovers, and other birds.

ADAMSON HOUSE: *23200 Pacific Coast Hwy., Malibu.* The gracious, Mediterranean-style Adamson House is set among broad lawns overlooking Surfrider Beach. Now a museum, the house was constructed beginning in 1929 by Merritt Adamson and his wife Rhoda, the daughter of Frederick and May K. Rindge. The house is lavishly decorated with tiles produced at Malibu Potteries, which operated from 1926 to 1932 and furnished Moorish-style tiles for many southern California buildings of the era.

Adjacent to the Adamson House is the Malibu Lagoon Museum, which contains materials reflecting the area's Chumash Native American heritage and its ranching and surfing history. The Adamson House and museum are bordered on three sides by the beach and Malibu Lagoon, but can be entered only through the gate on Pacific Coast Hwy.; park at Malibu Lagoon State Beach at Cross Creek Rd. and walk east to the gravel drive leading to the Adamson House. The grounds are open daily from 8 AM to sunset for self-guided tours. Docent-led house tours are offered from 11 AM to 2 PM, Wednesday to Saturday; closed major holidays; call: 310-456-8432. Museum and garden tours are also available. Visitor vehicles are allowed on the property only with a license plate displaying the disabled emblem; the museum and first floor of the house are wheelchair accessible.

SURFRIDER BEACH: *23050 Pacific Coast Hwy., Malibu.* Known for surfing, this strand also features swimming, fishing, and sand volleyball. There are restrooms and beach showers, off-street parking, and lifeguards on duty during daylight hours. Managed by Los Angeles County Dept. of Beaches and Harbors. Recorded information on surfing and diving conditions is updated regularly by lifeguards; call: 310-457-9701. No alcohol or fires on the beach; pets not allowed.

Decorative tiles at Adamson House

In the 1950s and 1960s, freeway planning and construction in the Los Angeles area operated at full tilt. A 1958 master plan shows projected freeways densely crisscrossing Los Angeles, including a route through Topanga Canyon and an east-west expressway through the Santa Monica Mountains near Mulholland Hwy. The planned Pacific Coast Freeway would have extended over 110 miles along the shoreline from Oxnard in Ventura County to Capistrano Beach in Orange County. The existing seven-mile-long Route 1 freeway from Oxnard to near Point Mugu was built as a first link in that route; the rest of it and many other planned freeways were never constructed, as dollar costs rose and environmental costs were recognized.

What might have been the most dramatic freeway in California, if it had ever been built, was the link contemplated between Malibu Beach and Santa Monica. One option that was studied by the Division of Highways was an offshore alignment that would have cut across Santa Monica Bay on a causeway or earthen fill. The U.S. Army Corps of Engineers found in a preliminary report in 1963 that such a route was feasible. Incredibly, the study stated that an offshore freeway could enhance recreational opportunities by creating new beaches on each side of the roadway. The report fails to mention negative effects on pre-existing beaches; the studied freeway alignment would have sliced right through the celebrated surf break at Malibu Point.

MALIBU PIER: *23000 Pacific Coast Hwy., Malibu.* The wooden Malibu Pier, punctuated by tidy twin buildings at the end, retains its old-time, mid-20th-century look. Come here to fish, to watch the surfers on the adjacent world-famous break, or enjoy the expansive views of sand, sea, and mountains. Anglers on the pier catch halibut and various species of croakers and perch, and occasionally thresher sharks are hooked. Ocean sportfishing and whale-watching excursions depart from the pier; for recorded information, call: 310-456-8031. The pier is wheelchair-accessible. Off-street parking is available in the commercial parking lot at 22809 Pacific Coast Hwy. on weekends and holidays from sunrise to sunset; parking fees apply.

CARBON BEACH: *22670 and 22132 Pacific Coast Hwy., Malibu.* Carbon Beach is a mile-long stretch of sandy shore, located east of Malibu Pier. Lined with houses and commercial buildings, the beach features two short public accessways from Pacific Coast Hwy. to the sand, both bordered by private property; do not trespass. The Zonker Harris Accessway, named for the beach-obsessed Doonesbury comic strip charac-

ter created in 1971 by Garry Trudeau, is at 22670 Pacific Coast Hwy. The gate is opened at dawn and locked at dusk daily by the Los Angeles County Dept. of Beaches and Harbors; however, visitors may exit at any time. On weekends from May 15 to September 15, off-street parking is available nearby in the second-story commercial lot at 22601 Pacific Coast Hwy.; pay fee downstairs at Pacific Coast Greens market.

At 22132 Pacific Coast Hwy. is another short path to the beach, this one maintained by a nonprofit organization, Access for All. The gate is unlocked at sunrise and locked at sunset; no exit after gate is closed. A map posted at the accessway shows portions of the nearby beach that are available for public recreation; in addition, the public may legally use all lands seaward of the mean high tide line. Look for shorebirds along the sandy beach and dolphins swimming nearby offshore. At the east end of Carbon Beach, the beach narrows and is covered with cobbles, some with large populations of mussels clinging to them. At low tide, beachgoers can continue east on the wet sand onto La Costa Beach.

Malibu Pier

The Malibu Pier is located in a cove named "Keller's Shelter" after its first American owner, Matthew Keller, who bought the cove in 1860. In 1903 Frederick Rindge built a 400-foot-long pier to serve as a loading dock for supplies for his ranch. In 1943 William Huber bought the cove and built the present pier to replace Rindge's, which had been destroyed by storms. Huber sold the 700-foot-long pier and the adjoining shoreline property to the state in 1980. Prior to the 1990s, the pier had been home for decades to a popular eatery called Alice's Restaurant, as well as sport-fishing boats, but severe storms in 1993 and 1995 caused the pier's closure. The California Department of Parks and Recreation renovated and reopened the pier in 2006; a restaurant has opened and a surf museum and additional restaurants are planned.

Carbon Beach

Rivers and Streams

ALONG THE COAST of southern California, rivers and streams are especially important resources. Not only is the annual rainfall relatively low, ranging from about 14 inches at Malibu to less than 10 inches at Imperial Beach, but precipitation tends to come only in the cool months. During the long, warm summers, rivers and streams are a source of essential moisture and sustenance for plants and animals.

Southern California's rivers and streams flow out of the Transverse and Peninsular Ranges, with watersheds that reach many miles inland from the coast. Streams pass through areas of forest, chaparral, scrubland, grassland, and marsh on their way to the sea. Along the banks of these watercourses is the area called the riparian zone, consisting of the land and organisms associated with the stream. The term "riparian" is derived from the Latin word *ripa*, meaning river bank. The riparian zone is a transition area between the water and land, between aquatic and terrestrial realms. Life in the riparian zone and in the adjacent watercourse is interdependent. Organisms in the riparian zone rely on the adjacent stream as a source of water, and organisms that live in the stream depend on the riparian habitat for food and shelter.

Watercourses convey not only water, but also nutrients. Leaves, twigs, decaying insects, and other organic matter from the riparian zone move into the watercourse and become available for use by organisms both locally and downstream. Riparian organic matter has the potential of supporting a diversity of food webs within both aquatic and terrestrial ecosystems. The movement of plant and animal materials along the watercourse represents a transfer of energy from inland, higher-elevation areas to the lower part of the stream, nearer the ocean. Streams also move plant propagules, including seeds and spores, and animal eggs, larvae, and juveniles downstream, where life can establish itself along the lower part of the watercourse.

Malibu Creek, Santa Monica Mountains

Watercourses serve as important corridors for wildlife migration and dispersal. Large and small mammals use the thickly wooded zones along streams to move in search of food sources or mates. Riparian vegetation shades streams, thus optimizing light and temperature conditions for aquatic plants, fish, and other animals. Overhanging willows and shrubs help shade streams from the warm southern California sun, benefiting species such as the southern steelhead, which requires relatively cool water temperatures. Vegetation growing along a streambank also helps to stabilize the bank and to retard erosion and, in some places, to create an overhanging bank that serves as a refuge for many organisms, including damselfly and dragonfly nymphs, frogs, salamanders, and fish in the water below.

Riparian soils filter excess nutrients, sediments, and pollutants from surface water runoff, while regenerating ground water supplies and improving stream water quality. Riparian vegetation plays a role in flood prevention. As flood waters flow through a vegetated area, the plants resist the flow and dissipate the energy, increasing the time available for water to infiltrate the soil and be stored for use by plants. Streams are vital components of the water cycle, delivering water, nutrients, and sediments to the ocean, including sand to beaches. Although aquatic and riparian ecosystems generally occupy only small areas on the landscape, they are usually much more biologically diverse than adjacent upland areas. In the western United States, riparian areas comprise less than one percent of the land area, but are among the most diverse, productive, and valuable natural resources.

In southern California, many watercourses that flow generously in winter are dry for a portion of the year, reflecting the Mediterranean climate with its cool, wet winters and long, dry summers. Some native organisms, such as the California newt, use a summertime adaptation called estivation, similar to hibernation, in which the animal becomes essentially dormant and able to survive months without water. Other species of animal, such as the California red-legged frog (*Rana aurora draytonii*), which has been extirpated in southern California but still inhabits riparian areas in northern California and Baja California, adapt to the long dry season by breeding early in the year. That way, larvae metamorphose before water supplies are exhausted. The insects commonly seen "walking" on streams or ponds, known as waterstriders, encapsulate their eggs in cysts that are capable of surviving several years of dry conditions.

Changes to riparian areas made by humans often have long-term adverse effects on biological resources. Dams, levees, and channelization of streams with concrete walls may have the most adverse impacts of all. These modifications significantly alter the movement and storage of water that is so important to the riparian system. Water withdrawal from a stream reduces its base flow, depriving its riparian zone and the plants and animals that inhabit it of moisture. Perhaps the most common disturbance to riparian areas consists of clearing vegetation and converting the area to another use, such as urban or agricultural development. Poorly designed recreational development, such as water parks, campgrounds, and trails, can destroy natural plant diversity and structure, lead to soil compaction and erosion, and disturb wildlife. However, if park facilities are carefully designed, these impacts can be avoided, minimized, or mitigated. Once introduced by humans, exotic plants such as the giant reed, or Arundo, take advantage of the good growing conditions found in riparian zones and the movement of plant materials downstream to invade the rest of the watershed. As some exotic plants tend to out-compete and dominate native plants, the overall vegetative diversity decreases, resulting in less favorable habitat for most wildlife species.

Southern California black walnut

The **Southern California black walnut** (*Juglans californica hindsii*) is a deciduous tree that grows up to 75 feet in height and is found along the edges of riparian woodlands as well as in open woodlands. The tree produces small, round walnuts with a strong odor. The leaves are pinnately compound, each having 11 or more leaflets. Walnut trees are often confused with the invasive and toxic tree-of-heaven, which has similar leaves. The tree-of-heaven (*Ailanthus altissima*), which originated in China, may be distinguished by its mostly smooth leaflets, whereas the leaflets of the native black walnut have serrated edges. During the fall the shiny, resinous, green walnut leaves turn soft shades of yellow. By dropping its leaves in the cold winter months, the tree recycles nutrients and saves carbohydrates that would otherwise be used to maintain those leaves.

Arroyo willow

The **arroyo willow** (*Salix lasiolepis*) is a common riparian plant. It is also known as "white willow" because it has light-colored bark and leaves with whitish lower surfaces. It can take on shrub or tree-like dimensions ranging from six to 30 feet in height. During the spring, the arroyo willow produces inconspicuous yellow flowers that grow on stems in bunches called catkins, which are shaped like chubby caterpillars. Willows provide habitat and protection for birds and other animals that use willows as nesting and feeding places. Some varieties of willow bark were used by Native Americans to help reduce fever and pain; willow bark contains salicin, which human bodies convert to salicylic acid, the active pain-relieving ingredient in aspirin.

Mugwort

Mugwort (*Artemisia douglasiana*) is a native perennial herb in the sunflower family that is commonly found within riparian habitats. It is an aromatic plant that reaches three to five feet in height, has gray-green stems, and toothed leaves that are pale green and hairless on the upper surface and gray with thick hairs on the underside. Mugwort boasts a long list of medicinal uses including prevention and treatment of fungal infections and poison oak rash, treated by rubbing mugwort leaves on the skin. Mugwort played a large role in Native American culture. The leaves were rubbed on the body to keep away ghosts, and a mugwort necklace was worn to prevent dreaming of the dead.

The **phainopepla** (*Phainopepla nitens*) has red eyes, a noticeable crest, and a long tail. Males are especially striking, because they have glossy black plumage and a white wing patch that is visible during flight. The female is less flashy, exhibiting gray plumage and a light gray wing patch. While this bird is commonly sighted near creeks and streams in coastal southern California, it is also found in foothills and deserts. Its main food is mistletoe berries, and it is an important vector for mistletoe seeds. It also eats other berries, such as elderberry, as well as insects. Interestingly, phainopepla imitate the calls of at least 12 other birds, including red-tailed hawks and northern flickers.

Phainopepla

The **unarmored threespine stickleback** (*Gasterosteus aculeatus williamsoni*) is found in only a few remaining watersheds in southern California. The stickleback is a small, scaleless fish that inhabits the quiet waters of streams. The fish has a greenish-gray dorsal surface and a pinkish belly. During the spawning season males develop a dark red coloration. The males construct nests from gravel and algae, held together by a glue-like secretion produced by the fish. Females then deposit eggs into the nests that the males actively aerate and guard until the fry leave the protection of the nest. This species reaches a maximum length of three inches. Stickleback are severely impacted by exotic predator species including sunfish and crawdads.

Unarmored threespine stickleback

"Cute" is a very apt term for the **California newt** (*Taricha torosa*), a large salamander with big eyes and a wide mouth. The California newt has warty skin, yellow-brown to dark orange-brown, that is not as slimy as that of most salamanders. You may know the California newt from having observed one crossing a road or field; in order to breed, the newts often migrate back to where they originally developed as larvae. California newts mate from December to early May, and their courtship involves a dance in which the male mounts the female and rubs his chin over her nose and shakes his tail. To ward off predators, a newt may raise its head and point its tail straight out to expose its bright yellow or orange chest and undersides as a warning. If the predator attacks, the newt can excrete a neurotoxin through the skin which can cause paralysis or death.

California newt

Big Rock Beach

Malibu East

	Sandy Beach	Rocky Shore	Trail	Visitor Center	Campground	Wildlife Viewing	Fishing or Boating	Facilities for Disabled	Food and Drink	Restrooms	Parking	Fee
La Costa Beach	•											
Big Rock Beach	•	•										
Las Tunas Beach	•									•	•	
Topanga Beach	•				•	•	•		•	•	•	•
Tuna Canyon Park			•		•							

LA COSTA BEACH: *21700 Pacific Coast Hwy., Malibu.* La Costa Beach is a narrow crescent of sand and cobbles that is currently accessible to the public only by walking downcoast from Carbon Beach, and then only at a low tide. From Pacific Coast Hwy., a view of the ocean and shoreline is available at a beachfront parcel owned by the State Coastal Conservancy. Facilities enabling access to the beach are planned for the future.

BIG ROCK BEACH: *20350 and 20000 Pacific Coast Hwy., Malibu.* This narrow beach lies seaward of a row of houses, as well as the highway and unstable slopes subject to landslides. A public beach stairway is located at 20000 Pacific Coast Hwy. Another stairway, at 20350 Pacific Coast Hwy. next to Moonshadows Restaurant, is closed indefinitely due to storm damage. Both accessways are maintained by the Los Angeles County Dept. of Beaches and Harbors, which opens beach access gates at dawn and locks them at dusk; however, visitors can exit at any time. Caltrans has installed a vista point with a bench and nice views of Santa Monica Bay at the intersection of Pacific Coast Hwy. and Big Rock Dr.; no beach access.

LAS TUNAS BEACH: *19444 Pacific Coast Hwy., Malibu.* Much of this narrow beach is lined with houses, but ocean views and unimproved public access from Pacific Coast Hwy. to the water's edge are available at several pull-outs on the seaward side of the highway. Use care in pulling off and onto the pavement, as traffic moves fast here. Facilities are limited to chemical toilets; a lifeguard tower is staffed by the Los Angeles

County Dept. of Beaches and Harbors during the summer.

TOPANGA BEACH: *18700 Pacific Coast Hwy., Malibu.* This serene beach park is located below busy Pacific Coast Hwy., west of Topanga Canyon Blvd. The wide, sandy beach lies on both sides of the mouth of Topanga Creek. Facilities include picnic tables, restrooms, beach showers, and food service. Topanga Beach is a noted surfing spot, and is also popular for swimming and fishing. Lifeguards are on duty during daylight

Public stairway to Big Rock Beach

Lagoon at mouth of Topanga Creek, Topanga Beach

hours. A beach wheelchair is available at the lifeguard station. The main parking lot occupies a narrow terrace on the blufftop. For visitors with disabled-person parking placards, there is also limited parking at beach level; the turn-off from Pacific Coast Hwy. is accessible to eastbound vehicles only and is very abrupt.

On the beach, California gulls, sandpipers, and killdeer rest and feed. Rock scallops, sea urchins, and numerous other invertebrates inhabit the rocky bottom offshore. This Los Angeles County-managed beach park, formerly known as Topanga State Beach, opened in 1973 after the state of California acquired the land and removed the beach houses located on the property. Across Pacific Coast Hwy. from Topanga Beach is Topanga State Park, linked to the beach by a pedestrian underpass beneath the highway. On the inland side of the highway, a trail leads inland along Topanga Creek, although it does not connect with the rest of Topanga State Park. The California State Parks Department has plans for future habitat restoration in Topanga Creek and recreational improvements to the park.

TUNA CANYON PARK: *Fernwood Pacific Dr., off Topanga Canyon Blvd., Topanga.* This undeveloped, open-space park encompasses two square miles of steep-sided canyons and ridges. Approach the park from Topanga Canyon Blvd.; turn west on Fernwood Pacific Dr. next to the fire station. Continue on Fernwood Pacific Dr. (which becomes Tuna Canyon Rd.) a distance of 3.9 miles to Big Rock Motorway, a fire road that is the entrance to the park. A white steel gate marks the spot, which is unsigned. Tuna Canyon Rd. continues down the canyon to Pacific Coast Hwy., becoming one-way southbound. Off Big Rock Motorway is a network of trails for hikers, bicyclists, and equestrians, offering striking views of distant mountains, the ocean, and the coastal slopes. Native plant communities include coastal sage scrub, grasslands, sycamore riparian woodland, and oak woodland; look for prickly pear cactus on the slopes and Southern California black walnut trees in the canyons. Bring plenty of water; no facilities. Dogs permitted on leash. Park managed by the Mountains Recreation and Conservation Authority; call: 310-456-7049.

Fire in Malibu, October 2007

Fire is a common occurrence in Malibu and the Santa Monica Mountains. Much of the steep slopes and canyons are covered with coastal sage scrub and chaparral, ecosystems that have evolved to depend on frequent fires. Many of the plants in these vegetation communities are well-adapted to fire. Some require open ground on which to germinate, while others, able to grow back quickly after fire, out-compete plants not so adapted. As urban development has encroached into these habitats, people have proved to be less adaptable. The combination of topography, fuel load, and wind makes the Santa Monica Mountains home to some of the most dramatic and damaging fires in the United States.

Although fires can occur throughout the year, "fire season" comes in late summer and early fall, when summer drought has dried out the vegetation and before the rains of the winter have begun. The infamous Santa Ana winds also commence at this time. These winds result when cool air in the high deserts of eastern California, Arizona, and Nevada cascades downslope toward the sea. As the air descends, it undergoes compression, heating the air and reducing its relative humidity. Funneled through canyons, these winds can hit the coast with speeds of 80 miles per hour or more, driving air temperatures to 90 degrees Fahrenheit, or above. Fires that start in the dry chaparral are driven through the rugged canyons of the mountains with astonishing speed.

Immediately following fire season, another hazard comes to the Santa Monica Mountains. Winter rains, falling on denuded slopes, can saturate soils, mobilizing them as soil avalanches. These avalanches can evolve into cascades of muddy water called debris flows. Often called "mud slides" by the media, debris flows have the consistency of wet concrete and can move down canyons at speeds of up to 60 miles per hour. The fire-and-debris-flow cycle has repeatedly struck the canyons of Malibu, with the Hume Fire of 1956, the Wright Fire of 1970, the Piuma Fire of 1985, the Old Topanga fire of 1993, and the Canyon fire of 2007.

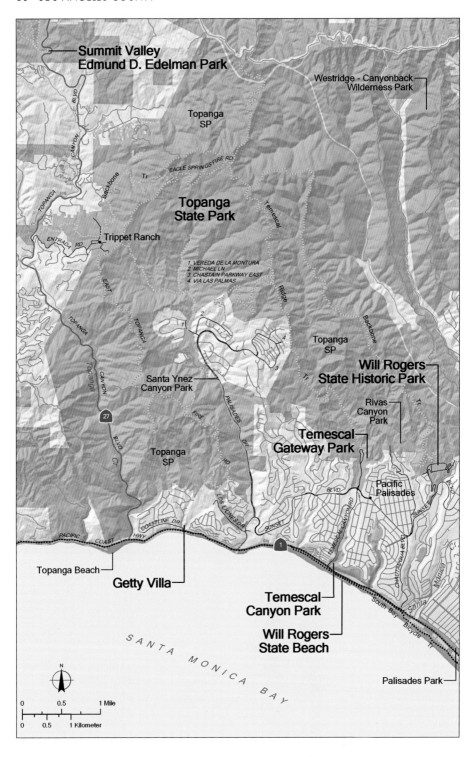

Summit Valley
Edmund D. Edelman Park

Westridge - Canyonback
Wilderness Park

Topanga
SP

EAGLE SPRINGS FIRE RD.

Tr

Topanga
State Park

Temescal

Trippet Ranch

ENTRADA RD.

EAST

TOPANGA

1. VEREDA DE LA MONTURA
2. MICHAEL LN
3. CHASTAIN PARKWAY EAST
4. VIA LAS PALMAS

Ridge

Backbone

Topanga
SP

Will Rogers
State Historic Park

Tr

Santa Ynez
Canyon Park

PALISADES

FIRE

Rivas
Canyon
Park

27

BLVD

Topanga
SP

RD

Temescal
Gateway Park

BLVD

Pacific
Palisades

BLVD

Cr

LOS LIONES DR.

COASTLINE DR.

PACIFIC

COAST

HWY

SUNSET

1

TEMESCAL CANYON RD.

SUNSET

CHAUTAUQUA BLVD

Maguea

Topanga Beach

Getty Villa

Temescal
Canyon Park

South Bay

Santa

Will Rogers
State Beach

Bicycle

Cr

SANTA

MONICA

BAY

Palisades Park

N

0   0.5   1 Mile

0   0.5   1 Kilometer

Topanga State Park to Will Rogers State Beach

	Sandy Beach	Rocky Shore	Trail	Visitor Center	Campground	Wildlife Viewing	Fishing or Boating	Facilities for Disabled	Food and Drink	Restrooms	Parking	Fee
Summit Valley Edmund D. Edelman Park			•						•	•	•	
Topanga State Park			•	•	•	•		•	•	•	•	
Getty Villa				•				•	•	•	•	
Temescal Gateway Park			•						•	•	•	•
Temescal Canyon Park										•	•	
Will Rogers State Beach	•		•				•	•	•	•	•	•
Will Rogers State Historic Park			•	•				•	•	•	•	•

SUMMIT VALLEY EDMUND D. EDELMAN PARK: *Off Topanga Canyon Blvd., 2.6 mi. S. of Mulholland Dr., Topanga.* Approach the park southbound on Topanga Canyon Blvd.; the turn-off is abrupt. There is a mile-long loop trail for hikers, equestrians, and mountain bikers; dogs on leash OK. Unpaved parking lot; chemical toilets.

TOPANGA STATE PARK: *Main entrance, end of Entrada Rd. off Topanga Canyon Blvd., 4.5 mi. N. of Pacific Coast Hwy., Topanga.* Imagine an enormous, scenic, and wild park within the boundaries of the West's largest city. Topanga State Park contains ridges where 360-degree views are dominated by undeveloped terrain, Santa Monica Bay, and Catalina Island. Besides open space, the park has facilities for picnics and hike-in and equestrian camping, along with 36 miles of trails.

The main entrance is at Trippet Ranch. Picnic tables, some under shady oaks, are near the large parking lot, along with interpretive panels and restrooms. There is a self-guided nature trail and a mile-and-a-half-long trail through Santa Ynez Canyon that leads to a 20-foot-high waterfall; look for tiger lilies and stream orchids. In the dry late summer landscape, look for prickly pear cactus in bloom and California black walnut trees bearing ripe nuts. Wildlife in the park includes coast horned lizards, California mountain kingsnakes, gray foxes, coyotes, bobcats, and mule deer.

Heading inland from Pacific Coast Hwy. on Sunset Blvd., turn left on Los Liones Dr. to reach one of several trails into Topanga State Park. Turn off Sunset Blvd. on Palisades Dr. and continue two miles to Santa Ynez Canyon Park, which borders Topanga State Park. One mile farther inland on Palisades Dr., turn west on Vereda de la Montura and park on the street; an opening in the fence leads to the Santa Ynez Canyon Trail. In the 1700 block of Michael Ln. a small sign marks a trail; park on the street. Past the point at which Palisades Dr. becomes Chastain Parkway East, turn on Via Las Palmas and go through a decorative archway, past private homes on both sides. A gated parking lot and restrooms for trail users is on the left. Hike up the paved path out of the residential area to the Temescal Fire Rd., which leads into Topanga State Park.

GETTY VILLA: *17985 Pacific Coast Hwy., Pacific Palisades.* The Getty Villa houses Greek, Roman, and Etruscan treasures at a dramatic site overlooking the sea. Admission is free, but an advance, timed ticket is required. The Getty Center in Los Angeles houses European and American art from the medieval period to the modern. For information about both museums, call: 310-440-7300.

TEMESCAL GATEWAY PARK: *End of Temescal Canyon Rd., N. of Sunset Blvd., Pacific Palisades.* This very lovely landscaped park offers tree-shaded lawns, picnic areas, and trail access into Topanga State Park. Summer camps for kids and conferences are held in Temescal Gateway Park's historic buildings. Fee for parking; leashed dogs OK within the park. Call: 310-454-1395, x103.

TEMESCAL CANYON PARK: *Temescal Canyon Rd. and Pacific Coast Hwy., Pacific Palisades.* A mile-long, landscaped park is located along both sides of Temescal Canyon Rd., inland of Pacific Coast Hwy. There are picnic areas shaded by sycamore trees, children's play equipment, lawns, and a native plant garden. Shoulder parking.

WILL ROGERS STATE BEACH: *Off Pacific Coast Hwy., Pacific Palisades.* This highly popular beach park, managed by Los Angeles County, occupies most of the ocean frontage along Pacific Coast Hwy. from Topanga Canyon Blvd. to Santa Monica. Large parking lots are located on both sides of the foot of Temescal Canyon Rd. and at Chautauqua Blvd. The parking lot at the foot of Sunset Blvd. is shared with Gladstone's restaurant; the deck is open to the public for ocean viewing. A small parking area with picnic tables, a view deck, and a ramp to the beach is located at the end of Coastline Dr. Some shoulder parking on the seaward side of the busy highway is available, but use caution. Restrooms, volleyball nets, and life-guard stations are spaced along the beach. The South Bay Bicycle Trail begins at Temescal Canyon Rd. and runs south to Torrance. Beach hours are 7 AM to 10 PM. No fires or pets on the beach. Call: 310-305-9503.

WILL ROGERS STATE HISTORIC PARK: *End of Will Rogers State Park Rd., off Sunset Blvd., Pacific Palisades.* Will Rogers and his family took up residence here in 1928. The grounds are spacious, containing a polo field, riding stables, and lawns. The home itself reflects Will Rogers's personality: gracious, expansive, and unpretentious.

Visitors can tour the restored home, have a barbecue at picnic tables overlooking the polo field, or hike a series of loop trails around the property. The Backbone Trail leads into adjacent Topanga State Park, and the Rivas Canyon Trail leads two miles to Temescal Gateway Park. Polo matches take place on weekends, and Will Rogers's films are shown at the visitor center. For a schedule and other information, call: 310-454-8212. The Will Rogers home is wheelchair accessible, although the approach across the lawn may require assistance. No smoking on trails. Dogs must be leashed, and are not allowed on the Backbone Trail. Open from 8 AM to sunset.

Temescal Gateway Park

Will Rogers was born on a cattle ranch in Indian Territory (now Oklahoma) in 1879 and went on to become a folk hero, "cowboy philosopher," movie star, and renowned writer and humorist. With his cowlicked hair and big ears, he endeared himself to the public through his sharp wit, cheerful disposition, and self-deprecating charm.

In 1902, while traveling in South Africa, Rogers entered show business performing impressive tricks with lassos and was dubbed "The Cherokee Kid." (Rogers was part Cherokee although the majority of his ancestors came from Great Britain.) He continued trick roping in the United States, grew even more popular after introducing jokes into his act (often at his own expense), and later added running humorous commentary about the daily headlines, for which he became famous. Over the years the targets of his critical wit included presidents, taxes, Prohibition, both houses of Congress, and other aspects of politics, news, and everyday life.

In 1919 Rogers moved to southern California to act in silent films. He started appearing in talking pictures in 1929, usually improvising his lines and generally playing himself. By 1931 he was Hollywood's highest paid star, and in 1935 he was the second-biggest box office draw after Shirley Temple.

Rogers also wrote a daily newspaper feature called "Will Rogers Says." Between his columns and a weekly radio show, his opinions and commentary were reaching over 40 million Americans a week, more than any other journalist. His writing often contained grammatical and punctuation errors which, combined with his common sense and conversational tone, made him seem an everyday man to whom the average American could relate.

Rogers was an aviation enthusiast and was killed in 1935 in a plane crash in Alaska, prompting shock and mourning all across the nation. By then he had famously written his own epitaph: "Here lies Will Rogers. He joked about every prominent man in his time, but he never met a man he didn't like."

Will Rogers (1879–1935)

Will Rogers State Historic Park

Lifeguards of Southern California

S WIMMING in the Pacific Ocean demands caution. A century ago, when no life-guards were on duty, the hazards on southern California's beaches were great. When a swimmer got in trouble, sometimes there was a volunteer who would toss a life ring or row from shore in a cumbersome lifeboat; a would-be rescuer gener-ally avoided getting in the water with a flailing victim. At some beaches there were ropes fixed to the shore; waders tried to hold on as they ventured out. Other beach visi-tors enjoyed the greater safety of saltwater swimming pools, called plunges, that were built at Redondo Beach and elsewhere.

It was at Redondo Beach that George Freeth pioneered new lifesaving techniques. In 1907 Freeth came to California from his native Hawaii, where the young man im-pressed visitors with his ocean skills, which included "surf-board riding." Good-look-ing, athletic, and possessor of all-around talents in the water, Freeth taught swimming at the Redondo Beach plunge, introduced water polo to Californians, and gave surfing demonstrations. He was also an innovative member of the U.S. Volunteer Lifesaving Corps. At a call for help, he would dash to the water's edge, swim through the surf, and pull the swimmer to safety. He introduced two rescue devices: the paddle board and the flotation device called the rescue can, both of which remain in use.

Freeth's speed and skill were highly effective. Newspapers proclaimed him the "hero of Venice, Ocean Park, and Santa Monica" after he reportedly saved or helped to save 50 lives near Venice in 1907–08. During a sudden December storm off Venice in 1908, several Japanese fishing boats were swamped or capsized. Volunteers responded. Three times Freeth swam out through the tumultuous surf to personally rescue seven fisher-men. Altogether, 11 lives were saved that day; none were lost. Afterwards, a chilled and exhausted Freeth was treated to a hot beverage. The *Los Angeles Times* reported, "Girls crowded around just to pat his tanned shoulders and smile at him."

The growing population along southern California's shore justified a professional life-guard service that could be available whenever and wherever needed. Long Beach assigned a lifeguard to the Police Department as early as 1908. In the 1920s the city of Los Angeles provided professional lifeguards at ocean beaches when the towns of Venice and San Pedro were annexed. Huntington Beach and San Diego hired lifeguards starting in 1918, and California State Parks began to provide lifeguard service in 1938 at Orange County beaches.

The professional lifeguard service of the Coun-ty of Los Angeles expanded in the 1930s to serve towns such as Hermosa Beach, Redondo Beach, and Manhattan Beach. Lifeguarding had its Hollywood connection. Johnny Weis-muller, who played Tarzan in the movies, was an honorary Santa Monica lifeguard, as was Buster Crabbe, who played Flash Gordon and Buck Rogers. Actor and state park advocate Leo Carrillo, whose name is memorialized at

George Freeth (1883–1919)

Leo Carrillo State Park in Los Angeles County, was once a working lifeguard in Santa Monica. Marilyn Monroe's boyfriend at one time was Hollywood stuntman and lifeguard, Tom Zahn. The vastly popular television series *Baywatch* was the creation of a Los Angeles County lifeguard.

Lifeguards were innovators in lifesaving techniques. The swim fin was adopted early by Santa Monica lifeguards, and the wetsuit was developed by Los Angeles County lifeguards. During World War II, the county's lifeguards trained U.S. Navy personnel in water survival and scuba diving, or volunteered for service. The first woman lifeguard in the service of Los Angeles County was hired in 1930.

Competitive sporting events among lifeguards are popular, and influential. At the first International Surf Lifesaving Competition held in 1956 near Melbourne, Australia, California lifeguards competed in open water swimming, dory racing, and paddleboard racing with their counterparts from other Pacific locales. The Californians brought with them to Australia the rescue cans, lightweight paddleboards, and cardiopulmonary resuscitation techniques they used at home. The honorary chairman of the Melbourne event was fabled surfer and swimmer "Duke" Kahanamoku, who had been coached decades earlier at the Los Angeles Athletic Club by none other than George Freeth, the hero of Santa Monica Bay beaches.

Today, lifeguards are not only trained for water rescues including diving and cliff rescues, but also are trained in emergency medical techniques such as the use of defibrillator units for heart attack victims. Thousands of rescues are performed annually at southern California beaches, most of them due to rip currents. More numerous still are preventive actions taken by lifeguards, to stop dangerous behavior from becoming life-threatening. In 2006 Newport Beach had 7.5 million beach visitors, and lifeguards reported 3,916 rescues and 84,949 preventive actions, with no fatalities. The U.S. Lifesaving Association estimates that the chance of a person drowning at a beach protected by Association-affiliated lifeguards is 1 in 18 million. This high level of safety can be contrasted with conditions a century ago. In 1918, before San Diego's lifeguard service was organized, 13 persons drowned at Ocean Beach in one day.

Enjoy the water, and always be careful. Do not turn your back on the ocean, keep an eye on your children, and always swim near a lifeguard.

Lifeguard, El Porto Beach

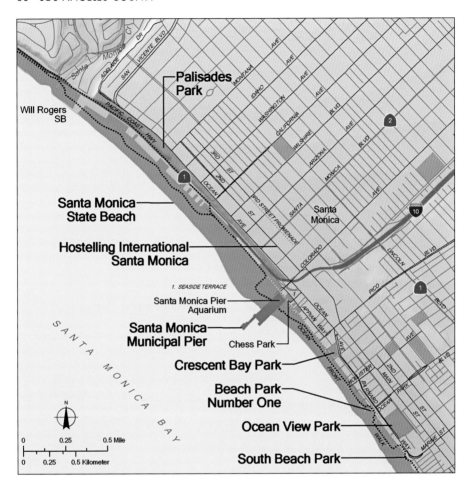

Santa Monica State Beach

Santa Monica

	Sandy Beach	Rocky Shore	Trail	Visitor Center	Campground	Wildlife Viewing	Fishing or Boating	Facilities for Disabled	Food and Drink	Restrooms	Parking	Fee
Palisades Park			•	•				•		•		
Santa Monica State Beach	•		•	•			•	•	•	•	•	•
Hostelling International Santa Monica								•	•	•		•
Santa Monica Municipal Pier				•		•	•	•	•	•	•	
Crescent Bay Park	•		•					•	•	•		
Beach Park Number One	•		•					•	•	•	•	
Ocean View Park										•		
South Beach Park	•		•					•	•	•	•	•

PALISADES PARK: *Along Ocean Ave., from Adelaide Dr. to Colorado Ave., Santa Monica.* In the 1920s, construction commenced on Route 66, a highway which linked Chicago, Illinois with Santa Monica. For generations of visitors, the first sight of the Pacific Ocean was from palm-fringed, blufftop Palisades Park. The view is still lovely. A plaque in the park at the foot of Santa Monica Blvd. commemorates old Route 66, later renamed the Will Rogers Highway. Modern-day visitors can find maps and assistance at the Santa Monica Visitor Information Kiosk near the end of Broadway; call: 310-393-7593. The linear park has nicely landscaped walkways, flowerbeds, shuffleboard courts, and restrooms, as well as vistas of Santa Monica Bay, the beach, and the Santa Monica Mountains. Beach access stairs or ramps are at the ends of Montana, Idaho, and Arizona Avenues.

Palisades Park view to Santa Monica Pier

During the 1920s and '30s, the stretch of oceanfront just north of Santa Monica Pier was known as the Gold Coast, because it was the location of fancy beach clubs and the elegant homes of Hollywood stars such as Cary Grant, Douglas Fairbanks, and Greta Garbo. The largest, most ornate of these homes by far belonged to film star Marion Davies, thanks to her paramour and professional supporter, William Randolph Hearst. Her beach house was actually five different houses all built in the Georgian Colonial style. They included a large three-story mansion with the structure designed by architect William Flannery and the interior designed by Julia Morgan; four other houses for family members, servants, and guests; and grounds with tennis courts, gardens, and two swimming pools. In all, there were 55 bathrooms, 37 fireplaces, and over 100 rooms. There were chandeliers of Tiffany crystal, gold-leaf ceilings, and many elements transported from buildings in Europe, including entire rooms from British mansions, three rooms lifted from an Irish castle, and a ballroom imported from Venice. Hearst spent an estimated $3 million building the complex and another $4 million to decorate it. Always a popular hostess, Davies made her Santa Monica beach house the frequent site of large parties entertaining movie stars, political dignitaries, and other members of society's elite.

Davies sold her estate in the mid-1940s, and the property underwent a number of transformations with different buildings being added and demolished over the years, operating alternately as a private beach club and a luxury hotel known as Ocean House, where guests could enjoy their stay among the antiques and opulent surroundings. It was purchased by the State of California in 1959 and leased to the Sand and Sea Club from the 1960s through 1990. It was then opened to the public for several years as a seasonal beach club and filming site, including serving as the fictional Beverly Hills Beach Club in television's Beverly Hills 90210. In 1994, the Northridge earthquake caused nearly everything on the property to become too damaged to occupy.

The site, located at 415 Pacific Coast Hwy. next to Santa Monica beach parking lot #10 North, is planned after renovation by the city to reopen in 2009 as the Annenberg Community Beach Club. The Club will provide convenient access to Santa Monica Beach and amenities that include beach boardwalks, locker rooms, special event venues, paddle tennis and volleyball courts, concessions, and a children's play area. North House (the original guesthouse) and the 110-foot long Italian marble swimming pool, both designed by architect Julia Morgan, are also being restored for use by the public. These are the two original structures still remaining from Marion Davies' time, offering present-day visitors a special glimpse into the days of Santa Monica's Gold Coast.

Marion Davies (1897–1961)

Santa Monica State Beach

SANTA MONICA STATE BEACH: *W. of Pacific Coast Hwy., Santa Monica.* The extremely wide, sandy beach stretches three and a half miles from Will Rogers State Beach to Venice Beach. Extensive facilities north and south of the pier include sand volleyball nets, playgrounds, and, scattered along the sand, more than a dozen restroom buildings with beach showers. Numbered fee parking lots are spaced along the beach. Skate, bike, and surfboard rentals and food service are available at Perry's Café's four locations at 930 and 1200 Pacific Coast Hwy. and 2400 and 2600 Ocean Front Walk. Other restaurants and snack stands are located near the beach and on the pier.

Grassy picnic areas are found south of the pier at three sites: Crescent Bay Park in the 2000 block of Ocean Ave., Beach Park Number One at the foot of Ocean Park Blvd., and South Beach Park at the south end of Barnard Way. Barbecuing is not allowed in the parks. Wheelchair-accessible boardwalks lead from parking areas onto the sand near the pier, both north and south. Beach wheelchairs can be checked out at no charge from two of the Perry's Café locations, north of the pier at 930 Pacific Coast Hwy. and south of the pier at 2600 Ocean Front Walk. For information, call: 310-452-2399.

Santa Monica State Beach is managed by the city of Santa Monica, which prohibits smoking, glass containers, fires, and temporary enclosures or tents. Dogs are not permitted on the beach. For information, call: 310-458-8974. Lifeguard service is provided by Los Angeles County, which maintains the world's largest professional lifeguard service, now a part of the county's Fire Department. Nearly 30 towers are spaced along the Santa Monica beach; some are staffed year-round on a daily basis, and others are staffed seasonally. Los Angeles County also maintains a fleet of twin-engine diesel rescue boats, and lifeguards are trained in use of defibrillator units for heart attack victims. For more information, call lifeguard headquarters: 310-394-3261.

HOSTELLING INTERNATIONAL SANTA MONICA: *1436 2nd St., Santa Monica.* This large renovated facility, with 254 beds, has a downtown location only two blocks from the beach. Family rooms available. Facilities include a shared kitchen, laundry, and Internet access. Linens included; meals available. Open 24 hours; wheelchair accessible. For information, call: 310-393-9913.

SANTA MONICA MUNICIPAL PIER: *Foot of Colorado Ave., Santa Monica.* South of the pier on Ocean Front Walk at Seaside Terrace is Chess Park, where tables with chess boards are available for use from sunrise to sunset. Also south of the pier on Ocean Front Walk is Muscle Beach, an array of parallel bars and other gymnastics apparatus, for first-come, first-served use. Originally named for the mussels attached to the pier pilings, Muscle Beach came to its altered name after a 1930s project turned the beach into a workout area for Depression-era children. Later, UCLA gymnasts, circus performers, and weightlifters practiced on the beach, until weightlifting equipment was removed in the late 1950s. Today, Venice Beach is known for outdoor bodybuilding and weight training, while the Santa Monica site is popular for gymnastics.

The Santa Monica Pier Aquarium is located on Ocean Front Walk at beach level, under the Carousel. There are interactive displays, touch tanks, and programs for school groups; open to the public Tuesday through Friday from 2:00 PM to 6:00 PM and Saturday and Sunday from 12:30 PM to 6:00 PM. Free admission for children under 12; donations encouraged for others. Fee for groups. Call: 310-393-6149. The aquarium is operated by Heal the Bay, a nonprofit organization that works to improve water quality in southern California's coastal waters, including Santa Monica Bay. Heal the Bay also issues annual, summer, and weekly California Beach Report Cards, grading hundreds of beaches on levels of bacterial pollution; for more information, see: www.healthebay.org.

Located on Appian Way, where it passes beneath the approach to Santa Monica Pier, is the Santa Monica Urban Runoff Recycling Facility. This structure treats dry-season water runoff from Santa Monica and parts of Los Angeles, much of which comes from yard irrigation or car washing. The runoff contains various contaminants, such

Ferris wheel on Santa Monica Pier

Santa Monica State Beach

as trash, oil and grease, and heavy metals. After treatment, the water is used for landscape irrigation or other non-public-contact purposes, rather than being dumped into Santa Monica Bay, as formerly occurred. The facility was designed as a piece of public sculpture, and visitors can view interpretive displays at the site.

CRESCENT BAY PARK: *2000 block, Ocean Ave., Santa Monica.* Green lawns, covered picnic areas, and a beachfront parking lot are located on Ocean Ave. at Bay St. Restrooms with beach showers are at the edge of the sand. A wheelchair-accessible boardwalk leads partway onto the beach.

BEACH PARK NUMBER ONE: *Foot of Ocean Park Blvd., Santa Monica.* A green, landscaped park with picnic tables, play equipment, restrooms, and Perry's Café is located

seaward of Barnard Way; bicycles and skates can be rented at the café. Large fee parking lots are located north and south of the park. A wheelchair-accessible boardwalk leads from the south parking lot out onto the sand.

OCEAN VIEW PARK: *2701 Barnard Way, Santa Monica.* This city park on the inland side of Barnard Way offers a basketball court, two junior paddle tennis courts, and six tennis courts. On weekdays the courts are open to all on a first-come, first-served basis; on weekends courts are monitored and use may be subject to reservation and fees.

SOUTH BEACH PARK: *Barnard Way at Marine St., Santa Monica.* A small strip of lawn next to the wide beach contains picnic tables and children's play equipment; restrooms are adjacent, on the beach, and a large fee parking lot is located to the north.

Santa Monica's beaches and attractions are popular all year. At peak times, traffic congestion can be formidable. Convenient ways to get around include the Tide shuttle bus, which runs in a continuous loop that links the Third Street Promenade, Santa Monica Pier, beaches, and Main St. shops and restaurants; buses run daily all year from noon until 8 PM (until 10 PM on Friday and Saturday). Santa Monica's Big Blue Bus system serves the larger community and neighboring parts of Los Angeles. For information on the Tide shuttle and the Big Blue Bus, call: 310-451-5444. The city of Santa Monica maintains a website that lists all beach parking lots north and south of the pier, downtown parking structures, and tips for best weekend beach parking. The website also provides real-time information, updated constantly, on parking availability in key lots surrounding the pier area; see http://parking.smgov.net.

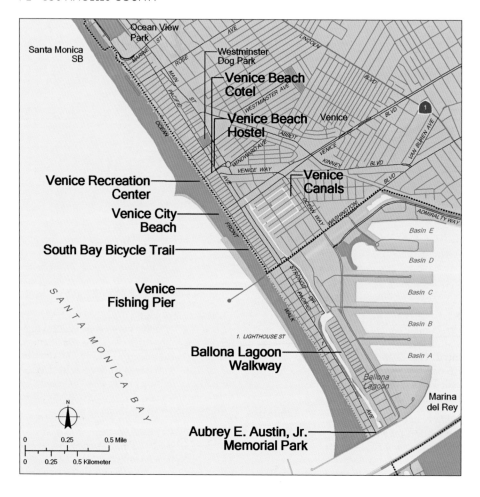

Ocean Front Walk, Venice City Beach

Venice

	Sandy Beach	Rocky Shore	Trail	Visitor Center	Campground	Wildlife Viewing	Fishing or Boating	Facilities for Disabled	Food and Drink	Restrooms	Parking	Fee
Venice Beach Cotel									•		•	
Venice Beach Hostel									•		•	
Venice Recreation Center								•	•	•	•	
Venice City Beach	•		•			•	•		•	•	•	
South Bay Bicycle Trail			•									
Venice Fishing Pier						•	•		•	•		
Venice Canals		•			•							
Ballona Lagoon Walkway		•			•							
Aubrey E. Austin, Jr. Memorial Park	•	•	•		•		•				•	

VENICE BEACH COTEL: *25 Windward Ave., Venice.* This hostel, located steps from the beach, offers both shared rooms and private rooms. Amenities include multi-lingual staff, Internet access, and recreational equipment. Guests must show a valid passport, US or foreign. Fee applies. For information, call: 310-399-7649.

VENICE BEACH HOSTEL: *1515 Pacific Ave., Venice.* Shared rooms sleep a total of 40 persons; there are also 12 private rooms. Facilities include a kitchen, laundry room, common room, and storage lockers. Overnight fee applies; open 24 hours. For information, call: 310-452-3052.

VENICE RECREATION CENTER: *End of Windward Ave., Venice.* The old Venice Pavilion, a recreation facility now demolished, once stood at the end of Windward Ave. Now located at the site are modern outdoor courts for basketball, volleyball, racquetball, and handball; a skate park; children's play area; and a picnic area. The renowned open-air Muscle Beach weight pen, which was renovated in 2008, includes weight-lifting and strength-training equipment. Fees apply for some activities.

The one-time "graffiti pit" that was located near the end of Windward Ave. has been replaced by the Venice Art Walls, which are concrete structures on which artists may express themselves; for a required painting permit, visit on a weekend, or call: 310-535-7729. Modern restrooms with showers are located near the ends of Venice Blvd. and Washington Blvd. For Venice Recreation Center information, call: 310-399-2775. A small, off-leash dog park maintained by the city of Los Angeles is located nearby, at 1234 Pacific Ave.

VENICE CITY BEACH: *Ocean Front Walk, Venice.* A very popular three-mile-long sandy beach is used by swimmers, surfers, divers, and kite-flyers. Fish commonly caught from shore include surf perch, corbina, and halibut. From mid-March through late August grunion spawn on the beach several nights a month immediately following a new or full moon. Sanderlings, gulls, and willets rest and feed on the beach. No fires or alcohol are permitted on the beach; pets are not allowed. Lifeguard service is provided by the County of Los Angeles; headquarters are at 2300 Ocean Front Walk in Venice, and lifeguards are on duty during daylight hours. A beach wheelchair is available at lifeguard headquarters. For surf and tide information, see: www.watchthewater.org.

Paralleling Venice Beach is lively Ocean Front Walk, a paved promenade which draws vendors, street musicians, colorful characters, and visitors from all over. Strolling, jogging, roller-skating, and skateboarding are popular, along with people-watching. Shops and eating establishments are located in the area. Bicycle and skate rentals are located adjacent to the beach, near the ends of Venice Blvd. and Washington Blvd. The parking lot closest to the beach is at the west end of Venice Blvd.; spaces in that fee lot fill up fast. Additional fee parking is available at Venice Blvd. where it intersects Pacific Ave., and, during the summer, at the west end of Rose Ave. and on Westminster Ave., east of Pacific Ave.

SOUTH BAY BICYCLE TRAIL: *Along the beach from Pacific Palisades to Torrance.* A paved, 20-mile-long bicycle route follows the beach closely from Will Rogers State Beach in Pacific Palisades to Torrance. In Venice, the bicycle route detours inland around Marina del Rey Harbor by running along Washington Blvd. and then generally along Admiralty Way and Fiji Way. The trail rejoins the beach south of the channel entrance to Marina del Rey Harbor and then continues south to Torrance County Beach. In Venice, bicyclists and pedestrians use separate, parallel paved alignments. Elsewhere, the South Bay Bicycle Trail is shared by bicyclists, skaters, and pedestrians; please be courteous in using the route.

VENICE FISHING PIER: *End of Washington Blvd., Venice.* In the summer of 1905 a pier,

pavilion, ship-hotel, and auditorium were built at the end of Windward Ave. The pier served as a meeting place and as a site for society dances. The original pier was destroyed by fire in 1920, and was later rebuilt as an amusement midway lined with rides and concessions. Mack Sennett, who made silent films featuring Charlie Chaplin and the Keystone Kops, used the pier for location shooting. After a series of disastrous fires, the pier was demolished in 1947.

A replacement pier was built in 1965, this time at the end of Washington Blvd. The 1,300-foot-long pier has fish cleaning stations, restrooms, and showers. Fish commonly caught from the pier include bonito, mackerel, jacksmelt, halibut, and various species of croakers and perch, as well as the occasional yellowtail or white seabass. The pier is open from 6 AM to midnight. Fee parking is available at the end of Washington Blvd. and also at the corner of Washington Blvd. and Pacific Ave. Additional summer-weekend parking is located at Washington Blvd. and Strongs Dr.

VENICE CANALS: *Between Pacific Ave. and Ocean Ave., S. of Venice Blvd., Venice.* The Venice Canals are bordered on both sides by public sidewalks. Carroll Canal, Linnie Canal, Howland Canal, and Sherman Canal

Venice Pier and Beach

Eastern Canal, Venice

run east and west, and the Grand Canal and Eastern Canal run north and south. Mallards paddle along the waterways, and you might spy a double-crested cormorant roosting on a boat. Parking in the neighborhood is extremely limited; visitors would do better to walk to the canals from nearby beach parking lots. No facilities.

BALLONA LAGOON WALKWAY: *E. side of Ballona Lagoon, Marina del Rey.* A dirt public walkway runs along the east side of the Ballona Lagoon. The landscaped path can be reached from Pacific Ave. via a pedestrian bridge at Lighthouse St. and from Aubrey E. Austin, Jr. Memorial Park. Bufflehead ducks and cormorants feed in the lagoon, and snowy egrets search for prey along its shallow margin. Look for belted kingfishers awaiting their next meal. Dogs must be kept on leash.

AUBREY E. AUSTIN, JR. MEMORIAL PARK: *S. end Pacific Ave., Marina del Rey.* A linear park, part of Marina del Rey but physically at the south end of Venice Beach, runs perpendicular to the end of Pacific Ave. The park is a great place to watch passing boats and crew rowing teams. There is a paved pathway, and benches overlook the Marina del Rey entrance channel. The paved path extends west onto the north jetty of the entrance channel, allowing anglers to reach the water and pedestrians to gain access to the adjacent sandy beach. Metered street parking; no facilities.

Venice Art Walls

In 1904, cigarette magnate Abbot Kinney purchased 160 acres of coastal marshland just south of Santa Monica (once part of the Ballona Wetlands) with the intention of developing a "Venice of America." Architects Norman Marsh and C. H. Russell, commissioned by Kinney to design his project, created the Grand Canal, two networks of smaller canals, and a central lagoon from wetlands that were historically used for hunting and fishing. Gondoliers and gondolas imported from Italy, arched Venetian bridges joining the canals, and the St. Mark's Hotel added authenticity and romance to the venture. Visitors were drawn to the beachfront promenade and the pier with its cafés and an auditorium for lectures and concerts, where such notables as author Helen Hunt Jackson, actress Sarah Bernhardt, and the Chicago Symphony performed. However, attendance soon waned at these cultural events, and from 1910 to 1920, visitors flocked to Venice's roller coasters, casinos, parades, and bathhouse instead. A period of decline began after the death of Abbot Kinney in 1920. Because of design flaws, the canals were often dirty and stagnant. The area's sewer system was inadequate for the growing population, and the narrow streets were designed primarily for pedestrians and not automobiles. By 1930, all but six canals had been paved over. Even during the years of the Great Depression, however, visitors headed for the beach during the heat of summer, and holiday parades and beauty pageants were popular.

A restoration project undertaken by the city of Los Angeles in the 1990s included stabilization of the canal banks, construction of new sidewalks, and landscaping. The public walkways along the canals provide a charming respite from the surrounding busy streets. The well-maintained neighborhood of small-scale, canal-front homes offers visitors a sort of mini-architectural walking tour of Los Angeles, with structures in what seems like every style from Craftsman cottage to the ultra-modern.

Venice dance marathon, ca. 1930s

Keeping Our Ocean Waters Clean

When rinsing a paintbrush, consider how it pollutes runoff into storm drains

C LEAN, CLEAR coastal waters have always contributed to the attractiveness of southern California's shoreline. And most of the time, at most of the beaches, the water is still clean and clear. But the large numbers of people and extensive urban development have taken a toll on the quality of coastal waters. The growth in population near the coast has brought more roads, houses, irrigated landscaping, air pollution, and domestic animals—all elements that contribute to polluted runoff, also referred to as nonpoint source pollution. While state and national initiatives have been successful at reducing water pollution coming from point sources such as factories and waste water treatment plants, polluted runoff has taken on more significance. So an appropriate question is: are the waters along the southern California coast clean enough to swim, fish, and play in?

The good news is that most of our beaches have been tested, and the water is fine for swimming or other forms of recreation, most of the time. California has the most comprehensive beach water quality monitoring in the nation and conducts ongoing efforts to improve testing and standards. Concerns about beach water quality led the California legislature in 1997 to require more frequent monitoring of heavily used beaches and to develop statewide beach water quality standards. As a result, decisions to close beaches and to post warning signs are being made more consistently statewide. More frequent monitoring has identified that, unfortunately, a few beaches often have poor water quality and that many beaches occasionally have poor water quality, especially after rain storms.

In general, you will find clean water in the ocean along California, but to minimize the health risk of swimming or wading, you can observe the following precautions. Avoid swimming in the ocean for two or three days after rainstorms, and always avoid swimming near flowing storm drains. Stay out of beach ponds that form at the ends of creeks

Cigarette butts are the most frequently found debris items on Coastal Cleanup Day in California

or storm drains. Since these ponds are usually shallow, waveless, and warmer than the ocean, they often attract children, but these water bodies are the ultimate recipients of contaminants from streets, yards, and pet waste. Minimizing contact with these pond waters is highly recommended, but if you cannot keep the kids out of the ponds, keeping the water out of their mouths and noses and rinsing off immediately after contact will reduce chances of getting sick.

How do you go about determining the water quality conditions at a beach you intend to visit on a particular day? Each of the southern California counties has a beach water quality information line that beachgoers can call in advance. In Los Angeles County, call: 1-800-525-5662; in Orange County, call: 714-433-6400; and in San Diego County, call: 619-338-2073. For current trends in the quality of coastal waters, you can check out the weekly Beach Report Card. This website is maintained by the nonprofit group, Heal the Bay, at www.healthebay.org/brc. It provides an easy-to-use map, showing beach water quality conditions throughout California. Southern California, where large numbers of people swim and play in the ocean year-round, has information on over 375 beach locations.

You can help make sure that more beaches have excellent water quality by doing your part to address the problem of polluted runoff. The pollutants that cause our beaches to fail the water quality standards come from many sources including our own neighborhoods. One of the biggest mistakes we can make is to confuse the storm drain system (used to prevent flooding) with our sewer system (used to collect and treat wastes). Waste from household plumbing flows through the sewer system and undergoes treatment, but runoff from our yards and streets goes through the storm drain system and then into creeks or the ocean without treatment (except in a handful of California communities). The slogan, "Only rain down the storm drain!" means that we should try to keep all wastes out of the storm drains and only use the storm drains for rainwater.

There are many potential sources of pollutants that can get into the storm drains from our own daily activities. Washing a car in the street sends soap, oil, and grease directly into creeks, and even if the soap is biodegradable over time, it can have a harmful impact on stream and ocean creatures before it breaks down. Improper application of fertilizer, such as applying too much, applying near water bodies, spilling the material onto the sidewalk or street, and applying it just before it rains, can allow the fertilizer to enter storm drains, leading to excessive algae and nuisance plant growth in our coastal waters. Improper application of pesticides can kill beneficial stream and ocean organisms. Leaving pet waste or litter on the ground often results in those pollutants entering storm drains and our coastal waters. We all need to do our part to pick up after our pets, use fertilizers and pesticides carefully, and avoid using storm drains as a place to wash away our wastes.

Like human swimmers, tidepool creatures are affected by polluted runoff. The impacts of storm drain flows that occur between rainstorms and during the summer, the so-called "dry-weather runoff," are particularly bad. While tidepool organisms have evolved to put up with short periods of rainwater, long exposure to fresh water can kill marine creatures. They depend upon the dry periods of the year to recover from the effects of the fresh water and to reestablish their numbers. Such opportunities for recovery are drastically reduced near storm drains that flow throughout the year due to irrigation of yards and gardens. In some areas, overwatering near coastal bluffs results in water discharging directly to the rocky intertidal zone, thus killing tidepool creatures and increasing the potential for bluff collapse. Although it takes some effort to design an efficient irrigation system, in most cases coastal residents can irrigate yards so that no excess water flows to storm drains. Other ways to prevent dry-weather runoff are sweeping, rather than hosing off, sidewalks and driveways and washing cars on the lawn or at a car wash instead of in the street. Remember that intertidal organisms, fish, marine mammals, and people too may end up swimming in whatever you send down the storm drain.

Car washing sends soap, oil, and grease directly into creeks and coastal waters

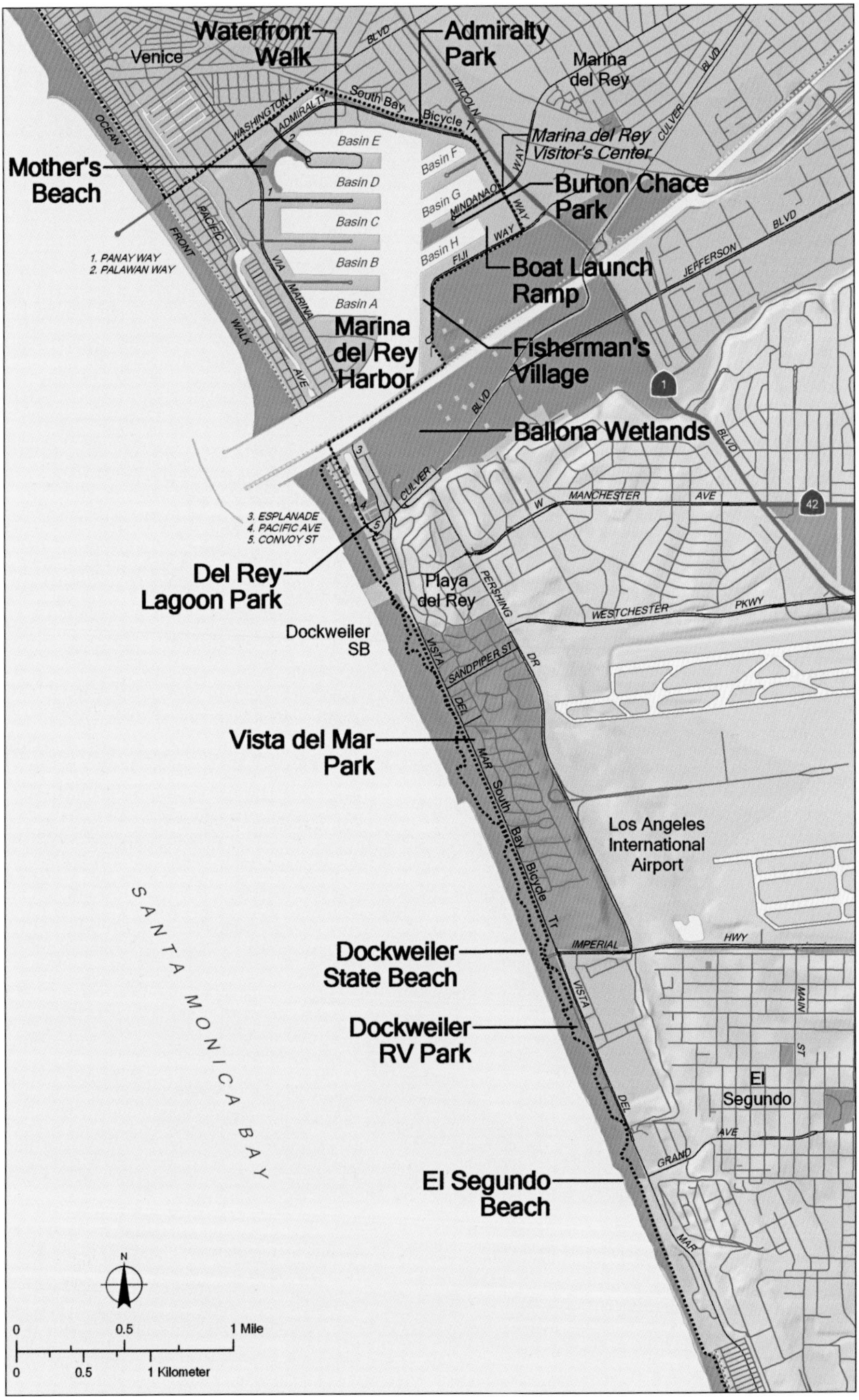

Waterfront Walk

Admiralty Park

Venice

Marina del Rey

Mother's Beach

Marina del Rey Visitor's Center

Burton Chace Park

Basin E

Basin F

Basin D

Basin G

Basin C

Basin H

Boat Launch Ramp

1. PANAY WAY
2. PALAWAN WAY

Basin B

Basin A

Marina del Rey Harbor

Fisherman's Village

Ballona Wetlands

3. ESPLANADE
4. PACIFIC AVE
5. CONVOY ST

MANCHESTER   AVE

Del Rey Lagoon Park

Playa del Rey

WESTCHESTER   PKWY

Dockweiler SB

Vista del Mar Park

Los Angeles International Airport

Dockweiler State Beach

IMPERIAL   HWY

Dockweiler RV Park

El Segundo

SANTA MONICA BAY

Dockweiler State Beach

El Segundo Beach

N

0   0.5   1 Mile

0   0.5   1 Kilometer

Marina del Rey to El Segundo

	Sandy Beach	Rocky Shore	Trail	Visitor Center	Campground	Wildlife Viewing	Fishing or Boating	Facilities for Disabled	Food and Drink	Restrooms	Parking	Fee
Marina del Rey Harbor				•			•	•	•	•	•	
Mother's Beach	•						•	•	•	•	•	•
Waterfront Walk				•			•	•				
Admiralty Park				•								
Burton Chace Park							•	•		•	•	
Boat Launch Ramp							•			•	•	
Fisherman's Village							•		•	•	•	•
Ballona Wetlands			•			•						
Del Rey Lagoon Park							•			•	•	
Vista del Mar Park											•	
Dockweiler State Beach	•		•			•	•		•	•	•	•
Dockweiler RV Park	•				•		•		•	•	•	
El Segundo Beach	•		•				•			•	•	•

MARINA DEL REY HARBOR: *S. of Venice, W. of Lincoln Blvd., Marina del Rey.* Marina del Rey is the largest small craft harbor on the West Coast. Along with over 6,000 boat slips, the harbor contains boat repair and fuel services, dry storage facilities, yacht clubs, parks, restaurants, shops, and hotels. There is a residential population of some 10,000. Public access is available along most of the marina's bulkheads. Pets must be leashed.

Summertime water bus service links Burton Chace Park, Fisherman's Village, Mother's Beach, and several other locations within Marina del Rey on Friday evenings, weekend days and evenings, and certain holidays. Fare applies. Bikes and strollers welcome; no pets. Call: 310-628-3219. The Los Angeles County Dept. of Beaches and Harbors offers a wide range of summer youth camps that teach about water safety and marine life along with surfing, sailing, kayaking, and junior lifeguard skills. Call: 310-305-9587.

What is now the marina was once known as the Playa del Rey inlet, where, from 1815 to 1825, the Los Angeles River emptied into the Pacific Ocean. (The river now flows into the

sea at Long Beach.) Dredging of the wetlands for construction of a recreational harbor began in 1960, and in 1962 the harbor opened. The harbor is all public property, owned by the County of Los Angeles, and long-term leases accommodate private developments. The Department of Beaches and Harbors is located at 13837 Fiji Way; call: 310-305-9546. The Marina del Rey Visitor's Center is located at 4701 Admiralty Way; open daily from 9 AM to 5 PM; or call: 310-305-9545.

MOTHER'S BEACH: *End of Basin D, Panay Way, Marina del Rey.* Generations of young people have learned to swim at Mother's Beach, which offers quiet water and daily lifeguard service. Check water quality reports before use; call the Los Angeles County Dept. of Public Health Beach Advisory Hotline at 1-800-525-5662 or 626-430-5360. Facilities include children's play equipment, volleyball nets, picnic shelters, and restrooms with beach showers. Fee parking lots are on Palawan Way and Panay Way. Kayaks and small, non-motorized boats can be hand-launched at no charge; for boat launchers, there is free short-term parking along Palawan Way. A beach wheelchair is suitable for loan from the lifeguard station; call: 310-394-3261. Dogs are not permitted on the beach.

WATERFRONT WALK: *Along N. edge of Marina del Rey.* A wide public walkway leads along the bulkhead, offering nice views of boats in the harbor. Enter the walkway from Palawan Way near Mother's Beach or from Admiralty Way through the Ritz Carlton Hotel or next to the fire station.

ADMIRALTY PARK: *Admiralty Way, Marina del Rey.* A landscaped linear park is located along the north side of Admiralty Way. A par course fitness circuit and a mile-long jogging loopare here, and the South Bay Bicycle Path runs through the park.

BURTON CHACE PARK: *W. end of Mindanao Way, Marina del Rey.* Ten-acre Burton Chace Park offers picnic facilities, harbor viewing, and many activities, including Fourth of July fireworks and boat parades. Free outdoor summer pops concerts are held; call: 310-305-9545. The Dept. of Beaches and Harbors offers fee kayaking and water safety instruction; call: 310-305-9587. A fishing dock and fish cleaning station are available. Cooking fires are allowed in the barbecue grills; no other fires allowed in Marina del Rey.

No-reservation guest boat docks are located next to the park, facing the main channel. Four-hour slips are free and require no registration; longer stays require a fee. Restrooms and showers available for boaters. Call: 310-305-9595. A pumpout station for use by all boaters is next to the guest docks.

BOAT LAUNCH RAMP: *13477 Fiji Way, Marina del Rey.* Trailered boats can be launched at the head of Basin H; enter from Fiji Way. Open 24 hours. Fee covers launch and retrieval plus 24-hour parking. For longer parking, call in advance: 310-305-9534.

FISHERMAN'S VILLAGE: *Fiji Way, Marina del Rey.* Shops, galleries, and eating establishments, with the look of a New England seaport. Fishing licenses and bait and tackle available. Harbor tours depart from Fisherman's Village; call: 310-301-6000. Sport fishing charters can be arranged; call: 310-822-3625. For boat rentals, call: 310-574-2822. A high-speed catamaran service operates seasonally to Catalina Island; call: 310-305-7250. Validated fee parking. The University of California at Los Angeles Marina Aquatic Center, next to Fisherman's Village, offers training in sailing, rowing, kayaking, surfing, and windsurfing, including introductory sessions for short-term visitors; for information, call: 310-823-0048.

BALLONA WETLANDS: *W. of Lincoln Blvd. along Culver Blvd. and Jefferson Blvd., Playa del Rey.* A restored freshwater marsh is at the corner of Lincoln Blvd. and Jefferson Blvd.;

Ballona Wetlands

park along Jefferson, eastbound. Public tours are offered by Friends of Ballona Wetlands; call: 310-306-5994. Future restoration of the adjacent saltmarsh is planned.

DEL REY LAGOON PARK: *6660 Esplanade, Playa del Rey.* A neighborhood park, Del Rey Lagoon Park has picnic tables with barbecue grills, a baseball diamond, basketball courts, and a playground; restrooms are not wheelchair accessible. Park open dawn to dusk. Parking on Pacific Ave. at Convoy St. or on surrounding streets. Call: 310-396-1615.

VISTA DEL MAR PARK: *E. of Vista del Mar, S. of Sandpiper St., Playa del Rey.* Picnic tables on a green lawn with palm trees are located on the inland side of Vista del Mar, opposite Dockweiler State Beach. Street parking.

DOCKWEILER STATE BEACH: *W. of Vista del Mar from Marina del Rey entrance channel to S. of Grand Ave., El Segundo.* The very wide, three-mile-long sandy beach has several main entry points. At the end of Culver Blvd. there are restrooms and a lifeguard station; fee parking lots are at the intersection of Convoy St. and Pacific Ave. and at the north end of Pacific Ave., and there is some street parking. Much more parking is available at the Dockweiler State Beach entrance at the end of Imperial Hwy., and an additional entrance is south of the Dockweiler RV Park. Altogether, there are over 2,000 parking spaces.

Picnic areas, snack bars, and restrooms with outdoor showers are spaced along the beach. Lifeguards on duty during daylight hours. Beach wheelchairs are available; call: 310-372-2162. For surf and tide information,

see: www.watchthewater.org. The South Bay Bicycle Trail runs the length of Dockweiler State Beach. Fires allowed in fire rings only. The beach is maintained by the Los Angeles County Department of Beaches and Harbors. The County of Los Angeles plans to open a new facility at Dockweiler Beach by 2009 for the Water Awareness, Training, Education, and Recreation (WATER) Program, which introduces at-risk youth to the ocean, marine life, and water safety.

DOCKWEILER RV PARK: *12001 Vista del Mar, Playa del Rey.* The only RV camping on the beach in Los Angeles County, located south of Imperial Hwy. Complete hook-ups, pump-out station, wheelchair-accessible hot showers, and laundromat. Open all year except January; call: 310-322-4951. Dogs OK.

EL SEGUNDO BEACH: *End of W. Grand Ave., El Segundo.* A wide, sandy beach is located opposite the foot of Grand Ave. Part of Dockweiler State Beach, El Segundo Beach has sand volleyball, fee parking, and chemical toilets.

El Segundo, whose name is Spanish for "the second," was named in 1911 for Standard Oil Company's second oil refinery in California. Inhabiting a small remnant dune at the Chevron Corporation's refinery is the El Segundo blue butterfly, colored blue and orange, and with a wingspan of only three quarters of an inch. The endangered El Segundo blue butterfly depends upon the coastal buckwheat plant. Native plant restoration has protected the butterfly at El Segundo and the dunes west of Los Angeles International Airport.

Dockweiler State Beach

Communities of herons and egrets are redefining what is considered wildlife habitat in southern California by establishing their nests and roosts in tall trees amidst the hustle and bustle of urban neighborhoods. In parking lots, alleyways, and outside apartment windows, close-knit groups of herons and egrets are perpetuating their populations in spite of the surrounding commotion. Each year, from late winter through spring, the sound of our car alarms and stereos is matched by avian squawks and chatter announcing the commencement of breeding season. Position yourself in March or April near one of the few heron and egret colonies in southern California, at Channel Islands Harbor, Marina del Rey, or Alamitos Marina, and you are likely to witness a heron alight on its sweeping wingspan in a skyscraping tree and pass an incongruously thin branch to a waiting mate. Twig by twig the heron crafts a platform nest high in the trees.

Wading birds, such as the great blue heron, black-crowned night heron, and snowy egret, are among the more conspicuous birds that nest in urban areas. Wading birds take their collective name from the slow stalking movement by which they tiptoe through placid lagoon waters on their stilt-like legs, hunting small fish and aquatic invertebrates. Rarely is a wading bird colony composed of a single bird species; typically, two or three species coexist noisily. In some locations, a few double-crested cormorants congregate on the fringes of the colony or a great egret mixes with the waders. Invariably, the stately great blue heron takes up residence high in the center of the colony tree.

Year after year, the birds congregate in familiar colony trees to nest. The trees that are most attractive to the feathered colonists are not necessarily native to southern California, but all are tall with dense foliage, including trees such as cypress, pine, eucalyptus, and palm. Years, even decades, of continual use make a colony tree easily identifiable by its guano-stained branches and trunk. Many herons and egrets are year-round residents of southern California and continue to flock to the colony trees outside of breeding season, return-

Great blue heron in breeding plumage near Fiji Way in Marina del Rey

ing nightly to the same trees to roost communally following a day of foraging. From the ground far below, the behavior known as roosting may be mistaken as mere loafing in the evening glow after a day's work, but the social benefits are believed to be critical to the lives of wading birds. Young birds especially benefit from their elders' familiarity with the locations of prime foraging areas in the favored hunting ground of wading birds, our vanishing wetlands.

A common characteristic of all wading-bird colonies is that the chosen site is only a short flight away from a nearby wetland. In southern California, wetlands originally occupied what both humans and herons consider prime coast-al real estate, and vast areas of those wetlands have been displaced for residential and commercial development.

Undeterred by this relatively recent turn of events, herons continue to look for nest sites near the lost or diminished wetlands. The development projects which have paved over wetlands and which often incorporate geographically anomalous, lush landscaping have, probably unintentionally, provided nesting opportunities for wading birds. Where once herons nested in native riparian trees in the streams feeding coastal wetlands, they now make do in the towering spires of such alien trees as Australian gums, African corals, and Arabian palms.

Marina del Rey

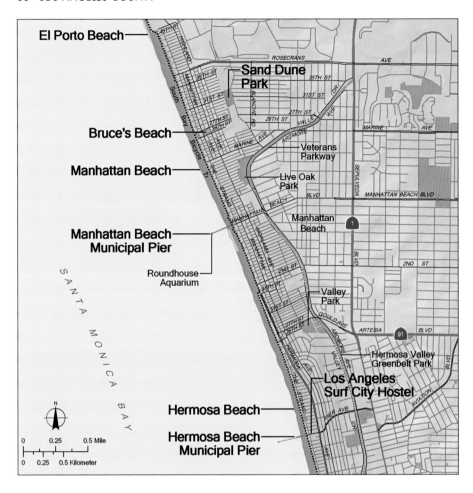

El Porto Beach

Manhattan Beach and Hermosa Beach

	Sandy Beach	Rocky Shore	Trail	Visitor Center	Campground	Wildlife Viewing	Fishing or Boating	Facilities for Disabled	Food and Drink	Restrooms	Parking	Fee
El Porto Beach	•	•					•		•	•	•	•
Sand Dune Park							•			•	•	
Bruce's Beach							•			•	•	•
Manhattan Beach	•	•					•		•	•	•	
Manhattan Beach Municipal Pier				•			•	•	•	•		
Hermosa Beach	•	•					•		•	•	•	
Hermosa Beach Municipal Pier							•	•	•	•		
Los Angeles Surf City Hostel									•		•	

EL PORTO BEACH: *W. end of 45th St., Manhattan Beach.* A highly popular surfing beach, El Porto also has volleyball nets, bicycle racks, and restrooms with beach showers; a food concession and equipment rentals are located near the midpoint of the parking lot. Year-round lifeguard service from dawn to dusk. To arrange use of a beach wheelchair, call the lifeguard station: 310-372-2162. Wheelchair-accessible restrooms are at the south end of the parking area. Metered beach parking with five-hour limit; lot closes at 8 PM.

SAND DUNE PARK: *31st St. W. of Blanche Rd., Manhattan Beach.* A remnant sand dune, 100 feet high, is located in this city park. Children enjoy sliding down, while fitness buffs climb up. The park also contains children's play equipment, picnic facilities, and restrooms. As the city of Manhattan Beach grew following incorporation in 1912, extensive sand dunes were leveled or built over; in the 1920s, some sand was even shipped to beaches in Hawaii.

BRUCE'S BEACH: *27th St. and Highland Ave., Manhattan Beach.* Nice coastal views can be had from this green, hillside city park. Formerly named Parque Culiacán for Manhattan Beach's sister city in Mexico, the park was renamed Bruce's Beach in 2006. A narrow basketball court and benches occupy the steep site; restrooms are at beach level. Metered off-street parking is on 26th St. at Manhattan Ave.

MANHATTAN BEACH: *W. of the Strand, Manhattan Beach.* Manhattan Beach has two miles of sandy shoreline, all of it accessible to the public and used for swimming, surfing, volleyball, and relaxing. The Strand, used by pedestrians, joggers, and skaters, extends the length of the beach, as does the parallel South Bay Bicycle Trail. Sand volleyball courts and restrooms with beach showers are located near the pier, and fee parking lots are at the foot of Manhattan Beach Blvd. Los Angeles County lifeguard stations are at the foot of Marine Ave. and at the pier; seasonal lifeguard towers are spaced along the sand. Lifeguards on duty during daylight hours. To arrange use of a beach wheelchair, call: 310-372-2162. For surf and tide information, see: www.watchthewater.org. Dogs are not permitted on the beach; no smoking, alcohol, or fires allowed. Many street ends provide access to the beach, but neighborhood parking can be tight.

MANHATTAN BEACH MUNICIPAL PIER: *Foot of Manhattan Beach Blvd., Manhattan Beach.* The 928-foot-long pier, renovated with funding from the State Coastal Conservancy, is maintained by the city of Manhattan Beach. Anglers fish from the pier for halibut, mackerel, and perch and croaker species. Open from 6 AM to midnight. Restrooms are at the foot of the pier. No dogs allowed.

The Roundhouse Aquarium at the west end of the pier exhibits garibaldi fish, Spanish shawl nudibranchs, sharks found in Santa

Monica Bay, sunflower stars, California sheepheads, and more. A touch tank contains tidepool creatures. Open to the public weekdays from 3 PM to sunset and weekends from 10 AM to sunset; the aquarium is used by school field trips at other times. Donations accepted. Call: 310-379-8117.

HERMOSA BEACH: *W. of the Strand, Hermosa Beach.* Hermosa Beach's two miles of sandy shoreline is all public beach. Volleyball nets are near the pier, and swimming and surfing are popular too. The paved walkway known as The Strand extends along the beach, continuing north into Manhattan Beach, but interrupted by stairs at 35th St. in Hermosa Beach. Lifeguard service on Hermosa Beach is provided by Los Angeles County. A beach wheelchair is available from the lifeguard station near the pier; for information from area headquarters, call: 310-372-2162. For information about surf and tide conditions, see: www.watchthewater.org. Dogs not permitted on the beach; no alcohol or fires.

HERMOSA BEACH MUNICIPAL PIER: *Foot of Pier Ave., Hermosa Beach.* The original wooden Hermosa Beach Pier was built in 1904 and destroyed by storms in 1913. A concrete replacement pier met a similar fate. The current, rebuilt pier is used for fishing and ocean-viewing. Anglers fish from the pier for halibut, mackerel, and perch and croaker species. At the foot of the pier is a bronze statue dedicated to the memory of Los Angeles County lifeguard Tim Kelly, a noted surfer and youth worker who died in 1964. Restrooms are nearby.

LOS ANGELES SURF CITY HOSTEL: *26 Pier Ave., Hermosa Beach.* Offering oceanview rooms, the hostel is located right on The Strand. Facilities include a shared kitchen, laundry, and Internet access; breakfast and linens are included. Call: 310-798-2323.

Hermosa Beach Municipal Pier

Mrs. Willa Bruce and her son, Charles A. Bruce, were African-American entrepreneurs who operated a beach resort near 26th St. in Manhattan Beach in the 1910s and 1920s. The California Constitution guarantees public access for all to the navigable waters of the state, but in the early 20th century few southern California beaches were open to African-Americans. (A beach in Santa Monica known as the Ink Well, from the end of Pico Blvd. south to Ocean Park Blvd., was another site where African-Americans were not restricted from going to the beach.)

At the Bruces' establishment, visitors enjoyed dining, dancing, and bathing in the sea. White residents objected to the increasingly popular spot, and in the 1920s the Bruces and other African American property owners nearby were ousted by the local government through condemnation proceedings. But African-American beachgoers continued to resist expulsion, and some were arrested for sitting on the beach or swimming. In 1927, the city of Manhattan Beach acknowledged the right of all to go to the beach and set aside its entire shoreline for the public. The African-American newspaper *Pacific Defender* reported at the time that the city's action would mean the beach would "forever remain open and free of access to the general public without restrictions." A plaque erected in 2006 by the city of Manhattan Beach in the hillside park now named Bruce's Beach notes the injustice of what took place there and states: "All are welcome."

Manhattan Beach

Manhattan Beach is home to a sport that epitomizes the southern California beach lifestyle—beach volleyball. The first beach volleyball courts reportedly were set up in Santa Monica in the 1920s, and the first official two-man tournament was held at Will Rogers State Beach in 1947. Sand volleyball courts are common now, but Manhattan Beach plays a special role in the sport: this beach holds the premier event on the professional beach volleyball tour—the Manhattan Open, which debuted in 1960. In this tournament, bragging rights are even more valuable than the prize money. To add to the honor, winners of the Manhattan Open are remembered by a volleyball-shaped bronze plaque mounted on the Manhattan Pier Volleyball Walk of Fame. Karch Kiraly, regarded as the "King of the Beach," has the most Manhattan Open titles with ten. Players say there is something special about Manhattan's tournament: the knowledgeable and spirited fans, the intense competition, and the ideal beach environment making the Manhattan Open the most anticipated beach volleyball tournament of the year.

Professional beach volleyball tournaments have grown in size and popularity. In the 1980s, visitors could just show up at the beach and set up beach chairs next to the main court. Now, there is a large stadium surrounding center court and sponsors' booths at the entrance. Charging an admission fee for a volleyball tournament on the public beach has raised some controversy between those who value free access onto the beach for all and those who support the business enterprise of the Association of Volleyball Professionals (AVP). Despite this debate, players and fans agree that beach volleyball is here to stay and Manhattan Beach will certainly remain the premier place to watch and play. The annual tournament occurs usually in August; see: www.avp.com.

Beaches

BEACHES and southern California go together. Think of southern California beach music, southern California beach movies, and southern California beach culture. Many of the beaches in southern California fit the classic image: wide stretches of sand, palm trees, volleyball courts, gentle waves, and sea breezes scented by a mixture of salt spray and coconut sun tan lotion. Sandy beaches are found along three-quarters of the 190 miles of coast in Los Angeles, Orange, and San Diego Counties, and these beaches are much-used recreational areas. On a warm summer weekend, over a million people may travel to the southern California coast to swim, jog, surf, play volleyball, fish, or just enjoy being outdoors. Few of these beach visitors may recognize how the urbanization they see around them has altered the beach itself.

In 1900, the shore of Santa Monica Bay was sparsely developed; only 170,000 people lived in all of Los Angeles County. The low-lying areas inland of the Santa Monica Bay beaches were covered with sand dunes formed over millennia. As new residents settled this area, most of the dunes were flattened to accommodate roads, building pads, or to provide construction materials. The small craft harbor at Marina del Rey was created through an enormous construction and excavation project. The jetties and breakwater that control the inlet channel to Marina del Rey have had a persistent influence on sand movement along the coast. A less obvious influence of this harbor on beaches stems from the disposal of all the sand that was excavated during harbor construction. Over ten million cubic yards of sand were excavated from the harbor and placed on Dockweiler Beach. An additional 20 million cubic yards of sand from construction of the Hyperion Sewage Treatment Plant and the Scattergood Power Plant, both located in El Segundo, and other major construction projects were put on the beaches at Dockweiler and Venice. This sand placement has resulted in an incidental, long-term beach nourishment effort for Los Angeles-area beaches. Much of the sand has moved from where it was originally placed but is still part of a southern California beach somewhere. Some beaches on Santa Monica Bay are wider now than they were a century ago.

Redondo County Beach

The beach that we notice as we walk along the coast includes the dry sand and the intertidal parts of the beach, but the sandy zone extends far offshore, out of sight. All the beach sand, whether on the dry beach or offshore, is sorted by grain size and moved by waves and currents. The general trend is for sand to be moved onshore by gentle spring and summer waves, to be moved offshore by larger winter storm waves, and to be moved along the coast following the direction of waves as they approach the shoreline. In Santa Monica Bay, waves tend to move sand in a clockwise direction, from Point Dume to the deep Redondo Submarine Canyon, which traps sand.

The long-term retention of sand that was placed along Santa Monica Bay stems in part from the many structures that were built to support boating—the Santa Monica breakwater, the jetties and breakwater at Marina Del Rey, the King Harbor breakwater, and others. These structures, while installed for navigation or other purposes, have had the unintended consequence of slowing the longshore transport of sand in the bay and thereby contributing to the long-term stability of many Santa Monica Bay beaches.

Whatever the source of sand, beaches provide unique ecological services, such as filtering water, recycling nutrients, and providing critical habitats for hundreds of species. The sand supports both microscopic and macroscopic (easily seen) creatures. The microscopic creatures live in the spaces around sand grains, and the macroscopic creatures live in the sand and around beach wrack, which consists of loose seaweed as well as seeds and plant debris from terrestrial sources. The wrack supports a dynamic food web of herbivores, omnivores, and carnivores. Amphipods, isopods, worms, pseudo-scorpions, beetles, and flies are a few of the creatures found in the wrack. These creatures, in turn, are prey for shorebirds. Sand crabs are abundant around the wrack, but a lot of other animals make a living here too, including polycheate worms, olive snails, and several species of clams.

Unlike other marine ecosystems, beaches produce very little food. A small amount of primary productivity occurs within the top few inches of sand where photosynthesis takes place among microscopic plants, such as diatoms and dinoflagellates. However, the bulk of nutrients and organic material are delivered to and from beaches via rip currents, nearshore currents, tides, waves, and wind. The jetties, seawalls, and harbors that affect sand transport along the coast also interrupt normal circulation patterns of organic materials onto and along the beaches.

The amount of organic material on the beach is affected by the beach management practice known as grooming, performed to present a "clean" and "attractive" appearance. But this practice can dramatically disrupt the natural ecology of beaches by removing wrack and its associated organisms. And during grunion season, beach grooming can destroy grunion eggs deposited in the sand. As more cities and counties have become aware of the importance of healthy, natural beaches, beach grooming practices have been adjusted to avoid grooming during grunion runs, to hand-rake instead of using heavy equipment, to groom only when an excessive amount of wrack is on the beach, or to simply leave some beaches ungroomed altogether. Beach grooming is practiced in Los Angeles County at Will Rogers State Beach; in Orange County at Huntington Beach and Newport Beach; and in San Diego County at Pacific Beach, Mission Beach, and Ocean Beach. Generally ungroomed beaches can be seen in Los Angeles County at Cabrillo Beach; in Orange County at Doheny State Beach; and in San Diego County at Torrey Pines City Beach. Research has documented that the diversity of both invertebrates and birds is significantly higher on ungroomed beaches.

Beach hopper

If you sit next to a pile of seaweed (wrack) on any California beach you are almost guaranteed to encounter a **beach hopper** (*Megalorchestia* sp.), one of the most abundant creatures found on sandy beaches. Scientists have counted as many as 25,000 per square meter. Also known as sand fleas, beach hoppers are a type of crustacean called an amphipod. Beach hoppers are aptly named because in spite of how small they are, only a few millimeters in length, they can hop as high as three feet. For the most part, beach hoppers stay hidden under sand and beach wrack during the day and emerge at night to go to work devouring kelp. Studies in South Africa have shown that beach hoppers can consume 70 percent of the kelp on the beach. Beach hoppers serve as an important prey item for predatory beetles and many species of shorebirds.

Pictured rove beetle

The **pictured rove beetle** (*Thinopinus pictus*) is a large, flightless, nocturnal beetle. Unless you dig in the sand under wrack piles or spend time on ungroomed beaches at night, you are unlikely to ever have the pleasure of seeing one. These handsome beetles emerge from the sand at night, often in large numbers, to hunt their prey, which consists of other insects and crustaceans, especially beach hoppers. Pictured rove beetles have specific habitat requirements—beaches with wrack. Although their range spans sandy beaches from Baja California to northern California, their distribution has been greatly reduced due to beach grooming.

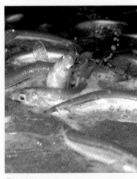

Grunion

Grunion (*Leuresthes tenuis*) participate in a striking behavior: male and female fish wriggle out of the water onto the dry beach to spawn. Under cover of darkness grunion flop onto southern California beaches following a full or new moon. After the peak of the high tide, a female grunion rides a wave onto the beach and vertically buries her posterior half in the sand; several males will then immediately curl around the female, fertilizing her released eggs. The adults then return to the ocean, while the eggs remain in the sand for the next two weeks until the next cycle of high tides pulls them back to the sea, stimulating the larvae to hatch. Adult grunion grow to a maximum length of seven inches. Grunion are not an abundant species, likely due to loss of spawning habitat.

The adult **California gull** (*Larus californicus*) is a me-
dium-sized gull with a white head, dark gray back,
and wings with black tips and white spots. The legs
are greenish-yellow, the eyes are dark brown, and the
bill is yellow with a red spot or, in winter, a black spot.
From late summer through winter California gulls are
commonly seen in southern California on beaches,
playfields, landfills, and parking lots. The gull's diet
includes fish, insects, small mammals, marine invertebrates, fruit, grain, and garbage. The California gull
breeds in colonies near inland bodies of water, including the Great Salt Lake, from northern Canada to the
central United States. Nests are built on the ground and
are tended by monogamous couples, or sometimes by
a pair or trio of females. *Larus californicus* is Utah's state
bird; in 1848 flocks of gulls saved the crops of pioneer
settlers from hordes of crickets.

California gull

The **black skimmer** (*Rynchops niger*) looks like a tern
but has a highly distinctive, and specialized, bill. The
lower mandible of the thin, red-and-black bill is longer
than the upper mandible, and the black skimmer feeds
by poking the lower mandible just below the surface
of a body of water while gliding above. Contact with a
fish results in the upper bill snapping shut instantly on
the prey. Hunting by feel allows the black skimmer to
forage readily at dusk and after dark, as well as during
the day. Black skimmers are found widely in migratory groups along the Atlantic coast of North and South
America, whereas southern California's resident black
skimmer population is relatively new (the first bird in
California was identified in Orange County in 1962).

Black skimmer

The **California least tern** (*Sterna antillarum browni*) mi-
grates from Mexico and South America to spend spring
and summer months along the California coast. This
is the smallest North American tern, further distinguished by a contrasting black cap and white forehead.
The California least tern nests in open sandy areas near
coastal waters where it dives for fish. The nests are not
elaborate, consisting of bits of shell or pebbles, and the
exposed speckled eggs, which blend in with the sand,
are often trampled. In recent years, the nesting sites of
breeding colonies have been fenced off and monitored
in an effort to protect these endangered birds.

California least tern

Redondo Beach Marina

Redondo Beach

	Sandy Beach	Rocky Shore	Trail	Visitor Center	Campground	Wildlife Viewing	Fishing or Boating	Facilities for Disabled	Food and Drink	Restrooms	Parking	Fee
SEA Lab				•	•	•			•	•		
King Harbor							•		•	•	•	•
Seaside Lagoon	•								•	•	•	•
Redondo Sportfishing Pier							•		•	•	•	
Plaza Park							•			•		
Redondo Beach Municipal Pier							•		•	•	•	
Monstad Pier						•	•			•		
Veterans Park							•		•	•		
Redondo County Beach	•	•					•		•	•		

SEA LAB: *1021 N. Harbor Dr., Redondo Beach.* SEA Lab is a short block south of Herondo St. Originally a marine research station, founded in 1974 by electric utility company Southern California Edison, this facility is now a coastal science education center managed by the Los Angeles Conservation Corps. School groups visit the SEA Lab, while a mobile Traveling Tidepool brings intertidal organisms to students at other locations. Visitors of all ages are welcome to visit the SEA Lab for 30-minute guided tours of the touch tanks, when school groups are not present; call ahead for tour availability.

Tidepool talks and fish feeding take place on Saturdays at noon. Aquariums contain treefish, blacksmith fish, moon jellies, and much more. SEA Lab also offers activities such as guided beach exploration walks and summer day camps for mini-mariners. Open Tuesday through Friday from 9 AM to 5 PM, Saturday from 10 AM to 4:30 PM, and Sunday from 11 AM to 4:30 PM. Donations encouraged. For information, call: 310-318-7438.

KING HARBOR: *W. of Harbor Dr., Redondo Beach.* King Harbor contains four marinas with a total capacity of more than 1,400 boats and a wide range of marine supplies and services, including fuel service and pumpout station. For information, call the harbor patrol at 310-318-0632.

King Harbor Marina has a capacity of 827 boats along with boating and commercial facilities. Call: 310-376-6926, and select "other services" for information on sailing lessons, boat rentals, marine repairs, fishing and sightseeing charters, boat fueling, and boat repair. Fee parking.

The Redondo Beach Marina is located adjacent to the Redondo Sportfishing Pier. Sportfishing and whale-watching trips are available, along with boat rides, boat charters, sailing classes, and bicycle rentals. There are two five-ton boat hoists and a launch

Redondo Beach Municipal Pier

for hand-carried watercraft; fee for service. Guest boat slips are usually available. For all services, call: 310-374-3481. King Harbor includes Port Royal Marina, 555 Harbor Dr., and Portofino Marina, on Portofino Way.

SEASIDE LAGOON: *200 Portofino Way, Redondo Beach.* Seaside Lagoon is a three-acre, warm-water swimming lagoon with lifeguard service, children's playground, lawns, volleyball courts, and snack bar. Fee for entry; call: 310-318-0681. The lagoon is a unique recreational facility, built in 1963 and made possible by the nearby Redondo Beach Generating Station. Sea water that cools the power plant passes through the lagoon before discharge into the ocean. Because of aging mechanical equipment and the requirements of modern water quality standards, the city of Redondo Beach in 2007 began to study rehabilitating or replacing the lagoon.

REDONDO SPORTFISHING PIER: *W. of Harbor Dr., N. of Basin 3, Redondo Beach.* A 200-foot-long wooden pier is located south of Seaside Lagoon. Fishing licenses, equipment sales and rentals, sportfishing charters, and food service; live bait is usually available. Restrooms on the pier are not wheelchair accessible. Surface parking lot is adjacent to the pier; fee applies.

PLAZA PARK: *Foot of Diamond St., Redondo Beach.* Also known as Czuleger Park, this grassy area on a bluff east of Harbor Basin 3 has benches, paved paths, and views. The park provides access via both stairs and a wheelchair-accessible elevator to pedestrian walkways in King Harbor. A parking structure is nearby; metered parking is available on Catalina Ave.

REDONDO BEACH MUNICIPAL PIER: *Foot of Torrance Blvd., Redondo Beach.* The roughly V-shaped, 1,550-foot-long Redondo Beach Municipal Pier is also known as the Horseshoe Pier. Shops and restaurants line part of the pier, and there are fine views of boats and the sea; free summertime evening concerts take place here. A bronze bust of George Freeth, California's first professional surfer and lifeguard, stands on the pier; a nearby street is named for him. On the adjacent lower level is the International Boardwalk, featuring bumper cars and arcade games. A parking structure is adjacent; enter at the foot of Torrance Blvd. The South Bay Bicycle Trail runs through the parking garage. For information about the pier, call the Redondo Beach Harbor Dept.: 310-318-0631.

MONSTAD PIER: *Foot of Torrance Blvd., Redondo Beach.* Mainly used for fishing, the Monstad Pier is connected to the south end of the Redondo Beach Municipal Pier. Anglers catch halibut, mackerel, bonito, and perch. Because of the adjacent submarine canyon, deepwater species that include

Redondo County Beach

Located offshore from Redondo Beach is the Redondo Submarine Canyon, which extends from the vicinity of the Redondo Beach Municipal Pier a distance of ten miles, in a south-westerly direction, to an intersection with the San Pedro escarpment at a depth of 2,000 feet. The discovery of the canyon, which provides ample depth for ocean-going vessels quite close to shore, contributed to Redondo Beach's one-time development in the late 19th century as the first port for Los Angeles, complete with an extensive railway and wharf system. The submarine canyon, however, provided no protection from winter storms and their associated surf and surge.

During the winter of 1919, storms left the pier and wharf system devastated; by then, the Port of Los Angeles had developed a more permanent home in San Pedro. King Harbor, completed in 1958 with a protective breakwater at the head of the submarine canyon, now serves the Redondo Beach community primarily as a harbor for fishing and recreational boating.

The Redondo Submarine Canyon brings nutrient-rich seawater from deep on the ocean floor to the near-shore coastal area, creating an area of enhanced marine biological production. Nutrients support the phytoplankton that serve to transfer energy throughout the food chain, fueling increased numbers of fish and other marine organisms. The canyon has also served as a channel for pelagic (open ocean) species to migrate into the southern part of Santa Monica Bay bringing a wide variety of fishes, sharks, and marine mammals close to shore.

Bluefin tuna were frequently hooked and occasionally landed from the old piers off Redondo Beach, and several local fishing boats regularly ferried customers a short distance offshore to target these valuable fish. The last reported catches of local bluefin tuna, however, were recorded in the late 1980s. Since that time, it is probable that increased fishing pressure on this species around the world has reduced its population to where it is scarce along its former migration routes.

hake, sanddabs, and some shark species are somewhat frequent catches. Bait and tackle are available, and there are bait-cutting and fish-cleaning stations. A wheelchair-accessible fishing platform is located at the end. The lighted pier is open 24 hours.

VETERANS PARK: S. side, foot of Torrance Blvd., Redondo Beach. Landscaped park with playground, bandshell, picnic area, paved paths, and restrooms. A senior center and community center are available for rental. Stairs lead from the park to Redondo Beach. Parking along the perimeter of the park or at the foot of Torrance Blvd.

REDONDO COUNTY BEACH: W. of Esplanade, Redondo Beach. South of the Redondo Beach pier are two miles of sandy beach.

Volleyball nets, restrooms, beach showers, and lifeguard towers are spaced along the beach. Lifeguards are on duty during daylight hours. Dogs not permitted on the beach; no alcohol or fires. Metered parking along Esplanade. For surf and tide report, see: www.watchthewater.org. To reach the lifeguard headquarters, call: 310-372-2166.

The paved South Bay Bicycle Trail continues from Redondo Beach south to Torrance, along the inland edge of the beach below the bluff. A separate paved walkway runs along the top of the bluff from Veterans Park south to the Torrance city boundary, with a break near the end of Knob Hill Ave. Stairs and steep ramps lead from the blufftop walk down to the beach.

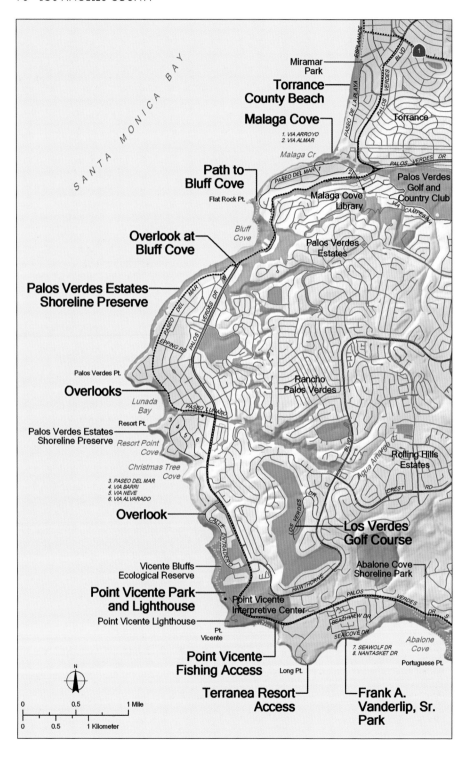

SANTA MONICA BAY

Miramar Park

Torrance County Beach

Malaga Cove

1. VIA ARROYO
2. VIA ALMAR

Malaga Cr

Path to Bluff Cove

Flat Rock Pt.

Overlook at Bluff Cove

Bluff Cove

Palos Verdes Estates Shoreline Preserve

Palos Verdes Pt.

Overlooks

Lunada Bay

Resort Pt.

Palos Verdes Estates Shoreline Preserve

Resort Point Cove

Christmas Tree Cove

3. PASEO DEL MAR
4. VIA BARRI
5. VIA NEVE
6. VIA ALVARADO

Overlook

Vicente Bluffs Ecological Reserve

Point Vicente Park and Lighthouse

Point Vicente Lighthouse

Point Vicente Interpretive Center

Pt. Vicente

Point Vicente Fishing Access

Long Pt.

Terranea Resort Access

PASEO DE LA PLAYA

ESPLANADE

PALOS VERDES BLVD.

Torrance

PALOS VERDES DR

Palos Verdes Golf and Country Club

PASEO DEL MAR

VIA CAMPESINA

Malaga Cove Library

Palos Verdes Estates

PASEO DEL MAR

VERDES DR

PALOS

LEPPING RD

Rancho Palos Verdes

PASEO LUNADO

BLVD

Agua Amarga

LOS VERDES DR

CREST RD

Rolling Hills Estates

Los Verdes Golf Course

Abalone Cove Shoreline Park

CALLE ENTRADERO

HAWTHORNE

PALOS VERDES DR S

BEACHVIEW DR

SEACOVE DR

7. SEAWOLF DR
8. NANTASKET DR

Abalone Cove

Portuguese Pt.

Frank A. Vanderlip, Sr. Park

N

0   0.5   1 Mile

0   0.5   1 Kilometer

Torrance to Rancho Palos Verdes

	Sandy Beach	Rocky Shore	Trail	Visitor Center	Campground	Wildlife Viewing	Fishing or Boating	Facilities for Disabled	Food and Drink	Restrooms	Parking	Fee
Torrance County Beach	•	•					•		•	•	•	•
Malaga Cove	•	•				•	•			•		
Path to Bluff Cove	•	•				•						
Overlook at Bluff Cove	•					•				•		
Palos Verdes Estates Shoreline Preserve	•					•						
Overlooks	•					•				•		
Los Verdes Golf Course									•	•	•	
Overlook	•	•				•				•		
Point Vicente Park and Lighthouse	•	•	•			•		•	•	•		
Point Vicente Fishing Access	•	•				•	•	•	•	•		
Terranea Resort Access	•	•				•		•	•	•		
Frank A. Vanderlip, Sr. Park						•				•		

TORRANCE COUNTY BEACH: *Along Paseo de la Playa, Torrance.* The wide, sandy beach is accessible by cement ramps leading down the bluff. There are two fee parking lots providing over 300 spaces located on Paseo de la Playa near Esplanade. Grassy Miramar Park, with benches and stairs to the beach, separates the parking areas. Concession stands and restrooms with outdoor showers are located at beach level. Native dune buckwheat plants, on which the endangered El Segundo blue butterfly is dependent, have been restored on the coastal bluffs. South of Torrance County Beach, the steep bluffs of the Palos Verdes Peninsula begin.

A beach wheelchair is available from the lifeguard station at Torrance County Beach; for information from area headquarters, call: 310-372-2162. For surf and tide information, see: www.watchthewater.org. Torrance Beach forms one end of the South Bay Bicycle Trail, also known as the Marvin Braude Bikeway; from here, bicyclists can ride 20 miles north along the shore to Will Rogers State Beach.

Lawn overlooking Torrance County Beach

MALAGA COVE: *End of Via Arroyo, off Paseo del Mar, Palos Verdes Estates.* Malaga Cove is also called Rat Beach, for "Right After Torrance." A gazebo overlooks the scenic cove, and a partially paved road leads from the parking lot down to the shoreline. The popular Malaga Cove beach is a mix of sand and cobbles. Walking north from Malaga Cove provides access to the south end of sandy Torrance County Beach, where there are restroom facilities. For information about the shoreline in Palos Verdes Estates, call: 310-378-0383. A trail in the 500 block of Paseo del Mar, opposite Via Chino, leads to the southern end of Malaga Cove, a surfing and diving spot known as Haggerty's.

PATH TO BLUFF COVE: *At Flat Rock Point, 600 block of Paseo del Mar, Palos Verdes Estates.* Two poles linked by a chain mark the start of a hard-to-see dirt path that leads one-half mile down to Bluff Cove, a rocky beach with tidepools and a popular surfing and diving spot. The cove is a resting and overwintering area for shorebirds such as willets, marbled godwits, and plovers. Street parking; no facilities.

OVERLOOK AT BLUFF COVE: *1300 block of Paseo del Mar, Palos Verdes Estates.* A blufftop parking area at the intersection of Paseo del Mar and Palos Verdes Dr. West affords views of Catalina Island and, on very clear days, San Nicolas and Santa Barbara Islands. A dirt trail begins at the parking area and continues south along the blufftop to the 1700 block of Paseo del Mar.

PALOS VERDES ESTATES SHORELINE PRESERVE: *Entire shoreline of Palos Verdes Estates.* The Palos Verdes Estates Shoreline Preserve extends along the full length of the city's four-and-a-half-mile shoreline. The preserve was established in 1969 by the city of Palos Verdes Estates, which combined 130 acres of undeveloped blufftop parkland and a 1963 state tidelands grant of the adjacent offshore area. The blufftop parklands are undeveloped and have no facilities; street parking only. Footpaths that are very steep and hazardous lead from scenic overlooks and blufftop trails down the cliffs to the rocky shore. The underwater topography is characterized by rocky boulders and reefs that form a series of ridges with sandy areas in between. Offshore kelp beds provide habitat for treefish, blue-banded gobies, and senorita fish. Tidepools are abundant, but look and do not touch; no rocks, plants, shells, or animals can be removed from the shoreline preserve.

OVERLOOKS: *1900 block, 2300 block, and 2800 block of Paseo del Mar, Palos Verdes Estates.* An

Malaga Cove

overlook providing a view of a rocky beach beneath the high bluff is opposite the end of Epping Rd., in the 1900 block of Paseo del Mar. The remains of the freighter *Dominator* can be seen to the south at Rocky Point, where it ran aground in 1961. In the 2300 block there is a view of Lunada Bay, located between Rocky Point and Resort Point. Unimproved trails lead along the bluff edge and offer fine views of the sea with its nearshore kelp beds, which provide habitat for crabs, tunicates, ghost shrimp, and blind gobies.

South of Paseo Lunado there are two overlooks, one opposite the end of Via Barri and another opposite Via Neve, in the 2800 and 2900 blocks of Paseo del Mar. Extremely steep, unimproved trails lead down to rocky cove beaches and tidepools; do not disturb plants or animals.

LOS VERDES GOLF COURSE: *7000 W. Los Verdes Dr., Rancho Palos Verdes.* This public 18-hole golf course is operated by the County of Los Angeles. The course occupies a dramatic setting overlooking the sea and Catalina Island. Call: 310-377-7370.

OVERLOOK: *Calle Entradero, Rancho Palos Verdes.* Off Palos Verdes Dr. West, at the northern end of Calle Entradero, is a small parking area and ocean overlook. A chemical toilet, not wheelchair accessible, is north of the parking lot. Dirt paths lead south from the parking lot along the bluff edge to Point Vicente Park.

POINT VICENTE PARK AND LIGHTHOUSE: *31501 Palos Verdes Dr. West, Rancho Palos Verdes.* This four-acre park north of the Point Vicente Lighthouse has picnic areas and a paved blufftop trail. The park is open from dawn to dusk; leashed dogs OK. Leading north from Point Vicente Park is a blufftop trail that leads through an area of restored coastal sage scrub habitat, part of the Vicente Bluffs Ecological Reserve. The trail continues north along the blufftop to the overlook on Calle Entradero, offering a very pleasant stroll along the coast.

In the park is the Point Vicente Interpretive Center, which includes a whale-watching deck, displays on local history and ecology, and a gift shop. Open daily from 10 AM to 5

Bluff Cove

Palos Verdes Estates is the oldest of the four cities on the Palos Verdes Peninsula. The community includes homes of Spanish Colonial Revival design, equestrian and hiking trails, and lush native and exotic vegetation. The town was designed in part by landscape architects Frederick Law Olmsted, Jr. and John Olmsted, sons of Frederick Law Olmsted, Sr. who designed Central Park in New York City. The golf course at the Palos Verdes Golf and Country Club, 3301 Via Campesina, is open to public play on weekday afternoons by advance reservation; call: 310-375-2759. The Palos Verdes Beach and Athletic Club, a members-only facility, is located at Malaga Cove; for information regarding day passes, call: 310-375-8777. The Malaga Cove Library at 2400 Via Campesina includes a local history room.

PM, except Thanksgiving Day, December 24 and 25, and January 1; call: 310-377-5370.

The adjacent Point Vicente Lighthouse is operated by the U.S. Coast Guard. Tours are given between 10 AM and 3 PM on the second Saturday of most months; for tour requirements, which include bringing picture identification, call in advance: 310-541-0334.

POINT VICENTE FISHING ACCESS: *E. of Point Vicente Park, 31300 Palos Verdes Dr. South, Rancho Palos Verdes.* A blufftop parking area, with restrooms and a short paved path overlooking the sea, is located east of the Point Vicente Lighthouse. Fifty additional parking spaces will be provided by the neighboring Terranea Resort, under construction in 2008. The fishing access is managed by the city of Rancho Palos Verdes; open from dawn until dusk. For information, call: 310-377-0360. A steep dirt path leads down to a rocky beach. Shore anglers catch fish off the reefs surrounding the Palos Verdes Peninsula, including opaleye, half moon, calico bass, halibut, and various perch and croaker species, as well as the oc-

casional white seabass. The beach is popular also for diving. Anemones and nudibranchs inhabit offshore kelp beds.

TERRANEA RESORT ACCESS: *At Long Point, off Palos Verdes Dr. South, Rancho Palos Verdes.* The Terranea Resort, under construction in 2008, will provide new public access facilities, including a wheelchair-accessible path to a scenic overlook, a perimeter blufftop trail linking Point Vicente Fishing Access to Frank A. Vanderlip, Sr. Park, and trails down the bluff to the shoreline. Snack stand, beach shower, and public restrooms to be provided on the resort property.

FRANK A. VANDERLIP, SR. PARK: *6500 Seacove Dr., Rancho Palos Verdes.* Turn off Palos Verdes Dr. South onto Seawolf Dr., then turn right on Beachview Dr. and left on Nantasket Dr. to reach Seacove Dr. This small blufftop park has benches and a lovely view of cliffs and offshore kelp beds; a short blufftop trail extends east and west of the park. No facilities; no beach access. Street parking along Seacove Dr. Dogs must be leashed; open dawn to dusk.

Point Vicente Lighthouse

Long-lasting poisons and short-sighted thinking have combined to produce high levels of the pesticide DDT and the industrial compounds known as PCBs (polychlorinated biphenyls) on the ocean floor off the Palos Verdes Peninsula. Beginning in the 1940s and continuing for three decades or more, companies that produced DDT and PCBs discharged heavily contaminated wastewater to the ocean through an outfall pipe at White Point. One major producer was the Montrose Chemical Corporation in Torrance. Even though their use in the US virtually ceased decades ago, DDT and PCBs persist and are ingested by various organisms, ending up in fish and the humans and birds that consume fish. DDT and PCBs build up over time in body fat. They may cause cancer, liver disease, and immune system effects. Because DDT and PCBs build up in sediments rather than ocean water, there is no known health risk to swimmers associated with these chemicals.

Lawsuits by state and federal agencies led to legal settlements that have funded programs to protect human and environmental health. The interagency Montrose Settlements Restoration Program is one such effort, and another is led by the federal Environmental Protection Agency,

which has designated the Palos Verdes "shelf" as a "Superfund Site."

Another response to the problem has been to advise anglers about consuming certain fish. A study of fish samples taken along the coast from Malibu to Newport Beach in 2002 showed big differences in DDT and PCB contamination, based on both fish species and the location where the fish were caught. Bottom-feeding white croaker is a fatty fish that exhibits especially high contamination by DDT and PCBs; the Fish Contamination Education Collaborative recommends that white croaker caught off the Palos Verdes Peninsula not be eaten. The Collaborative also recommends limiting consumption of rockfishes, surfperch, and other species that are caught in specific locations in southern California. See the Collaborative's website at www.pvsfish.org.

Hazardous substances such as DDT, PCBs, and mercury are found in fish elsewhere in California, too. When fishing along the coast, observe warning signs at fishing sites, and refer to the consumption guidelines contained in the annually updated California Sport Fishing Regulations, available wherever fishing licenses are sold. For more information, call the California EPA: 510-622-3166.

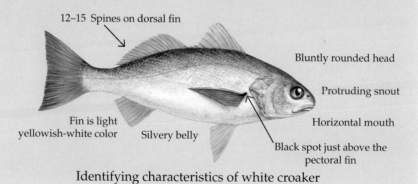

12–15 Spines on dorsal fin

Bluntly rounded head

Protruding snout

Fin is light yellowish-white color

Silvery belly

Horizontal mouth

Black spot just above the pectoral fin

Identifying characteristics of white croaker

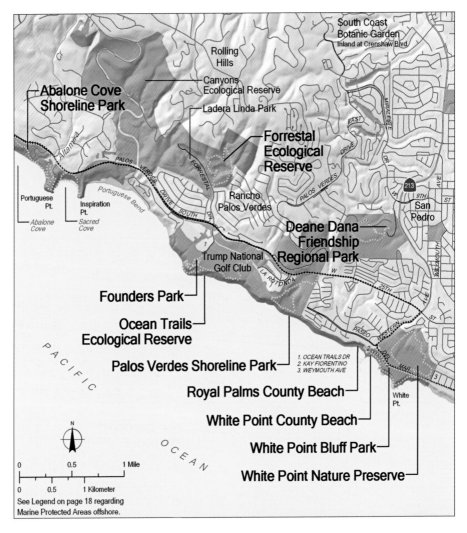

South Coast
Botanic Garden
Inland at Crenshaw Blvd.

Rolling
Hills

Canyons
Ecological Reserve

Ladera Linda Park

**Abalone Cove
Shoreline Park**

**Forrestal
Ecological
Reserve**

Portuguese
Pt.

Inspiration
Pt.

*Abalone
Cove*

*Sacred
Cove*

Rancho
Palos Verdes

San
Pedro

**Deane Dana
Friendship
Regional Park**

Trump National
Golf Club

Founders Park

**Ocean Trails
Ecological Reserve**

Palos Verdes Shoreline Park

1. OCEAN TRAILS DR
2. KAY FIORENTINO
3. WEYMOUTH AVE

Royal Palms County Beach

White
Pt.

White Point County Beach

White Point Bluff Park

White Point Nature Preserve

N

0   0.5   1 Mile

0   0.5   1 Kilometer
See Legend on page 18 regarding
Marine Protected Areas offshore.

PACIFIC   OCEAN

Abalone Cove Shoreline Park

Rancho Palos Verdes to San Pedro

	Sandy Beach	Rocky Shore	Trail	Visitor Center	Campground	Wildlife Viewing	Fishing or Boating	Facilities for Disabled	Food and Drink	Restrooms	Parking	Fee
Abalone Cove Shoreline Park	•	•	•			•	•			•	•	•
Forrestal Ecological Reserve			•			•				•		
Founders Park							•			•	•	
Ocean Trails Ecological Reserve			•			•		•		•	•	
Palos Verdes Shoreline Park			•									
Deane Dana Friendship Regional Park			•	•		•		•		•	•	
Royal Palms County Beach	•					•				•	•	•
White Point County Beach	•					•				•	•	•
White Point Bluff Park						•				•	•	
White Point Nature Preserve			•			•		•			•	

ABALONE COVE SHORELINE PARK: *5970 Palos Verdes Dr. South, Rancho Palos Verdes.* The park includes Abalone Cove, located west of Portuguese Point, and smaller Sacred Cove, east of Portuguese Point. A steep dirt path leads from the parking area down to Abalone Cove Beach, about a five-minute walk. The beach is a mix of sand and cobbles. Restrooms are located at the beach, and lifeguards are on duty daily during the summer and on weekends at other times.

To reach Sacred Cove, walk east from the parking area along Palos Verdes Dr. South past Portuguese Point to find two dirt trails that lead down the steep bluff. No facilities or lifeguards at Sacred Cove. A sea cave extends under Portuguese Point, which separates Abalone Cove from Sacred Cove. On top of Portuguese Point, which was graded for residential development that never took place, are informal dirt trails and fine views of Catalina Island.

Abalone Cove Shoreline Park is open on weekends from 9 AM to 4 PM, year-round. On weekdays, the park is open from 9 AM to 4 PM during the summer and from 12 noon to 4 PM the rest of the year; closed on Thanksgiving Day, December 24 and 25, and January 1.

Ocean Trails Ecological Reserve

No barbecues or fires; dogs not allowed. The park is managed by the city of Rancho Palos Verdes; for information, call: 310-377-1222. Abalone Cove and Sacred Cove are part of a marine protected area, where all marine plants and invertebrates are protected.

FORRESTAL ECOLOGICAL RESERVE: *Upper end of Forrestal Dr., Rancho Palos Verdes.* Forrestal Dr. is gated to vehicles opposite the entrance to Ladera Linda Community Park. Next to the gate is a trailhead for several steep, uphill paths through the Forrestal Ecological Reserve. In spring, the slopes are bright with wildflowers. The Quarry Bowl Trail is a mile-long loop, and the Pirate Trail is a shorter out-and-back route. Leashed dogs allowed on trails; pick up after your pet. The Forrestal Ecological Reserve is owned by the city of Rancho Palos Verdes

and managed by the nonprofit Palos Verdes Peninsula Land Conservancy; for information, call: 310-541-7613. Ladera Linda Community Park has spacious coastal views, children's play equipment, a basketball court, and restrooms.

Portuguese Point

The Palos Verdes Peninsula consists of a giant arch-like fold in the rocks of the Earth's crust. Although a variety of rocks occur at depth, at the surface of the Peninsula nearly everywhere are rocks of the Monterey Formation. This rock unit generally consists of shale and siltstone, including numerous silica-rich beds made up of the remains of tiny marine plants called diatoms. Interspersed with these sedimentary deposits are layers of volcanic ash, wafted into the area from gigantic volcanic eruptions to the north that occurred between 10 and 20 million years ago. These thin layers of volcanic ash have been altered into the slippery clay known as smectite, and the beds themselves are known as bentonites.

The uplift of the arch forming the Palos Verdes Peninsula has been, geologically speaking, fairly rapid and recent. As sea level has fluctuated up and down over the last two million years or so, as a result of repeated ice ages, a series of marine terraces has been cut into the uplifting peninsula. Terraces were formed when sea level was relatively constant, or at least rising at a rate comparable to that of the land. Coastal erosion then formed relatively flat wave-cut terraces. When sea level fell, or the land started rising faster than the sea, these terraces rose above the waves, and sea cliffs were formed. Over geologic time, the land continued to rise, and as sea level varied, a whole flight of relatively flat (although tilted) terraces were developed, separated by steep slopes. The highest terraces are the oldest, and the lowest terraces are the youngest. The "present" marine terrace is that terrace being carved today offshore, below the sea cliff and in the area subject to the waves. Land development, grading, and other landform alteration have obscured the classic flight of marine terraces once evident on the peninsula, but the discerning eye can still pick out flat areas separated by steeper slopes, stepping outwards toward the sea.

The upwarping of the rocks of the Monterey Formation into an arch-like shape has had another profound effect on the Palos Verdes Peninsula. As the rocks were tilted seaward, and seacliffs were cut at the margins of the arch, the rocks had a tendency to slide downwards toward the sea. This tendency is exacerbated by the presence of the relatively thin, but very weak, bentonite layers from ancient volcanic eruptions.

At numerous places around the Peninsula, the rocks have slid along these bentonite layers into the sea, forming some of the largest and most spectacular landslides along the California coast. The 200-acre Portuguese Bend landslide, triggered in the 1950s by a combination of irrigation and road construction, has been sliding seaward ever since. The entire area lies in a "geologic moratorium zone" imposed by the city of Rancho Palos Verdes, prohibiting all development on the unstable landslide. Indeed, when crossing the landslide on Palos Verdes Dr. South, drivers are cautioned not to stop because of the risk of sudden movement. The flexible, above-ground sewage line is apparent bordering the street. The street is under constant repair and relocation as the land beneath it slides toward the sea.

Other somewhat smaller landslides in the area are equally impressive–the "Sunken City" at Point Fermin is a portion of San Pedro that slid seaward in the 1920s and likewise is closed off to development and even public access, and Abalone Cove Shoreline Park is at the toe of another 80-acre landslide. Indeed, that so much of Palos Verdes has been set aside for public parks and nature preserves is partly due to the fact that these areas are just too dangerous to develop for urban uses. Although they are slowly sliding seaward, they are excellent places to (cautiously) enjoy hiking and explore some prime habitat in the Los Angeles area.

Above-ground utilities on unstable ground, Palos Verdes Dr. South near Abalone Cove

FOUNDERS PARK: *1 Ocean Trails Dr., Rancho Palos Verdes.* A five-acre public park is located seaward of the clubhouse of the Trump National Golf Club. The park has picnic areas, bicycle racks, and spectacular views of the sea. Public trails lead from the park to the shoreline; dogs must be leashed. Open dawn to dusk. Free parking in the lot just east of the clubhouse. Public restrooms are located in the clubhouse. The ocean-view Trump National Golf Club course is open to the public; fee for play. Call: 310-265-5000.

OCEAN TRAILS ECOLOGICAL RESERVE: *Between Trump National Golf Club and Pacific Ocean, Rancho Palos Verdes.* Trails lead through a 125-acre reserve that features formerly degraded coastal sage scrub habitat, now undergoing restoration; breeding pairs of threatened coastal California gnatcatchers have been identified here. From Founders Park, a short, paved loop trail leads out to the bluff edge; from there, one can continue down to the beach.

A separate trailhead for the Ocean Trails Ecological Reserve is located at the end of La Rotonda Dr., where there is a 50-space parking lot, restrooms, and drinking fountain. The Lakeview Trail leads from the parking lot through golf greens to the edge of the ocean bluff, and from there a steep trail winds down to the beach. The Lakeview Trail also continues west to Founders Park, next to the Trump National Golf Clubhouse. Do not remove shells or living organisms from the Ecological Reserve. The Ocean Trails Ecological Reserve is managed by the Palos Verdes Peninsula Land Conservancy; call: 310-541-7613.

PALOS VERDES SHORELINE PARK: *Palos Verdes Dr. South, Rancho Palos Verdes.* This unsigned open space park is undeveloped, but offers excellent scenery. Access to the park is adjacent to the city boundary, where Palos Verdes Dr. South becomes W. 25th St. in San Pedro. A mile-and-a-half-long loop trail leads from Palos Verdes Dr. South through restored coastal sage scrub habitat to a small canyon and back. Shoulder parking on the frontage road in the eastbound direction; no facilities. Call: 310-544-5260.

Founders Park

DEANE DANA FRIENDSHIP REGIONAL PARK: *1805 W. 9th St., San Pedro.* The park includes 123 acres for picnicking and hiking, with scenic paths and views of Los Angeles Harbor. Some trails are wheelchair accessible. The park is open from 7 AM to sunset. A natural history museum on the property contains displays and live animals; open daily from 9 AM to 5 PM. Bird walks, classes, and summer camps for young people are offered; call: 310-519-6115.

ROYAL PALMS COUNTY BEACH: *1799 Paseo del Mar, San Pedro.* This park shares an access road with White Point County Beach; at the bottom of the bluff, turn right to Royal Palms County Beach. The Royal Palms Hotel was situated here until it was washed out by a storm in the 1920s. Majestic palms and garden terraces remain, making the site popular for picnics. Popular diving and surfing spot, too; Los Angeles County lifeguards on duty during daylight hours. For surf and tide report, see: www.watchthewater.org. No fires or alcohol on the beach; pets not allowed. Park hours are from 7 AM to 10 PM.

WHITE POINT COUNTY BEACH: *1799 Paseo del Mar, San Pedro.* At White Point County Beach, there are steep, rugged cliffs located above a shoreline of contorted rock formations and tidepools. There is much to see here, but do not touch or disturb organisms in the tidepools. No fires or alcohol on the beach; pets not allowed.

WHITE POINT BLUFF PARK: *S. Paseo del Mar, 300 yards E. of Western Ave., San Pedro.* This blufftop park overlooks White Point County Beach. The park includes picnic facilities, children's play equipment, a baseball diamond, restrooms, and no-fee parking.

WHITE POINT NATURE PRESERVE: *Inland of S. Paseo del Mar, between Western Ave. and Weymouth Ave., San Pedro.* A 100-acre open space site, owned by the city of Los Angeles and operated by the Palos Verdes Peninsula Land Conservancy, features restored wildflower grasslands and coastal sage scrub habitat. The threatened coastal California gnatcatcher is a resident bird in the preserve, and the western meadowlark is a common visitor in fall and winter. A wheelchair-accessible trail with interpretive panels loops around the site. No-fee parking; dogs on leash OK. Call: 310-541-7613. A nature educational center is planned by 2009.

The South Coast Botanic Garden, at 26300 Crenshaw Blvd., Palos Verdes Peninsula, is well worth an inland detour. From the coast, take Palos Verdes Dr. East to Palos Verdes Dr. North, then turn left to Crenshaw Blvd. and right to the garden, a total distance of about eight miles. There are gardens of roses, dahlias, fuchsias, and other showy flowers, along with a Japanese garden, cactus garden, and a waterwise garden of landscaping plants with low water requirements. The garden includes both exotic plants and California natives. There are shady, wheelchair-accessible paths and abundant butterflies and birds. Once the site of an open-pit mine that produced diatomaceous earth and later a sanitary landfill, the South Coast Botanic Garden since 1961 has been an example of successful land restoration. Open daily from 9 AM to 5 PM; closed December 25. Fee for admission. Call: 310-544-1948.

Mormon Island

Vincent Thomas Bridge

Catalina Terminal

Smith Island

Berth 93

S.S. *Lane Victory*

Cruise Ship Promenade

Terminal Island

Los Angeles Maritime Museum

Fish Harbor

Ports O'Call Village

San Pedro

Cabrillo Marina

Watchorn Basin

Los Angeles Harbor

Hostel Los Angeles South Bay

Fort MacArthur Military Museum

Marine Mammal Care Center

International Bird Rescue Research Center

Lookout Point Park

W 34TH ST

Launch Ramp

Cabrillo Marine Aquarium

Cabrillo Beach

W 36TH ST

1. S BARBARA ST
2. W 36TH ST
3. ROXBURY ST
4. LEAVENWORTH DR
5. STEPHEN M WHITE DR

Cabrillo Fishing Pier

San Pedro Breakwater

Angels Gate Park

Joan Milke Flores Park

Pt. Fermin

Blufftop View Area

Point Fermin Park

Friendship Bell

Point Fermin Lighthouse

SAN PEDRO BAY

N

0   0.25   0.5 Mile

0   0.25   0.5 Kilometer
See Legend on page 18 regarding
Marine Protected Areas offshore.

San Pedro

	Sandy Beach	Rocky Shore	Trail	Visitor Center	Campground	Wildlife Viewing	Fishing or Boating	Facilities for Disabled	Food and Drink	Restrooms	Parking	Fee
Angels Gate Park						•				•	•	
Joan Milke Flores Park										•	•	
Point Fermin Park			•			•	•			•	•	
Point Fermin Lighthouse	•	•	•					•				
Lookout Point Park											•	
Cabrillo Beach	•					•	•	•	•	•	•	•
Cabrillo Marine Aquarium				•		•		•		•	•	
Ports O'Call Village							•	•		•	•	•
Los Angeles Maritime Museum				•		•	•			•	•	
Cruise Ship Promenade							•	•			•	
Catalina Terminal							•	•		•	•	

ANGELS GATE PARK: *3601 S. Gaffey St., San Pedro.* The park is on a high promontory with superlative views. There are lawns, basketball courts, a children's play area, and a pagoda housing the Friendship Bell given by the people of the Republic of Korea in 1976 to commemorate the U.S. Bicentennial and honor Korean War veterans. The bell is rung three times a year, on the Fourth of July, August 15 (Korean Independence Day), and New Year's Eve. Angels Gate Park is managed by the city of Los Angeles; call: 310-548-7705.

The Fort MacArthur Military Museum, located in the park off Leavenworth Dr., maintains a collection that documents the U.S. Army's defense of the mainland and Los Angeles harbor from this location throughout much of the twentieth century. Open Saturday and Sunday, from noon to 5 PM; donations encouraged. Call: 310-548-2631.

The Angels Gate Cultural Center, also off Leavenworth Dr., offers art galleries, open studio events, and school education programs; call: 310-519-0936. The Marine Mammal Care Center on Leavenworth Dr., which cares for sick or injured marine mammals, is open to the public daily from 8 AM to 4 PM. For information, call: 310-548-5677. The

adjacent International Bird Rescue Research Center treats birds oiled by spills and operates a small visitor center and gift shop; call: 310-514-2573.

Within Angels Gate Park is the 60-bed Hostel Los Angeles South Bay, part of the Hostelling International network. The hostel is in Building 613 on Leavenworth Dr., off S. Gaffey St. The hostel features dorm and private rooms, ocean views, a fully equipped kitchen, laundry facilities, Internet access, and library. From mid-June to mid-September, the hostel is open to individual travelers and groups; from October to May, open to groups of 20 or more persons only. Call: 310-831-8109.

JOAN MILKE FLORES PARK: *Inland of S. Paseo del Mar, W. of Point Fermin, San Pedro.* This grassy park has benches and views of the sea; parking and non-wheelchair-accessible chemical toilets.

POINT FERMIN PARK: *Shoreline from S. Barbara St. to E. of Point Fermin, San Pedro.* The point was named by British navigator George Vancouver in 1793 for Father Fermin Francisco de Lasuén, who established nine of the 21 Spanish missions in what is now California. The park named for Father Lasuén is landscaped with Moreton Bay fig

Angels Gate Park

trees and overlooks the ocean. Facilities include a bandshell, picnic tables with barbecue grills, playground, and restrooms. Migrating whales can be seen offshore. Monarch butterflies overwinter in groves in the park. A Los Angeles city park; open from 6 AM to 10 PM. Call: 310-548-7705. Part of the park, but entered from the south end of Pacific Ave., is a blufftop viewing area with parking; no shoreline access.

A paved walkway runs from Point Fermin Park along the seaward side of South Paseo del Mar to White Point Park, a distance of about a mile and a half. A grassy linear park borders part of the walkway, from Roxbury St. to Barbara St. Two paved but steep paths, opposite Barbara St. and Meyler St., lead to the narrow, rocky beach.

POINT FERMIN LIGHTHOUSE: *S. end of S. Gaffey St., San Pedro.* The Point Fermin Lighthouse was built in 1874 and stands in Point Fermin Park. The lighthouse operated with an oil lamp, then a vapor incandescent light, and finally an electric light until 1928, when an automated light was installed on the point; during World War II, the lighthouse was converted to a radar station. The original Fresnel lens is on display. Open daily from 1 PM to 4 PM, except Monday. Donations encouraged. Partially wheelchair accessible. Call: 310-241-0684.

LOOKOUT POINT PARK: *S. Gaffey St. between 34th and 36th Streets, San Pedro.* Small overlook area with an elevated view of Los Angeles Harbor; coin-operated telescopes.

CABRILLO BEACH: *Steven M. White Dr., E. of S. Pacific Ave., San Pedro.* There is a wide, sandy, stillwater beach inside the San Pedro Breakwater and also a surf beach facing the ocean. Facilities include picnic tables, grills, restrooms, showers, dressing rooms, and playground; parking is subject to fee seasonally. The Mediterranean-style bathhouse, built in 1932 and restored in 2002, overlooks the beach; for information, call: 310-548-7554. Lifeguards on duty during daylight hours. A summertime junior lifeguard program is offered at Cabrillo Beach. City of Los Angeles lifeguards instruct young people in lifesaving techniques, swimming, paddling, surfing, kayaking, and first aid; for information, call the lifeguard station: 310-548-2909. Beach wheelchairs are available from the information booth at the Cabrillo Marine Aquarium. Beach fires OK in provided fire rings; no alcohol or pets on the beach. Park hours: 7 AM to 10 PM; managed by the city of Los Angeles. For surf and tide information, see: www.watchthewater.org.

Offshore kelp beds provide habitat for sea stars, abalones, and kelp surfperch. At the east end of Cabrillo Beach, inside the breakwater, is the Cabrillo Fishing Pier. Fish commonly caught from this pier include croakers and jacksmelt. The California Office of Environmental Health Hazard Assessment warns that several species of locally caught fish show high concentrations of the pesticide DDT and the compound known as PCB in their flesh. The Office recommends that no white croaker caught from the pier be eaten. In addition, anglers should limit themselves to only one meal every two weeks of the following species: queenfish, black croaker, and surfperch.

At the north end of the Cabrillo Beach parking lot is a concrete public boat launch ramp, open 24 hours; for information, call: 310-548-2909. North of the boat launch is a small saltmarsh with a public viewing platform. The Cabrillo Beach Youth Waterfront Sports Center offers day camps and classes in water sports, water safety, first aid, and other subjects; call: 310-831-1984.

CABRILLO MARINE AQUARIUM: *3720 Stephen M. White Dr., San Pedro.* Exhibits and aquaria at this city of Los Angeles facility feature the resources of the Southern Cali-

The Cabrillo Marina, on Via Cabrillo Marina off W. 22nd St., has 885 slips, fuel dock, and pumpout facilities, plus a hotel and shops; call: 310-732-2252.

Harbor cruises in Los Angeles Harbor are offered by several vendors at Ports O'Call Village and at Cabrillo Marina, including 22nd Street Landing Sportfishing, call: 310-832-8304; Fiesta Harbor Cruise, call: 310-831-1906; L.A. Harbor Sportfishing, call: 310-547-9916, and Spirit Cruises, call: 310-548-8080.

fornia Bight, rocky shores, and more; look for kelp forest denizens such as kelp bass, tree fish, and California sheephead. Facilities include a touch tank, auditorium, and gift shop. Open Tuesday through Friday from noon to 5 PM, and weekends from 10 AM to 5 PM. Closed on Thanksgiving and Christmas; donations encouraged. Park at Cabrillo

Cabrillo Beach inside breakwater

The Waterfront Red Car Line is a mile-and-a-half-long streetcar route that links attractions along the San Pedro waterfront. Trolley cars like those of the old Pacific Electric Railway run from the World Cruise Center south to 22nd St., with stops at 6th St. and Ports O'Call Village. One vintage car operates on the line, while others are nearly exact replicas, down to the exterior paint color and the fine interior woodwork. Cars run from 10 AM to 6 PM, Friday through Monday and other days when cruise ships are in port; fare is good all day. The Cabrillo Beach shuttle bus meets the Red Car trains at 22nd St. and continues south to the Cabrillo Marine Aquarium.

Beach, where fee applies seasonally, or park free at 22nd St. and Miner St. and take the Cabrillo Beach Shuttle; call: 310-732-3473. The aquarium sponsors grunion programs and excursions to marine locations, including the Channel Islands; call: 310-548-7562. Whale watch boat trips depart daily during winter months; call: 310-548-8397.

PORTS O'CALL VILLAGE: *Berth 77, L.A. Harbor, San Pedro.* Facing the main harbor channel, Ports O'Call Village offers good views of shipping activity, as well as restaurants and fish markets. Harbor tours and whale watching excursions depart from the wharf.

LOS ANGELES MARITIME MUSEUM: *Berth 84, foot of 6th St., San Pedro.* The museum is housed in the historic ferry terminal that was used by passengers going to Terminal Island before the Vincent Thomas Bridge opened in 1963. The large building displays ship models, navigational equipment, and exhibits about the history of Los Angeles Harbor, including San Pedro's role through much of the 20th century as the nation's leading fishing port. The tugboat *Angels Gate* is part of the museum's collection. Open Tuesday through Saturday from 10 AM to 5 PM and Sunday from noon to 5 PM; donations suggested. Call: 310-548-7618.

Los Angeles Maritime Museum with tugboat *Angels Gate*

In front of the Maritime Museum is the striking American Merchant Marine Veterans Memorial, which honors merchant seamen who served in the nation's wars.

CRUISE SHIP PROMENADE: *Berth 93, L.A. Harbor, San Pedro.* Passenger cruise ships from more than a dozen lines call at the Port of Los Angeles. The quarter-mile-long Cruise Ship Promenade, outfitted with comfortable wooden deck chairs, overlooks the cruise ships and the harbor. At the end of the promenade is the S.S. *Lane Victory*, a fully operational World War II victory ship, now a museum. Open daily from 9 AM to 3 PM; fee for entry. Not accessible to wheelchairs or strollers. Call: 310-519-9545. Overhead is the Vincent Thomas Bridge, which is lighted from dusk to midnight with thousands of tiny, blue, light-emitting diode lights, powered by solar-generated electricity. The bridge figured prominently in the 1985 film, *To Live and Die in L.A.*, which includes an adrenaline-spiking bungee-jumping scene.

CATALINA TERMINAL: *Berths 94 and 95, L.A. Harbor, San Pedro.* Catalina Express provides service to Avalon and Two Harbors year-round, more frequent in summer; call: 1-800-481-3470. Island Express provides helicopter trips to Catalina Island; call: 310-510-2525.

The diminutive Palos Verdes blue butterfly (*Glaucopsyche lygdamus palosverdesensis*), considered a subspecies of the silvery blue butterfly and found historically only on part of the Palos Verdes Peninsula, was thought by 1984 to be extinct. A decade later, the butterfly was rediscovered at a U.S. Department of Defense fuel depot near Ken Malloy Regional Park in San Pedro. During its lifetime, the butterfly stays close to its host plants, which include deerweed and locoweed. Native plant restoration at the fuel depot, started in 1994, has supported the continued existence of the Palos Verdes blue butterfly, as well as other vulnerable coastal sage scrub dwellers, such as the coastal California gnatcatcher. The fuel depot site is not publicly accessible, but efforts have been made to reintroduce the Palos Verdes blue butterfly at other publicly owned sites on the Palos Verdes Peninsula.

Cruise Ship Promenade

Ports of Los Angeles and Long Beach

THE PORTS of Los Angeles and Long Beach are the busiest in the United States. The value of the trade passing through the two harbors exceeds $300 billion annually; more than 40 percent of the nation's goods shipped in containers flow through these two ports in San Pedro Bay. Besides container transshipment, the harbors move dry and liquid bulk cargos, automobiles, and other goods. The facilities of the ports include not only piers for cargo ships, but also rail lines, trucking facilities, a commercial fishing fleet, marinas and boater services, passenger terminals, a popular swimming beach, and even a nesting area for the endangered California least tern.

What was once an estuary of mudflats and salt marshes has been transformed dramatically by dredging and filling activities that commenced in the 1870s and have created the largest artificial harbor complex in the world. Before California became a state in 1850, San Pedro was a port. In *Two Years before the Mast*, Richard Henry Dana wrote of loading cattle hides onto a waiting ship there in the 1830s. In 1869, southern California's first railroad linked the port at San Pedro to Los Angeles, then nearly 20 miles away. To better accommodate ships, San Pedro's Main Channel was dredged to a depth

Port of Los Angeles

of ten feet in 1871, and a breakwater was built in 1873 between Rattlesnake Island, now Terminal Island, and Deadman's Island, which no longer exists. In 1897, expansion of the harbor at San Pedro won out over competing proposals to develop a major harbor at Santa Monica, Marina del Rey, or Redondo Beach, and in 1909, the city of Los Angeles annexed a 16-mile-long "shoestring" strip of land that connected the city with San Pedro, Wilmington, and Terminal Island. The nearly nine-mile-long breakwater that protects the San Pedro Bay ports was built between 1899 and the 1940s.

In the early 20th century, tens of thousands of laborers worked in the port of Los Angeles, moving goods on and off vessels, building and repairing ships, and fishing or processing the catch. As Los Angeles grew from a population of 102,479 in 1900 to 576,673 in 1920, construction boomed, and the port of Los Angeles became the world's largest lumber importer. In 1911, the port of Long Beach began operations, and the opening of the Panama Canal in 1914 was a stimulus to both San Pedro Bay harbors, which were the closest major American ports to the canal.

Bananas may seem like one of life's incidentals, but in the 19th century the importation of the fruit from South America and the Caribbean was a revolutionary advance at a time when most American consumers had limited choices in fresh produce. Banana imports meant hard work for stevedores, who shouldered the easily damaged banana stalks, weighing between 30 and 125 pounds apiece, and carried them off the ships. By the 1930s, a conveyor system put into use at the port of Los Angeles eased the heavy lifting. Bananas were still among the major imports at the port of Los Angeles in that decade, along with oil and lumber.

Exports from the port of Los Angeles in the early 20th century were dominated by crude oil, much of it produced in southern California's oil fields. Oil production in the Los Angeles Basin amounted to one-fifth of the world's production in 1923, and Los Angeles was then the world's leading oil port. Oil was shipped out of Los Angeles to the U.S. east coast, Hawaii, Asia, and elsewhere. Other leading exports from Los Angeles were cotton and citrus fruits grown on California's farms and borax from California's mines.

The ports of Los Angeles and Long Beach act as landlords, building terminal facilities and leasing them to shipping and stevedoring companies. Upon arrival in port, goods are moved out by trucking companies and railroads. In the 1960s, shipping containers largely replaced the motley crates, drums, and bags that were used before then. Containers meant that goods were moved more quickly from ships to trains or trucks, while fewer workers were required. One modern container ship can carry the equivalent of 8,000 20-foot-long shipping containers, with more than enough consumer goods to stock an entire shopping center. By 2007, over ten million loaded containers moved in and out of the two San Pedro Bay ports in one year.

The ports have expanded their facilities to accommodate the large ships that require deep waterways; the main channel of the port of Los Angeles was deepened in 1983 to 45 feet and, starting in 2003, to 53 feet. To accommodate larger and heavier shipping containers, concrete wharves equipped with large cranes have replaced wooden piers. An enormous dredging project at the Port of Los Angeles, commenced in 1994, resulted in the production of 29 million cubic yards of dredged soil and the construction of 265 acres of new land at Pier 400.

Long Beach is the West Coast's leading port for imported automobiles. Other leading imports at Long Beach include bulk petroleum, electronics, vehicles, furniture, and clothing; leading exports include machinery, plastic, meat, waste paper, chemicals, and scrap metal. Measured by tonnage, imports exceed exports by almost four to one. More than 300,000 jobs in southern California, and more than one million jobs nationwide, are related to Long Beach trade alone. San Pedro Bay's trading partners are all over the world; the leading partner is China, and other Pacific Rim nations are important, too.

In 2006 the ports of Los Angeles and Long Beach began a series of steps, called the Clean Air Action Plan, to improve air quality in and around the harbors. A major source of air pollutants in the harbor area is trucking. Along with other air pollutants, diesel trucks generate potentially cancer-causing particulates, which are fine particles of soot, dust, metals, and other materials suspended in the air. Over 16,000 diesel trucks move in

Port of Long Beach

and out of the harbors regularly. The ports now encourage use of newer-model diesel trucks, which burn 90 percent cleaner than older models. By 2012, the oldest trucks will be phased out, and others will be retrofitted.

The ports are also seeking to limit air pollution from ships, trains, cargo-handling equipment, and harbor craft. Even as ever-increasing amounts of cargo are handled, port plans call for reducing particulates, oxides of nitrogen and oxides of sulfur, and greenhouse gases such as carbon dioxide. Cleaner-burning, low-sulfur fuels will be required for ocean-going vessels while operating in and near the harbors. While in port, a ship can draw power from the electrical grid onshore rather than from shipboard diesel generators. For each day that a ship is in port, one ton of nitrogen oxides and half a ton of sulfur oxides can be kept out of the atmosphere. Railroad locomotives will use cleaner-burning diesel fuels and limit idling time. Tugboats will use clean electrical power while at the dock, and even maintenance dredging in the harbors can be powered by electricity. Looking ahead, the ports plan to explore new, renewable energy sources for their power needs.

The busy ports have tested new methods of conveying goods that minimize the production of air pollutants. A new, Internet-based technology called the "virtual container yard" has been tried at the San Pedro Bay ports. To minimize the transportation of storage containers once they have been emptied at their ultimate destination, the virtual container yard allows companies with goods to export to pinpoint the location of nearby, recently emptied containers to load up for the return trip to the port. Reducing truck container traffic helps reduce air pollution and traffic congestion, too.

Other environmental measures are in place to address water pollution. Both San Pedro Bay ports treat storm water runoff to reduce contamination of waters in the harbor and nearby beaches. Other measures include efforts to reduce water pollution from recreational boaters and to avoid oil spills. In San Pedro Bay, water quality is much improved compared to 1967, when local monitoring began, and the diversity of fish species and abundance of birds have both increased since the 1970s.

Along with busy port activities, San Pedro Bay supports natural habitats, too. The outer harbor includes shallow water habitat, an important rearing area for juvenile fish. Beds of eelgrass grow in the harbor, serving as a rough indicator of water quality, because the marine plants will not grow in heavily polluted areas. In deeper water, the port of Los Angeles has successfully established a giant kelp forest. California least terns nest on 15 acres of the Los Angeles port's Pier 400, a huge area of landfill. During some years, the least tern nesting colony has been the second most populous in California. Near the Cabrillo Marine Aquarium is a saltwater marsh restored by the port of Los Angeles and used for educational programs. To offset the unavoidable impacts of filling harbor areas for new facilities, the Port of Los Angeles has funded habitat restoration in Batiquitos Lagoon in San Diego County, and the two San Pedro Bay ports financed the restoration of the Bolsa Chica wetlands in Orange County.

The port of Long Beach offers free summertime boat tours for a close-up look at activity in the harbor; see: www.polb.com or call: 562-437-0041. Visitors can view harbor activity at the port of Los Angeles from the promenade near Slip 93, where cruise ships tie up and large container ships can be seen in the harbor's Main Channel. Planned public improvements include an expanded promenade leading from Slip 93 south to Ports O'Call Village, incorporating a segment of the California Coastal Trail, and new boat harbors with short-term visitor docks. For information, call: 310-732-7678.

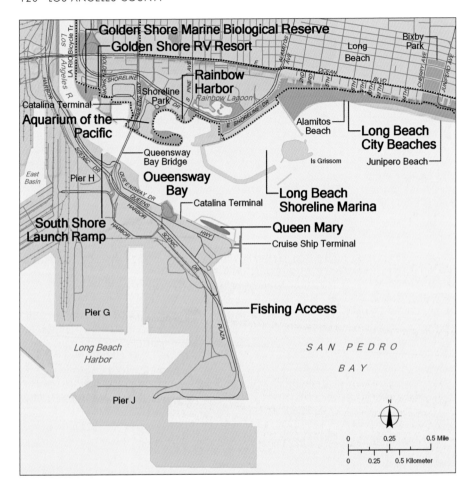

Fishing Access, great blue heron on rock above fisherman

Long Beach

	Sandy Beach	Rocky Shore	Trail	Visitor Center	Campground	Wildlife Viewing	Fishing or Boating	Facilities for Disabled	Food and Drink	Restrooms	Parking	Fee
Fishing Access							•			•	•	
Queen Mary				•			•		•	•	•	•
Queensway Bay						•	•			•	•	
South Shore Launch Ramp							•		•	•	•	
Aquarium of the Pacific				•		•	•		•	•	•	•
Golden Shore Marine Biological Reserve						•				•		
Golden Shore RV Resort					•	•			•	•	•	•
Rainbow Harbor		•				•	•		•	•	•	
Long Beach Shoreline Marina							•		•	•	•	
Long Beach City Beaches	•	•				•	•		•	•	•	

FISHING ACCESS: *Harbor Scenic Dr. South, Long Beach Harbor.* Public access to the shoreline for fishing or viewing is available south of the *Queen Mary.* There is parallel parking and a paved sidewalk along the shoreline, which is lined with riprap, and a chemical toilet; no other facilities. Easiest access is from the south end of the Long Beach Freeway (I-710). Follow signs to Harbor Scenic Dr. South; near the end of the road, make a sharp left turn into the fishing access parking area. Or, from Magnolia Ave. near downtown Long Beach, take the Queensway Bay Bridge south and get in the middle lane. South of the bridge, take the left fork toward the *Queen Mary*, then immediately exit right to Harbor Plaza East, toward Pier J. At Harbor Scenic Dr. South, turn right to reach the fishing access. Watch out for busy truck traffic to and from harbor terminals.

QUEEN MARY: *Pier J, Long Beach Harbor.* The *Queen Mary*, once the largest luxury liner afloat, was launched at Clydebank, Scotland in 1934. The Art Deco interior features extensive wood paneling and splendid murals. During World War II, the ship carried Allied troops, Winston Churchill on his way to war-time conferences, and thousands of American servicemen's brides and children. Passenger service resumed in 1947; in all, the ship made 1,001 transatlantic voyages. The ship was retired in 1967 and permanently berthed in Long Beach as a tourist attraction and hotel, with restaurants and shops. Guided and self-guided tours are available. Every October, there are haunted ship tours through the maze of long corridors. The ship is wheelchair accessible. Open daily from 10 AM to 6 PM; fee for entry. Restaurants and lounges stay open later, and entry fee is not charged after 6 PM, or for hotel guests. For information, call: 562-435-3511.

QUEENSWAY BAY: *Mouth of the Los Angeles River, Long Beach.* Where the Los Angeles River meets San Pedro Bay is a water area devoted to recreational boating. On the downtown side of Queensway Bay are parks, a marina, an aquarium, and other facilities, and on the other side of the bay is the *Queen Mary*, along with additional boating facilities. There is public access to much of the waterfront. The Los Angeles River, or LARIO, bicycle path runs along the east bank of the Los Angeles River from the Golden Shore Marine Biological Reserve northwards. The route continues some 20 miles to downtown Los Angeles, although portions of the path may not be fully improved; see: www.bicyclela.org.

SOUTH SHORE LAUNCH RAMP: *Queensway Dr., W. of Queensway Bay Bridge, Long Beach.* One of three public launch ramps in Long

Catalina Express boats depart from Long Beach daily, year-round for the approximately hour-long trip to Catalina Island. There are two terminals in Long Beach, the Downtown Catalina Landing at 320 Golden Shore St. and a second terminal at 1046 Queen's Hwy., next to the *Queen Mary*. Most boats go to Avalon on Catalina Island; some stop at Two Harbors. There is extra service on weekends and holidays. Reduced fares for seniors and children; extra fee applies for bicycles and surfboards. Reservations are recommended. Call: 1-800-481-3470.

Catalina Express boats also serve Catalina from San Pedro and Dana Point, and other carriers serve Catalina from Marina del Rey and Newport Beach.

Aquarium of the Pacific

Beach for trailered boats; the other two are in Alamitos Bay. From Magnolia Ave., take the Queensway Bay Bridge south and keep to the right. Make an abrupt right turn into Queensway Dr., then turn left to the launch ramp. Open 24 hours; fee for parking. For Information, call: 562-570-8636.

AQUARIUM OF THE PACIFIC: *100 Aquarium Way at Shoreline Park, Long Beach.* The dramatic Aquarium of the Pacific offers close-up looks at many denizens of the ocean off southern California and Baja California, along with creatures from the tropical Pacific and north Pacific. There are sea lions and harbor seals, and a lagoon features sharks, some of which visitors can touch. Brilliantly colored lorikeets occupy an outdoor, walk-through aviary, and a shorebird sanctuary features typical birds and wetland plants of coastal southern California. A theater in the aquarium complex shows 3-D films about the deep ocean and other subjects. There are many special events and changing exhibits.

Open from 9 AM to 6 PM daily, except December 25 and the weekend of the Long Beach Grand Prix, which is typically in April. Timed ticketing is employed at busy times, such as summer weekends. Café and gift shop. Fee for entry; free loaner wheelchairs available on request. Aquarium parking is available in a parking structure on the water side of Shoreline Drive, between Chestnut Place and Aquarium Way; fee applies. For information, call: 562-590-3100.

GOLDEN SHORE MARINE BIOLOGICAL RESERVE: *Adjacent to Golden Shore RV Resort, Golden Shore St., Long Beach.* This area of mudflat and saltmarsh is the best place in Long Beach to view wading birds; look for willets and whimbrels, along with Caspian terns and pied-billed grebes. Bring binoculars or spotting scope; entry to the reserve is not allowed. From Ocean Blvd., turn south on Golden Shore St.; metered public parking is located next to the wetlands. For information, call: 562-570-1600.

GOLDEN SHORE RV RESORT: *101 Golden Shore St., Long Beach.* The RV campground overlooks the Golden Shore Marine Biological Reserve. There are 80 RV sites with full hook-ups, a swimming pool, kitchen, laundry, and store. Dogs allowed. For information, call: 562-435-4646.

RAINBOW HARBOR: *Foot of Pine Ave., S. of Shoreline Dr., Long Beach.* Rainbow Harbor is where downtown Long Beach meets the shoreline, and there is public access to the water's edge all around. The waterfront promenade that follows the perimeter of Rainbow Harbor is a delightful place for a stroll on a summer evening, or anytime. Restaurants and shopping are nearby, along with the Aquarium of the Pacific and other attractions.

Landscaped Shoreline Park has fishing platforms, a working lighthouse, bicycle and pedestrian paths, picnic areas, parking, and restrooms. Sport fishing charters, whale-watching trips, boat rentals, scenic cruises, and educational trips to the Channel Islands are available on the docks that ring Rainbow Harbor. Rainbow Harbor Marina includes a 200-foot-long guest dock, with a three-hour time limit, and other docks for commercial vessels. For information on Rainbow Harbor Marina, call: 562-570-8636.

Separate from Rainbow Harbor is Rainbow Lagoon, an enclosed water body located north of Shoreline Dr. and east of Pine Ave. The saltwater lagoon is home to fish and marine invertebrates, despite its manicured appearance; a paved public path surrounds it. A paved promenade, partially elevated above street level, connects Rainbow Harbor, Rainbow Lagoon, and the pedestrian-only mall that runs through downtown Long Beach.

LONG BEACH SHORELINE MARINA: *450 E. Shoreline Dr., E. of Rainbow Harbor, Long Beach.* The Long Beach Shoreline Marina,

From Dock 4 in Rainbow Harbor, Long Beach Transit provides Aqua Bus water taxi service to the *Queen Mary* and other destinations around Queensway Bay, and Aqua Link catamaran service to Alamitos Bay Landing. Long Beach Transit also operates the Passport bus service from Catalina Landing on Golden Shore St. to Belmont Pier, and from Queensway Bay to Pine Ave.; for information on all services, call: 562-591-2301. The Metro Blue Line rail service runs from the Transit Mall near the foot of Pine Ave. to downtown Los Angeles.

Rainbow Harbor

with 1,844 slips for recreational boaters, is one of three operated by the city of Long Beach. The other two are the Rainbow Harbor Marina and the Alamitos Bay Marina. The Long Beach Shoreline Marina includes guest slips for recreational boaters; call ahead for availability. There is also a fuel dock, a pumpout station, a boat repair facility, and a yacht club. For information about Long Beach Shoreline Marina, call: 562-570-4950. Shoreline Village is a tourist attraction located between the marina and Rainbow Harbor with shops, restaurants, and a carousel.

LONG BEACH CITY BEACHES: *Seaward of Ocean Blvd., Long Beach.* A very wide beach extends from east of downtown to 72nd Place, at the tip of the Alamitos Peninsula. Alamitos Beach is the name applied to the stretch from E. Shoreline Dr. to Cherry Ave., and Junipero Beach extends from Cherry Ave. east to Belmont Pier. There is lots of sand but small surf, as the beach is largely protected by the harbor breakwater. Lifeguards patrol year-round; some towers staffed only seasonally. The Long Beach lifeguard service also maintains three rescue boats. Dogs not allowed on the beach; no smoking or glass containers.

From the downtown end of the beach to the Belmont Pier, the beach lies below a bluff. The beach can be reached by stairways down the bluff at the ends of 2nd, 3rd, 5th, 8th, 9th, 10th, and 14th Places; a stairway and ramp are located at 11th Place. There is limited parking along Ocean Blvd. At the end of Junipero Ave. there is a large, metered parking lot located at the beach level, and restrooms are at both ends of the lot. East of Junipero Ave., there are stairways from Bluff Park down to the beach, located at every other block. A paved bicycle path runs the length of the beach.

Although Los Angeles is advertised as the entertainment capital of the world, there is a lesser-known industry powering the city. In 2005 alone, more than six million barrels of oil and five billion cubic feet of natural gas were produced from more than 700 wells beneath the city. Add to these figures the oil that is produced from the geologically related fields underlying parts of Long Beach, Seal Beach, Huntington Beach, and Newport Beach, and it becomes apparent how important the "Los Angeles Basin" is to the state's economy.

The Los Angeles Basin is the name geologists give to the stack of rocks, mostly marine in origin, that accumulated in fault-bounded basins over the past 70 million years or so. Beneath downtown Los Angeles these deposits are nearly six miles deep. Tiny marine algae that were present in the seas filling these basins accumulated in the sediments as they were deposited.

As the sediment pile thickened, older sediments were pushed downward, where they were heated by the Earth's heat flux from below. This heat broke down the complex organic molecules, converting them to oil and, if heated sufficiently, to gas. The oil and gas moved upward through cracks and interconnected pore spaces to accumulate in the pore space of "reservoir" rocks, where natural traps were formed by overlying impermeable rocks. Where the upward migration of oil or gas was not inhibited, it continued to the surface, forming seeps such as at the famous La Brea tar pits. Elsewhere, oil and gas fields remained trapped underground, awaiting their discovery by entrepreneurs in the nineteenth century.

The tar from pits at Rancho La Brea was used by Native Americans as a sealant for their canoes, but it was not until 1892 that the first producing oil well was excavated by pick and shovel near present-day Dodger Stadium. Three years later there were more than 300 wells in the city of Los Angeles, producing 730,000 barrels of oil per year. Between 1892 and 1936 some 43 fields in the Los Angeles Basin were discovered, extending along a northwest-southeast trend as far south as Newport Beach. Today there are some 4,000 actively producing wells, both onshore and offshore at Long Beach and Seal Beach. Four artificial islands off Long Beach were built in the 1960s to disguise oil wells. The architect, who had worked at Disneyland, created surreal "condominium towers" with palm trees, waterfalls, and colorful night lighting. Production on the four islands has ranged from 100,000 barrels per day to a more recent figure of 30,000 barrels. Production from the Los Angeles Basin has been declining since 1990, when 49 million barrels were produced. In 2004, over 30 million barrels were produced—still an important contribution to California's energy supply.

Oil field development has not been without its environmental costs. In addition to occasional spills, extraction of oil from the largest of the Los Angeles Basin's oil fields, the Wilmington Field, caused subsidence of the ground surface by as much as 30 feet. This subsidence has largely been halted, and even locally reversed, by the re-injection of water into the subsurface reservoir.

Belmont Veterans Memorial Pier with oil development Island White offshore at center

Bayshore Beach on Alamitos Peninsula

Belmont Shore to Naples

	Sandy Beach	Rocky Shore	Trail	Visitor Center	Campground	Wildlife Viewing	Fishing or Boating	Facilities for Disabled	Food and Drink	Restrooms	Parking	Fee
Bixby Park							•			•	•	
Bluff Park			•									
Belmont Veterans Memorial Pier						•	•		•	•	•	
Belmont Plaza Olympic Pool										•	•	•
Belmont Shore	•		•				•			•	•	•
Alamitos Peninsula	•		•				•					
Alamitos Bay							•					
Naples			•				•					
Marine Park	•						•			•	•	
Marine Stadium							•			•	•	•
Colorado Lagoon	•									•	•	
Alamitos Bay Marina			•				•			•	•	•

BIXBY PARK: *Ocean Blvd. between Cherry and Junipero Avenues, Long Beach.* This 12-acre Long Beach city park is located across Ocean Blvd. from the beach. The park has picnic tables on tree-shaded lawns, playground equipment, a skateboard area, and shuffleboard courts. A band shell is used for frequent outdoor concerts. A recreation center offers programs for youth and seniors. For information, call: 562-570-1601.

BLUFF PARK: *Seaward of Ocean Blvd., from Lindero Ave. to E. of Redondo Ave., Long Beach.* Bluff Park is landscaped and outfitted with benches and a paved sidewalk that runs the length of the mile-long park. From the sidewalk, there are expansive views of the beach and harbor, and there are stairways down to the sand at every other block. At the west end of Bluff Park, at 2300 E. Ocean Blvd., is the Long Beach Museum of Art. The museum is open Tuesday to Sunday, from 11 AM to 5 PM; call: 562-439-2119.

BELMONT VETERANS MEMORIAL PIER: *Foot of 39th Place, Long Beach.* The 1,620-foot-long, T-shaped pier is popular for sightseeing and fishing. Anglers fish from the pier for halibut, mackerel, and perch and croaker species. On the pier are a snack stand, bait shop, and restrooms. Open dawn to dusk.

Fee parking is at the foot of S. Termino Ave., off E. Ocean Blvd.

The California Office of Environmental Health Hazard Assessment offers advice to the public about eating various species of game fish. At Belmont Pier and the vicinity, the recommendation is that no more than one meal of locally caught surfperch be consumed within a two-week period. This advisory is due to elevated levels of the pesticide DDT and the compounds known as PCBs. Because these chemicals are found in sediments on the ocean floor at certain locations, rather than in ocean water, there is no known risk to swimmers from DDT and PCBs. For more information, see the website of the Fish Contamination Education Collaborative: www.pvsfish.org.

BELMONT PLAZA OLYMPIC POOL: *E. of Belmont Veterans Memorial Pier, Long Beach.* Indoor pool, on the beach, designed for Olympic-class swimming and diving events; used in training U.S. athletes for international events. The facility is also used for public recreational swimming and diving, swimming lessons, and water exercise classes, and there is a weight room. Fee for entry; for open hours, call: 562-570-1806. Metered parking adjacent.

Belmont Shore

BELMONT SHORE: *Seaward of E. Ocean Blvd., between 39th Place and 54th Place, Long Beach.* Part of Long Beach City Beach, extending from east of the Belmont Veterans Memorial Pier to the Alamitos Peninsula. The wide sandy beach has year-round lifeguard service, sand volleyball, shore fishing, and fee parking in several large lots. Dogs permitted on the beach only between Prospect and Granada Avenues, where they are allowed off leash. Smoking and glass containers are prohibited on the beach. A paved bike path runs along the beach from the downtown area to 54th Place. From that point, the bicycle path turns inland along Bay Shore Ave., which is closed to vehicle traffic during the summer. A beach wheelchair is kept at Alfredo's concession opposite Granada Ave.

There are two places on Ocean Blvd. in Belmont Shore for launching small vessels into San Pedro Bay. One boat launch, opposite LaVerne Ave., is for sailboats; there is metered off-street parking. A nearby launch, opposite S. Granada Ave., is for jet skis that can be rolled across the beach; parking fee is payable upon entry. Open from 8 AM to dusk, year-round.

ALAMITOS PENINSULA: *Off E. Ocean Blvd., from 54th Place to 72nd Place, Long Beach.* Alamitos Peninsula extends from Belmont Shore to the entrance channel of Alamitos Bay; the peninsula separates Alamitos Bay from San Pedro Bay. The jetty at the end of the peninsula is a popular fishing spot. The sandy beach on the San Pedro Bay side of the peninsula is part of Long Beach City Beach. Along the beach is a wooden pedestrian boardwalk called Seaside Walk. Landscaped street ends between 54th Place and 69th Place provide access from Ocean Blvd. to Seaside Walk.

On the northern side of the peninsula facing Alamitos Bay is Bay Shore Walk, a public path that runs along the water from 55th to 65th Place. Bayshore Beach and Playground at 54th Place off E. Ocean Blvd. has calm waters, a children's playground, and courts for basketball, handball, racquet ball, and paddle tennis; call: 562-570-1715. Next to Bayshore Beach is a dry boat storage area for kayaks and other small craft, located at E. Ocean Blvd. and 54th Place and accessible to Alamitos Bay. Managed by the city of Long Beach; call: 562-570-3239.

ALAMITOS BAY: *W. of the San Gabriel River, Long Beach.* Alamitos Bay was once an extensive estuary and wetland with sloughs, mudflats, and marshland; it was dredged around the turn of the 20th century for the development of the Naples island community. The bay provides habitat for spotted bay bass, jacksmelt, perch, and halibut and acts as a nursery for various coastal and offshore fish species. There are two boat launch ramps in Alamitos Bay operated by the city of Long Beach. Launch fee applies; for information, call: 562-570-8636. The Davies launch ramp is under the E. Second St. bridge; from E. Second St., turn north onto Marina Dr. and then immediately left to the launch ramp; open 24 hours. On the opposite (west) side of the Marine Stadium channel is a launch ramp at 5255 Paoli Way. Open from 8 AM to dusk, but check ahead for closures during special events in Marine Stadium, call: 562-570-3203.

NAPLES: *Along E. 2nd St. in Alamitos Bay, Long Beach.* Named after the city in Italy, Naples is a residential community composed of three islands in Alamitos Bay that are linked by bridges and separated by the Rivo Alto and Naples Canals. Public walkways run along each canal and encircle most of the islands. Along E. Sorrento Dr. are several narrow public walkways leading to the water's edge. A small landscaped park at the foot of E. Naples Plaza has benches and a nice view of the bay. Street parking. The annual Christmas Boat Parade, held in early December in Alamitos Bay, can be viewed from Naples.

MARINE PARK: *E. Appian Way at E. 2nd St. overcrossing, Long Beach.* North of E. 2nd St. and facing calm bay waters is a sandy beach known as Mothers Beach, with a marked swimming area, seasonal lifeguard service, and a small boat dock at the north end. Amenities include picnic tables, play equipment, paved paths, sand volleyball courts, and tree-shaded lawns. A city of Long Beach park; call: 562-570-3100.

MARINE STADIUM: *N. of E. 2nd St. and east of Appian Way, Long Beach.* The site of the 1932 Olympics rowing races, Marine Stadium is a narrow, two-mile-long body of water now used for recreational boating and special

Mothers Beach at Marine Park

events. Marine Stadium can be reached from E. 3rd St., near Appian Way, or off Boathouse Ln. Open from 8 AM to sunset, with separate hours for water skiing and rowing. Boat launch fee applies; for information, call: 562-570-3203. Boaters gather on summer evenings to attend waterside concerts at Marine Stadium.

On Boathouse Ln., along the east side of Marine Stadium, there is trailerable boat storage (fee applies), and farther south there is public parking (no fee). At the south end of Boathouse Ln. is the Pete Archer Rowing Center, which offers rowing programs for young people and adults; for information, call: 562-438-3352.

Walk left and behind the Rowing Center to reach the Jack Dunster Marine Biological Reserve, a small restored mudflat and salt marsh surrounded by residential and recreational development. A pathway and observation platforms provide quiet places to look for waders and other birds; open from sunrise to sunset. A city of Long Beach park; for information, call: 562-570-3100. The Los Cerritos Wetlands Stewards, a nonprofit organization, conducts a nature walk and habitat restoration program on the second Saturday of each month at 10 AM.

COLORADO LAGOON: *5119 E. Colorado St. at E. Appian Way, Long Beach.* Colorado Lagoon is a tidal water body with inflow from Marine Stadium. There are sandy beaches linked by a floating causeway, picnic tables with barbecue grills, and playgrounds, open all year; lifeguard service is seasonal. A model boat shop is open during the summer, and model sailboat races are held every Friday. Metered parking on E. Appian Way and off E. 6th St. Call: 562-570-1720.

North of Colorado Lagoon is Recreation Park with two municipal golf courses, tennis center, lawn bowling, ball fields, and a teen center; call: 562-570-1670. For information on the nine-hole golf course; call: 562-438-4012; for the 18-hole course, call: 562-494-5000. South of Colorado Lagoon, on E. Eliot St. off E. 6th St., is Marina Vista Park, with ball fields, tennis courts, and picnic areas.

ALAMITOS BAY MARINA: *205 Marina Dr., Long Beach.* A municipal marina, with an enviable location that is well-protected by breakwaters but close to open water. There

Marine Stadium

Naples Plaza

are more than 1,975 boat slips, including slips available for guest boaters (fee applies); reservations are taken but are not required. Fuel dock and pumpout facilities available. For marina information, visit the Long Beach Marine Bureau at 205 Marina Dr., or call: 562-570-3215. The Marina Shipyard offers boat repairs and maintenance; call: 562-594-0995.

Alamitos Bay Landing is a restaurant and shopping complex located at the entrance to Alamitos Bay, near the Marina Dr. bridge across the San Gabriel River channel. Brightly painted Aqua Link catamarans ferry passengers from Alamitos Bay Landing to the Aquarium of the Pacific and the *Queen Mary* in Queensway Bay; for information, call Long Beach Transit: 562-591-2301. Long Beach Transit also provides service by land, via the Passport bus, to Pine Ave. in downtown Long Beach and intermediate points in Belmont Shore.

Rancho Los Alamitos, located at 6400 Bixby Hill Rd. in eastern Long Beach, is a historic ranch house surrounded by gardens, a delightful reminder of southern California's rural past. The property is owned by the city of Long Beach and operated by the nonprofit Rancho Los Alamitos Foundation. The site was occupied by Native Americans as early as about 500 A.D.; the adobe ranch house was built around 1800 by the Nieto family. There are farm animals and a working blacksmith shop. There are guided tours of the ranch house and barns and self-guided tours of the gardens. Free admission; open Wednesday through Sunday from 1 PM to 5 PM. For information, call: 562-431-3541.

SAN PEDRO

Santa Catalina Island

Wrigley Res

Hamilton Cove
Playa Azul

SAINT

CATHERINE WAY

Descanso Beach

Casino Point Marine Park
Casino Pt.

STAGE

Avalon Casino

Avalon Bay

Pleasure Pier
Crescent Beach

Abalone Pt.

CHANNEL

RD

CRESCENT AVE

Avalon
Island Plaza

CATALINA AVE

CLARISSA AVE

TREMONT ST

PEBBLY BEACH RD

Pebbly Beach

Hermit Gulch Campground

N

AVALON CANYON RD

0   0.25   0.5 Mile
0   0.25   0.5 Kilometer
See Legend on page 18 regarding Marine Protected Areas offshore

Nature Center at Avalon Canyon
Wrigley Memorial and Botanical Garden

Avalon Bay

Avalon, Santa Catalina Island

	Sandy Beach	Rocky Shore	Trail	Visitor Center	Campground	Wildlife Viewing	Fishing or Boating	Facilities for Disabled	Food and Drink	Restrooms	Parking	Fee
Hamilton Cove	•	•	•							•		
Descanso Beach	•						•		•	•		•
Casino Point Marine Park		•				•						
Pleasure Pier						•	•	•	•	•		
Avalon Bay						•	•					
Crescent Beach	•					•	•		•	•		
Nature Center at Avalon Canyon				•		•		•		•		
Hermit Gulch Campground			•		•				•	•		•
Wrigley Memorial and Botanical Garden			•			•		•		•		•

HAMILTON COVE: *1 mi. N. of Avalon Bay.* Small, pebbly cove adjacent to condominium complex. Amenities include restrooms and drinking water. Accessible from Avalon by traveling to guardhouse, where visitors sign in and then walk down the steep hill on Playa Azul. Also accessible by kayak.

DESCANSO BEACH: *N. of Avalon Casino.* This private beach club is open to the public for a daily fee from mid-April through mid-October. There is a seaside restaurant, and facilities include volleyball courts, dressing rooms, restrooms, and outdoor showers. Kayaks, beach umbrellas, and snorkeling gear can be rented. Call: 310-510-7410.

CASINO POINT MARINE PARK: *Offshore from the Casino, Avalon.* The underwater park, established by the city of Avalon, includes kelp forests, shipwrecks, and marine life.

Great snorkeling and diving. Stairs north of the Casino lead directly into the bay.

PLEASURE PIER: *Foot of Catalina Ave., Avalon.* Known as the Green Pier but painted a vivid turquoise color, the Pleasure Pier is where tour boats depart, while ferries from the mainland land at the concrete pier at the east end of the bay. Also on the Pleasure Pier are concessions, equipment rentals, dinghy docks, and boat hoist. Diving supplies, marine supplies, bait and tackle, and fishing licenses are available. The Harbormaster's office is on the Pleasure Pier.

Catalina Express passenger ferries serve Catalina Island from mainland harbors at San Pedro, Long Beach, and Dana Point; for information, call: 1-800-481-3470.

Other ferry services operate from Marina del Rey, 310-305-7250, and Newport Harbor, 1-800-830-7744.

The 1929 Avalon Casino, featuring spectacular Art Deco-style murals, is a historic entertainment venue. A ballroom on the upper level is used occasionally for big-band dances, as it was in the days when live, nationwide radio broadcasts came from the Casino. A theater on the lower level shows first-run films, daily. For information about Casino tours, call: 800-626-5440. Tour fee applies; it includes entry to the Catalina Island Museum, located in the Casino.

AVALON BAY: *E. end of the island, on the leeward side.* Avalon Harbor is within the bay. There are no berths; boaters moor to buoys. For first-come, first-served mooring assignments, check in upon arrival with the Harbor Patrol boat; for information, call: 310-510-0535. A fuel dock and convenience store is next to the Casino, open daily; call: 310-510-0046. Sewage pumpout station is nearby. Water-skiing and diving are permitted beyond the breakwater.

CRESCENT BEACH: *N. and S. of the Pleasure Pier, Avalon.* A surf-free swimming beach is next to the Pleasure Pier. At the north end of the beach facilities include restrooms, outdoor shower, and towel rental. Lifeguards on duty during the summer.

NATURE CENTER AT AVALON CANYON: *1202 Avalon Canyon Rd., Avalon.* The Nature Center features self-guided exhibits and hands-on activities for kids, and also hosts the popular Evening Nature Program lecture series. The work of the Catalina Island Conservancy to protect and restore the Island's wild lands is featured. The Nature Center and the Wrigley Memorial and Botanical Garden make a perfect introduction to Catalina Island's natural history. Docent-led tours are available. Open daily from 10 AM to 4 PM; closed on Thursdays from Labor Day to Memorial Day. Call: 310-510-0954.

HERMIT GULCH CAMPGROUND: *Avalon Canyon Rd., 1.5 mi. from Pleasure Pier.* The Hermit Gulch Campground in a wooded setting offers tent campsites and tent cabins, with picnic tables and barbecue grills. Running water, showers, restrooms, and vending machines; charcoal, ice, fire logs, and propane for sale. Walk from Avalon or take a taxi. Fees for camping and equipment rentals. Call: 310-510-8368.

WRIGLEY MEMORIAL AND BOTANICAL GARDEN: *Avalon Canyon Rd., 1.7 mi. from Pleasure Pier.* The Memorial is built almost entirely with native materials, including blue flagstone rock from Little Harbor and glazed tiles made by hand on the island by Catalina Pottery, a local producer that operated in the 1920s and 1930s. The Botanical Garden features cacti, succulents, and other dry-climate plants. The original collection started in the 1930s under the direction of Ada Wrigley, wife of William Wrigley, Jr., has come to focus on Catalina Island plants, including some found nowhere else, such as the Santa Catalina ironwood and Santa Catalina manzanita. Open from 8 AM to 5 PM, year-round; fee for entry. Call: 310-510-2595.

Hamilton Cove

Avalon is a compact, walkable town with many lodging and dining options. To get about, visitors use bicycles or golf carts; for taxi service, call: 310-510-0025. Tours in and beyond Avalon are available from Discovery Tours, 310-510-8687, and Catalina Adventure Tours, 877-510-2888. The Safari Bus runs from Avalon to Two Harbors, with stops at the trailhead for Black Jack Campground, Airport-in-the-Sky, and Little Harbor. For schedule, fares, and reservations, call: 310-510-2800.

The Catalina Island Conservancy, which manages much of the island as a preserve, offers private and group tours in open-air, four-wheel-drive vehicles; visitors must be ambulatory, at least six years old, and not in a booster seat. The Conservancy also operates the Wildlands Express shuttle to the Airport-in-the-Sky, with stops for hikers and picnickers. For information, call: 310-510-2595 Ext. 0.

From Avalon Canyon, the Hermit Gulch Trail leads to the spine of the island, where there are striking views of the windward side; the route climbs some 1,500 feet within three miles. The Trans Catalina Trail extends 26 miles from Avalon to Parson's Landing. Free, same-day hiking permits are required to explore the island's trails; apply in person at 125 Clarissa Ave. between 8:30 AM and 3:30 PM daily, 310-510-2595;

at Airport-in-the-Sky, 310-510-0143; or at Two Harbors, 310-510-4205. To explore by bicycle outside Avalon, obtain a required bike permit (fee applies) at one of the same three locations; helmets must be worn. Bring your own mountain bike (check with the ferry operator for fees) or rent one on the island at Brown's Bikes, 310-510-0986, or Catalina Auto & Bike, 310-510-0111; golf carts and strollers are also available for rent. You can bring a bike on the Safari Bus; extra fee applies. Whether hiking or bicycling, bring plenty of drinking water. Pets are not allowed in the interior of the island or in any campground, and smoking is allowed only in designated areas.

Guided kayak tours are available from Descanso Beach Ocean Sports; call: 310-510-1226. Kayaks, and other craft can be rented from Joe's Rent-a-Boat; call: 310-510-0455. Kayak and snorkel equipment rentals are available from Wet Spot Rentals; call: 310-510-2229. There is good snorkeling in Lover's Cove, located east of Crescent Beach.

Ocean waters off Catalina Island are very clear. Diving trips and instruction are offered by Scuba Luv; call: 310-510-2350. Sales and rentals of dive gear, air fills, and dive tours and instruction are offered by Catalina Divers Supply; call: 310-510-0330. Guided fishing trips are available; call: 323-447-4669.

Avalon Bay

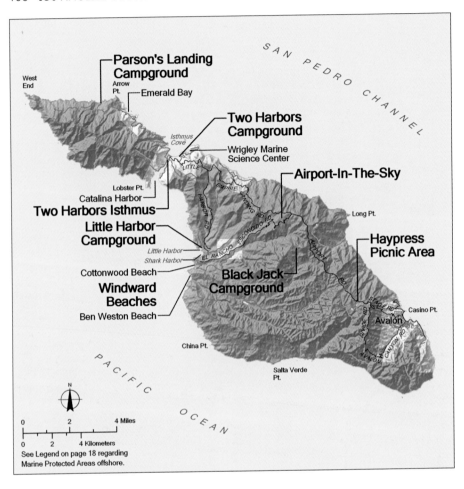

Parson's Landing
Campground

West
End

Arrow
Pt.

Emerald Bay

SAN PEDRO CHANNEL

Two Harbors
Campground

Isthmus
Cove

Wrigley Marine
Science Center

LITTLE

Airport-In-The-Sky

Lobster Pt.
Catalina Harbor
Two Harbors Isthmus

Little Harbor
Campground

HARBOR RD

EMPIRE

LANDING RD

ESCONDIDO RD

Long Pt.

Little Harbor
Shark Harbor

EL RANCHO

Cottonwood Beach

Windward
Beaches

Ben Weston Beach

Black Jack
Campground

AIRPORT RD

Haypress
Picnic Area

STAGE RD

Casino Pt.

Avalon

DIVIDE RD

CANYON RD

AVALON

China Pt.

Salta Verde
Pt.

PACIFIC OCEAN

N

0   2   4 Miles

0   2   4 Kilometers

See Legend on page 18 regarding
Marine Protected Areas offshore.

Isthmus Cove

Santa Catalina Island

	Sandy Beach	Rocky Shore	Trail	Visitor Center	Campground	Wildlife Viewing	Fishing or Boating	Facilities for Disabled	Food and Drink	Restrooms	Parking	Fee
Parson's Landing Campground	•	•	•		•	•	•			•		•
Two Harbors Campground	•	•	•		•	•	•			•		•
Two Harbors Isthmus	•	•	•			•	•	•	•	•		
Little Harbor Campground	•	•	•		•	•	•			•		•
Windward Beaches	•	•	•			•						
Airport-in-the-Sky				•					•	•	•	
Black Jack Campground			•		•	•				•		•
Haypress Picnic Area				•		•				•		

PARSON'S LANDING CAMPGROUND: *Parson's Landing, N.W. end of the Island.* Perhaps the most remote campground in coastal southern California, Parson's Landing offers a camping experience far from the urban bustle. Get there by hiking seven miles from Two Harbors or two and a half miles from the boat landing at Emerald Bay. There are eight campsites with picnic tables, barbecue grills, and fire rings. Chemical toilets available, but no drinking water and no natural shade. An initial supply of firewood and drinking water is included in the camping fee. Arriving campers must check in at Two Harbors Visitor Services. For information and reservations, call: 310-510-8368 or see: www.visitcatalinaisland.com.

TWO HARBORS CAMPGROUND: *Little Fisherman's Cove, Two Harbors.* Overlooking the ocean are 42 individual campsites and three group campsites. Also available are tent cabins equipped with cots, camp stove, barbecue grill, lantern, and picnic table. Fresh water, showers, lockers, and chemical toilets are provided. Fees for camping and equipment rental. Call: 310-510-8368.

TWO HARBORS ISTHMUS: *N.W. part of the Island.* The Two Harbors area is a very popular draw for boating enthusiasts. On the leeward side of the isthmus is Isthmus Cove with 257 moorings and additional anchorages, and on the windward side nearby is Catalina Harbor, with 117 moorings plus anchorages. The hamlet of Two Harbors has a permanent population of about 200, a general store, restaurant, bar, and snack stand. Arriving boaters must call the Harbor Patrol on VHF Channel 9 for mooring assignments. Boating facilities at Isthmus Cove include a fuel dock, dinghy dock, boat and motor rentals, and shore boat service. For information, call the Harbor Dept.: 310-510-4253. Divers and snorkelers are drawn by the exceptionally limpid waters off Catalina; equipment rentals and tours can be arranged at the foot of the pier in Isthmus Cove, or call: 310-510-4272. Public restrooms, showers, and laundry are also available, as are fishing licenses and bait and tackle.

Near Two Harbors is the University of Southern California's Wrigley Marine Science Center, where researchers pursue ma-

Campers with their own boats have a choice of boat-in campsites at 11 roadless sites scattered along the east side of the island. Campers are required to bring their own supplies and equipment, including self-contained restroom facility; a VHF radio is recommended. Rangers visit campsites daily. Camping fees apply, and reservations are essential; call: 310-510-8368.

rine and terrestrial investigations. Public science camps are held in the summer for young people, adults, and families; for information, call: 213-740-5679. Elderhostel courses, for participants 55 years of age and older, are offered in ecology, archaeology, and other subjects; call: 310-510-4021. Lectures and tours ranging in length from one hour to all day may also be available, with advance notice, for all visitors to the island; for information, call the Wrigley Marine Science Center: 310-510-0811.

LITTLE HARBOR CAMPGROUND: *Little Harbor, on the windward side of the Island.* This campground is located above a secluded, sandy, crescent-shaped beach. There are 16 campsites, including eight group sites, equipped with picnic tables, barbecue grills, fire rings, and lockers. Drinking water, rinse-off showers, and chemical toilets available. Get there by Safari Bus from Avalon or Two Harbors; check in first at Island Plaza in Avalon or at Two Harbors Visitor Services. Fee for camping; call: 310-510-8368.

WINDWARD BEACHES: *Windward side of the Island.* Experience the gorgeous windward shore of Catalina Island by having a picnic on a beach near Little Harbor. During the summer when the Safari Bus makes more than one daily trip, make an out-and-back excursion to the Windward Beaches from

either Avalon or Two Harbors; bus reservations are essential. Ride the Safari Bus to Little Harbor Campground and hike one-eighth mile to Shark Harbor or one mile to Cottonwood Beach.

AIRPORT-IN-THE-SKY: *On Airport Rd., 10 mi. N.W. of Avalon.* Charter services and private planes use this airport located atop the island. The Catalina Island Conservancy's Nature Center at the airport features displays about the natural history of Catalina Island. The Conservancy's Wildlands Express shuttle bus links the Airport-in-the-Sky to Avalon; call: 310-510-2595 Ext. 0.

BLACK JACK CAMPGROUND: *9.4 mi. N.W. of Avalon.* This inland campground is situated at 1,600 feet above sea level, with distant views of the ocean beyond scattered trees. There are 11 campsites, outfitted with picnic tables, barbecue grills, and fire rings; fresh water, showers, lockers, and chemical toilets. Get there by Safari Bus or airport shuttle from Avalon. Fee for camping and equipment rental. Check in first at Island Plaza in Avalon or at Two Harbors Visitor Services. Call: 310-510-8368.

HAYPRESS PICNIC AREA: *On Airport Rd., 3.9 mi. from Avalon.* Picnic area; water available. Hike from Avalon, or take the Safari Bus or the Wildlands Express bus.

Two Harbors Campground at Little Fisherman's Cove

Blueschist at Isthmus Cove

Catalina Island is dominated by two distinct rock types. The first is a rock that is very unusual in California, known as a blueschist. This rock, as its name implies, is deep blue in color and metamorphic in origin. The blue color is due to the mineral glaucophane, which forms only at intense pressures, but at relatively low temperatures. Its presence is usually a clue that the rock formed in a subduction zone, where an oceanic plate, diving beneath a continental plate, carried rocks to great depths before they were allowed to heat significantly. These rocks are some 130 to 60 million years old.

Intruding and surrounding these rocks are much younger dark-colored igneous rocks, 10 to 20 million years old, that were injected into the crust during a period of regional extension and volcanism. This volcanism introduced hot fluids into the crust, many of them carrying valuable metals. These fluids also altered the blueschist rocks, forming the minerals talc and steatite. These secondary products have long been exploited by humans. For thousands of years, Native Americans on Catalina mined the soft and carveable, but durable, steatite for use in bowls and cooking utensils, which were valuable goods used in trade with mainland tribes. In the 1860s, miners found lead and silver deposits, but the rugged and remote island setting made production uneconomic. William Wrigley, Jr., after acquiring the island in 1919, successfully extracted lead, zinc, and silver from the Black Jack area for a few years, until prices for commodity metals crashed worldwide.

Southern Channel Islands

CALIFORNIA'S Channel Islands have been labeled "the American Galapágos" because of their value as natural laboratories and their amazing biodiversity. The Channel Islands also contain some of the earliest sites of human occupation in North America, and the islands' colorful history is replete with pirates, shipwrecks, sea monsters, cattle rustling, Hollywood stars, Navy mysteries, bootlegging, smuggling, and many legends.

There are eight Channel Islands, four northern and four southern islands. The northern Channel Islands are influenced by cold ocean waters, known as the Oregonian Oceanic Province, while the southern Channel Islands are more influenced by the warmer Californian Oceanic Province. The northern Channel Islands get more rain and fog and have plant communities different from those of the southern Channel Islands. The northern islands exhibit an east-west orientation and are an extension of the Santa Monica Mountains, separated from the mainland by the Santa Barbara Channel, whereas the southern Channel Islands exhibit a northwest-to-southeast orientation and are separated from the mainland by the San Pedro Channel. The four southern Channel Islands are Santa Catalina (commonly called Catalina), San Clemente, San Nicolas, and Santa Barbara Islands. Santa Barbara Island is part of Channel Islands National Park, along with all four northern islands, and is covered in the California Coastal Commission's companion volume, *Beaches and Parks from Monterey to Ventura*.

Catalina is the third largest of the Channel Islands, after Santa Cruz and Santa Rosa Islands. Catalina is 21 miles long and eight miles across at its widest, and it lies nearly 20 miles from the nearest mainland point, the Palos Verdes Peninsula. Catalina Island is quite mountainous. A high central ridge runs its length, and Mount Orizaba, at 2,097 feet, is the highest point. Narrow canyons drain steep slopes on both sides of this ridge, and small coves with beaches mainly of cobblestones lie at canyon mouths. A few sandy beaches are found below larger canyons. Catalina's large size, high elevations, deep canyons, diverse geology and soil types, differing slope orientations, and varying micro-climates combine to support a wide diversity of plant communities, plant types, and ecological niches.

Catalina is home to approximately 600 species of plants, 400 of which are native. The island supports six main plant communities and seven endemic plant species, meaning they are found nowhere else in the world. The Catalina mountain mahogany is the rarest shrub in California; at one time there were only seven naturally growing specimens in the world. Catalina Island has the highest diversity of any Channel Island for reptiles (nine species) and amphibians (three species). Given the large number of residents and visitors, perhaps it is not surprising that Catalina has the largest number of non-native animals, including bison, commonly but incorrectly called "buffalo." The non-native goats, pigs, and deer destroy native plants; feral cats prey on native birds, mammals, reptiles, and amphibians; and the bison, with their large size and wide-roaming habits, tear up terrain, causing erosion. Island land managers have removed some non-native animals (such as the goats and pigs) and limited the numbers of the bison, but management of mule deer and feral cats remains controversial. The tiny island shrew, no bigger than a penny, is likely to face extinction due to feral cat predation.

Catalina Island is the only one of the eight Channel Islands that supports two year-round settlements: Avalon, population 3,000, and Two Harbors, population 200. Although Avalon is the only one of California's 500-plus cities that you cannot reach by car, Catalina does have regular ferry service and the popular Airport-in-the-Sky. Over one million people visit Catalina each year.

San Nicolas Island is owned by the U.S. Navy and is off limits to the general public. San Nicolas is used for testing and training exercises. The main San Nicolas Island Navy Base provides complete housing, dining, recreation, transportation, and public works support. Facilities include a 10,000-foot-long runway, an air terminal, a power plant, and a fuel farm depot. The west end of San Nicolas Island provides a secured area that serves as a target for missile tests.

San Nicolas Island was made famous by Scott O'Dell's popular children's story, *Island of the Blue Dolphins*. The tale is based on actual events that began in 1835, when a schooner was sent by the California mission padres to pick up the San Nicolas Island Indians, allegedly to protect them from Aleutian sea otter hunters. As the story is commonly recounted, while the ship was being loaded, a woman discovered her child had been left in the village and went back to find her. Meanwhile a strong wind arose, and the ship was forced to sail. The woman was abandoned on the island; her child is thought to have been killed by wild dogs. The schooner's captain was unable, or unwilling, to go back for her, and she spent 18 years alone on the barren, windswept island. She never saw her fellow islanders again.

In 1853 a party headed by sea otter hunter George Nidever found the woman alive and well on San Nicolas. Clad in a dress of cormorant skins sewn together, she lived in a shelter made from whale bones. Nidever brought her home to live with him and his wife in Santa Barbara, where she caused quite a sensation. Sadly, she contracted dysentery and died after she had been on the mainland for only seven weeks. The Native American woman is buried in an unmarked grave at Mission Santa Barbara.

San Clemente Island is the most southerly of the Channel Islands, located 68 nautical miles west of San Diego. San Clemente is 21 miles long and four-and-a-half miles across. Archaeological data indicate the presence of a maritime-oriented hunter-gatherer population on San Clemente as far back as 9,000 years ago. Over 7,600 archaeological sites have been mapped, but only a small percentage has been excavated, revealing many ancient artifacts. Native American occupation continued through the early historic period, until

Eelgrass survey off San Clemente island

about 1820. Since 1934 the island has been owned by various U.S. Naval commands. The island is now administered by the Naval Air Station North Island, located in Coronado. San Clemente Island is the only surface fire support range on the West Coast and the Navy's only ship-to-shore, live-fire range. Training of personnel and evaluation of equipment take place on and around the island.

Despite its use for military activities, San Clemente Island harbors more endangered species than all the other Channel Islands together, including six plants, three birds, the island fox, and the night lizard. The San Clemente loggerhead shrike is one of the rarest birds in North America and is found only on San Clemente Island. The Navy initiated a recovery effort for the bird in 1991, in partnership with the U.S. Fish and Wildlife Service, the state Department of Fish and Game, and the San Diego Zoo. The San Clemente Island fox is a state-listed rare species; there are approximately 800 foxes left on the island.

Santa Catalina ironwood

Island ironwood is differentiated into two subspecies: the **Santa Catalina ironwood** (*Lyonothamnus floribundus floribundus*), which is found only on Santa Catalina Island, and the island ironwood or fern-leaved ironwood (*Lyonothamnus floribundus* ssp. *aspleniifolius*), which is found on San Clemente, Santa Cruz, and Santa Rosa Islands. Both subspecies of ironwood are relictual endemics that had much wider distributions during the Pleistocene Epoch. Santa Catalina ironwood grows only on volcanic soils between 400 and 1,400 feet elevation, in steep canyons on the north-facing, San Pedro Channel side of the island. Santa Catalina ironwoods form dense groves, and each grove is a single clone of genetically identical individuals. The trees are connected underground by long-lived colonial roots.

Southern Channel Is. tree mallow

The **Southern Channel Island tree mallow** (*Lavatera assurgentiflora* ssp. *glabra*), also called malva rosa, stands three to seven feet in height and has maple-like leaves. The showy flowers are about three inches across, and the petals are white to pale purple with purple veins. The tree mallow prefers flat areas with sandy to rocky soil. This beautiful shrub is in the mallow family (Malvaceae), which also includes the hibiscus. *Lavatera assurgentiflora* ssp. *glabra* is endemic to San Clemente and Santa Catalina Islands, but has been planted on the mainland and many of the other islands, including the northern Channel Islands, where the northern Channel Island tree mallow (*Lavatera assurgentiflora* ssp. *assurgentiflora*) is native. On Santa Catalina Island, tree mallow now grows only on Bird Rock and Indian Rock, safe from browsers such as mule deer and bison.

The **bald eagle** (*Haliaeetus leucocephalus*) was found historically on all the Channel Islands and on the mainland of southern California. The mainland population disappeared in the 1930s, although bald eagles remained on the Channel Islands until the mid-1950s to early 1960s. Shooting, egg collecting, nest destruction, poisoning, and removal of young from nests all contributed to the bald eagle's population decline. Even more significant was the use of the industrial pesticide DDT. The use of DDT was banned in the United States in 1972, and in 1980 a bald eagle reintroduction program was initiated on Santa Catalina Island. Between 1980 and 1986, 33 eagles were released on the island, and many of the birds formed mating pairs. In 1987, the first eggs were laid, but unfortunately they broke soon afterwards, due to high concentrations of DDE (a metabolite of DDT). In 1989, a labor-intensive egg collection and artificial incubation program commenced, whereby viable eggs were collected from nests and replaced with fake eggs. The viable eggs were then incubated in a laboratory until just before hatching, when they were replaced in nests, sometimes by helicopter. Since 1980, more than one hundred bald eagles have been released or fostered into nests on Catalina Island.

Bald eagle

Most of the young eagles leave the island in the late summer of their first year, perhaps returning when they reach breeding age (about four or five years old). A few young eagles have remained on the island, moving about for several years before settling down in a territory. Five breeding pairs and four to six younger eagles have resided on the island in recent years. In 2007, a very exciting event happened: two bald eagle chicks hatched unaided by humans. The parents are a 21-year-old male, originally from British Columbia and released on the island in 1986, and an eight-year-old female, hatched at the San Francisco Zoo and released on the island in 1999.

Three-day-old bald eagle chicks hatched at the San Francisco Zoo, April 2004. Their DDT-contaminated eggs were retrieved from Catalina Island by the San Francisco Zoo Avian Conservation Center. Soon after hatching, the chicks were returned to the wild nest to be raised by their eagle parents.

Loggerhead shrike

The **loggerhead shrike** (*Lanius ludovicianus*) is a gray bird with black and white markings, resembling a stocky mockingbird with a black mask. This songbird has a small hook on the end of its beak, which gives it the appearance of a small raptor. However, the shrike does not have talons. Loggerhead shrikes maintain breeding populations on seven of the eight Channel Islands, and genetic research has confirmed the distinctiveness of the San Clemente Island loggerhead shrike, the Santa Catalina Island loggerhead shrike, and the loggerhead shrike found both on the northern Channel Islands and the mainland. Loggerhead shrikes are carnivores, and their prey includes insects, rodents, snakes, and small birds. Loggerhead shrikes have earned the name "butcher birds," because they often impale prey on thorns, stems, or barbed wire, to eat or store for later. The birds hunt in open or brushy areas, diving from perches and swiftly rising to the next lookout.

American bison

The **American bison** (*Bison bison*) was first introduced to Santa Catalina Island in 1924 when 14 animals were used in the filming of Zane Grey's movie, *The Vanishing American*. In 1934, 11 more bison were added to the herd, and 15 bull calves were introduced in 1969 to counteract the deleterious effects of inbreeding. The population peaked at 500 animals, although the goal of the Catalina Conservancy, the local land manager, is to maintain the population at 200 or below, in order to maintain a balance between island natural resources and the health of the herd. Bison are large herbivores and are left alone to freely graze on much of the island. While the bison certainly cause some negative impacts, especially to riparian habitats, they are much less damaging than non-native deer, goats, and pigs. The Catalina Conservancy offers island tours on which one is almost guaranteed to see bison, and "buffalo" burgers are available at the island's Airport in the Sky café.

Page opposite: Path to Strand Beach, part of Salt Creek Beach, located off Selva Rd., Dana Point

Orange County

Orange County

ORANGE County, named for the oranges that were once cultivated in vast orchards, was formed in 1889 from the southeastern portion of Los Angeles County. The county's northern coastal area, from Seal Beach to Newport Beach, is situated on the edge of the Los Angeles Basin, and is characterized by broad, sandy beaches backed by low bluffs and mesas, and lowland areas that once held extensive wetlands. At Corona del Mar the coastal plain ends and the San Joaquin Hills, part of the Peninsular Ranges, begin; from here to Dana Point, steep cliffs rise above picturesque sandy coves bounded by rocky points and tidepools and fringed by offshore rocks. South of Dana Point the coastline consists of a high marine terrace above a ribbon of narrow, sandy shoreline.

In the 1870s and 1880s, the growth of railroads opened the southern California coast to development. One of the first large settlements along Orange County's coast was at Newport Beach, where a shipping center was established in 1873. North of Newport Beach, new settlers drained the marshlands for farming; to the south, farmers homesteaded coastal areas from Laguna Beach to Dana Point. Residents of inland towns discovered the recreational possibilities of the coast, and summer resorts appeared at Laguna Beach and South Laguna. By 1906, Henry Hunting-

ton had extended his Pacific Electric Railway, an interurban system that served the Los Angeles Basin, into Orange County and down the coast to the Balboa Peninsula. To accommodate vacationers from Los Angeles and beyond, the resort towns of Seal Beach, Sunset Beach, Huntington Beach, and Balboa were created.

Orange County was known then and now for its magnificent beaches. The county is a prime destination for surfing, sunning, and playing on the sand. The city of Huntington Beach, which faces miles of spacious beaches, draws ten million visitors annually. Among California's ten most popular state park units, three are shoreline parks in Orange County: Bolsa Chica State Beach, Huntington State Beach, and Doheny State Beach. Orange County also offers boating facilities at Huntington Harbour, Newport Beach, and Dana Point Harbor, as well as fishing trips, whale-watching tours, and transportation to Catalina Island. And although the landscape has changed drastically as Orange County has urbanized, the county retains valuable natural resources. The north coast contains some of the healthiest and largest remaining wetlands in southern California. And some of California's premier wildlife viewing destinations are found in Orange County, including Bolsa Chica Ecological Reserve and Upper Newport Bay.

Anaheim/Orange County Visitor and Convention Bureau, 714-765-8888.

Laguna Beach Visitors Bureau, 252 Broadway, Laguna Beach, 1-800-877-1115.

Orange County Transit provides bus service to coastal destinations; Bus No. 1 travels the length of the county along Pacific Coast Hwy. Call: 714-636-7433.

Laguna Beach Transit serves Laguna Beach and Dana Point; for information, call: 949-497-0746.

Metrolink rail service links Union Station in downtown Los Angeles with Anaheim (home of Disneyland), San Juan Capistrano, and San Clemente, and Oceanside in San Diego County. Call: 1-800-371-5465.

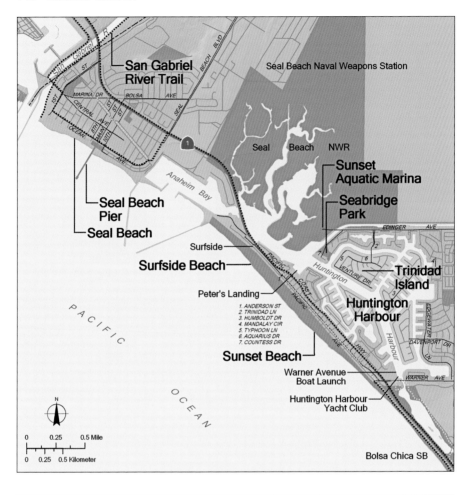

San Gabriel
River Trail

Seal Beach Naval Weapons Station

Seal   Beach   NWR

Sunset
Aquatic Marina

Seabridge
Park

Seal Beach
Pier

Seal Beach

Surfside

Surfside Beach

Peter's Landing

1. ANDERSON ST
2. TRINIDAD LN
3. HUMBOLDT DR
4. MANDALAY CIR
5. TYPHOON LN
6. AQUARIUS DR
7. COUNTESS DR

Trinidad
Island

Huntington
Harbour

Sunset Beach

Warner Avenue
Boat Launch

Huntington Harbour
Yacht Club

Bolsa Chica SB

PACIFIC   OCEAN

N

0   0.25   0.5 Mile

0   0.25   0.5 Kilometer

Seal Beach

Seal Beach and Huntington Harbour

	Sandy Beach	Rocky Shore	Trail	Visitor Center	Campground	Wildlife Viewing	Fishing or Boating	Facilities for Disabled	Food and Drink	Restrooms	Parking	Fee
Seal Beach	•					•	•		•	•	•	
Seal Beach Pier						•	•		•	•	•	
San Gabriel River Trail			•							•		
Surfside Beach	•											
Sunset Beach	•						•			•	•	
Huntington Harbour						•	•		•	•	•	
Trinidad Island							•					
Seabridge Park	•					•	•			•	•	
Sunset Aquatic Marina						•	•		•	•	•	•

SEAL BEACH: *Seaward of Ocean Ave., Seal Beach.* Seal Beach is located between the mouths of the San Gabriel River and the entrance to Anaheim Bay. A mile-long and very wide reach of sand is centered on Main St., which terminates at the Seal Beach Pier. Seal Beach is popular for surfing, swimming, and fishing. Beach parking lots are located off Ocean Ave. at the ends of 1st, 8th, and 10th Streets; pay for parking between 6 AM and 10 PM at self-service machines. Restrooms are located at the foot of 1st St. and at the Seal Beach Pier.

Year-round lifeguard service is provided by the city of Seal Beach. To borrow a beach wheelchair, inquire at lifeguard headquarters at the foot of the Seal Beach Pier, lower level; for information, call: 562-430-2613. Glass bottles and smoking are prohibited on the sand in Seal Beach; dogs are not allowed. A paved path runs south from the Seal Beach Pier along the inland edge of the beach.

SEAL BEACH PIER: *Foot of Main St., Seal Beach.* The Seal Beach Pier points directly at Catalina Island, located some 26 miles across the San Pedro Channel. Besides a view of Catalina, which on a clear day seems improbably close, the pier offers vistas of the downtown Long Beach skyline to the north and a wide expanse of sand to the south. A restaurant is located at the seaward end of the pier, which also has fish-cleaning stations and restrooms. There is good fishing for a variety of different croaker species; catches of perch are common, while the occasional halibut is also caught. No smoking on the pier. Restrooms are located at the foot of the pier on the lower level, where there are also outdoor showers, and a sandy playground with children's play equipment. A grassy park adjoins Ocean Ave. at the foot of the Seal Beach Pier.

Seal Beach Pier

Kite Day at Seal Beach

SAN GABRIEL RIVER TRAIL: *E. bank of the San Gabriel River.* A paved bicycle path runs from the Orange County coast along the east side of the San Gabriel River through urbanized Los Angeles County to Azusa and the San Gabriel Mountains, a distance of more than 30 miles. Park at the foot of 1st St. in Seal Beach, where the trail begins.

SURFSIDE BEACH: *Anderson St. and Pacific Coast Hwy., Surfside.* Pedestrian and bicycle access only are available through the Anderson St. gate of the private Surfside residential community. No public parking or restroom facilities. Lifeguard service is provided by the city of Seal Beach; call: 562-430-2613.

SUNSET BEACH: *W. of Pacific Ave., Huntington Beach.* A broad beach of soft sand extends from Anderson St. to Warner Ave., with public access available at street ends. Restrooms and shower facilities are located one short block inland of the beach, in a landscaped linear park that runs down the median of Pacific Ave.; restrooms at 2nd St. and 19th St. are wheelchair accessible. The park also includes a bike path and more than 600 parking spaces. The beach area has volleyball nets and surfing areas that are designated by flags. Lifeguard service is provided by the county of Orange. Dogs not allowed;

no alcohol or glass bottles on the beach. For information, call: 949-923-2250.

HUNTINGTON HARBOUR: *E. of Pacific Coast Hwy., Huntington Beach.* Huntington Harbour combines boating facilities, including five marinas with space for over 3,000 boats, with residential and commercial uses. Some facilities are open to the public. At Peter's Landing Marina, located opposite Anderson St., two-hour guest boat slips are available on a first-come, first-served basis, and longer-term guest slips are sometimes available by advance reservation; call: 714-840-1387. Boating facilities for tenants at Peter's Landing include laundry, showers, restrooms, and a pumpout station. Kayak rentals are available from vendors along Pacific Coast Hwy., and there are motels, restaurants, and shops. A one-lane public boat launch ramp is located near the Huntington Harbour Yacht Club, on the north side of Warner Ave. just east of Pacific Coast Hwy.; the launch is free, but parking fee applies. Small parks are dotted across Huntington Harbour's five islands; some parks have play areas or tennis courts. Respect private property; do not trespass.

TRINIDAD ISLAND: *Trinidad Ln., Huntington Beach.* This small, mostly residential island has a waterfront park on Trinidad Ln. north of Aquarius Dr. The park includes a sandy beach, outdoor shower, playground, and restrooms. From the foot of Trinidad Ln. a greenbelt continues across the island to Venture Dr., where there is a small public fishing dock that is open from 5 AM to 10 PM. A paved path for bicycles and pedestrians parallels Venture Dr. and Typhoon Ln. along the harbor, and meanders through the center of the island.

SEABRIDGE PARK: *End of Countess Dr., off Edinger Ave., Huntington Beach.* Seabridge Park has a sandy beach, playground, grassy areas, picnic tables, restrooms, an outdoor shower, and ample parking. A harbor-view walkway is located around the perimeter of the condominium complex at the end of Countess Dr.; to enter the walkway during daytime hours, push open the time-lock gate on the north side of the condominiums. Additional small public beaches are located on Davenport Dr. just west of Edgewater Ln. and on Humboldt Dr. west of Saybrook Ln.

SUNSET AQUATIC MARINA: *End of Edinger Ave., Huntington Beach.* A public small-boat harbor is at the west end of Edinger Ave.; from Warner Ave., turn north on Bolsa Chica St., then west on Edinger Ave. Grassy areas with pathways and picnic tables, some wheelchair accessible, overlook the bay. There are 300 privately owned boat slips; eight rented guest slips are available. A seven-lane concrete boat ramp is open 24 hours a day. Fee for use; register at office. Dry storage, haul-out, and repair facilities available.

Sunset Aquatic Marina is adjacent to Seal Beach National Wildlife Refuge, which comprises 1,200 acres of salt marshes that are within the boundaries of the U.S. Naval Weapons Station. There is no public access to the Wildlife Refuge. Ocean access from Sunset Aquatic Marina is through Anaheim Bay; non-powered boats are not permitted to pass through the Naval Weapons Station.

View from Seal Beach Pier to Long Beach

Renowned swimmer Lynne Cox has braved extreme cold-water environments in Antarctica and the Bering Strait, but Seal Beach is also very familiar to her. In 1974, at the age of 17, she broke the world's record for swimming from Seal Beach to Catalina Island with a time of 8 hours, 48 minutes. A training swim off the Seal Beach Pier one winter dawn inspired her to write *Grayson,* a book about her playful encounter with a baby California gray whale that had become separated from its mother while migrating from Baja California to Alaska. The book is a vivid account of swimming in the early-morning hours among schools of silvery juvenile anchovy, grunion, and albacore tuna.

Swimming in the ocean, as opposed to a pool, is known as rough water swimming. At Seal Beach, the annual Rough Water Swim has been held in mid-summer for four decades. The open-water swims begin at the Seal Beach Pier. Distances range from 200 yards to 1,200 yards for young people and up to five kilometers for adults. Other open-water swims off southern California's piers include the La Jolla Rough Water Swim, which has taken place nearly every year since 1916. That year seven men swam from the Scripps Pier to La Jolla Cove; more than 2,000 swimmers have participated in recent years. Open-water swims in Los Angeles and Orange Counties are publicized by the Southern Pacific Masters Association; see: www.spma.net. The San Diego-Imperial Masters provides information about open-water swims at La Jolla and elsewhere; see: www.simasterswim.org.

Endangered least terns at Bolsa Chica Ecological Reserve; male tern presents fish to female as courtship ritual

Bolsa Chica

	Sandy Beach	Rocky Shore	Trail	Visitor Center	Campground	Wildlife Viewing	Fishing or Boating	Facilities for Disabled	Food and Drink	Restrooms	Parking	Fee
Bolsa Chica Interpretive Center			•	•		•		•		•	•	
Bolsa Chica State Beach	•		•	•		•	•		•	•	•	•
Bolsa Chica Ecological Reserve			•	•		•		•		•	•	
Bolsa Chica State Beach Campground	•		•	•			•	•	•	•	•	•
Dog Beach	•		•							•	•	•

BOLSA CHICA INTERPRETIVE CENTER: *3842 Warner Ave. at Pacific Coast Hwy., Huntington Beach.* On the southeast corner of Warner Ave. and Pacific Coast Hwy. is a small visitor center operated by the Bolsa Chica Conservancy. The Conservancy operates educational and research programs for young people and organizes non-native vegetation removal efforts in the adjacent wetlands. The visitor center, which is wheelchair accessible, is open to the public Tuesday to Friday from 10 AM to 4 PM, Saturday from 9 AM to noon, and Sunday from 12:30 PM to 3:30 PM and contains displays about the plants, birds, and other wildlife of the Bolsa Chica wetlands. The parking lot is open every day from 6 AM to 8 PM for users of the trails that overlook the Bolsa Chica Ecological Reserve; dogs and bicycles are not allowed on the trails. For information, call: 714-846-1114.

BOLSA CHICA STATE BEACH: *W. of Pacific Coast Hwy., S. of Warner Ave., Huntington Beach.* Consistently among the top state beaches in number of visitors, along with nearby Huntington State Beach, Bolsa Chica State Beach features three miles of sand and surf. Volleyball, swimming, and sunning are popular. Anglers fish in the surf for perch, corbina, croakers, and occasional shark species. Grunion spawn on the beach during the summertime.

Bolsa Chica Ecological Reserve

The main entrance to the beach is on Pacific Coast Hwy. between Warner Ave. and Seapoint Ave. There are large fee parking lots, along with picnic areas, firepits, food concessions, beach showers, and restrooms. State park lifeguards are on duty year-round, and lifeguard towers are staffed from about Memorial Day weekend to Labor Day. For a beach wheelchair, contact a lifeguard, or call: 714-846-3460. Park hours are from 6 AM to 10 PM year-round; entrance gates close at 9 PM. A paved multi-use path runs the length of the beach and continues south through Huntington Beach, connecting to the Santa Ana River Trail.

BOLSA CHICA ECOLOGICAL RESERVE: *E. of Pacific Coast Hwy., S. of Warner Ave., Huntington Beach.* The reserve, operated by the California Dept. of Fish and Game, has benefited from a major expansion and enhancement program. In all, nearly one square mile of marine and wetland habitat restoration has taken place, the largest such effort in southern California. In 2006, an entrance channel connecting the wetland to the ocean was completed, restoring the ample supply of saltwater that formerly flowed through the wetland complex. Habitat areas for use by nesting and feeding birds have been enhanced, and old oil extraction facilities have been removed.

Originally a 2,300-acre estuary, Bolsa Chica, meaning "little pocket" in Spanish, was largely drained for farming beginning in 1890. In the late 1890s, sportsmen built a dam to restrict tidal flow from the ocean into the marsh and constructed ponds and levees to facilitate duck hunting. When the original ocean opening silted up completely, a channel was dug from the bay into Anaheim Bay, by way of what is now Huntington Harbour, leaving the wetlands with only limited saltwater influence.

Bolsa Chica is a great place to observe California least terns. The terns nest on islands in the wetland during spring and summer and can be seen swooping over the water as they dive for fish. The birds' shrill voices are distinctive. Park in the lot one mile south of Warner Ave., on the east side of Pacific Coast Hwy. opposite the main entrance to Bolsa Chica State Beach. The entrance to the Bolsa Chica Ecological Reserve parking area is accessible only from the northbound lanes of Pacific Coast Hwy. Walk east over a bridge for close-up looks at marsh birds and distant views of water and sky. A trail continues north, looping around part of Bolsa Bay. Chemical toilets are at the parking area. Another parking area is farther north, adjacent to the Bolsa Chica Interpretive Center.

Dog Beach

The Bolsa Chica Ecological Reserve and the marshes in nearby Anaheim Bay contain stands of cordgrass that are among southern California's largest. Other marsh plants include saltgrass, pickleweed, and jaumea. In addition to California least terns, other endangered species inhabiting the wetlands include Belding's savannah sparrow and the light-footed clapper rail. The reserve is open daily from sunrise to sunset. Pets must remain inside a vehicle. Call: 858-467-4201.

BOLSA CHICA STATE BEACH CAMPGROUND: *W. of Pacific Coast Hwy., S. of entrance to Bolsa Chica State Beach, Huntington Beach.* Fifty-seven enroute campsites for self-contained RVs are located south of the main entrance to Bolsa Chica State Beach; electrical and water hookups are available, as are coin-operated hot showers. No tent camping. An RV dump station is located near the campground. Reservations are required; call: 1-800-444-7275.

DOG BEACH: *W. of Pacific Coast Hwy., from Seapoint Ave. to Goldenwest St., Huntington Beach.* Dogs are allowed on this part of Huntington City Beach. Metered parking is available in two lots, one south of Seapoint Ave. and the other north of Goldenwest St.; enter either lot from southbound Pacific Coast Hwy. The parking lots open at 5 AM, and meters are enforced from 8 AM to 10 PM daily. Picnic tables are on top of the bluff at the north end of Dog Beach. Chemical toilets, not wheelchair-accessible, are next to the parking areas.

Ramps lead down to the beach from the ends of the parking lots. Huntington Beach city lifeguards patrol year-round, from dawn to dusk, and lifeguard towers spaced along the beach are staffed seasonally. A paved multi-use path runs the length of Huntington Beach, paralleling the shore. For beach information, call: 714-536-5281.

Passing through the Bolsa Chica wetlands is one of California's most notorious faults. As its name implies, the active Newport-Inglewood Fault extends from offshore Newport Beach to Inglewood, running northeast of the Palos Verdes Peninsula. To the south, the Newport-Inglewood Fault joins the Rose Canyon Fault offshore and comes ashore in La Jolla. Altogether, this fault system extends some 100 miles and runs either through, or lies just offshore of, some of the most densely populated areas of California. The fault was the locus of the 1933 Long Beach earthquake, which killed 115 persons and resulted in over $40 million of damage (in 1933 dollars). Most of the deaths occurred when people ran out of buildings and were struck by falling bricks or debris. Many Long Beach schools collapsed, and the death toll could have been much worse if the quake had occurred earlier in the day, while children were still at their desks. After the earthquake, the state legislature adopted a law requiring stronger building codes for school construction.

Urbanization has obscured the fault trace along most of its onshore route; indeed the extent of development near or across the fault trace has led many geologists to consider this one of the most potentially damaging faults in California. One of the few places that it can be seen clearly today is at the Bolsa Chica mesas in Huntington Beach. Although the fault primarily carries land on its west side horizontally to the northwest, minor compression results in some vertical uplift to the east of the fault. At Bolsa Chica, an undeveloped "lower mesa" just above the Bolsa Chica Interpretive Center at Warner Ave. and Pacific Coast Hwy. rises to the new residential development located some 30 feet above on the "upper mesa." The slope separating the upper and lower mesas marks uplift associated with the Newport-Inglewood Fault, which lies at the base of the slope.

Salt Marsh in Southern California

THE SALT MARSHES of the southern California coast were remarked upon by many early writers for the enormous numbers of waterfowl that visited during seasonal migrations. Today these marshes are less obvious, reduced to islands of habitat in an urban sea. Nevertheless, they continue to provide many of the same ecological benefits.

The low marsh is characterized by tall cordgrass within which clapper rails go about their hidden business. Where the marsh plain slopes gently upward, it is dominated by pickleweed. Robust stands of pickleweed in the high intertidal zone are likely to be tightly divided into territories by Belding's savannah sparrows, one of the few bird species that is resident year-round in the salt marsh. Within the marsh plain, a change in elevation of three or four inches can result in an abrupt shift in floral composition and dominance relationships. Therefore, topographic heterogeneity in the middle marsh is reflected in increased vegetation diversity. The high marsh typically has the greatest floral diversity and, besides pickleweed, includes such transitional species as saltgrass and sea lavender that may only infrequently be wetted by the tides.

Fringing the vegetated marsh and separating it from deep water are sand and mudflats that provide critical foraging habitats for a host of migratory shorebirds. Bird abundance and viewing opportunities are especially high during the fall. Birds of all sizes, from willets and long-billed curlews to plovers and petite sandpipers, gather on mudflats and in sinuous channels exposed by the ebbing tide to feed on worms and other small creatures. As the tide returns, all but those with the longest legs congregate in drier refuges within the marsh or adjacent shore.

Buried in the sand and mud are a variety of clams and other organisms. Some feed on the plankton suspended in the waters above, and others make meals of detritus. Competition for a place in the mud is partially resolved by the tendency of different species to occupy different depths. The muddy surface of flats and channels is often covered with dense aggregations of horn snails, which share this frequently submerged habitat

Common yellowthroat, Upper Newport Bay

with fiddler crabs and other small animals. The animals of the flats and channels are food for fish when submerged, and when the tide goes out, they trade one set of diners for another as the birds return.

It is estimated that southern California was once graced with some 50,000 acres of rich coastal salt marsh. Urbanization has reduced that acreage by about 75 percent. Yet, despite over 100 years of human alterations, southern California's lagoons and estuaries still manage to provide critical ecological functions for hundreds of species. Even diked areas that are cut off from ocean waters continue to support pickleweed and sometimes Belding's savannah sparrows. We can do much better where the land is still available for restoration, although as the Bolsa Chica restoration in Huntington Beach illustrates, it is a complicated and expensive undertaking.

Anaheim Bay and Bolsa Bay were separated as late as 1894 at the Bolsa Chica Mesa. These estuaries, totaling perhaps 4,600 acres, were created over geologic time by the meandering San Gabriel and Santa Ana Rivers, now confined to armored manmade channels. Around the turn of the 19th century, estuaries along the Pacific Flyway were of great interest for sporting opportunities, and some 23 duck clubs were established in coastal Los Angeles and Orange Counties. One club owned much of the wetlands in Bolsa Bay and, beginning about 1898, closed the ocean inlet, built dikes to convert the salt marsh to freshwater ponds for waterfowl, and dug a channel to drain the Bolsa Chica system into Anaheim Bay. That channel now connects the manmade Huntington Harbour and outer Bolsa Bay. A culvert within the dike separating the outer and inner bays allows some tidal exchange. In the 1920s, oil was discovered and over the next three decades the Bolsa Chica wetlands were filled and further diked to create roads, pipelines, and drilling pads for hundreds of wells, some of which are still in production. After tidal waters were blocked, portions of the historical marsh were converted to agriculture, and the more inland areas were later filled for residential subdivisions.

At one time, it was envisaged that the Bolsa Chica lowlands be the site of a marina, commercial development, and some 900 homes. That this did not come to pass is due in no small part to the diligent efforts of local citizens with a vision to preserve the remnants of southern California's salt marshes. Restoration efforts began in 1970 when the California Department of Fish and Game gained ownership of about 300 acres in outer Bolsa Bay and the adjacent inner Bolsa Bay. As part of the restoration, islands were constructed, which have become a significant nesting location for several species of sea and shore birds. Designated the Bolsa Chica Ecological Reserve, this area is a favorite destination for birders and photographers.

Eventually, over 1,000 acres of historic marshlands were purchased by the State of California for restoration and preservation. Due to the magnitude of past alterations, there was no attempt to recreate historical conditions. Rather, the intent of restoration was to create a diversity of ecological values by creating a large, fully tidal basin with fringing mudflats and vegetated marsh and by enhancing much of the existing seasonally wet salt marsh by introducing muted tidal waters. Removal of oil infrastructure, including over 121,000 feet of pipeline and 64 wells, began in 2003. Later came the excavation and dredging of 2.7 million cubic yards of earth and construction of an ocean inlet, jetties, new bridges, water control structures, bird nesting islands, and groundwater barriers to protect nearby residential neighborhoods. In 2006, tidal waters entered the Bolsa Chica wetlands for the first time in over 100 years at a cost of about $148 million, most of which came from the Ports of Los Angeles and Long Beach to pay their mitigation bills for the inevitable environmental impacts of handling the nation's cargo.

Cordgrass

Cordgrass (*Spartina foliosa*) is a perennial grass one to four feet high that is endemic to coastal salt marshes of central and southern California and Baja California. It grows only in the low zone of salt marshes, because it requires daily flushing of surface salts. This ability to grow in a saline environment earns it the label "halophyte." An important cordgrass adaptation is the ability of its roots to take in seawater while excluding salts. Cordgrass forms large and often dense stands due to its ability to rapidly spread by vegetative reproduction. It tends to grow in pure stands, as it is a poor competitor with other plant species.

Sea lavender

Sea lavender (*Limonium californicum*) is a perennial herb that is characteristic of the upper salt marsh community. Although not a member of the lavender family, it gets its common name from its showy flowers, which catch the visitor's eye because they are held above the surrounding vegetation by a robust stalk. It is one of many species that are known as "everlastings" because the dried flowers retain their color and form. Ornamental species of *Limonium* are usually called "statice," an older name for the genus. Some of these ornamental species have escaped from gardens or nurseries and can be found growing in or adjacent to California salt marshes.

Belding's savannah sparrow

Belding's savannah sparrow (*Passerculus sandwichensis beldingi*) is endemic to the coastal salt marshes along the Pacific Coast, ranging from Morro Bay, California, to El Rosario, Baja California. This subspecies of the savannah sparrow is distinguished by its small size, heavy streaking, and less-prominent yellow lores (the area between the bill and the eyes). Its preferred habitat is tall, dense pickleweed (*Salicornia virginica*), where it can nest above the high tide line and forage in the surrounding marsh. The Belding's savannah sparrow is distinctive among songbirds in its ability to drink seawater. Even the way it does this is unique; it lacks the salt-filtering nasal glands that enable marine birds to drink seawater, relying instead on a highly efficient urinary system. The decline of southern California's coastal salt marshes has led to a significant loss of habitat for these wetland-dependent birds. The Belding's savannah sparrow is listed as an endangered species.

The **light-footed clapper rail** (*Rallus longirostris levipes*) is resident in only a few southern California marshes vegetated with cordgrass, rushes, or cattails. In size, the rail is like a small, very thin chicken. It feeds on snails, crabs, and other invertebrates. Well-concealed nests are made of hollow cordgrass, making the nest buoyant when the tide rises. Although rarely seen, the light-footed clapper rail is quite vocal; observers count the birds by listening at dawn or sunset for the "clappering" duets of mated pairs. Probably no more than 600 individuals exist, many of them at Upper Newport Bay in Orange County and Tijuana Estuary in San Diego County. To disperse the birds and increase genetic variability, since 1999 biologists have released some birds bred in captivity and translocated viable eggs to other marshes with very small populations.

Light-footed clapper rail

The **California horn snail** (*Cerithidea californica*) is a common inhabitant of intertidal channels and mudflats. Each square meter of mud may contain hundreds of individuals grazing on microalgae; the snails measure from one-quarter to one inch in length. California horn snails may provide clues to the biodiversity of the saltmarsh. The horn snails, which are easily collected by researchers, are parasitized by various species of trematodes, or "flukes." Trematodes are parasitic worms with a complex life-cycle whose larval stages commonly use snails as an intermediate host; at least 20 species of trematodes converge on horn snails as their first intermediate host. Adult trematodes use many different species of birds as a final host. Since the flukes are functionally related by their complicated life-cycle to a variety of vertebrate and invertebrate species, it is hoped that the abundance and species diversity of these parasites easily collected in horn snails can serve as an inexpensive indicator of the biodiversity of other species in the salt marsh.

California horn snail

Huntington City Beach

Huntington Beach

	Sandy Beach	Rocky Shore	Trail	Visitor Center	Campground	Wildlife Viewing	Fishing or Boating	Facilities for Disabled	Food and Drink	Restrooms	Parking	Fee
Huntington Beach International Surfing Museum				●					●			
Huntington Beach Pier						●	●	●	●	●	●	
Huntington City Beach	●	●		●		●	●		●	●	●	●
Wetlands and Wildlife Care Center				●		●				●		
Huntington Beach Wetlands			●			●						
Huntington State Beach	●	●				●	●	●		●	●	●
Santa Ana River Trail			●			●						

HUNTINGTON BEACH INTERNATIONAL SURFING MUSEUM: *411 Olive Ave., Huntington Beach.* The museum's collection includes materials about surfing legend and Olympic gold-medal-winning swimmer Duke Kahanamoku, as well as massive old-time surfboards and surf music memorabilia. Subjects of changing exhibits range from skin diving to skateboards to the history of the ukulele. Gift shop on the premises. Open daily during the summer and weekends the rest of the year, from 11 AM until 6 PM. Donations welcome; call: 714-960-3483.

HUNTINGTON BEACH PIER: *Main St. at Pacific Coast Hwy., Huntington Beach.* The 1,850-foot-long concrete pier is popular for fishing and for watching surfers and the waves. The pier is floodlit at night and wheelchair accessible. Stores on the pier sell bait, souvenirs, and kites, and there is a diner. No license is required for fishing from the pier, although regular catch limits apply. Fee parking lots are located seaward of Pacific Coast Hwy., both north and south of the pier. Additional fee parking is available in a parking structure on the east side of Main St., a block inland from the pier, between Walnut and Olive Avenues.

Events on the pier include a Friday afternoon farmer's market and an auto show every Saturday. Surfing lessons are available north of Pier Plaza. No smoking, skateboarding, or bicycling on the pier; dogs not allowed. The pier is open from 5 AM to midnight.

HUNTINGTON CITY BEACH: *W. of Pacific Coast Hwy., from Goldenwest St. to Beach Blvd., Huntington Beach.* This long and very wide beach draws over 10 million visitors per year. The soft sand is appealing, the relatively warm waters encourage swimmers, and the breakers have drawn surfers since the sport gained popularity in California in the early 20th century. Huntington Beach is home to the U.S. Open Surfing Championship, held annually in July.

Sand volleyball courts, fire rings, and outdoor showers are available, and restrooms and concession stands are spaced along the sand; beach wheelchairs are available at the concessions. Metered parallel parking is on Pacific Coast Hwy., and a 2,400-space beachfront parking lot can be entered at First St., Huntington St., or Beach Blvd.; fee is charged. Another fee beach parking lot north of the Huntington Beach Pier is entered at 6th St. No smoking on the beach; dogs are not allowed, except north of Goldenwest St. For beach information, contact the Marine Safety office at 103 Pacific Coast Hwy., or call: 714-536-5281.

Huntington Beach city lifeguards patrol year-round, from dawn to dusk. There are 23 lifeguard towers, some of which are staffed seasonally. Huntington Beach lifeguards maintain an admirable record of safety on the city's beaches. Lifeguards are trained in emergency medical techniques and search-and-rescue diving.

A paved multi-use path runs the entire length of the city of Huntington Beach along the inland side of the sand, extending also through the state beaches to the north and south of town. Off-season RV camping is allowed in the city's big beach parking lot south of the pier from October 1 through May 31st. Reservations available; fee for camping. Call: 714-536-5281.

WETLANDS AND WILDLIFE CARE CENTER:
Newland St. at Pacific Coast Hwy., Huntington Beach. A wildlife care facility is located in a structure built in 2007. Volunteers at the center care for sick, injured, and orphaned wildlife and educate the public about the importance of coastal wetlands. Human contact with animals undergoing rehabilitation is kept to a minimum, but the Wetlands and Wildlife Care Center plans to allow visitors to view the animals using video cameras. For information, call: 714-374-5587.

HUNTINGTON BEACH WETLANDS: *Inland of Pacific Coast Hwy., from Beach Blvd. to Santa Ana River mouth, Huntington Beach.* A series of marshes inland of Pacific Coast Hwy. reminds visitors of the huge wetland complex that once existed when the unchannelized Santa Ana River flowed into Lower Newport Bay. The river mouth was constrained to its present location in 1921. The marshes have no direct hydrologic connection with the river now, but seawater flows in through the ocean opening north of the Santa Ana River. The productive wetlands support pickleweed, saltgrass, bulrush, and cattail, and provide feeding grounds for gulls, least terns, shorebirds, and waterfowl. A multipurpose trail runs along the inland side of Talbert Marsh from Brookhurst St. to the Santa Ana River Trail; there is no parking at the Brookhurst gate. Dogs must be leashed.

HUNTINGTON STATE BEACH: *Seaward of Pacific Coast Hwy. from Beach Blvd. to the Santa Ana River, Huntington Beach.* This day-use park features two miles of sand with picnic areas, fire rings, beach volleyball, food concessions, restrooms, and outdoor showers. Six paved access ramps provide wheelchair access across the sand, and a beach wheelchair is also available; contact a lifeguard. A paved multiuse path runs parallel to the shore, the length of Huntington State Beach. Fee parking lots and pedestrian entries are at Beach Blvd., Newland St., Magnolia St., and Brookhurst St.; vehicle entrance gates close at 9 PM. Limited street parking nearby. For beach information, call: 714-536-1454.

The south end of Huntington State Beach near the mouth of the Santa Ana River is a sanctuary for breeding California least terns. Respect signage and fencing, and obey volunteer docents who protect summertime nests. Western snowy plovers also nest on the sand.

SANTA ANA RIVER TRAIL: *Both sides of the Santa Ana River, starting at Pacific Coast Hwy., Newport Beach.* One of Orange County's longest bicycle routes, this paved trail follows the river 27 miles to the Chino Hills in Riverside County. One mile inland from Pacific Coast Hwy. the trail borders the Talbert Nature Preserve, an Orange County park that includes picnic areas as well as wetlands and riparian woodlands. Look for water birds in Victoria Pond, a freshwater pond south of Victoria St. (which becomes Hamilton Ave. on the Huntington Beach side of the Santa Ana River).

Great egret at Talbert Marsh

The name "Huntington" appears in various locations around southern California. The first famous Huntington was Collis Huntington, a shipping magnate and one of the "Big Four" railroad barons of the nineteenth century. Collis was president of the Southern Pacific Railroad, and Henry Huntington was his nephew, employee, and protégé. Henry's second wife was his uncle's widow, Arabella, reputed to be the wealthiest woman in America at the time. Today the Huntington Library, Art Collections, and Botanical Gardens contain numerous valuable items that the couple collected at their mansion in San Marino.

Henry Huntington developed a rail system of electric trolleys that competed locally with the steam-powered Southern Pacific trains. His new company, Pacific Electric Railway, aggressively spread its network of "Big Red Cars" that provided convenient interurban transportation. Huntington controlled businesses owning the railway, land around the tracks, and the utilities serving these areas. His railway and real estate empire shaped southern California's development from Redondo Beach to Riverside.

When community leaders saw how people flocked to towns that were linked by the popular trolleys, they lobbied for tracks too. Such was the origin of Huntington Beach. Originally called "Shell Beach," it was renamed "Pacific City" in 1901 by developers wanting to build a resort they hoped would rival Atlantic City. As the new town was relatively isolated, they convinced Huntington to continue the Long Beach trolley south to Pacific City. He agreed after receiving enticements including renaming the town after him.

In 1914 the local land company sold property to an Encyclopedia Americana salesman. People who purchased an encyclopedia set received a free parcel of land in Huntington Beach; the city's long, narrow "encyclopedia lots" originate from that promotion. These properties became valuable when oil was discovered in 1920, and that is when the community's population began to boom. Oil strikes continued into the 1950s, and during that same decade the city's first surf shop opened. Huntington Beach is now known as a surfing capital and features an outdoor surfing hall of fame, walk of fame, and the International Surfing Museum.

Pacific Electric Railway car that currently runs in San Pedro

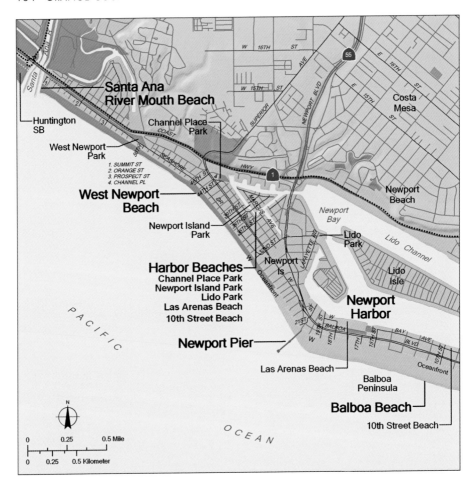

Off West Newport Beach jetty near 40th St.

Newport Beach

	Sandy Beach	Rocky Shore	Trail	Visitor Center	Campground	Wildlife Viewing	Fishing or Boating	Facilities for Disabled	Food and Drink	Restrooms	Parking	Fee
Santa Ana River Mouth Beach	•					•					•	
West Newport Beach	•						•	•		•	•	
Newport Pier							•	•	•	•	•	
Balboa Beach	•	•					•	•	•	•	•	
Harbor Beaches	•					•	•	•		•	•	
Newport Harbor							•	•	•	•	•	

SANTA ANA RIVER MOUTH BEACH: *Both sides of Santa Ana River, seaward of Pacific Coast Hwy., Newport Beach.* A narrow strip of sand borders the mouth of the Santa Ana River. The county of Orange provides lifeguard service. Mainly a surfing spot, but for experienced surfers only, due to the strong rip currents. Access is from Huntington State Beach or from the north end of Seashore Dr. Call: 949-923-2250.

WEST NEWPORT BEACH: *Santa Ana River mouth to Newport Pier, Newport Beach.* A long sandy beach stretches from the mouth of the Santa Ana River past the Newport Pier

> The infamous Santa Ana winds are named for the Santa Ana Canyon, but occur throughout the Los Angeles Basin. The winds form in fall and winter when air in the interior deserts piles up against the Transverse Ranges and begins streaming down the mountain passes toward the coast. The air heats due to increasing pressure at lower elevation, and temperatures at the coast may rise to over 100 degrees Fahrenheit. Because coastal hills are driest in the fall, the hot, arid winds pose a serious fire hazard. The winds may reach gale strength—up to 60 miles per hour—and can create dangerous waves offshore.

along the Balboa Peninsula. The beach is maintained by the city of Newport Beach. Most street ends lead to the beach.

West Newport Park, a landscaped, linear park, is located along Seashore Dr., a short block from the sand. The park has picnic tables, play equipment, and restrooms. Beach showers are located at street ends, next to the beach. West Newport Park hours are from 6 AM to 11 PM; dogs must be leashed. Three metered parking areas are within West Newport Park; for the first lot, turn off Coast Hwy. on Orange St. and then turn right again on Seashore Dr. For the second parking lot, turn off Coast Hwy. on Prospect St., then right on Seashore Dr., and for the third lot, turn off W. Balboa Blvd. on 46th St., then right on Seashore Dr. Note that north of 46th St., Seashore Dr. is one-way northbound, and south of 46th St., Seashore Dr. is one-way southbound.

A series of groins cross the sand between 56th St. and the Newport Pier and contribute to good surf breaks. The groins were built to counteract extensive erosion that occurred during the 1960s due to reduced sand supply from local streams. Much of the sand that moves along the coast in the area is eventually lost in the deep Newport Submarine Canyon, which begins offshore near the end of the Newport Pier. Surfing is very popular at Newport Beach and is regulated by season; flags designating conditions fly at each lifeguard station. Volleyball nets are on the beach. Ask at the lifeguard station at the Newport Pier for a beach wheelchair, or

Balboa Beach

call: 949-644-3047. Restrooms and outdoor showers are located at the base of the Newport Pier. Dogs are not allowed on bay or ocean beaches in Newport Beach from 9 AM to 5 PM; leashed dogs allowed at other times. No glass bottles or alcohol; no smoking on beaches or piers.

NEWPORT PIER: *Near W. end of 21st St., Newport Beach.* The oldest pier on the southern California coast, Newport Pier was built in 1888 as a wharf for trains carrying farm products and passengers from Santa Ana, and soon became the center of a small fishing village. In 1922 the City of Newport Beach bought the wharf and redesigned it as a public fishing pier. The inland end of the pier produces typical catches of perch and croaker species. The outer end of the pier extends close to a submarine canyon, and anglers catch pelagic species, such as mackerel and bonito, as well as deep water species, including sanddabs and hake. There are fish cleaning stations on the pier.

A restaurant is located at the pier's seaward end. The pier is paved and wheelchair accessible; open from 6 AM to 10 PM daily. For information, call: 949-644-3047. Several parking lots are located off W. Balboa Blvd. north of Newport Pier, and another smaller parking area is on 15th St. next to the beach.

BALBOA BEACH: *From Newport Pier to Balboa Pier, Newport Beach.* A very wide sandy beach stretches all along the Balboa Peninsula, and street ends provide beach access.

Six-hour metered parking is located in the median of Balboa Blvd. From 36th St. east to E St., a paved boardwalk called Oceanfront runs along the edge of the sandy beach. Oceanfront is used by walkers, skaters, and bicyclists. For recorded surf and weather report, call: 949-673-3371.

HARBOR BEACHES: *Bay side of Balboa Peninsula, Newport Beach.* There are numerous vest-pocket parks, vistas, and public walkways around Newport Harbor. Sheltered water makes harbor-facing beaches popular with families. Many street ends adjoining Newport Harbor provide views and access to the water's edge, including 13 street ends on Lido Isle.

A sandy cove beach is located at Channel Place Park, where there is also a grassy area with covered picnic tables, restrooms, and play equipment. The park is on Channel Place at 44th St.; very limited street parking. Newport Island Park, another neighborhood park, is on Marcus Ave. between 38th St. and 39th St. and features a playground, lawn, palm trees, and a small sandy beach.

Lido Park is a bay-viewing area at Lafayette Rd. and 32nd St. Las Arenas Beach is a three-block-long stretch of sand on the bay side of the Balboa Peninsula that can be reached at the end of 18th St., where there is metered parking. Nearby Las Arenas Park, between 17th St. and 15th St. at the end of W. Bay Ave., has covered picnic tables, grills, basketball and tennis courts, and a playground.

10th St. Beach is a small sandy area at 10th St. along W. Bay Ave. Small, hand-carried boats can be launched at Balboa Peninsula street ends between 11th St. and 15th St. Public docks where boaters may load and unload passengers and gear are located at the ends of 19th St. and 15th St.

NEWPORT HARBOR: *N.E. of Balboa Peninsula, Newport Beach.* America's largest small-craft harbor, Newport Harbor accommodates over 9,000 boats. There are more than 2,100 slips and side ties at public and private marinas, 1,230 residential piers, and over 1,200 bay moorings, some along the beaches and some offshore. A guest mooring area is offshore from the Harbor Patrol facility. A free public anchorage area is located off Lido Isle, outside navigation channels. Guest boat slips can be found in some of the marinas located in Newport Harbor. The harbormaster office is at 1901 Bayside Dr., Corona del Mar; for information, call: 949-723-1002. Facilities in Newport Harbor include dry boat storage, fuel docks and service stations, shipyards, engine and hull maintenance, marine supplies, and sewage pumpouts. Many waterfront shops and restaurants incorporate public pedestrian areas overlooking the harbor.

Just north of Newport Pier is an outdoor seafood market started by a Portuguese fisherman in 1891. It is run by the Newport Beach Dory Fleet. The fishing fleet and its market are recognized as a local historical landmark, and the fleet is known as the only such beachside fishing cooperative existing in the United States.

Keeping the tradition going is a group of fishermen who leave in their dories (small, flat-bottomed boats) in the middle of the night and return in the morning to sell freshly caught fish, lobster, crab, and other types of seafood directly to the local public, tourists, and restaurants. The fishermen haul their boats onto the sand and, weather permitting, can be found filleting and selling their fresh catch right on the beach every day between approximately 6 AM and 10 AM, while supplies last.

Cleaning fresh fish from the Newport Beach Dory Fleet

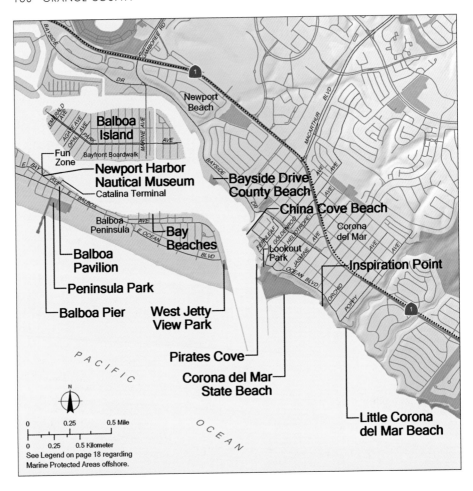

Newport Beach

Balboa Island

Fun Zone

Bayfront Boardwalk

Newport Harbor Nautical Museum

Catalina Terminal

Balboa Peninsula

Bay Beaches

Balboa Pavilion

Peninsula Park

Balboa Pier

West Jetty View Park

Bayside Drive County Beach

China Cove Beach

Corona del Mar

Lookout Park

Inspiration Point

Pirates Cove

Corona del Mar State Beach

Little Corona del Mar Beach

PACIFIC

OCEAN

N

0   0.25   0.5 Mile

0   0.25   0.5 Kilometer

See Legend on page 18 regarding Marine Protected Areas offshore.

Newport Harbor with *Catalina Flyer*

Balboa to Corona del Mar

	Sandy Beach	Rocky Shore	Trail	Visitor Center	Campground	Wildlife Viewing	Fishing or Boating	Facilities for Disabled	Food and Drink	Restrooms	Parking	Fee
Balboa Island	•	•				•	•	•	•		•	
Newport Harbor Nautical Museum				•		•		•	•	•	•	
Balboa Pavilion						•	•		•	•	•	
Peninsula Park											•	
Balboa Pier		•				•	•		•	•	•	
Bay Beaches	•					•	•					
West Jetty View Park						•					•	
Bayside Drive County Beach	•					•	•			•	•	
China Cove Beach	•					•						
Pirates Cove	•	•										
Corona del Mar State Beach	•	•				•	•	•	•	•	•	•
Inspiration Point						•						
Little Corona del Mar Beach	•	•				•		•		•		

BALBOA ISLAND: *Marine Ave., Newport Beach.* Balboa Island, located within Newport Harbor, has a mix of residences and commercial uses, along with public waterfront access. Parking is tight, but the small, level island is very walkable. The Bayfront Boardwalk circles the island, providing access to small public beaches. Street ends also provide access to the bay, and hand-launching of small craft is allowed at 22 of the street ends. Four street ends lead to the interior Grand Canal, which bisects the island. Small public boat docks for loading and unloading passengers and gear are located at the south ends of Emerald Ave. and Opal Ave.; docks also popular for fishing. Mudflats near the island attract shorebirds at low tide; look for willets, marbled godwits, and plovers feeding along the water's edge.

Only one vehicle bridge, at the end of Jamboree Rd., connects Balboa Island to the mainland. On the south side of the island, the Balboa Island Ferry carries pedestrians, bicyclists, and autos across the channel to Balboa Peninsula, saving a long drive around the bay. To reach the ferry slip from Marine Ave. on Balboa Island, head west on Park Ave., then south on Agate Ave. Ferries operate from 6 AM to 2 AM daily; fee charged.

NEWPORT HARBOR NAUTICAL MUSEUM: *600 E. Bay Ave., Newport Beach.* The museum, housed in three separate buildings, includes ship models, a virtual deep-sea fishing experience, and a small touch tank with tidepool animals. Family events include treasure hunts and storytelling. Open daily from 10 AM to 6 PM, except Tuesday; some exhibits are closed at lunchtime and during special events. Donations suggested. For information, call: 949-675-8915. Restrooms are at Bay Ave. and Washington St.

Surrounding the Newport Harbor Nautical Museum is the Fun Zone, a small permanent carnival with a carousel, Ferris wheel, and arcades. There are shops, food concessions, and restaurants, and boat trips and sport-fishing excursions can be booked in the area. Also available are rentals of boats, bicycles, bodyboards, and skates.

BALBOA PAVILION: *400 Main St., Balboa Peninsula, Newport Beach.* The cupola-topped Victorian building was once the terminus for the Pacific Electric Railway. The landmark pavilion was a dance hall during the Big Band Era of the 1930s and became the center of seaside recreation in Newport Beach. The building houses a restaurant, fishing tackle shop, and boat rental shop. Daveys Locker offers sport-fishing and whale-watching trips; call: 949-673-1434. Next to the pavilion is the terminal for the *Catalina Flyer*, serving Catalina Island; call: 1-800-830-7744. The landing for the vehicle and pedestrian ferry to Balboa Island is at the end of Palm St.

PENINSULA PARK: *Main St. at E. Oceanfront, Balboa Peninsula, Newport Beach.* A palm-studded park with picnic tables, barbecue grills, children's play equipment, and ample lawns is located at the foot of the Balboa Pier. Wheelchair-accessible Oceanfront boardwalk and several disabled parking spaces are adjacent.

BALBOA PIER: *W. of Balboa Blvd. at Main St., Balboa Peninsula, Newport Beach.* The Balboa Pier is used for fishing and viewing and is open from 5 AM to midnight; dogs not allowed. Restrooms and a 650-space fee park-

ing lot are near the foot of the pier. A marker on Balboa Pier commemorates the 1912 flight of Glenn L. Martin from the pier to Catalina Island. The flight was the first water-to-water flight, and the longest and fastest overwater flight to that date. Spacious, sandy Balboa Beach extends both upcoast and down from Balboa Pier. For recorded surf and weather report, call: 949-673-3371.

BAY BEACHES: *Harbor side, Balboa Peninsula, Newport Beach.* A bayfront walkway starts at Main St. on the Balboa Peninsula and extends to the northwest about two-thirds of a mile, offering nice views of boats and the water. At the end of Island Ave. is a narrow strip of sand known as Montero Beach. Hand-carried kayaks and small craft can be launched at numerous street ends on the north side of the Balboa Peninsula, including those from B St. to K St. Public docks where boaters may load and unload passengers and gear are located at the ends of Fernando St., Main St., and E. Balboa Blvd.; the latter location also features a small sandy beach. In Newport Beach, dogs are not allowed on bay or ocean beaches from 9 AM to 5 PM; leashed dogs allowed at other times. No glass bottles or alcohol; no smoking on beaches or piers.

WEST JETTY VIEW PARK: *End of Channel Rd., Balboa Peninsula, Newport Beach.* This small park is located at the far end of wide, sandy Balboa Beach. The site faces the West Jetty at the entrance to Newport Harbor and overlooks the Wedge, a popular, highly challenging surfing spot. From late spring through fall, generally from 10 AM to 5 PM, body surfing only is allowed. Benches, drinking water, and a paved path along the water.

BAYSIDE DRIVE COUNTY BEACH: *Adjacent to 1901 Bayside Dr., Corona del Mar.* A small sign on the inland side of Bayside Dr. marks this hard-to-see beach park. The parking area is small, but some spaces are reserved for beach visitors only. Walk on the left side of the buildings to reach a sandy, triangular-shaped beach fronting Newport Harbor. Volleyball net, jetty for fishing, picnic tables, beach showers, and restrooms are available. Hand-carried boats can be launched, except at busy beach times. Call: 949-923-2250.

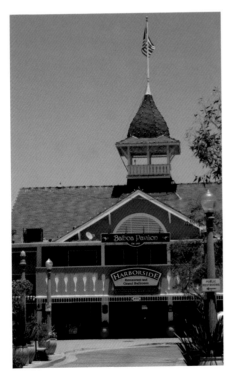

Balboa Pavilion

Little Corona del Mar Beach

CHINA COVE BEACH: *Along Harbor Channel, W. of Fernleaf Ave., Corona del Mar.* A pair of small sandy coves are along the harbor channel. Parking in the area is very tight; pedestrian access from Ocean Blvd. is via a pedestrian stairway at the end of Fernleaf Ave. A volleyball net is on the sand, and hand launching of small boats is possible.

PIRATES COVE: *Along Harbor Channel, S. of China Cove Beach, Corona del Mar.* A sandy cove with many small wave-formed caves can be reached by stairs down the bluff from Lookout Park, located on Ocean Blvd. between Goldenrod and Heliotrope Avenues. A separate stairway on the north side of Lookout Park winds down the hill to China Cove Beach.

CORONA DEL MAR STATE BEACH: *Ocean Blvd. opposite end of Jasmine Ave., Corona del Mar.* The sandy beach is popular for swimming, fishing, and diving; the East Jetty is a popular surfing spot. Beach facilities include parking, seasonal concession stands, restrooms, and nine sand volleyball nets. At the south end of the beach are tidepools that are exposed at low tide; the rocks are covered with California mussels. Shore anglers

may catch perch, croakers, bass, and halibut. The East Jetty attracts fish such as garibaldi and California sheephead, as well as lobster and octopus.

Corona del Mar State Beach is managed by the City of Newport Beach; a parking fee is charged, and State Parks Annual Day Use Pass does not apply. Parking lot hours are 6 AM to 10 PM. Pedestrian access to the beach is available via stairs opposite the end of Heliotrope Ave. and a ramp opposite Jasmine Ave. For beach information, call: 949-644-3151. Contact a lifeguard to borrow a beach wheelchair. For recorded surf and weather report, call: 949-673-3371.

INSPIRATION POINT: *Ocean Blvd. at Orchid Ave., Corona del Mar.* A grassy blufftop park with benches. A pedestrian ramp leads down the hill to Corona del Mar State Beach.

LITTLE CORONA DEL MAR BEACH: *Ocean Blvd. and Poppy Ave., Corona del Mar.* A picturesque sandy cove beach with rocky reefs and tidepools lies at the bottom of the bluff. A paved ramp leads down to the beach from the foot of Poppy Ave. Restrooms are located part-way down the slope. On-street parking only.

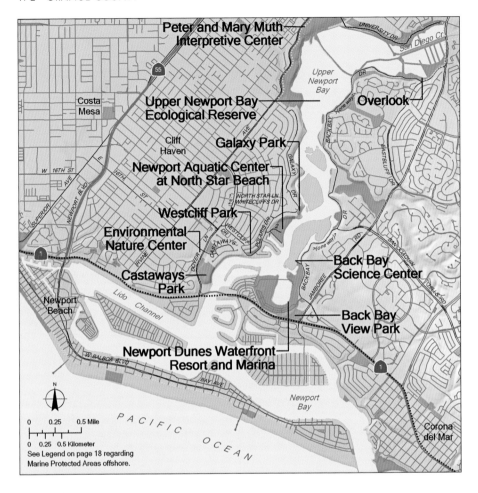

Upper Newport Bay, high tide

Upper Newport Bay

	Sandy Beach	Rocky Shore	Trail	Visitor Center	Campground	Wildlife Viewing	Fishing or Boating	Facilities for Disabled	Food and Drink	Restrooms	Parking	Fee
Castaways Park			•			•					•	
Environmental Nature Center			•	•		•		•		•	•	
Westcliff Park											•	
Newport Aquatic Center at North Star Beach	•					•	•			•	•	
Galaxy Park											•	
Upper Newport Bay Ecological Reserve			•			•				•	•	
Peter and Mary Muth Interpretive Center			•	•		•		•		•	•	
Overlook			•			•						
Newport Dunes Waterfront Resort and Marina	•		•		•	•	•	•	•	•	•	•
Back Bay View Park			•									
Back Bay Science Center				•		•		•		•	•	

CASTAWAYS PARK: *Castaways Ln. at Dover Dr., Newport Beach.* Turn sharp right off Castaways Ln. into the first parking lot. Paved paths lead through native plantings restored with funds provided by the State Coastal Conservancy to an overlook above Upper Newport Bay. There is a wildflower meadow, colorful in spring, and plants of the coastal sage scrub community. Drinking water and benches; no other facilities.

Great blue heron

ENVIRONMENTAL NATURE CENTER: *1601 16th St., Newport Beach.* The Environmental Nature Center features walking trails through 15 California native plant communities. Programs in science and Native American history are offered to student groups from kindergarten through sixth grade. Also available are full-moon hikes for families and birding trips for adults. A butterfly house, open from May to October, Monday through Saturday from 10 AM to 3 PM, offers a unique look at native Orange County butterfly species, including the mourning cloak, Lorquin's admiral, cloudless sulphur, and the brightly colored California dogface, the state butterfly of California. Call: 949-645-8489.

WESTCLIFF PARK: *Polaris Dr. off Westcliff Dr., Newport Beach.* There are bay views from this hillside park. Parking lot; no other facilities.

NEWPORT AQUATIC CENTER AT NORTH STAR BEACH: *1 Whitecliffs Dr., off Polaris Dr., Newport Beach.* Turn onto North Star Ln., then Whitecliffs Dr. to reach North Star Beach, a broad, sandy area adjacent to the quiet waters of Upper Newport Bay. The nonprofit Newport Aquatic Center offers a variety of boating programs for human-powered craft. Bring your own kayak or canoe to hand-launch here, or rent one by the hour. Rowing and kayaking classes are offered to the public, and the center offers summer youth camps and hosts the annual Newport Autumn Rowing Festival, call: 949-646-7725. Naturalist-led kayak tours through the Upper Newport Bay Ecological Reserve are available; call: 949-923-2269.

GALAXY PARK: *1400 block of Galaxy Dr., Newport Beach.* Views of the bay from a high bluff. Benches; no other facilities.

UPPER NEWPORT BAY ECOLOGICAL RE-SERVE: *W. of Backbay Dr., Newport Beach.* The Upper Newport Bay Ecological Reserve, managed by the California Dept. of Fish and Game, and the adjoining Nature Preserve, managed by Orange County, together include nearly 1,000 acres of estuary, intertidal mudflat, and salt marsh. Considered one of the best birding sites in North America, the estuary is a key southern California stopover for birds migrating along the Pacific Flyway. Ducks, including buffleheads, shovelers, and pintails, along with other water birds and shorebirds, number in the tens of thousands during the winter months. Most of the shallow bay is exposed at low tide, and consists of intertidal mudflats and an extensive salt marsh community of cordgrass, pickleweed, saltgrass, and the endangered salt marsh bird's beak. The light-footed clapper rail and Belding's savannah sparrow, both endangered, are year-round residents of the marsh, and owls, raptors, songbirds, small mammals, and reptiles inhabit the adjacent uplands. Ocean-dwelling fish such as California halibut, white croaker, and barred sandbass depend on the bay as a spawning and nursery ground.

Backbay Dr. along the east margin of the bay provides the best opportunities for close-up viewing of the reserve. Backbay Dr. is one-way northbound; enter off Jamboree Rd. to follow the entire route. A viewpoint with interpretive panels, parking, and restrooms is located on Backbay Dr. north of San Joaquin Hills Rd. Backbay Dr. is part of the ten-and-a-half-mile-long Back Bay Loop hiking and bicycling trail, which encircles the entire Upper Bay. The public can also experience the Ecological Reserve by participating in a California Coastal Commission-sponsored habitat restoration day, removing exotic plants and planting native vegetation; for information, call: 949-640-0286.

PETER AND MARY MUTH INTERPRETIVE CENTER: *2301 University Dr., Newport Beach.* The airy, modern structure, tucked into a hillside site, offers attractive exhibits, a children's activity room with pint-sized display

Light-footed clapper rail, Upper Newport Bay

cases, and a short, multi-screen film about the birds and wildlife of the Upper Newport Bay Ecological Reserve. Programs include "raptor raps" for junior naturalists, nature walks for all ages, and habitat-restoration days. For information, call: 949-923-2290. Open Tuesday to Sunday, 10 AM to 4 PM; closed major holidays. Free admission to the Interpretive Center; fee for some programs.

OVERLOOK: *Backbay Dr. and Eastbluff Dr., Newport Beach.* A planned overlook will provide distant views of Upper Newport Bay; roadside parking. Nearby, on the bayward side of Jamboree Rd. at Eastbluff Dr., is the terminus of a paved bicycle and walking path that follows San Diego Creek through Irvine to Tustin and beyond.

NEWPORT DUNES WATERFRONT RESORT AND MARINA: *1131 Backbay Dr., Newport Beach.* This privately operated resort has a 15-acre swimming lagoon with a sandy bay beach. Facilities include beach equipment rentals, a swimming pool, exercise room, dressing rooms, outdoor showers, picnic tables, and playground. Paddleboard, kayak, sea cycle, wind surfboard, and sailboat rentals are available. Activities include water sport lessons and large-screen movies on the beach. Restaurant and gift shop open daily.

The marina has boat slips (including guest slips), pumpout facilities, dry storage, and a multi-lane boat ramp open 24 hours; boat launch fee. The RV campground includes 406 sites with full hookups; tent camping OK. Cottages are also available for rent. Reservations required; fee for overnight and day use. The entire facility is wheelchair accessible. For information, call: 949-729-3863. For reservations, call: 1-800-765-7661.

BACK BAY VIEW PARK: *Corner of Jamboree Rd. and Coast Hwy., Newport Beach.* Great sunset views of Newport Bay can be seen from this park, which features an area of restored coastal sage scrub habitat. The park can be glimpsed from adjacent Jamboree Rd. and Coast Hwy., but there is no stopping on the shoulder of those busy streets. Instead, park on Backbay Dr. north of Jamboree Rd.; a paved path leads from the south side of the Newport Dunes Resort entrance gate to the park. Benches; no other facilities.

BACK BAY SCIENCE CENTER: *Shellmaker Rd., off Backbay Dr., Newport Beach.* The Science Center offers educational programs for 7th through 12th-grade students and teachers. The programs, which incorporate California state science standards, emphasize estuarine ecology of Upper Newport Bay, marine biology, and water quality issues. Research on ecological and water quality monitoring is also a focus. For the general public, the Back Bay Science Center offers a variety of naturalist-led tours and programs. For information on education and research programs, call: 949-640-9956. For information about tours by electric boat, canoe, or on foot, call: 949-923-2269. For kayak tours, call: 1-800-585-0747. Many programs at the Back Bay Science Center and the Peter and Mary Muth Interpretive Center are offered by a partnership of the California Dept. of Fish and Game, Orange County Parks, and the Newport Bay Naturalists and Friends, a nonprofit group formed in 1967 by citizen activists to call attention to the ecological significance of Upper Newport Bay.

The largest coastal freshwater marsh complex in southern California includes the San Joaquin Wildlife Sanctuary. A series of water treatment ponds are set among willow thickets, with miles of shady trails; restrooms and some trails are wheelchair accessible. Come here to view birds of freshwater marshes, including green herons, common moorhens, and red-winged blackbirds. From the I-405 freeway, take Jamboree Rd. south and turn left on Michelson Dr. Proceed to Riparian View St. and turn right; continue past the water reclamation plant and watch for signs to the Sanctuary. Open daily from dawn to dusk. Sea and Sage Audubon volunteers staff the visitor center; open daily from 8 AM to 4 PM; call: 949-261-7963. No dogs allowed.

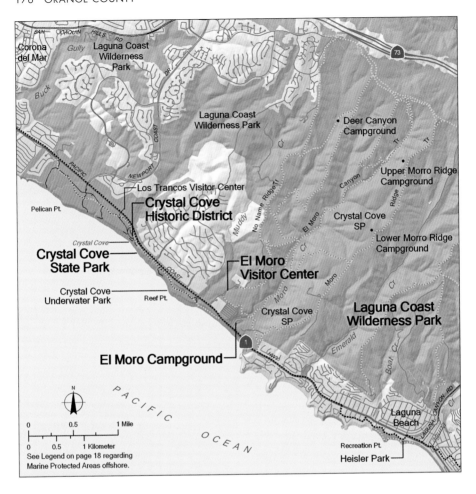

No-Name Ridge Trail, Crystal Cove State Park

Crystal Cove State Park

	Sandy Beach	Rocky Shore	Trail	Visitor Center	Campground	Wildlife Viewing	Fishing or Boating	Facilities for Disabled	Food and Drink	Restrooms	Parking	Fee
Crystal Cove State Park	•	•	•	•	•	•	•	•	•	•	•	•
Crystal Cove Historic District	•	•	•	•	•	•	•	•	•	•	•	•
El Moro Visitor Center			•	•		•		•		•	•	
El Moro Campground					•		•				•	•
Laguna Coast Wilderness Park		•				•					•	•

CRYSTAL COVE STATE PARK: *Along Coast Hwy. between Corona del Mar and Laguna Beach.* Crystal Cove State Park, one of the gems in California's outstanding state park system, offers over four square miles of scenic open space and over three miles of undeveloped shoreline. Below the sandstone bluffs are a series of sandy coves with a remarkably remote feel. Visitor facilities include picnic areas; campgrounds; trails for hiking, biking, and equestrian use; and, a rarity on the California coast, historic cottages at the beach that can be rented by the public at moderate rates. Inland of Coast Hwy., the state park encompasses most of the Moro Canyon watershed in the San Joaquin Hills. The adjacent Laguna Coast Wilderness Park wraps around Crystal Cove State Park, and trails link the two recreational areas.

The Pelican Point entrance to Crystal Cove State Park is at the signalized intersection of Newport Coast Dr. and Coast Hwy. There are four separate parking lots, each with restroom facilities. A paved multi-use path links all the parking areas and continues south past Reef Point. A boardwalk leads from the second of the four parking lots through coastal sage scrub habitat to the bluff edge at Pelican Point. There is pedestrian access to the beach at several points.

Another park entrance is at Reef Point; parking and restrooms are on the bluff, overlooking a popular surfing spot. Park day-use hours are 6 AM to sunset. No fires are allowed on the beach; beach barbecues can be used, but coals must be taken out of the park. Leashed dogs are allowed only on paved trails on the seaward side of Coast Hwy. and not on the beach. For park information, call: 949-494-3539.

The Crystal Cove Underwater Park encompasses the nearshore ocean waters from north of Pelican Point to the south end of El Moro Beach. Several popular dive sites are located within this area. All resources are protected, including marine plants, animals, rocks, and archaeological artifacts.

CRYSTAL COVE HISTORIC DISTRICT: *Seaward of Coast Hwy. at the mouth of Los Trancos Canyon.* The Los Trancos parking area, inland of Coast Hwy., is the main access point for the Crystal Cove Historic District. The beach is a ten-minute walk from the Los Trancos parking lot, via a pedestrian tunnel beneath the highway or a signalized crosswalk. A motorized shuttle service runs from 7 AM to 10 PM, linking the Los Trancos visitor center to the Crystal Cove Historic District.

Twenty-two of the vintage cottages in the Crystal Cove Historic District have been refurbished inside for various purposes, while the exteriors still reflect the 1930s through the 1950s, when they were built. Eleven of the cottages are open to the public as individual accommodations, and three are dorm-style facilities. Renovation of 17 additional cottages for overnight stays is planned. The highly popular cottages must be reserved well ahead of time (a maximum of seven months in advance); call: at 1-800-444-7275 or go to www.reserveamerica.com and search for "Crystal Cove Beach Cottages." Three of the cottages are accessible to the disabled, who receive priority in bookings. The Shake Shack on the blufftop and the Beachcomber Café at the beach serve food, and a small park store is located near the beach. A marine research facility operated by the University of California at Irvine is housed in one of the refurbished cottages at the cove; a beach museum and outdoor education facility are planned. The beach near the historic cottages is wide and sandy, and when the tide is exceptionally low, nearby tidepools are exposed.

EL MORO VISITOR CENTER: *Inland of Coast Hwy., 1.3 mi. S. of Los Trancos Canyon.* El Moro Visitor Center, open daily from 9 AM to 5 PM, contains interpretive displays and is the place to pick up wildlife checklists and trail maps. A series of loop trails begins at the parking lot; mountain biking is highly popular. Bring plenty of water.

EL MORO CAMPGROUND: *Inland of Coast Hwy. at the mouth of El Moro Canyon.* A new campground with 60 sites for tents or RVs is planned for completion by 2010, along with new picnic facilities and day-use parking. A pedestrian underpass beneath Coast Hwy. provides access to El Moro Beach. A private

mobile home community once occupied land leased from the state; now the park's land holdings are open to all.

Thirty-two hike-in campsites with picnic tables and pit toilets are also available in El Moro Canyon, but located about three miles inland (and uphill) from Coast Hwy. Register at El Moro ranger station; for reservations, call: 1-800-444-7275. Carry your own water. Horses allowed; no dogs. Due to the risk of fire, no open flames are permitted in the back country, although backpack stoves can be used.

LAGUNA COAST WILDERNESS PARK: *Off Laguna Cyn. Rd., 3 mi. inland from Coast Hwy., Laguna Beach.* A small, gravel parking area is located on the west side of Laguna Canyon Rd. Trails for hikers, equestrians, and mountain bikers lead into the hills, among coastal sage scrub vegetation and dramatic sandstone boulders eroded by wind and water. Parking area opens at 8 AM; gate is locked at 4 PM; fee for parking. Dogs not allowed; no fires or smoking. For information, call: 949-923-2235. The Wilderness Park extends inland past the San Joaquin Hills Toll Rd.

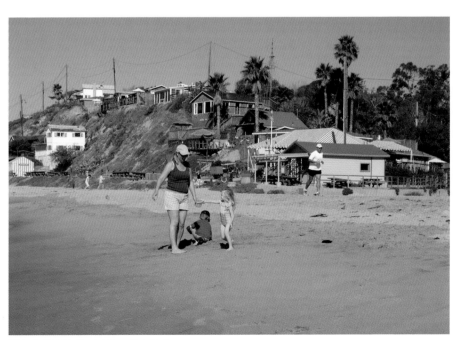

Historic District, Crystal Cove State Park

Historic District, Crystal Cove State Park

The small beach community of Crystal Cove sprang up around 1917 on land that was then part of the vast Irvine Ranch. At first, the Irvine Company permitted beach visitors to put up tents and simple cabins. Then Pacific Coast Hwy. was built along the bluff, and Southern California's burgeoning film industry discovered Crystal Cove as a stand-in for more exotic locales. More cottages were built in the 1930s. In 1979 the State Park system took over the little hamlet of Crystal Cove with its 46 cottages and the rest of the land that is now the state park. Despite all the changes, Crystal Cove still reflects an era of low-key beach holidays in modest surroundings, and the Historic District is listed on the National Register of Historic Places.

The Historic District in Crystal Cove State Park is an example of innovation in state parks management. The beachfront restaurant, blufftop snack stand, and the old-time cottages, some available since 2006 as overnight accommodations, are run by the Crystal Cove Alliance and its partners. Like some 80 other California state park cooperating associations, the Crystal Cove Alliance provides volunteer labor and conducts fund-raising to support the resource protection and education functions of its associated state park.

The Crystal Cove Alliance also holds the concession contract, the first in the state park system held by a nonprofit organization, to provide goods and services to visitors. After expenses, all proceeds from the cottages, food service, and sales in the park interpretive store help support future improvements to the park, including the planned renovation of more cottages for overnight visitors. The Crystal Cove Alliance was formed as a response to an earlier and ultimately rejected proposal to convert the cottages to 73 luxury resort units.

Coastal Sage Scrub and Chaparral

THE NATIVE PLANT communities that are most characteristic of southern California's coastal counties are various types of scrub, or woody shrub, vegetation that are adapted to low rainfall (10 to 15 inches per year), extreme summer drought, and periodic fire. During the summer, scrub-covered hillsides appear brown and lifeless but are transformed to a vibrant green by winter rains. For a few years after a wildfire, these same hills may be painted with splashes of color each spring by fire-following herbs that flower among the charred remains of shrubs. Inevitably, the shrubs regain their dominance, and, except in scattered light gaps, the herbaceous species must again persist as seeds until fire initiates a new cycle of change.

These communities are broadly classified as either coastal sage scrub or chaparral. Coastal sage scrub is made up of various low-growing shrubs that generally occur on finer textured soils, have adaptations to avoid the effects of summer drought, and produce persistent seeds that germinate in response to fire. Some species may also resprout from root crowns if the fire is not too intense. By contrast, chaparral plants generally occur on coarser textured soils, are larger and woodier, and have adaptations, such as tough waxy leaves, that reduce moisture loss and enable them to grow longer into the hot, dry summer. Although chaparral species also have long-lived seeds that sprout in response to fire, many of the dominant species, especially the ubiquitous chamise, are strong resprouters that quickly grow back from the root crown, or basal burl. Others, like some species of mountain lilac, rely entirely on their seed bank to recover from fire.

Coastal sage scrub is dominated by shrubs that have evolved various distinctive adaptations to avoid the desiccating effects of drought. These species may produce smaller leaves in the summer or even drop their leaves, die back, and enter a period of dormancy. Many of the characteristic species of this community are highly aromatic. The scents of California sagebrush and the true sages, or Salvias, of the mint family, such as black sage, white sage, and purple sage, are highly regarded by aromatherapists. A walk in coastal sage scrub after a rain is an olfactory delight, and the therapy is free.

Coastal sage scrub vegetation

Coastal sage scrub is home to many rare species of animals and birds, such as the coastal California gnatcatcher. The urbanization of southern California has resulted in severe losses of this habitat and a concomitant decline in the gnatcatcher population, which resulted in its being listed as "threatened" under the federal Endangered Species Act in 1993. This created immediate conflicts in southern California between the needs for resource protection and continued urban development. In response, state and federal agencies and local governments embarked on a grand experiment in resource conservation called "natural community conservation planning," the first example of which was instituted in San Diego in 1998. Under such a plan, large contiguous areas of habitat and important wildlife corridors are placed in a protected status and, in return, development within other areas is facilitated. In concept, this approach is attractive because it offers predictability to development interests and avoids the habitat fragmentation that often accompanies partial protection of habitat on a parcel-by-parcel basis. However, since both development and habitat preservation take place over time, it may be decades before the effectiveness of these plans can be properly evaluated.

Chaparral is made up of woody species that, in contrast to those of coastal sage scrub, may reach a height of 15 feet or so and often forms a nearly impenetrable thicket. Chaparral is one of the most abundant and widespread vegetation types in California. Nevertheless, as common as chaparral is, where it is part of an intact matrix of community types, its loss can result in significant environmental impacts. This is the case in the Santa Monica Mountains, where chaparral forms a patchwork of habitats with coastal sage scrub, oak woodland, grassland, and riparian forest in a wonderfully intact ecosystem, which is all the more remarkable for being next door to some ten million people. Wildlife relies on the predictable mix of these natural communities for sustenance through the seasons and during different portions of their life cycles. For example, many animals have evolved to exploit the flowering and growth cycles of coastal sage scrub and chaparral, which differ in a complementary and sequential way. Whereas coastal sage scrub is shallow-rooted and responds quickly to seasonal rains, chaparral plants are typically deep-rooted, having most of their flowering and growth later in the rainy season after the deeper soil layers have been saturated. Honeybees, butterflies, moths, and other insects tend to follow these cycles of flowering and new growth, moving from coastal sage scrub in the early rainy season to chaparral in the spring. The insects, in turn, are followed by insectivorous birds.

Chaparral comes in a great variety of combinations whose names generally derive from the relative proportions of chamise, mountain lilac (*Ceanothus* species), manzanita, oaks, and other large shrubs or small trees. One type of chaparral is "southern maritime chaparral," which is a very special community that only occurs close to the ocean, from Laguna Beach south to Mexico. Maritime chaparral is restricted to well-drained sandy or gravelly soils of low fertility within the summer fog zone and is characterized by the presence of one or more rare species of oak, manzanita, or mountain lilac intermixed with more common shrubs. The floral composition of the community, including the identity of the narrowly distributed rare species, changes with latitude. Above the residential areas of Laguna Beach, many of the ocean-facing slopes that can be seen from Coast Highway are dominated by southern maritime chaparral that is distinctive due to the presence in the canopy of bushrue, scrub oak, and a peculiar form of mountain lilac that is thought to be either a distinct sub-species of big-pod ceanothus or perhaps a hybrid with the more southern, and rarer, warty-stemmed ceanothus. The habitat also supports rare herbs such as Laguna Beach dudleya and big-leafed crownbeard, a native aster.

Mountain lilac

Mountain lilac is the common name of about 40 species of shrubs or small trees in the genus *Ceanothus*. Whereas the ornamental lilac is a member of the olive family, mountain lilac is contained in the buckthorn family. Mountain lilac gets its name from its clusters of blue or white flowers and its lovely fragrance, both reminiscent of its better known lilac "cousins." Some species of mountain lilac are "obligate seeders," meaning they grow only from germinated seeds and cannot respond to fire by resprouting from the root crown. Therefore, the unnaturally frequent fires that are associated with human activities can consume the seed bank and prevent its replenishment, thereby removing these beautiful shrubs from our native communities.

Laguna Beach live-forever

Plants of the species *Dudleya* are commonly called "live-forevers," because they are reputed to live for up to 100 years. Although an undisturbed individual may have an impressive lifespan, it could take a miracle for the species known as the **Laguna Beach live-forever** (*Dudleya stolonifera*) to survive another century. This threatened species is now confined to just six locations in the San Joaquin Hills in or near Laguna Beach. Laguna Beach live-forever's microhabitat is weathered sandstone rock outcrops on cliffs within coastal sage scrub or chaparral. Although there is a "natural community conservation plan" in effect that "covers" Laguna Beach live-forever, most of the world's population occurs on land owned by non-participants in the plan. This rare live-forever demonstrates the hazards of endemism in the face of relentless urbanization.

Coastal California gnatcatcher

A kitten-like mew is the best indication that the **coastal California gnatcatcher** (*Polioptila californica californica*), a threatened species, is nearby. For much of the day, this small insectivore remains hidden beneath coastal sage scrub's waist-high canopy, gleaning insects from the foliage of sagebrush and buckwheat. When the gnatcatcher forays to an exposed perch, its distinctive black cap may be visible. The coastal California gnatcatcher is endemic to southern California and Baja California. Within that limited range, the California gnatcatcher's habitat is restricted to coastal sage scrub. To ensure the survival of this imperiled bird, large areas of coastal sage scrub have been protected from development.

The **Pacific pocket mouse** (*Perognathus longimembris pacificus*) is a tiny, nocturnal mammal endemic to coastal California from Los Angeles to Mexico. Cute by any standard, it has light pinkish-brown fur and a bi-colored tail, and the soles of its hind feet are hairy. Seeds are the staple of the Pacific pocket mouse's diet, which it supplements with leafy material and the occasional insect. Unfortunately for the mouse, its preferred habitat is fine, sandy soil in open coastal sage scrub, close to the ocean—a habitat also coveted for urban development. As a result, the mouse has lost most of its habitat.

Pacific pocket mouse

The **mountain lion** (*Puma concolor*), also known as a cougar, is the only large cat native to California. An average adult male weighs about 140 pounds and measures up to eight feet from nose to tip of tail, making it the fourth largest cat in the world, behind the tiger (500 pounds), the African lion (400 pounds) and the jaguar (200 pounds). Taxonomists do not group the cougar with lions and tigers, because cougars lack the specialized anatomical features that enable the "big cats" to roar. Cougars must be content to hiss and scream, although humans tend to find those vocalizations similarly intimidating. Cougars are solitary predators that stalk and ambush rather than chase their prey. Although a mountain lion may eat a deer each week, it also consumes small mammals and even insects. If a habitat supports deer, cougars are probably present.

Mountain lion

Male mountain lions maintain huge territories, ranging from about 50 to 300 square miles. The presence of mountain lions in areas like the Santa Monica Mountains is a good sign that large areas of habitat are still connected. The bad news is that an increase in both human and cougar populations has increased the risk of a dangerous encounter. Although cougar attacks are still rare, they have increased in the last several decades. Be cautious; hike with a companion and do not leave children unsupervised, even in a campground. If you see a cougar, stay together, make noise, appear big, and do not run. In the unlikely event of an attack, the best response is to fight back with anything at hand. To put this risk in perspective, in the US and Canada since 1990, there were about 50 documented attacks and ten deaths. By comparison, every year in the US alone, about 12 people die from rattlesnake bites, about 40 from bee stings, and about 82 from lightning strikes.

Mountain lion

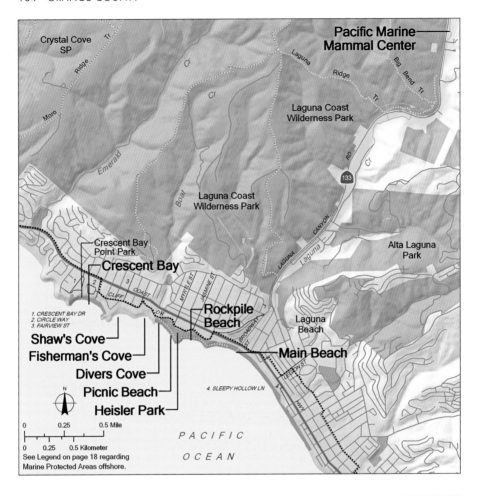

Pacific Marine Mammal Center

Crystal Cove SP

Laguna Coast Wilderness Park

Laguna Coast Wilderness Park

Crescent Bay Point Park

Crescent Bay

Alta Laguna Park

1. CRESCENT BAY DR
2. CIRCLE WAY
3. FAIRVIEW ST

Rockpile Beach

Laguna Beach

Shaw's Cove

Fisherman's Cove

Divers Cove

Main Beach

Picnic Beach

4. SLEEPY HOLLOW LN

Heisler Park

0   0.25   0.5 Mile

0   0.25   0.5 Kilometer
See Legend on page 18 regarding
Marine Protected Areas offshore.

PACIFIC OCEAN

View of Crescent Bay from overlook

Laguna Beach North

	Sandy Beach	Rocky Shore	Trail	Visitor Center	Campground	Wildlife Viewing	Fishing or Boating	Facilities for Disabled	Food and Drink	Restrooms	Parking	Fee
Crescent Bay	•					•	•			•		
Shaw's Cove	•	•				•	•					
Fisherman's Cove	•	•				•	•					
Divers Cove	•	•				•				•	•	
Picnic Beach	•	•				•				•	•	
Heisler Park		•					•			•	•	
Rockpile Beach	•	•				•						
Main Beach	•						•	•	•	•		
Pacific Marine Mammal Center				•		•					•	

CRESCENT BAY: *Off Cliff Dr. at Circle Way, Laguna Beach.* A sandy, curved beach, one quarter-mile long, lies below the cliffs. A steep ramp leads down from Cliff Dr. at Circle Way; restrooms and beach showers are at the bottom. A beach stairway from Circle Way is located one block north of the ramp. Popular with skimboarders, divers, and body surfers. Lifeguard service provided by the city of Laguna Beach; lifeguard towers are staffed seasonally. Dogs are not allowed on the beach from June 1 to September 16, between 8 AM and 6 PM; leashed dogs OK at other times. No smoking or bottles on the beach at any time.

Crescent Bay Point Park at the end of Crescent Bay Dr. overlooks the beach; no beach access. The park is a good whale-watching spot, and Santa Catalina and San Clemente Islands may be spotted.

SHAW'S COVE: *Off Cliff Dr., opposite Fairview St., Laguna Beach.* The sandy 500-foot-long pocket beach is hemmed in by rocky promontories; a stairway leads down to the sand. Popular for swimming, diving, and tidepooling; skimboarding not allowed. Rocky intertidal areas of Laguna Beach are inhabited by California mussels, limpets, snails, barnacles, shore crabs, and several species of algae. Subtidal reefs support forests of giant kelp and provide a habitat for fish such as the kelp rockfish, California sheephead, and senorita fish. Reef-dwelling fish caught by anglers include opaleye, halfmoon, calico bass, halibut, various perch and croaker species, and the occasional white seabass. Cormorants, California brown pelicans, and California sea lions rest on offshore rocks.

FISHERMAN'S COVE: *600 block of Cliff Dr., Laguna Beach.* A hard-to-see stairway, on the north side of the large condominium complex, leads down to a tiny, sandy beach bordered by a rocky reef. Surf fishing is permitted on the beach.

DIVERS COVE: *600 block of Cliff Dr., Laguna Beach.* The stairway to this beach is located just 20 yards south of the stair to Fisherman's Cove. Metered parking spaces are located next to the beach accessway. Surf fishing is not allowed here. The beach is steep, and strong rip currents are often in evidence.

PICNIC BEACH: *Off Cliff Dr., opposite Myrtle St., Laguna Beach.* A ramp leads down the slope from Cliff Dr. to the sandy beach located below Heisler Park. Diving is popular here, but no fishing or skimboarding allowed. Restrooms and beach showers are located in adjacent Heisler Park.

HEISLER PARK: *400 block of Cliff Dr., Laguna Beach.* This beautifully landscaped park atop the cliffs provides wonderful views of the ocean, rocky shoreline, and hills rising behind Laguna Beach. Facilities include picnic areas, restrooms, outdoor showers, and stairs and pathways leading to the beach. Metered parking on Cliff Dr.

ROCKPILE BEACH: *Off Cliff Dr., opposite Jasmine St., Laguna Beach.* Rockpile Beach has sandy and rocky stretches, and there are tidepools to investigate at low tide. All marine resources are protected, so look, but do not disturb marine creatures and plants. A city-designated, summertime surfing beach; swimming not permitted in summer.

MAIN BEACH: *W. end of Broadway St., Laguna Beach.* This wide expanse of sand is the heart of Laguna Beach's shoreline. Coast Hwy. passes by the beach nearly at sea level, providing easy pedestrian access to the sand. There are highly popular sand volleyball courts, basketball courts, a children's playground, benches and tables, and restrooms and outdoor showers at the north and south ends of the beach. A boardwalk runs along the sand, and a beach wheelchair is available at the lifeguard headquarters at the north end of the beach. Surfing is not allowed during the summer months. Limited pay parking is available in city lots off Broadway St. near Coast Hwy., and metered spaces are on area streets.

PACIFIC MARINE MAMMAL CENTER: *20612 Laguna Canyon Rd., Laguna Beach.* Operated by a nonprofit organization, the center rehabilitates sea lions and seals that are stranded on Orange County beaches due to injury or illness. Healthy marine mammals are later released. The public can visit and observe any animals being treated. Free parking in front of the center. Located on Laguna Canyon Rd., two-and-a-half miles from the beach. Open 10 AM to 4 PM daily. Free admission, but donations welcome. For information, call: 949-494-3050.

Shaw's Cove

Beaches within the city of Laguna Beach are very scenic, highly popular, and, except for Main Beach, fairly modest in size. Certain rules apply, in order to make the beach experience pleasant for everyone. Tents, large umbrellas, and beach fires are not allowed on city beaches, and smoking is prohibited on beaches and beach accessways. Dogs are prohibited on the beach between 8 AM and 6 PM, from June 1 to September 16; leashed dogs are OK at other times. From June 15 to September 15, surfing is not allowed at most of the city's beaches; yellow flags with a black ball indicate surfing closures. In designated surfing areas, swimming is prohibited between June 15 and September 15. Lifeguards signal swimming conditions by use of green, yellow, or red flags. Lifeguard towers on all of the city's popular beaches are staffed seasonally; lifeguards patrol year-round. The city of Laguna Beach offers a summertime junior lifeguard program that is both recreational and educational. Call: 949-494-6572. For a recorded surf and tide report, call: 949-494-6573

Main Beach

The first non-native settlers of Laguna Beach were homesteaders in the 1870s and 1880s. They were encouraged to move there by the Timber Culture Act of 1873, which allowed people to receive 160 free acres of federal land in the West if they grew trees on 40 of those acres (later lowered to ten of those acres). The eucalyptus trees still found today in the area originate from the planting done during that era.

The trees, coast, picturesque cliffs, and comfortable weather helped to attract and inspire artists, notably Norman St. Clair, a watercolorist from San Francisco, and landscape painters William Wendt and George Gardner Symons. These artists played an important role in the community's development in the early 1900s as an artists' colony. The community became known for plein air painting and fine examples of California Impressionism. In 1918, painter Edgar Payne organized the Laguna Beach Art Association, the colony's first gallery opened, and Laguna's popularity as an art destination was on its way.

Laguna Beach continues to be a hotspot for artistic activities. It is home to many local artists, the Laguna Art Museum, and the Laguna College of Art and Design. An evening "Art Walk" on the first Thursday of every month attracts visitors to some of the city's dozens of galleries. Laguna Beach also hosts several large annual artistic events. The Festival of Arts is a juried exhibition held each summer, and it also includes the Pageant of the Masters, a popular show featuring people in costume posing to replicate actual statues and paintings.

The Art-A-Fair Festival also takes place during the summer and features selections from different international artists. Finally, the summertime Sawdust Art Festival is a show by both professionals and amateurs, all Laguna Beach residents, who build booths in a village-like setting where visitors can walk on sawdust-lined paths among the various arts and crafts. For information on local events, see the website maintained by the Laguna Beach Alliance for the Arts at www.lagunabeacharts.com.

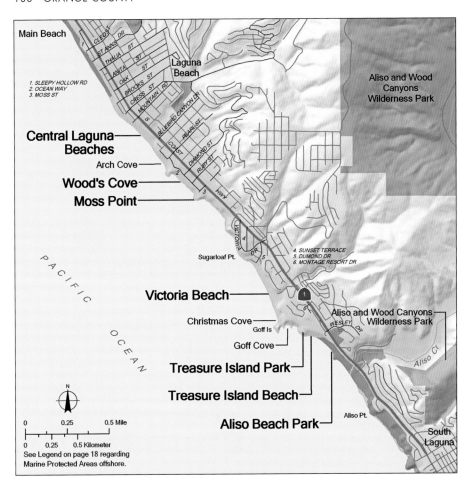

Main Beach

Laguna Beach

Aliso and Wood Canyons Wilderness Park

1. SLEEPY HOLLOW RD
2. OCEAN WAY
3. MOSS ST

Central Laguna Beaches

Arch Cove

Wood's Cove

Moss Point

PACIFIC OCEAN

Sugarloaf Pt.

4. SUNSET TERRACE
5. DUMOND DR
6. MONTAGE RESORT DR

Victoria Beach

Christmas Cove

Goff Is

Goff Cove

Treasure Island Park

Treasure Island Beach

Aliso Beach Park

Aliso and Wood Canyons Wilderness Park

Aliso Pt.

South Laguna

N

0   0.25   0.5 Mile

0   0.25   0.5 Kilometer
See Legend on page 18 regarding
Marine Protected Areas offshore.

Wood's Cove, at end of Diamond St.

Laguna Beach to Aliso Beach Park

	Sandy Beach	Rocky Shore	Trail	Visitor Center	Campground	Wildlife Viewing	Fishing or Boating	Facilities for Disabled	Food and Drink	Restrooms	Parking	Fee
Central Laguna Beaches	•	•				•	•		•			
Wood's Cove	•	•				•						
Moss Point	•	•				•						
Victoria Beach	•	•				•	•					
Treasure Island Park		•					•		•	•	•	
Treasure Island Beach	•	•				•	•					
Aliso Beach Park	•	•				•	•	•	•	•	•	•

CENTRAL LAGUNA BEACHES: *S. of Main Beach, Laguna Beach.* A chain of sandy beaches, separated by rock outcroppings, is located south of Main Beach. Most street ends provide beach access via stairs or ramps. Metered parking is along S. Coast Hwy. Lifeguards are on duty year-round; towers are staffed seasonally. Some pocket beaches are quite narrow when the tide is high.

A beach stairway is at the north end of Sleepy Hollow Ln. next to the Vacation Village Hotel. Another stairway at the end of Cleo St. leads to a narrow, rocky stretch of beach. Stairs to the sand are at the ends of St. Ann's Dr. and Thalia St., the latter with a wheelchair-accessible viewing platform on the bluff. The beach between St. Ann's Dr. and Thalia St. is designated by the city of Laguna Beach as a summertime surfing area. Rocky reefs make some areas unsuitable for swimming. For a recorded surf and tide report, call: 949-494-6573.

Continuing south, there is a stairway at the end of Anita St. and another at Oak St., where there is a wheelchair-accessible viewing platform and bench. A stairway at Brooks St. leads to a popular surfing beach. At the ends of Cress St. and Mountain Rd. there are stairways to a sandy beach with rock outcroppings; popular for surf fishing, diving, and body surfing. Use caution entering the water, due to submerged rocks.

At the end of Bluebird Canyon Rd. there is a ramp from S. Coast Hwy. to the sandy beach

in front of the Surf and Sand Hotel. A stairway at the end of Agate St. leads to a beach that is designated for surfing from sunup until 12 noon and from 4 PM until sunset. A stairway at the end of Pearl St. leads to Arch Cove, popular with body surfers, divers, anglers, and tidepoolers. Because of hazardous conditions, do not climb on Arch Rock.

WOOD'S COVE: *W. of Coast Hwy., between Pearl St. and Diamond St., Laguna Beach.* Wood's Cove and adjacent Lover's Cove are tiny curves of sand punctuated by rock outcroppings and accessible from two stairways, one at the end of Diamond St., and one a short block north of Diamond St. on Ocean Way. Rocks and rip currents present hazards; use caution in entering the water and do not dive or jump off the rocks. At the end of Ruby St. is a small landscaped park on the bluff overlooking the rocky shore.

MOSS POINT: *W. of Coast Hwy., end of Moss St., Laguna Beach.* A small sandy pocket beach bounded by rocks at each end is accessible from the end of Moss St.

VICTORIA BEACH: *S. of Victoria Dr., Laguna Beach.* Victoria Beach is a quarter-mile-long, relatively wide stretch of sand south of the rock outcropping known as Sugarloaf Point. A popular skimboarding, diving, and surf fishing beach. Lifeguard service provided by the city of Laguna Beach. From S. Coast Hwy. walk down Victoria Dr. to a stairway near the end of Sunset Terrace or continue to the end of Dumond Dr. to another access-

Treasure Island Beach

way. Very limited on-street parking; respect private property. To the south of Victoria Beach is a rocky promontory known as Goff Island. Because of hazardous conditions, climbing on the rocks is prohibited, and collecting shells or rocks is also prohibited.

TREASURE ISLAND PARK: *Seaward of Montage Resort, Laguna Beach.* A gorgeous landscaped park on the blufftop provides benches, picnic tables, drinking fountain, restrooms, outdoor showers, and both paved and dirt paths along the bluff. A fee parking structure is at the signalized intersection of S. Coast Hwy. and Wesley Dr.; three-hour time limit is enforced from 8 AM to 7 PM daily. A path leads from the parking structure past the hotel along the bluff, and a stairway and two ramps lead down to the sand and tidepools. There is also pedestrian access to Treasure Island Park from Montage Resort Dr.

TREASURE ISLAND BEACH: *S. of the Montage Resort, Laguna Beach.* A quarter-mile-long stretch of sand extends south of Treasure Island Park. Lifeguard service is provided year-round by the city of Laguna Beach; towers are staffed seasonally. For recorded surf and tide information, call: 949-494-6573. The sandy beach extends toward Aliso Beach Park, south of the mouth of Aliso Creek.

ALISO BEACH PARK: *31000 block of S. Coast Hwy., Laguna Beach.* Aliso Beach Park, managed by the county of Orange, features both a popular sandy beach and a woodland area along Aliso Creek, inland of Coast Hwy. A pedestrian underpass connects the two parts of the park. Seaward of the highway, the beach is long, wide, and sandy. Popular activities include surfing, bodyboarding, and surf fishing. The waves often break close to shore, so this is not a major swimming beach. Facilities include parking, restrooms, beach showers, a children's play area, picnic area with tables and grills, and a bike trail. A concession stand sells food and beverages and fishing supplies and rents recreational equipment. A diamond-shaped fishing pier that once stood on Aliso Beach was removed following storm damage in 1998.

A beach wheelchair is available from the lifeguard. No alcohol or glass containers on the beach; dogs not allowed. Beach fires are permitted only in provided fire rings. The parking area is open from 6 AM to 10 PM; parking fee applies year-round. For information, call: 949-923-2280. Inland of S. Coast Hwy., park facilities include parking, picnic facilities, and restrooms. There are nice views of the lower reach of Aliso Creek.

The steep hillsides of parts of Orange County are inherently unstable and subject to landslides. As urban development has crept up the ridges and canyons, increasing numbers of homes—and lives—have been placed at risk. Bluebird Canyon in Laguna Beach has been an especially unlucky spot. In the early morning of October 2, 1978 the hillside near the mouth of the canyon gave way, carrying 19 homes and parts of 14 others downhill at an initial rate of 40 feet per hour. The rate finally slowed to a few inches per day before movement ceased; by then, some 50 homes had been affected. The landslide followed near-record-setting rains the previous winter, which had raised the water table and reduced frictional forces on the slide plane. Although many landslides occur during rainstorms, others are delayed as it can take months for water to percolate deep into the earth.

History repeated itself on the morning of June 1, 2005. At about 7 AM, the hillside immediately east of the 1978 failure slipped. The slide apparently moved much faster than the 1978 slide, but not so fast that residents were not alerted, and all were able to get out of their homes and off the moving landslide. Only four minor injuries were sustained. The landslide resulted in a near-coherent mass of earth moving approximately 100 feet laterally and 50 feet vertically down the slope. Everything on top of this mass, including Flamingo Rd., 15 houses, and utilities, simply rode the block downwards. Over the next two years, massive grading operations, "undergrounding" of the stream, and the construction of two large retaining walls was undertaken. Although the engineering undertaken to shore up the sites of these landslides makes it unlikely that they will slip again, many areas not so reinforced remain at peril. Areas that are most at risk are areas, like the north flanks of Bluebird Canyon, that are underlain by weak rocks, where the layers of bedding dip parallel to the slope, and stream action over the millennia has undermined the toe of those beds.

Laguna Beach landslide, June 1, 2005

Rocky Shore

THE INTERTIDAL rocky shore is an environment of extremes—a place where some plants and animals are adapted to survive in both air and water. As the tide goes out, free-living marine life usually goes out with it, but some organisms are permanently attached to the rocks (that is, sessile). These plants and animals must be adapted to withstand not only desiccation (drying out), but also the effects of storms, wind, and rain. The ability of organisms to withstand dryness and their interactions with each other (eating, being eaten, competing for space, reproducing) help determine which ones dominate within the different micro-habitats of rocky intertidal areas.

The physical characteristics of each site also contribute to the mix of free-living and sessile marine life existing there. The physical factors most important in determining the distribution and abundance of shore life in a given area are the degree of wave shock, tidal exposure, and type of bottom or substrate. Important substrate qualities include size (ranging from cobble to boulder to bedrock), vertical relief (low or high), composition (sandstone, shale, basalt, or granite), and surface texture (smooth, pitted, or cracked). Habitats with diverse substrate characteristics generally host the richest assemblage of marine species.

While most of the shoreline of northern and central California is rocky (54 percent and 61 percent, respectively), the dominant substrate along the coast from Los Angeles County to the Mexican border is sand, gravel, or cobble. Intertidal reefs composed of bedrock are only a small component of the Los Angeles, Orange, and San Diego County coastlines, taking up 34 percent, 7 percent, and 14 percent, respectively, of the shoreline. In addition, the sandstone and siltstone substrate that makes up the south-

Sea stars and mussels at Leo Carrillo State Beach, Los Angeles County

ern California rocky shore tends to be less solid and stable than the hard granite reefs of central and northern California. It is not uncommon for large sections of southern California rocky reefs to break away. Furthermore, the rocky reefs in southern California are influenced by sand burial and sand scour because of the large sandy areas surrounding them. Rocky reef organisms that thrive in southern California have evolved adaptations to these disturbances.

Even though rocky reefs in southern California are not as stable as more northerly rocky reefs, they are still more resistant to erosion than sand, gravel, and cobble and therefore tend to occur at headlands, points, or peninsulas. Some of the more prominent rocky shorelines in southern California are Long Point, White Point, and Point Fermin on the Palos Verdes Peninsula; Reef Point at Crystal Cove State Park; and, in San Diego County, Point La Jolla, Nicholson Point Park, and Point Loma.

Rocky shores in southern California and in central and northern California differ not only in geology, but also in climate. The average temperature in southern California is higher than that in central and northern California, and rocky shores are more subject to heating and drying out. Especially stressful conditions occur when hot temperatures coincide with spring and fall Santa Ana wind conditions and low tides. Southern California is also exposed to the Southern California counter current—a northward-trending current that brings warm water into the Southern California Bight. The ocean temperature off Los Angeles, Orange, and San Diego Counties averages from two to five degrees warmer than the ocean off central and northern California.

Sessile organisms that thrive in southern California rocky shores include limpets, mussels, anemones, barnacles, seaweeds, and surfgrass. To enable them to attach to hard substrates, mussels produce protein fibers called "byssal threads." The byssal threads are five times tougher and 16 times more extensible than a human tendon. The threads are secreted by a special gland in the mussel's muscular foot. Scientists have unlocked the chemical mystery of the byssal thread protein, and it is thought to be the first known protein with both collagenous and elastin-like domains. Seaweeds avoid being ripped from the rocks by their elastic holdfasts, which are the part of the seaweed that attaches to the substrate, similar to the roots of terrestrial plants, and their elastic stipes, which are like plant stems. Holdfast and stipe elasticity is due in part to the presence of carrageenan or alginate, commercially valuable polysaccharides that are infused in seaweed cell walls. Other adaptations that enable sessile organisms to survive are hard shells, the ability to withstand sand burial, and rhizomous roots.

While exposed rocks may be devoid of creatures, tidepools can be teeming with life. It is not unusual to find sea anemones, sea urchins, sea stars, nudibranchs, snails, chitons, octopuses, hermit crabs, monkeyface eels, and tidepool sculpins all occupying one pool. Tidepools are the places where pools of water collect in depressions at low tide. They usually contain lots of nooks and crannies in which creatures can hide. Tidepools ameliorate some of the harsh conditions in the intertidal zone, although with their constantly fluctuating temperatures and salinity, they still provide serious challenges to intertidal life. Two basic survival rules for tidepool inhabitants are: avoid being washed away at high tide, and keep from being eaten.

Surfgrass

Surfgrass (*Phyllospadix scouleri*) lives in the intertidal zone and marks the zero tide mark. When you see surfgrass exposed you know you are experiencing a low tide. Surfgrass is not an alga, but rather is an angiosperm, or flowering plant, with true leaves, stems, and rootstocks. Surfgrass habitat is highly productive, providing shelter for many invertebrates and supporting many species of algae. Surfgrass also provides nursery habitat for fishes and invertebrates, such as the California spiny lobster. *Phyllospadix* is susceptible to desiccation and heat stress during low midday tides and it is sensitive to sewage and oiling. If the rhizome systems remain viable, then recovery following disturbance can be fairly rapid; however, recovery is slow if the entire bed is lost, because recruitment is irregular. Furthermore, restoration projects have been unsuccessful.

Tidepool sculpin

The **tidepool sculpin** (*Oligocottus maculosus*) is one of several small members of the sculpin family that you may encounter while investigating the intertidal zone. Masters of camouflage, they use varying patterns of reds, greens, browns, and grays to hide. A tidepool sculpin may inhabit one tidepool for over a year, and use its sense of smell to identify its home pool on the reef. As a defense mechanism, tidepool sculpins can also detect the scent of predators or injured comrades. This species has evolved to tolerate the large temperature variations that occur within its turbulent environment, and if a wave sweeps a tidepool sculpin up onto a rock, the fish is able to breathe air briefly until it wriggles back to the sea.

Sand castle worm

The **sand castle worm** (*Phragmatopoma californica*) is a colonial polycheate that lives in the intertidal zone from northern California to Baja California. The worms create enormous sand tube colonies, or "castles." The sand castle worm is able to do this because it has a gland that secretes a glue-like substance that it uses to coat sand grains, which are then added to the tubes. The feeding and sensory tentacles of the sand castle worm are dark purple, and when the tentacles are underwater and extended, the colony looks like it is carpeted in purple. The worms feed by waving their sticky tentacles in the water and capturing plankton.

The **southern spiny chiton** (*Nuttallina fluxa*) is thumb-sized and cream-colored, with reddish-brown hairs. It attaches itself to an intertidal rock. Its girdle, or mantle, nearly covers the eight shell plates that make up its skeleton. *Nuttalina* is one of many species of chitons that live in the intertidal zone. The chiton is an omnivore that scrapes rocks with a tongue-like radula, eating whatever sessile organism is in its path.

Southern spiny chiton

The **owl limpet** (*Lottia gigantea*) inhabits the high-to-middle intertidal zones of the southern Californian rocky coastline. The large owl limpet reaches over four inches in total length and may live up to 15 years. This species, sometimes referred to as the farmer limpet, has a unique adaptation to remove competition for valuable substrate and food in the harsh intertidal environment. The owl limpet tends to a "plot" of reef substrate by actively pushing out or scraping off competing barnacles, limpets, and other invertebrates that attempt to colonize the area. These plots average close to a square yard in area. The clearing behavior of the owl limpet promotes the growth of algae within the plot, which the herbivorous limpet then grazes for food.

Owl limpet

The **gooseneck barnacle** (*Pollicipes polymerus*) is distributed along the rocky shorelines of the U.S. Pacific coast. This crustacean thrives in the middle intertidal zone, often associated with clusters of California mussels. The gooseneck barnacle can be identified by its long, flexible, neck-like structure, called a "peduncle." The peduncle extends the appendages known as "cirri," which are used for feeding and breathing, out from the rock on which the invertebrate is permanently anchored. Larval barnacles drift in the water column, along with other plankton, and then settle onto hard substrate, in the process permanently gluing their "heads" down and extending their "feet," or cirri, into the water column. Gooseneck barnacles may reach four inches in total length and may live up to 20 years. Some Mediterranean diners consider the peduncle of this barnacle to be a delicacy.

Gooseneck barnacle

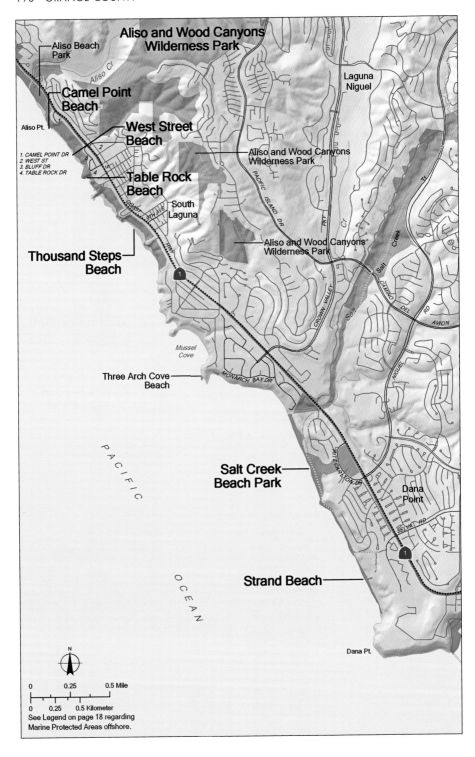

Aliso Beach Park

Aliso and Wood Canyons Wilderness Park

Laguna Niguel

Camel Point Beach

Aliso Cr

Aliso Pt.

West Street Beach

1. CAMEL POINT DR
2. WEST ST.
3. BLUFF DR
4. TABLE ROCK DR

Aliso and Wood Canyons Wilderness Park

Table Rock Beach

South Laguna

Aliso and Wood Canyons Wilderness Park

Thousand Steps Beach

COAST HWY

Mussel Cove

Three Arch Cove Beach

MONARCH BAY DR

CROWN VALLEY

Salt Creek

CAMINO DEL AVION

NIGUEL

PACIFIC ISLAND DR

PKY

Salt Cr

Salt Creek Beach Park

Dana Point

RITZ CARLTON DR

PACIFIC

SELVA RD

OCEAN

Strand Beach

Dana Pt.

N

0   0.25   0.5 Mile

0   0.25   0.5 Kilometer
See Legend on page 18 regarding
Marine Protected Areas offshore.

South Laguna

	Sandy Beach	Rocky Shore	Trail	Visitor Center	Campground	Wildlife Viewing	Fishing or Boating	Facilities for Disabled	Food and Drink	Restrooms	Parking	Fee
Camel Point Beach	•	•								•		
West Street Beach	•	•										
Table Rock Beach	•											
Thousand Steps Beach	•									•		
Aliso and Wood Canyons Wilderness Park			•	•	•		•			•	•	•
Salt Creek Beach Park	•		•				•	•	•	•	•	•
Strand Beach	•						•	•		•	•	

CAMEL POINT BEACH: *End of Camel Point Dr., South Laguna.* A wide sandy beach is accessible through a pedestrian gate at the end of Camel Point Dr. off S. Coast Hwy.; park along the highway shoulder. Two additional public walkways to the same beach are located between residences in the 31300 block of S. Coast Hwy. Do not trespass on private property. On the beach there are volleyball nets and portable toilets. Camel Point Beach is part of Aliso Beach Park, and lifeguard service is provided by Orange County.

WEST STREET BEACH: *Opposite end of West St., South Laguna.* A stairway leads to a long, sandy beach with rock outcroppings and scattered tidepools. Another stairway is located at the Coast Royale condominium building located 200 feet north of West St. Be cautious of submerged rocks. Lifeguard service is provided by Orange County. Limited shoulder parking on S. Coast Hwy.; use caution, as traffic moves fast here.

TABLE ROCK BEACH: *Off Table Rock Dr., South Laguna.* At the end of Table Rock Dr., two blocks south of West St., is a stairway to a small sandy cove bounded by spectacular rock formations. The beach is steep, and the surf can be rough. Lifeguard service; no facilities. Limited street parking.

THOUSAND STEPS BEACH: *Opposite 9th Ave., South Laguna.* Actually, 223 steep steps lead from S. Coast Hwy. at the foot of 9th Ave. down the bluff to the sand. At the base of the steps is a long sandy beach, and there are restrooms and a beach shower. Ask a lifeguard about swimming conditions, which can change rapidly. Limited shoulder parking along S. Coast Hwy.

ALISO AND WOOD CANYONS WILDERNESS PARK: *28373 Alicia Parkway, Laguna Niguel.* More than 30 miles of trails for hikers, equestrians, and mountain bikers lead through this open space park in an inland setting, open daily from 7 AM to sunset. For park information, call: 949-923-2200. The Orange County Natural History Museum at the park entrance is open Wednesday through Sunday from 11 AM to 5 PM.

Thousand Steps Beach

Salt Creek Beach Park

SALT CREEK BEACH PARK: *Off Ritz-Carlton Dr., Dana Point.* Salt Creek Beach Park includes a mile and a half of sandy and rocky shore. The beach is a popular surfing spot. The main access point to the beach is off Ritz Carlton Dr., which forms a semi-circular loop off Pacific Coast Hwy. Within the loop is a large fee parking area with restrooms; the parking lot is open from 5 AM to 12 midnight. Walk through an underpass and down the slope to the beach; visitors with disabled-person parking placards may drive down the hill for passenger drop-off. On the slope overlooking the sea is seven-acre, grassy Bluff Park, which has benches, barbecue grills, picnic tables, and restrooms. Paths and trails lead north and east through a golf course and into Salt Creek Regional Park, featuring several miles of trails for hiking, biking, and horseback riding.

Located at the edge of Salt Creek Beach are concessions, additional restrooms, and beach showers; additional facilities are located to the south, at the base of the bluff below the hotel. Lifeguard service is provided by Orange County. Dogs are not allowed on the beach; no alcohol or glass containers. For information, call: 949-923-2280. To the north of Salt Creek Beach is the private Monarch Beach community; public access is along the wet sand at low tide only. Do not trespass on private property.

A scenic path overlooks Salt Creek Beach from the top of the bluff. A pedestrian gate, open 24 hours, is located off Ritz-Carlton Dr. on the south side of the hotel's service entrance. The path leads around the perimeter of the hotel property, past benches and overlooks providing views of gray whale migration routes, Catalina Island, and the coastline. At its northern end, the path joins a paved multi-use trail leading north along the shoreline past Bluff Park.

STRAND BEACH: *Off Selva Rd., Dana Point.* An entrance to the southerly, and narrower, part of Salt Creek Beach is off Selva Rd., where there is a large parking area, restrooms, and a stairway down the steep slope to the beach. New beach access facilities from the parking area are planned, including a funicular down the high bluff and new stairways; additional restrooms and beach showers are also planned.

One of the most striking varieties of rock on the California coast is named the San Onofre Breccia. This rock is resistant to erosion, and it supports the bold headlands at Dana Point. Although rock units are usually named for the locality where they are best exposed, the most dramatic outcroppings of the San Onofre Breccia are found not near San Onofre (San Diego County), but in the coastal bluffs between Laguna Beach and Dana Point.

One of the best places to view this rock unit is Aliso Beach, located four miles north of Dana Point. From the parking area at Aliso Beach Park, walk 350 yards south along the sand and look at the base of the bluff. The rock here consists of tan-colored sandstones interspersed with beds of Breccia—conglomerate with sharp, angular fragments, varying from cobble to boulder size. Many of these fragments consist of blueschist, a bluish metamorphic rock containing the mineral glaucophane. Glaucophane forms only at extremely high pressures in the earth's crust, but at relatively low temperatures. Such blueschist is rare in southern California, outcropping only on Catalina Island and the Palos Verdes Peninsula. Large angular boulders do not travel far from their place of origin, and grain size generally decreases with distance from source. The blueschist fragments in the San Onofre Breccia decrease in size eastward, away from the coast.

So what was the source of these blueschist fragments? No blueschist lies anywhere close to coastal southern Orange County today. But 15 to 20 million years ago, when these rocks were deposited, Catalina Island or the Palos Verdes Peninsula might have been situated west of southern Orange County. Movement along the Newport-Inglewood Fault and other offshore faults over the past 30 million years has carried these land masses northwestward to their current locations. Clues such as the mysterious blueschist fragments in the San Onofre Breccia help geologists determine what movement has occurred along faults over geologic time.

San Onofre Breccia at Aliso Beach

Ken Sampson Lookout

San Juan
Capistrano

Dana
Point

Heritage Park

Lantern Bay
Park

CAMINO LAS RAMBLAS

Baby
Beach

San
Clemente

Dana Pt.

Doheny
State Beach

1. ST OF THE OLD
   GOLDEN LANTERN
2. DEL PRADO AVE
3. ST OF THE PARK LANTERN
4. ISLAND WAY
5. PALISADES DR

Capistrano
Beach

Picnic
Park

Catalina Express
Terminal

Ocean
Institute

Dana Point
Harbor

Capistrano
Beach Park

Dana Point
Headlands

PACIFIC

OCEAN

N

0   0.5   1 Mile

0   0.5   1 Kilometer
See Legend on page 18 regarding
Marine Protected Areas offshore.

Dana Point Harbor

Dana Point to Capistrano Beach

	Sandy Beach	Rocky Shore	Trail	Visitor Center	Campground	Wildlife Viewing	Fishing or Boating	Facilities for Disabled	Food and Drink	Restrooms	Parking	Fee
Dana Point Headlands			•	•		•						
Ken Sampson Lookout						•					•	
Heritage Park			•								•	
Lantern Bay Park						•				•	•	
Dana Point Harbor						•	•	•	•	•	•	
Catalina Express Terminal										•	•	
Ocean Institute				•		•		•	•	•	•	•
Doheny State Beach	•		•	•	•	•	•	•	•	•	•	•
Capistrano Beach Park	•					•	•		•	•	•	•

DANA POINT HEADLANDS: *Off Pacific Coast Hwy. at end of Street of the Green Lantern.* New residential development going up at Dana Point Headlands will be accompanied by new public facilities including a hostel, a park on Pacific Coast Hwy. at Street of the Green Lantern, and a visitor center at the end of Scenic Dr., off Street of the Green Lantern. A blufftop trail is planned to wrap around the headlands.

KEN SAMPSON LOOKOUT: *S. end of Street of the Blue Lantern, Dana Point.* There is a high-level view of the boats in Dana Point Harbor from sheltered benches at the lookout. Additional viewpoints are located at the south end of Street of the Amber Lantern and Street of the Violet Lantern.

HERITAGE PARK: *End of Street of the Old Golden Lantern, off Del Prado Ave. (eastbound Pacific Coast Hwy.), Dana Point.* Grassy blufftop park with benches and paved paths. A stairway leads down to the harbor.

LANTERN BAY PARK: *End of Street of the Golden Lantern, Dana Point.* This landscaped park, with tables, barbecue grills, and restrooms, is a pleasant spot for a picnic. There are wheelchair-accessible parking spots, although the ground slopes somewhat steeply. Vehicles enter off Dana Point Harbor Dr.; turn onto Street of the Park Lantern, then sharp right to a no-fee parking lot. Pedestrians can enter the park also via stairs from

Street of the Golden Lantern at Dana Point Harbor Dr. Park open from 6 AM to 10 PM.

DANA POINT HARBOR: *S. of Dana Point Harbor Dr., Dana Point.* Boating facilities at Dana Point Harbor include two marinas with

Dana Point's unique and colorful street names, such as "Street of the Golden Lantern," come from the 1920s, when roads were installed with lamps replicating kerosene lanterns found on sailing ships. Some of these streetlights were specially colored, glowing in hues such as blue, green, ruby, violet, and amber, each color on a different road, where early developers also planned matching flowerbeds and addresses painted in corresponding colors on the houses.

While the colorful street names remain, the colored lanterns do not. However, a small number of the original streetlights resembling ship lanterns have been saved and can be seen in Dana Point Plaza, which is located at Pacific Coast Hwy. and La Plaza in the city's downtown.

2,500 boat slips. For information about guest slips, which can be reserved in advance, call 949-496-6137. Short-term anchorages in the harbor are assigned by the Harbor Patrol; call: 949-248-2222.

The Embarcadero Marina operates a 10-lane boat launch ramp (fee applies) and a boat hoist and dry boat storage and also offers sailing lessons, boat rentals, and other services; call: 949-496-6177. Other harbor facilities include a fuel dock, 949-496-6113 and a shipyard with repair facilities, 949-661-1313. Captain Dave's Dolphin Safari offers ocean boat trips; call: 949-488-2828. Dana Wharf Sportfishing offers ocean trips for whale watching or sport fishing; call: 949-496-5794. Additional services, harbor-view restaurants, and shops are located at the foot of Street of the Golden Lantern.

Off the west end of Dana Point Harbor Dr. is the stillwater "Baby Beach," popular for swimming or wading; lifeguard service available. Baby Beach is also a good place to launch human-powered craft; kayak rentals are adjacent. Park in the no-fee lot next to the OC Sailing and Events Center, which offers public programs for young people and adults in sailing, rowing, and marine safety, including summer camps; call: 949-923-2215. A wheelchair-accessible fishing platform is located west of Baby Beach. At the end of Island Way is a grassy, waterfront "picnic park," with tables, barbecue grills, and restrooms. Nice views of boats in the harbor, but the breakwater obscures the ocean beyond.

Doheny State Beach

CATALINA EXPRESS TERMINAL: *34675 St. of the Golden Lantern, Dana Point.* Year-round boat service is available to Avalon on Catalina Island; for information and reservations, call: 310-519-1212.

OCEAN INSTITUTE: *24200 Dana Point Harbor Dr., Dana Point.* The Ocean Institute offers classes, educational programs, and boat trips. On weekdays most programs are for school groups, but public tours of the Institute are offered on weekends from 10 AM to 3 PM; fee applies. The gift shop is open daily from 9 AM to 5 PM. For schedules or reservations, call: 949-496-2274. Walk seaward around the Ocean Institute to reach a lovely beach next to the Dana Point Harbor breakwater; do not disturb tidepool creatures.

DOHENY STATE BEACH: *Shoreline E. of Dana Point Harbor, Dana Point.* This crescent of sand ringed by tall palm trees evokes the South Seas. Enter from Park Lantern, off Dana Point Harbor Dr. The day-use area near the entrance has spacious, well-tended lawns with picnic tables, fire rings, and food concessions. There are also sand volleyball courts and wheelchair-accessible boardwalks; ask at the entrance kiosk for a beach wheelchair, or call: 949-496-6162. The small aquarium and visitor center at the entrance is planned for renovation by 2009. The San Juan Creek Bikeway, which runs along the west side of the creek, begins just north of Doheny State Beach and continues inland past San Juan Capistrano.

The state beach campground has 120 family sites, some beachfront, including hike and bike sites and four wheelchair-accessible sites. Wheelchair-accessible showers; RV dump station. For camping reservations, call: 1-800-444-7275. For park information, call: 949-496-6172. South of the campground is another day-use beach, accessible from Pacific Coast Hwy. via a pedestrian overpass above the railroad tracks; shoulder parking.

CAPISTRANO BEACH PARK: *Pacific Coast Hwy. and Palisades Dr., Capistrano Beach.* This compact park fronts a part-sand, part-cobble beach. Pay-station parking, basketball court, summertime concession stand, restrooms, beach showers; lifeguard service is provided. Call: 949-923-2280.

"San Juan is the only romantic spot on the coast," wrote Richard Henry Dana, Jr. in *Two Years Before the Mast*, his famous book chronicling life as a sailor in the 1830s. "The country here for several miles is high table-land, running boldly to the shore, and breaking off in a steep cliff, at the foot of which the waters of the Pacific are constantly dashing." Enjoying a short rest with his crewmates at the spot now called Dana Point in his honor, he got caught up in his rocky, wave-splashed surroundings and was full of praise: "What a sight, thought I.... There was a grandeur in everything around.... Not a human being but ourselves for miles, and no sound heard but the pulsations of the great Pacific! ... Compared with the plain, dull sand-beach of the rest of the coast, this grandeur was as refreshing as a great rock in a weary land," he enthused.

Dana had landed in "San Juan" (near the mission of San Juan Capistrano) at the beginning of May, 1835. He was sailing aboard the *Pilgrim*, a brig which had left Boston in 1834 when Dana was 19 years old, surviving stormy seas rounding Cape Horn, and then traveling up and down the California coast between San Diego and San Francisco. The *Pilgrim's* crew spent the trip collecting huge quantities of cattle hides and tallow and trading many assorted wares brought from Boston, including wine, shoes, and "everything under the sun," as Dana described.

A full-sized replica of the *Pilgrim* is now berthed at Dana Point Harbor next to the Ocean Institute and is open for tours on most Sundays between 10 AM and 2:30 PM. Visitors can climb aboard, sing sea chanteys, and learn from docents in period costume how to raise the sails. Public programs on the ship are given by the Ocean Institute and they also include summer theatrical shows as well as living history programs for school children on board the *Pilgrim* and another tall ship, the *Spirit of Dana Point*. For more information, call: 949-496-2274.

Dana Point Ocean Institute, *Spirit of Dana Point* berthed

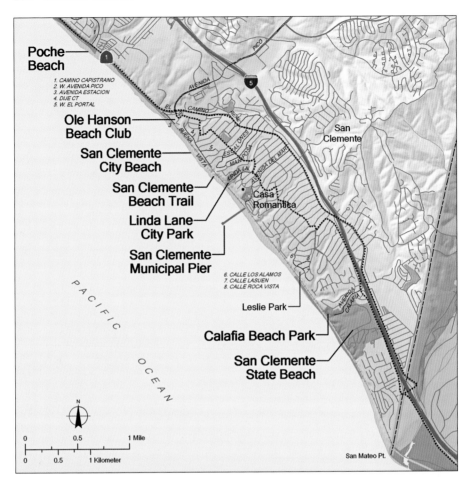

Poche Beach

1. CAMINO CAPISTRANO
2. W. AVENIDA PICO
3. AVENIDA ESTACION
4. DIJE CT
5. W. EL PORTAL

Ole Hanson Beach Club

San Clemente City Beach

San Clemente Beach Trail

Linda Lane City Park

San Clemente Municipal Pier

Casa Romantica

San Clemente

6. CALLE LOS ALAMOS
7. CALLE LASUEN
8. CALLE ROCA VISTA

Leslie Park

Calafia Beach Park

San Clemente State Beach

PACIFIC OCEAN

San Mateo Pt.

N

| 0 | 0.5 | 1 Mile |
| 0 | 0.5 | 1 Kilometer |

San Clemente Beach Trail

San Clemente

	Sandy Beach	Rocky Shore	Trail	Visitor Center	Campground	Wildlife Viewing	Fishing or Boating	Facilities for Disabled	Food and Drink	Restrooms	Parking	Fee
Poche Beach	•											
Ole Hanson Beach Club									•	•		
San Clemente City Beach	•	•				•	•		•	•		
San Clemente Beach Trail			•				•					
Linda Lane City Park	•									•		
San Clemente Municipal Pier		•				•	•		•	•	•	
Calafia Beach Park	•	•					•		•	•	•	•
San Clemente State Beach	•	•	•	•	•		•			•	•	•

POCHE BEACH: *Foot of Camino Capistrano at Pacific Coast Hwy., Capistrano Beach.* A beach of mixed sand and cobbles is located opposite the end of Camino Capistrano. Beach access is by foot only; cross Pacific Coast Hwy. and walk down the stairway under the railroad tracks. Accessway hours are 6 AM to 10 PM. No alcohol or glass containers on the beach; dogs not allowed. There is metered parking along Camino Capistrano. For information, call: 949-923-2280.

OLE HANSON BEACH CLUB: *105 W. Avenida Pico, San Clemente.* The beach club features a 25-yard-long heated outdoor swimming pool given to the community by Ole Hanson in 1928. Swim trials were held here in preparation for the 1932 Los Angeles Olympic games. The city of San Clemente operates the pool for swim classes and also for public recreational and lap swimming. The Spanish colonial-style club building and the landscaped grounds are available for parties and weddings. For swim hours or facility information; call: 949-361-8264.

SAN CLEMENTE CITY BEACH: *Beach area from Avenida Estacion to San Clemente State Beach, San Clemente.* Over two miles of beach extend from North Beach, near the Ole Hanson Beach Club, south to San Clemente State Beach. Railroad tracks run close to the shore, and beach-goers use designated crossings to get from the San Clemente Beach Trail to the water's edge. North Beach has children's play equipment, lifeguard towers staffed during the summer, concession stand, restrooms, beach showers, and metered parking at beach level; there is a controlled pedestrian crossing at the railroad tracks. Farther south, the west ends of Dije Court and W. El Portal, both off Buena Vista, have steep stairs leading down to the San Clemente Beach Trail, and there is a railroad undercrossing at W. El Portal. The end of W. Mariposa has a steep paved ramp to the shoreline. Other beach accessways north of the San Clemente Municipal Pier include Linda Lane City Park and the end of Corto Ln., where there is a long, steep stairway.

South of the Municipal Pier, there is beach access at the end of Avenida Esplanade, where a pedestrian railroad overpass and stairway lead to the beach; lifeguard, restrooms, showers, picnic facilities, and metered parking are available. A half-mile farther south, access to the San Clemente Beach Trail is available via a steep stairway starting at 2006½ Calle Los Alamos (called the Lost Winds accessway) and a short, nearly level path from the north end of Plaza a la Playa (called Riviera accessway); a railroad undercrossing to the beach is located at the Riviera accessway. Another railroad undercrossing (called Montalvo) is 200 yards farther south. On the blufftop, on Calle Los Alamos at the end of Calle Roca Vista, is Leslie Park, a small landscaped area with an ocean view but no beach access or facilities.

Glass containers, smoking, open fires, alcohol, and dogs are prohibited on the beach in San Clemente. For beach information or to reserve a beach wheelchair, call: 949-361-8219. For information about San Clemente's Junior Lifeguard Program, call: 949-361-8261. For a recorded surf and weather report, call: 949-492-1011.

SAN CLEMENTE BEACH TRAIL: *Shoreline from North Beach to Calafia Beach Park, San Clemente.* The multi-use San Clemente Beach Trail extends more than two miles along the shore, inland of the oceanfront railroad tracks. (The coast highway in San Clemente, called El Camino Real, runs even farther inland.) The Beach Trail, funded in part by the State Coastal Conservancy, links all of the city's shoreline access points and serves as part of the California Coastal Trail. Boulders and fences separate trail users from the railroad tracks, and beach-goers cross at underpasses or signalized grade crossings. The trail is part boardwalk and part packed earth and is wheelchair accessible; leashed dogs are allowed.

Railroad crossing at San Clemente City Beach

LINDA LANE CITY PARK: *Linda Lane, San Clemente.* An upland park, with lawns, a playground, picnic area, and metered parking, slopes down to the beach. From El Camino Real take Avenida Palizada to Encino Ln. and turn right to Linda Ln. A pedestrian underpass provides access to the beach.

SAN CLEMENTE MUNICIPAL PIER: *W. end of Avenida del Mar, San Clemente.* A popular fishing pier with food concessions, fish-cleaning sinks, a bait and tackle shop, restrooms, and lifeguard tower; open from 4 AM to midnight. Fish caught here include common perch and croaker species, mackerel, and bonito; anglers at this pier also capture a good number of sharks and rays. The beach adjacent to the pier has picnic facilities, outdoor showers, swings, and restrooms. There is metered parking on Avenida del Mar and pay-station parking lots nearby. Amtrak trains stop right at the pier. There is one underpass to the beach; other beach access is across the tracks. Full-service restaurant at the base of the pier. For information, call: 949-361-8219.

CALAFIA BEACH PARK: *Foot of Avenida Calafia, San Clemente.* Picnic areas, a snack bar, restrooms, outdoor shower, and a large metered parking area at beach level are available at this unit of San Clemente State Beach. There is access to the narrow sandy beach via a controlled pedestrian crossing over the railroad tracks. Lifeguard tower staffed during the summer.

SAN CLEMENTE STATE BEACH: *Off Avenida Calafia, San Clemente.* This state park provides both day-use and camping facilities. On the bluff there are 85 tent and 72 RV campsites, the latter with full hookups. Three tent and three RV campsites are wheelchair accessible, as are hot shower facilities. There is also a group campsite. For site-specific camping reservations, call: 1-800-444-7275.

A visitor center, in a beautiful Spanish colonial-style structure, is near the day-use parking area; open daily during the summer. Two steep trails lead down to the beach through eroded sandstone bluffs. Day-use and camping fees apply. Ask at the entrance kiosk for a beach wheelchair. For park information, call: 949-492-3156.

"I vision a place where people can live together more pleasantly than any other place in America. I am going to build a beautiful city on the ocean," wrote Ole (pronounced "Olee") Hanson, founder of the city of San Clemente. "The whole picture is very clear before me. I can see hundreds of white walled homes bonneted with red tile, with trees, shrubs, hedges of hibiscus, palms, and geraniums lining the drives. . . I want people to have more than a piece of land; I want them to have location, environment, development. . . .This will be a place where a man can breathe!"

That was how Hanson described his vision for the "Spanish Village by the Sea" that he began developing in 1925, when he set up a pair of tents and sold parcels of land for a master-planned community before such places were common. All buildings were white stucco with peaked red tile roofs, building plans had to be approved by an architectural board, and winding streets intentionally preserved the contours of the hillsides.

Hanson bought this land years after he had spied it from a passing train and thought of developing a village there. Before he created that village, he had moved from Wisconsin to Seattle by walking behind a covered wagon; had become mayor of Seattle; had gained widespread fame for ending a general strike and speaking out far and wide against "Bolshevism," and had even been considered as a presidential candidate in 1920. He succeeded in attracting buyers to San Clemente despite warnings that it wasn't a desirable location (being too distant from other major cities). By the late 1920s before the stock market crash, San Clemente had the reputation as the wealthiest city per capita in America.

Hanson's family home was built on a bluff overlooking the ocean and is now called Casa Romantica, operating as a cultural center open to the public. It was designed by architect Carl Lindbom, who also designed La Casa Pacifica in San Clemente; this was the estate of Hanson's business partner, Henry Hamilton Cotton, and later became known as the Western White House after President Richard Nixon purchased it in 1969. Ole Hanson's legacy includes the San Clemente Municipal Pier, the Beach Club, and the San Clemente Community Center (since rebuilt), all given by him to the city to help make it the ideal community he envisioned.

Visitor center at San Clemente State Beach

Geology of Coastal Southern California

THE NORTHWEST-to-southeast-trending mountain ranges of Orange and San Diego Counties are part of the geologic province known as the Peninsular Ranges. Only the northern tip of this province is located in California; the bulk of the province encompasses the long spine of Baja California. The salient feature of this province is a series of igneous rocks known as the Peninsular Ranges batholith. These rocks were emplaced between 140 and 80 million years ago and, like the Sierra Nevada batholith to the northeast, are part of the great chain of Mesozoic plutons, or solidified magma bodies, that extends from British Columbia to Baja California. They represent the roots of an ancient volcanic belt that formed as a result of the subduction of the now-extinct Farallon Plate beneath the North American Plate. Through this process, dense oceanic rocks of the Farallon Plate descended beneath lighter continental rocks of the westward-drifting North American Plate.

The eastern part of the Peninsular Ranges batholith is made up of silica-rich rocks, such as granodiorite, that are generally 100 to 95 million years old. To the west, rocks containing less silica, such as gabbro, are found, and the rocks have been dated to as much as 140 million years old. In addition, geochemical evidence clearly indicates that the rocks on the western and eastern sides of the batholith came from distinct sources. This has led many geologists to believe that the Peninsular Ranges batholith in southern California formed in two stages. First, an oceanic volcanic arc (similar to modern day Japan) collided with North America and was accreted to it. Later, subduction of the Farallon Plate led to the generation of magma that, being less dense than the surrounding solid rock, ascended through it. As the magma ascended, it incorporated continental rocks into itself, producing silica-rich magmas. The generation of magma shifted to the east as subduction continued, leading to the formation of the younger, eastern belt of silica-rich igneous rocks.

The igneous rocks of the Peninsular Ranges were intruded into older rocks that can still be found preserved in San Diego County. Metamorphosed volcanic rocks, including the Santiago Peak Volcanics, are found in the Santa Ana Mountains and in the hills of western San Diego County. To the east of these rocks are metamorphosed sandstones and siltstones representing submarine canyon deposits some 175 million years old. These rocks give way to the east to the metamorphosed remnants of a carbonate platform, an accumulation of limestone formed primarily from the shells of marine sea creatures, that is found throughout southeastern California. This platform represents the tectonically quiet western margin of North America that existed before subduction began on the western margin of North America some 400 million years ago.

At the same time as the igneous rocks of the Peninsular Ranges were being emplaced, the rocks overlying them were being eroded and the resultant sediments carried to the sea. The coastline was somewhat east of its present location at that time, and these sediments, now transformed to sedimentary rocks and lifted above the sea by tectonic activity, can be seen in the bluffs at La Jolla and Point Loma. For the most part, they represent submarine canyon and submarine fan deposits. These rocks, the Point Loma and Cabrillo Formations, were deposited on the sea floor by turbidity currents, dense mixtures of water and sediment that periodically cascaded down submarine canyons. A similar process is occurring today in nearby La Jolla and Scripps Submarine Canyons. Some of the best-preserved rocks represent ancient channel deposits, and contain accumulations of coarse sediments rich in pebbles, cobbles, and boulders. A spectacular exposure of such rocks is visible in the bluffs at Tourmaline Surfing Park.

Along the coast between La Jolla and Oceanside the most prominent rocks are younger formations, deposited during the Eocene Epoch (which extends from 56 to 34 million years ago). This varied assemblage represents shallow marine, estuarine, beach, and dune deposits. Rocks of the Del Mar Formation are mostly fine-grained rocks such as shale and siltstone, and contain abundant fossils representative of lagoons and nearshore marine environments. The overlying Torrey Sandstone is a beautiful buff-colored rock made up of steeply cross-bedded layers indicating it was formed from wind-blown dunes, originally located on a barrier island beach. A layer of nearly solid oyster shells lies at the base of this unit and is exposed both at the northern and southern ends of the shoreline of Solana Beach, because the rocks are broadly folded into an arch at these locations. The oyster-shell bed is more resistant to erosion than both the overlying sandstones of the Torrey Formation and the underlying shales of the Del Mar Formation, and forms prominent reefs at these locations. Waves breaking on these reefs make two of North County's finest surfing breaks.

A period of nearly 40 million years went by during which it appears that no rocks were deposited in the San Diego area, or, if they were deposited, they have been removed by subsequent erosion. Such gaps are common in rock sequences, complicating the job of geologists intent on understanding the geologic history of a region. The last few hundred thousand years of geologic history is told in the landforms and sedimentary deposits near the present shoreline. Between the foothills of the Peninsular Ranges and the sea are a series of flat terraces, separated by steep slopes. Each terrace formed at a time of stable, or slightly rising, sea level. Waves cut an offshore platform and a sea cliff that marched landward through time as waves attacked the sea cliff at its base. A similar terrace is being cut offshore today, and a dramatic sea cliff rises above the waves throughout much of coastal southern California. During periods when sea level fell, the shoreline moved seaward. In tectonically active coastal California, the land is rising, elevating these terraces above sea level. As sea level has risen and fallen through geologic time, a whole flight of terraces has formed, with the highest being the oldest.

Cross-bedded layers in the Torrey Sandstone at Encinitas indicate deposition in a dune environment

These terraces are covered with ancient beach and marine deposits, in turn mantled by terrestrially derived sediments. These deposits range in age from about 1.2 million years on the highest terraces, to 80,000 years on the lowest terrace overlooking the sea.

There is one more geologic province that we must consider in order to understand the geology of coastal southern California. Extending nearly 200 miles offshore of Los Angeles, Orange, and San Diego counties, and from the northern Channel Islands to midway down the Baja California Peninsula, is a realm of great undersea mountain ranges, separated by deep basins. Some of these ranges reach above sea level, forming Santa Catalina, San Nicolas, San Clemente, and Santa Barbara Islands, as well as several sets of islands off Baja California. The basins between these ranges are as deep as 6,000 feet below the surface of the sea. This region, known as the Southern California Borderland, owes its rugged topography to a number of active faults, such as the Newport-Inglewood-Rose Canyon Fault, the Coronado Bank Fault, the San Diego Trough Fault, and the San Clemente Fault, along which the ranges have been uplifted. The western edge of the Southern California Borderland is marked by the Patton Escarpment, where the seafloor plunges to depths of 12,000 feet, marking the abyssal plain of the Pacific Ocean. This escarpment is a relict accretionary wedge presumably underlain by rocks similar to those of the Franciscan Complex of northern California. The geology of the Southern California Borderland is poorly understood, partly because it is almost entirely underwater and partly because many of the rocks are deeply buried beneath submarine fans derived from the ridges and from onshore. Nevertheless, gaining a better understanding of the tectonic setting of the Borderland is important for an understanding of the seismic risk associated with the many active faults in the area.

Ocean waves carve sea caves into rocks of the Cabrillo and Point Loma Formation at La Jolla Cove

Page opposite: Torrey Pines Gliderport, San Diego County

San Diego County

San Diego County

MISIÓN San Diego de Alcalá, the first of the 21 Alta California missions, was founded by Father Junípero Serra in 1769 on what later became known as Presidio Hill. On the same spot, the first presidio or fort in California was also established. Agricultural crops including olives, oranges, grapes, plums, corn, and wheat were planted, and herds of cattle were raised to supply food for the missionaries and the mission's Native American residents. Native peoples, called Diegueños by the Spanish missionaries, had by more than 10,000 years preceded the Spanish in settling the area, establishing permanent settlements at sites that included modern La Jolla, the bay side of Point Loma, and the shores of Mission Bay and San Diego Bay.

The village that developed adjacent to Mission San Diego, known today as Old Town, became the center for Spanish domain in Alta California and, briefly, the northern terminus of El Camino Real, which eventually led farther north to San Francisco. In the 1870s, the center of town shifted from Old Town to the "new town" on San Diego Bay, which soon became the nucleus of the present city.

San Diego County is rich in history and geographic diversity. Extending south 76 miles from the Orange County line to the Mexican border, the county lures tourists with its temperate, sunny climate, extensive sandy beaches, deserts, mountains, museums, marinas, parks, and the world-famous San Diego Zoo. North of La Jolla are raised marine terraces and beach ridges, coastal marshes and lagoons, canyon-cut mesas, and seaside villages. South of La Jolla, the coast forms lowlands with estuaries, sandy beaches, tidepools, and coves. Inland valleys, oak woodlands, and deserts spread east, rising to mountain ranges over 6,000 feet high.

San Diego is among the nation's most urbanized counties, and yet in 2006 the county had the nation's 12th-largest agricultural economy. Most farms in San Diego County are small, measuring less than 10 acres each, and over 90 percent are family-owned. Nearly one-quarter of the farmland in the county is held by Native Americans. High-value crops predominate; San Diego County leads the nation in production value of avocados, indoor flowering and foliage plants, and cut flowers.

Walk-in visitor centers run by the San Diego Convention and Visitors Bureau are found at the following locations:

Near downtown San Diego at 1040 West Broadway, near Harbor Dr. (619-236-1212).

In La Jolla at 7966 Herschel Ave., near Prospect St. (619-236-1212).

The privately owned San Diego Visitor Information Center is located on Mission Bay at 2688 East Mission Bay Dr. (619-276-8200).

The Coaster Train runs from San Diego to Oceanside, where Metrolink trains depart for Los Angeles. Coaster stops near the beach include Carlsbad, Encinitas, and Solana Beach. Comprehensive information about buses, trains, and all transit options for the San Diego region is available; call: 619-233-3004 or see: www.transit.511sd.com.

Ferryboats link Coronado and downtown San Diego, and water taxis serve San Diego Bay points, including the Padres' PETCO Park; call: 1-800-442-7847.

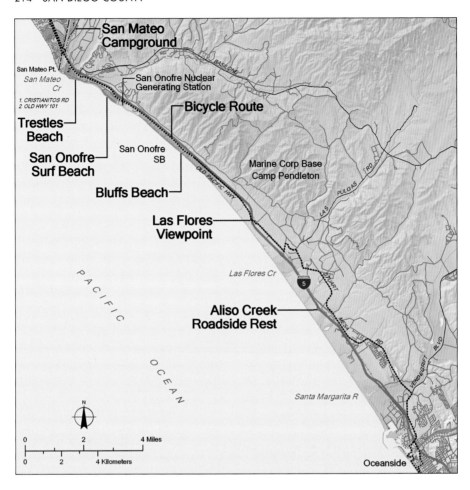

Trestles Beach

San Onofre

	Sandy Beach	Rocky Shore	Trail	Visitor Center	Campground	Wildlife Viewing	Fishing or Boating	Facilities for Disabled	Food and Drink	Restrooms	Parking	Fee
San Mateo Campground			•		•	•		•		•	•	•
Trestles Beach	•		•							•		
San Onofre Surf Beach	•							•		•	•	•
Bluffs Beach	•		•		•			•		•	•	•
Bicycle Route			•									
Las Flores Viewpoint										•		
Aliso Creek Roadside Rest								•		•	•	

SAN MATEO CAMPGROUND: *Off Cristianitos Rd. 1 mi. inland of Hwy. I-5, San Onofre.* One of two campgrounds at San Onofre State Beach, San Mateo Campground has 67 RV campsites with water and electrical hookups and 90 tent campsites in a lovely setting among trees. Coin-operated hot showers, wheelchair-accessible campsites, campfire programs, and junior ranger programs are offered. RV dump station available. For campground information, call: 949-492-4872. Reservations accepted year-round; call: 1-800-444-7275.

A mile-and-a-half-long trail leads from the campground to Trestles Beach. The trail follows San Mateo Creek, an intermittent stream with a drainage basin extending into Riverside, Orange, and San Diego Counties. Along the creek is riparian woodland, with trees such as sycamore, white alder, canyon live oak, and black willow. At the mouth of the creek are both freshwater and saltwater marshes. Chaparral growing on nearby slopes includes lemonadeberry, toyon, chamise, and laurel sumac.

TRESTLES BEACH: *Near mouth of San Mateo Creek, San Onofre State Beach.* Very popular and famous among surfers around the world are the long-ride surf breaks known collectively as Trestles. Surfers distinguish several sub-areas, including Middles, Lowers, and Uppers, with characteristic wave types that call for varying board lengths and different skills; an illustrated sign along the access path provides an overview. The main path to Trestles starts at a parking lot at Cristianitos Rd. and El Camino Real, near the southern boundary of San Clemente. The parking lot is open from 5 AM until 10 PM; a paved path leads under the I-5 freeway to the beach, about a three-quarter-mile walk. Another popular surf spot, known as Cottons, is reached by walking upcoast from Trestles on the sand, around San Mateo Point.

SAN ONOFRE SURF BEACH: *Off Basilone Rd., San Onofre.* Exit the freeway at Basilone Rd., head south on the old Pacific Hwy., and follow signs to Surf Beach, a long curving stretch of sand. At the beach are restrooms and beach showers, surfboard racks, and an unpaved parking area; ask at the entrance station for a beach wheelchair. Upcoast of Surf Beach is the Marine Corps recreational beach, which is not open to the public.

BLUFFS BEACH: *Seaward of Hwy. I-5, on Old Pacific Hwy. 2.5 mi. S. of Basilone Rd. off-ramp, San Onofre.* From the Basilone Rd. off-ramp, drive south two miles past the San Onofre Nuclear Generating Station to the Bluffs Beach unit of San Onofre State Beach. Day-use facilities are open year-round, from 6 AM to sunset; camping is allowed only from May to October. There are 173 campsites in a three-mile-long paved strip near the railroad tracks. There are no hook-ups and showers are cold only, but there is an RV dump station. Fees for day use and camping. Six trails lead down the steep bluff to the beach; dogs are allowed on Trails 1 and 6. For information, call: 949-492-4872.

BICYCLE ROUTE: *Seaward of Hwy. I-5 from San Clemente through San Onofre State Beach.* A paved bike route runs from Cristianitos Rd. through the Bluffs Beach unit of San Onofre State Beach. Security conditions permitting, bicyclists may proceed on old Hwy. 101 through Marine Corps Base Camp Pendleton to Las Pulgas Rd. Turn left on Las Pulgas Rd., then enter Camp Pendleton gate and continue south on Stuart Mesa Rd. to Oceanside gate. Riders must carry picture ID, wear a helmet, and ride single file.

LAS FLORES VIEWPOINT: *W. of Hwy I-5, 5 mi. S. of San Onofre.* Parking area with a view of the adjacent bluffs and the beach.

ALISO CREEK ROADSIDE REST: *W. of Hwy. I-5, 6 mi. N. of Oceanside.* Landscaped area with picnic tables, a dog run, and a map display showing local points of interest.

The southern California steelhead (*Oncorhynchus mykiss*) is an anadromous fish, meaning that it hatches in freshwater streams, spends its adult life in the ocean, and then returns to fresh water to spawn. The steelhead population in southern California can be distinguished from other population groups found as far north as Alaska. Southern California steelhead have adapted physiologically to withstand the dry and warm conditions present in this region. Juvenile southern California steelhead grow faster than more northerly steelhead, due to the elevated water temperatures, and they enter the sea at a younger age. Juveniles typically migrate to the ocean in their first year, and adult fish return to spawn after a period of one to four years in the ocean. Adults also show a greater ability to "stray" from their home stream when they return to spawn, a trait necessary to survive the unpredictable stream water levels of southern California.

Steelhead populations have been significantly depleted from all rivers and streams within their historical range. The southern California steelhead population was listed as a federally endangered species in 1997. The southern boundary for this species was established at Malibu Creek in Los Angeles County, because no steelhead had been described in any watersheds south of this creek in the previous 20 years. In 1999, after hearing tales of the steelhead that his grandfather once caught in a local stream, a young fisherman decided to try his luck and proceeded to catch a steelhead in San Mateo Creek in northern San Diego County. This event prompted further investigation, which turned up several more steelhead from this watershed and eventually led in 2002 to an extension of the range of southern California steelhead south to the Mexican border.

Nowhere in coastal California can you see a geologic fault with greater clarity than at San Onofre State Beach. Take any of the trails leading from the Bluffs Beach campground down to the beach. At the northern end of the beach there is a good view of the bluff, with the San Onofre Nuclear Generating Station in the background. The lower 30 to 40 feet of the bluff consists of two types of rock, separated by the Cristianitos Fault. To the northwest is white San Mateo Sandstone, four to five million years old. To the southeast, across the slightly curving fault trace, is a brownish shale of the 15-to-20-million-year-old Monterey Formation. The rocks have been brought together by movement on this fault. But when did this movement occur? Clearly, it must have occurred after the youngest rocks were deposited, about four million years ago. The fault must be older, however, than any undisturbed rocks that we find across it. The upper part of the coastal bluff at this location consists of nearly 100 feet of sand and gravel, the lowest six feet or so being a well-defined bed of boulders. These materials are deposited on a wave-cut platform that was elevated as the land rose. Notice that the boulder bed directly over the wave-cut platform is continuous and not offset by the fault. Clearly the fault had stopped moving by the time these boulders were deposited. Geologic dating of fossil shells found in these deposits indicates that the wave-cut platform—and the boulder layer—are about 125,000 years old. Thus, the fault has not moved since that time, and can safely be considered inactive.

A bench lies well below the top of the coastal bluff. This bench, like others to the south, is the top of a massive landslide. The coastal bluff in the southern part of San Onofre State Beach is breaking away in a series of such landslides, forming benches and curved amphitheaters in the bluff. The toes of these landslides lie offshore and can be recognized as reefs on which the waves break. These landslides occur where the bluff is made up of shales of the Monterey Formation—a notoriously weak rock. The Monterey Formation lies south and east of the Cristianitos Fault; to the west and north are the stronger sandstones of the San Mateo Formation. The nuclear power plant rests firmly on these stronger rocks and is not likely to be subject to the kind of landslides we see to the south.

Part of the Cristianitos Fault can be observed as the darkest diagonal line running upward from lower left to middle right, approximately at center of photo

Oceanside Harbor

THERE ARE few natural harbors along the California coast. Many of the ports and boat harbors along the coast have been constructed specifically to provide safe anchorage areas for commercial and recreational vessels. These harbor construction projects provide safe anchorage; but they have altered the way waves and currents meet the shore and how sand moves along the coast. In northern San Diego County, the construction of Oceanside Harbor and the Camp Pendleton Turning Basin has modified "coastal processes," in ways both predictable and unpredictable.

The initial harbor at Oceanside, the Camp Pendleton Turning Basin, was developed beginning in the early 1940s, after the Marine Corps acquired the Rancho Santa Margarita y Las Flores, located just north of the present City of Oceanside and between the Santa Margarita and the San Luis Rey Rivers. The Marine Corps needed a small craft harbor for training exercises and to off-load large landing craft. The Rancho land provided ocean access, but presented challenges for navigation. First, harbors need to have deep water areas in the channels and berthing areas to allow safe navigation. Furthermore, shoaling (filling in with sediment) can be a significant concern when a harbor is located adjacent to a river. Both of the rivers adjacent to Rancho Santa Margarita carry large volumes of sediment to the coast, which would cause the harbor areas to shoal. However, during World War II, the war-time need for a military training area outweighed the potential problems with locating this facility between two sources of sediment.

The Marine training area, including the Camp Pendleton turning basin, was excavated from a lowland area along the coast and was connected to the ocean by a navigation channel. It began to shoal almost as soon as the navigation channel was constructed. The Marine Corps built "arrowhead" jetties at the channel entrance in an attempt to reduce the shoaling. As their name suggests, these jetties were built widest at the shoreline and narrower toward the ocean. This configuration was supposed to reduce wave energy and keep the waves from carrying sand into the turning basin. But the jetties did little to prevent the filling of the turning basin, and soon the north jetty was

Camp Pendleton Turning Basin, 2006

Oceanside Harbor, 2006

redesigned and extended, forming the attached breakwater that exists at Oceanside today. Construction of the breakwater, however, resulted in the shoaling location being moved to the end of the breakwater. The turning basin was used for training maneuvers, but by the end of World War II, due to shoaling, deep draft vessels could enter or leave the harbor only during times of high tide.

After World War II, new residents and visitors flocked to San Diego County for jobs and to enjoy mild weather, beautiful beaches, and year-round opportunities for water sports. In the mid-1950s, the jetties at Oceanside were expanded one last time in an effort to deal with the sedimentation problems. At the same time, the City of Oceanside began planning the construction of a small craft harbor close to the turning basin. The City of Oceanside tried for a number of years, without success, to interest the Marine Corps in sharing the breakwater with a non-military, city-run marina. One day, as the story has it, the mayor of Oceanside and a Marine Corps general went duck hunting together, and the conversation turned to the Marine Corps's turning basin. The result was that the general agreed to consider some mutually beneficial use of the breakwater, provided that there would be no adverse consequences to the turning basin or military maneuvers. The City obtained about 67 acres of land from the Marine Corps, added these 67 acres to another 33 acres already owned by the City, and subsequently excavated the Oceanside Small Craft Boat Harbor that is located immediately south of the turning basin. The City's small craft boating facility and entrance channel are south of, and separated from, the turning basin; both the small craft harbor and the entrance channel are in the lee of the Marine Corps-built breakwater.

Immediately after the new turning basin was built, the beaches south of Oceanside Harbor started to erode. Local beaches had reportedly been almost 300 feet wide in the late 1880s, but they began eroding soon after installation of entrance controls for the turning basin. Between 1942 and 1980, approximately ten million cubic yards of sand and cobble were excavated to create the boating facilities or were dredged from the facilities to keep them functioning. Almost all of the sediment that was excavated to create the turning basin and the city's small craft harbor was placed on the beaches downcoast of Oceanside Harbor and the mouth of the San Luis Rey River. The sediment moved quickly through the littoral cell, and despite this large volume of nourishment material, those beaches downcoast of the Oceanside Harbor are now only narrow ribbons of sand, and homes along the beach often experience wave damage during the winter season. By contrast, north of the breakwater, the beach is fairly wide during much of the year, the sand being held on the beach by the breakwater.

One reason the impacts from the creation of Oceanside Harbor have been extensive is due to its location within the Oceanside Littoral Cell. "Littoral cell" refers to a segment of coast and its supply of sand and is used to describe sediment transport. The Oceanside Littoral Cell extends from Dana Point in Orange County to the La Jolla Submarine Canyon off La Jolla; Oceanside Harbor is near the "start" of the cell, where sand enters from farther north. The influence on sediment transport of changes to the shoreline at Oceanside can be noted throughout much of the littoral cell to the south.

The modifications of long-shore sediment transport patterns and the shifts in the width of beaches that have occurred near the Oceanside Breakwater are changes that have been seen in connection with many groins, jetties, and breakwater structures along the California coast. Examples include the breakwaters at Venice and Santa Cruz and Santa Barbara Harbors, the Marina del Rey jetties, and the groins at Will Rogers State Beach and El Segundo. The area of sand accretion upcoast of these structures has been called a "fillet." There is no comparable name for the down coast erosion spot; however, it has sometimes jokingly been referred to as the "empty-it."

In addition to changes in beach width, a second phenomenon that is developing at Oceanside Harbor is the accumulation of large volumes of sand in an extensive offshore sand bar. The bar seems to have accumulated over ten million cubic yards of sand, although due to the high cost of repeated studies of offshore bathymetry, some information on this bar is only estimated from sporadic and infrequent surveys. As scientists study this area, one theory about the Oceanside area is that the breakwater is diverting longshore currents into deeper water, carrying much of the sediment to the huge offshore bar. There it seems to be accumulating and not returning to the downcoast beaches that possibly received that sand before the breakwater was built. This phenomenon is not one that had been anticipated when the Oceanside Harbor was first developed.

Oceanside Harbor Fishing Pier

A rip current is an offshore current of ocean water that can carry large volumes of sand into deep water and, occasionally, endanger unwary swimmers. Rip currents often develop near coastal structures, such as breakwaters or groins, that project into the surf zone. Rip currents are a major pathway by which sand, wrack, decomposed organic matter, and other beach or shoreline material is moved from the beach to the nearshore zone. Structures perpendicular to the beach can set up small seaward currents and eddies that often develop into rip currents.

Rip currents that develop near structures are often considered "stable rips," since they tend to remain in one place. By contrast, rip currents that occur spontaneously along sand beaches will often change locations and not always occur in the same spot.

Rip currents are an important safety concern for recreational beach users. They are channels of water that move perpendicular to shore at speeds of one to two feet per second. Since rip currents carry water, floating material, and suspended solids offshore, the currents often can be identified by a break in the pattern of incoming waves, a change in water color or water surface, or by a seaward-moving line of seaweed, debris, or foam. Swimmers know to be wary of them and not struggle, but to swim parallel to shore if they get caught in one. Surfers know to take advantage of the breaks in the surf zone for a quick ride out to deeper water to wait for the next good ride.

North   South

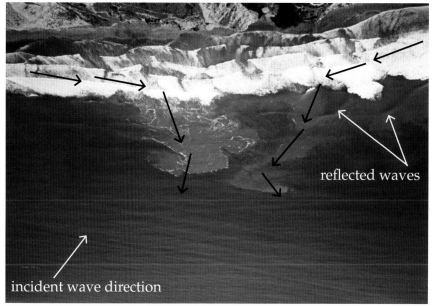

Two rip currents shown off the La Jolla bluffs. The currents, distinguished by their lighter color, are conveying sediment offshore. Black arrows indicate direction of rip current movement.

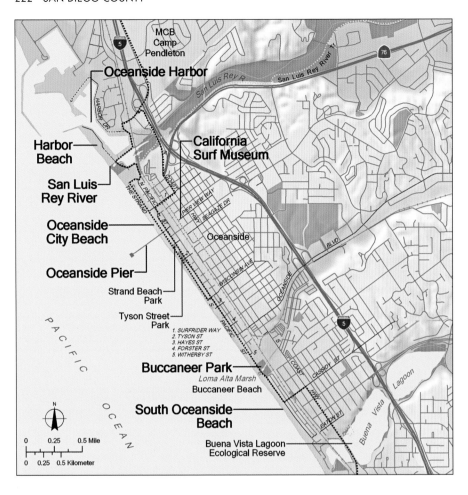

Oceanside City Beach with lifeguard vehicle

Oceanside

	Sandy Beach	Rocky Shore	Trail	Visitor Center	Campground	Wildlife Viewing	Fishing or Boating	Facilities for Disabled	Food and Drink	Restrooms	Parking	Fee
Oceanside Harbor			•	•	•	•	•		•	•	•	•
Harbor Beach	•			•		•	•		•	•	•	•
San Luis Rey River			•			•						
Oceanside City Beach	•	•		•	•	•			•	•	•	
Oceanside Pier				•		•	•		•	•	•	
California Surf Museum				•				•	•	•		
Buccaneer Park					•		•		•	•	•	
South Oceanside Beach	•					•	•				•	

OCEANSIDE HARBOR: *Along Harbor Dr., Oceanside.* The small-craft refuge at Oceanside Harbor was once beach and dunes. The harbor has berths for about 950 vessels and offers a wide range of boating and fishing services. A small commercial fishing fleet is also located at the harbor. Harbor facilities and services include a fuel dock, fishing pier, marine supplies, haul-out yard, charter sport fishing boats, fishing licenses, bait and tackle, lockers, and sailing instruction. A boat launching ramp on the west side of the harbor, with four concrete lanes, is open 24 hours; launching is free. There are 50 transient berths, which can be reserved in person at the Department of Harbor and Beaches office at 1540 Harbor Dr. North, Oceanside. For information, call: 760-435-4000.

A paved path runs along the harbor, providing views of the boats and of the sea. Picnic tables and restrooms are located along the path. Whale-watching trips are available from November to March, call: 760-722-2133. There are restaurants, shops, and hotels within the harbor. Some parking limited to boat slip holders; free public parking is off Harbor Dr. on the east side of the harbor.

HARBOR BEACH: *N. end of N. Pacific St., Oceanside.* Harbor Beach, facing the ocean on the south side of Oceanside Harbor, is Oceanside's widest beach. Volleyball and surf fishing are popular, and summertime ocean swells from the southwest produce good surfing conditions. There are cov-

ered picnic tables with firepits, playground equipment, and restrooms. Lifeguard towers are staffed during the summer months; ask for a beach wheelchair. Camping for self-contained RVs is available overlooking the harbor mouth; self-pay machines collect camping and day-use parking fees. For information, call: 760-435-4000.

SAN LUIS REY RIVER: *Harbor Dr. South and N. Pacific St., Oceanside.* The San Luis Rey River originates in the foothills of Mount Palomar. Common riparian tree species along the upper reach of the river include willow, western sycamore, and Fremont cottonwood. Songbirds, raptors, waterfowl, and small mammals use the riparian habitat for food and shelter. Where the river empties into the Pacific Ocean and forms a small lagoon, there is coastal saltmarsh vegetated with pickleweed and saltgrass. Fish such as bass, sunfish, chub, and mosquito fish inhabit the marsh waters, and the California least tern and the black-crowned night heron feed and rest near shore and in the lagoon waters. On the south bank of the river, the paved San Luis Rey River Trail extends from N. Pacific St. eastward a distance of more than seven miles, with underpasses at major roads.

OCEANSIDE CITY BEACH: *Along The Strand and S. Pacific St., between San Luis Rey River and Buccaneer Beach, Oceanside.* Oceanside City Beach extends along most of the city's ocean frontage, south of the mouth of the San Luis Rey River. The beach is very wide at the north end and narrower farther south. From Wisconsin Ave. south, residences line the sand, but the beach seaward of the homes is public. From Wisconsin Ave. north along Pacific St., a landscaped linear park lies on a low bluff, and ramps or stairways lead down to the beach at street ends. There is a vehicle turnaround north of Oceanside Pier at the end of Surfrider Way, where passengers can be dropped off, and south of the pier there are turnarounds at the ends of Hayes St. and Forster St. and beach access at the end of Oceanside Blvd. There are parking lots near the beach at the end of Seagaze Dr. and Wisconsin Ave., and additional lots are along Pier View Way, near Oceanside Pier; fee charged at some lots. Metered street parking also available.

Beach facilities include picnic tables, barbecue grills, outdoor showers, and restrooms. Lifeguard service is provided by the city of Oceanside; contact a lifeguard to use a beach wheelchair, including a manual model that can be used without assistance and also a motorized chair. A landscaped concrete walkway with benches runs along The Strand north of Oceanside Pier; dogs on leash are allowed on the Strand, but dogs are not allowed on Oceanside beaches. South of the pier are Strand Beach Park, at the end of Seagaze Dr.; and Tyson Street Park, at the end of Tyson St. Tyson Street Park is a grassy area with benches, a playground, and restrooms; the park is also accessible via stairs from S. Pacific St. Call: 760-435-4000.

OCEANSIDE PIER: *W. end of Pier View Way, Oceanside.* With a length of 1,954 feet, this municipal pier is the longest wooden pier on the West Coast. The pier is open 24 hours a day for fishing and viewing. Facilities include a bait and tackle shop, lifeguard station, and restrooms. Fishing poles can be rented on the pier; no fishing license required to fish from the pier, although catch limits apply. There is a full-service restaurant at the far end of the pier, a nice place to enjoy a meal and the view.

Strand Pier Plaza at the base of the pier includes a community center with meeting rooms and gym facilities; the center can be rented for special events, and the gym facilities are open to the public for a small fee. Fee parking. Call: 760-966-1406.

Oceanside Pier

Oceanside Harbor

CALIFORNIA SURF MUSEUM: *312 Pier View Way, Oceanside.* This museum, which moved in early 2009 to expanded facilities near the Oceanside Pier, displays dramatic surfing photos and vintage surfboards, some of which are huge and unwieldy looking. The museum's exhibits change annually. Gift shop; information about local surfing spots is available. Open from 10 AM to 4 PM daily; donations welcome. Call: 760-721-6876.

BUCCANEER PARK: *1500 block of S. Pacific St., Oceanside.* Grassy Buccaneer Park lies on the inland side of S. Pacific St., facing a fairly wide sandy beach. The park has a large no-fee parking lot, basketball court, children's play equipment, food concession, and restrooms. There is a path overlooking Loma Alta Marsh, where herons and snowy egrets may be seen feeding; dabbling ducks, ruddy ducks, and coots use the small lagoon.

SOUTH OCEANSIDE BEACH: *W. of Pacific St., between Buccaneer Park and Eaton St., Oceanside.* South Oceanside Beach is a continuation of Oceanside's city beach, which is increasingly narrow as you move south. The beach is largely out of sight from S. Pacific

California Surf Museum

St. due to a row of homes, but public beach access is available at several locations. One accessway is located opposite Buccaneer Park, and others are located one-half block north of Buccaneer Park and opposite Witherby St. Additional beach access points are adjacent to 1639 S. Pacific St., at the end of Cassidy St., and at 1919 S. Pacific St.; check a tide table before visiting, to estimate beach availability. For information on Oceanside beaches, call: 760-435-4000.

Coastal Lagoons

ALONG the southern California coast are a series of estuaries, from Malibu Lagoon in the north through Anaheim Bay and Upper Newport Bay in Orange County to the lagoons of San Diego County. The large, beautiful, and biologically complex lagoons along the San Diego coast include Buena Vista, Agua Hedionda, Batiquitos, San Elijo, San Dieguito, and Los Peñasquitos Lagoons, and the Tijuana River Estuary. The lagoons are mixed regimes of salt water and fresh water.

The behavior of these lagoons reflects southern California's long annual dry season. Most of the year, streams and small rivers have insufficient water volume and energy to counteract the tendency of ocean waves to push sand onshore. The sand forms a berm that the low flow of a river cannot breach, and the small volume of water delivered to an estuary throughout most of the year seeps out to sea through the berm. As summer wears on, river flow declines and the elevation of the water in the lagoon decreases. At the same time, water quality may be naturally impaired as oxygen is consumed and the shallow water warms up. With the first rains in the fall, the water level in the lagoon begins to rise, typically to the point that the sand berm is breached and water in the lagoon quickly flows to the sea. The lagoon may remain open to the sea, subject to tidal activity, for weeks or months as winter flows and tidal currents maintain the opening to the sea. As winter storms cease and river flows decline, the waves push sand up on the beach once again and close off the lagoon mouth.

The dynamics of a lagoon, where a river meets the ocean, are strongly influenced by the level of the sea. Sea level has been rising for the last 18,000 years. Due to global climate change, it seems likely that the current rate of sea level rise—about three millimeters per year—will increase in the future. The current rate, however, is minor compared to the rate at which sea level has changed in the recent geologic past. 18,000 years ago, sea level was as much as 400 feet lower than it is today. Over the past two million years, sea level has alternated between this level and more or less its present level.

Agua Hedionda Lagoon

San Elijo Lagoon

The effect of sea level change on the southern California estuaries has been profound. During periods of low sea level, the shoreline was a dozen or more miles west of its current location and as much as 400 feet lower than at present. Rivers responded to the change in sea level by incising their valleys downward, creating deep valleys at their mouths and pushing coarse sediment farther seaward than at high sea levels. During periods of relatively high sea level, such as the present, these valleys were flooded, and coarse sediment was deposited closer to the present shoreline. The resulting layers of sediment deposited at any one place in a lagoon thus alternate between sandy layers and finer layers consisting of silts and clays. The sandy layers hold water and make good aquifers, whereas the silts and clays are more impermeable to ground water. Where impermeable layers are near the surface, they support creation of wetlands, even where not inundated by lagoon waters. Deep below the surface, sandy aquifers carry groundwater to the sea, completing the hydrologic cycle.

Coastal lagoons and associated wetlands convey and dissipate floodwaters, reduce erosion by slowing runoff velocities, deposit flood-suspended sediments, stabilize the shoreline, recharge groundwater, and store surface water. The lagoons filter suspended sediments, remove organic and inorganic nutrients, remove toxic substances, and facilitate cycling of nitrogen and minerals. The coastal lagoon ecosystem is particularly important, because it exhibits very high primary and secondary biological productivity. Lagoons are both a source and a sink for nutrients and organic particulates. This productivity supports very diverse communities of aquatic invertebrates, fish, benthic species, and resident and migratory birds. In addition to physical and biological values, wetlands provide opportunities for recreation, education, and research, along with historic and archaeological values, and open space.

The San Diego County coastal lagoons represent approximately one-third of the remaining estuarine acreage in southern California. The San Diego County lagoons have been seriously affected by major transportation routes, including Interstate Hwy. I-5, the railroad corridor, and Pacific Coast Hwy. The lagoons are also heavily influenced by their urbanized watersheds. Runoff from surrounding developed areas, coupled with reduced tidal influence from restricted inlets, has resulted in problems such as low dissolved oxygen, excessive algal growth, eutrophication, presence of pathogens, excessive sedimentation, and suspended sediment. Nevertheless, the lagoons provide critical natural habitat for terrestrial and aquatic species. They serve as foraging areas and breeding grounds for a number of threatened and endangered species, and they are spawning and nursery habitats for commercial and non-commercial fish species.

Saltgrass

Saltgrass (*Distichlis spicata*) is characteristic of the upper marsh and transition zone in lagoons and estuaries but is also found growing in salty soils in inland areas. It is well adapted to a variety of environmental stresses. It has air spaces in its roots that enable them to obtain oxygen even when submerged. In areas that are frequently under water, most of the root mass is close to the surface, but in drier areas roots may grow deep to tap the water table. The leaf surface is dotted with crystals formed from salt excreted by salt glands. Most reproduction is vegetative, meaning clones of the original plant are formed by spreading rhizomes whose sharp tips are hardened with silica, aiding in soil penetration. Clones are able to colonize harsh microhabitats where seeds would never establish.

Killdeer

Killdeer (*Charadrius vociferus*) are the great actors of the local bird world. An adult killdeer drags a seemingly broken wing through the sand, to draw unwanted attention away from a nearby nest. Because the killdeer has adapted well to sharing its territory with human interlopers—among the killdeer's preferred nesting habitats are gravel parking lots—the audience for killdeer displays is often a human one. The foraging habitat of killdeer, a type of plover, is often no less peculiar; this is the plover that southern Californians are most likely to see flocking on vacant athletic fields. The *kill-dee* call and two black breast bands further identify these diminutive soccer players as killdeer.

Striped mullet

The **striped mullet** (*Mugil cephalus*) is one of the most characteristic fishes of tropical and subtropical lagoons and estuaries worldwide. When you see a big fish leap through the air and disappear with a splash in a southern California lagoon, it is probably a mullet. Large schools congregate near the mouths of estuaries in the fall. In answer to some unknown environmental cue, they then move en masse to deep, offshore spawning grounds. Their larvae migrate back to the estuary, where they inhabit the shallow, warmer waters of the intertidal zone. Even as tiny juveniles they form schools, which appears to reduce the risk of predation. When they reach about one inch in length they begin the transition from feeding on plankton to relying primarily on detritus and benthic algae for food.

The **fat innkeeper worm** (*Urechis caupo*) builds a U-shaped burrow in the soft, muddy sand located within low-zone mudflats along the California coast, near lagoons, tidal channels, and marshes. The worm derives its innkeeper moniker from the fact that several other organisms, including arrow gobies, pea crabs, and scale worms, also inhabit the burrow constructed and maintained by their "host" innkeeper worm. The innkeeper worm feeds by extending a mucous net over one end of its burrow, and then pumping water through the net and out the other end of the burrow. Small food particles are trapped in the net, which is then retracted and consumed by the innkeeper worm. The guest organisms in the burrow receive shelter from the burrow as well as food and running water from their host's feeding activities. Fat innkeeper worms average seven inches in length.

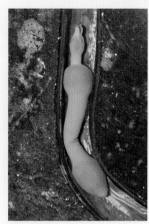

Fat inkeeper worm

The **ghost shrimp** (*Callianassa californiensis*), one of the most common inhabitants of mudflats, is seldom seen because it spends most of its life tunneling through the muddy bottom. This hyperactivity is related to the habit of processing sediments for detrital food. Ghost shrimp mine sand and mud from their tunnel walls, ingest the small bits, and cast off the larger particles, which they periodically gather up and deposit on the surface near the burrow entrance. In one square yard of mudflat, there may be well over 100 ghost shrimp, which together can entirely turn over the upper 18 or 20 inches of mud in a few months. These turbulent activities exclude some bottom-dwelling species, but help others. Small crabs and arrow gobies seek shelter in the burrows, whereas the filter-feeding California soft-shelled clam pokes its short siphons into burrows to take advantage of the continuous stream of surface water that the ghost shrimp pumps to supply its respiratory needs. A striking characteristic of ghost shrimp is the one huge claw of the males, which is useful for disputes involving space or females.

Ghost shrimp

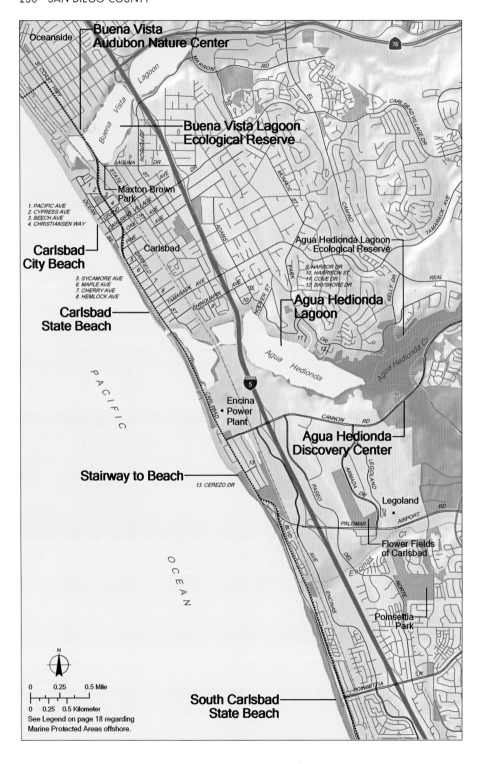

Oceanside

Buena Vista Audubon Nature Center

Buena Vista Lagoon Ecological Reserve

Maxton Brown Park

1. PACIFIC AVE
2. CYPRESS AVE
3. BEECH AVE
4. CHRISTIANSEN WAY

Carlsbad City Beach

Carlsbad

5. SYCAMORE AVE
6. MAPLE AVE
7. CHERRY AVE
8. HEMLOCK AVE

Carlsbad State Beach

Agua Hedionda Lagoon Ecological Reserve

9. HARBOR DR
10. HARRISON ST
11. COVE DR
12. BAYSHORE DR

Agua Hedionda Lagoon

PACIFIC

Agua   Hedionda

Encina • Power Plant

Agua Hedionda Discovery Center

Stairway to Beach

13. CEREZO DR

Legoland

AIRPORT

Flower Fields of Carlsbad

OCEAN

Poinsettia Park

N

0   0.25   0.5 Mile

0   0.25   0.5 Kilometer
See Legend on page 18 regarding
Marine Protected Areas offshore.

South Carlsbad State Beach

Carlsbad

	Sandy Beach	Rocky Shore	Trail	Visitor Center	Campground	Wildlife Viewing	Fishing or Boating	Facilities for Disabled	Food and Drink	Restrooms	Parking	Fee
Buena Vista Audubon Nature Center			•	•		•		•		•	•	
Buena Vista Lagoon Ecological Reserve			•			•	•			•		
Carlsbad City Beach	•					•				•		
Carlsbad State Beach	•	•				•	•	•	•	•	•	
Agua Hedionda Lagoon			•			•	•					
Agua Hedionda Discovery Center			•	•		•		•		•	•	
Stairway to Beach	•					•					•	
South Carlsbad State Beach	•	•	•		•	•	•	•	•	•	•	•

BUENA VISTA AUDUBON NATURE CENTER: *2202 S. Coast Hwy., Oceanside.* The Buena Vista Audubon Nature Center is located north of the lagoon, on South Coast Hwy. in Oceanside (the same road becomes Carlsbad Blvd. south of the lagoon, in the city of Carlsbad). The Nature Center offers displays of birds and other wildlife, docent-led walks at Buena Vista Lagoon and other lagoons, nature storytime for tots, and summer camps for older kids. There is a short trail along the lagoon shoreline. The Nature Center is open Tuesday to Saturday from 10 AM to 4 PM and on Sunday from 1 PM to 4 PM; for information, call: 760-439-2473.

BUENA VISTA LAGOON ECOLOGICAL RESERVE: *E. and W. of I-5, 2.5 mi. S. of downtown Oceanside.* Buena Vista Lagoon is an important resting and feeding site for migratory waterfowl on the Pacific Flyway. Ducks, geese, avocets, stilts, snowy egrets, black-crowned night herons, plovers, turnstones, and dowitchers are often seen in the lagoon. The lagoon also provides breeding sites for three endangered species: the light-footed clapper rail, California least tern, and Belding's savannah sparrow. Brackish water marsh plants such as pickleweed, saltgrass, cattail, and alkali bulrush grow along the margins of the lagoon.

Buena Vista Lagoon from Maxton Brown Park

Buena Vista Lagoon is segmented into four coastal ponds by transportation routes, including Carlsbad Blvd. and the I-5 freeway. Unlike San Diego County's other coastal lagoons, Buena Vista Lagoon receives no salt water inflow. The lagoon's opening to the ocean has become blocked since the 1940s, and sediment inflow has made it increasingly shallow. Cattails and bulrushes now heavily dominate parts of the lagoon. Without the influence of salt water, habitats are much less varied than they once were, or could be again. Possible restoration, to allow tidal influence and a saltwater environment at the west end of the lagoon while maintaining freshwater marsh at the east end, is under study. The lagoon is managed as an ecological reserve by the Dept. of Fish and Game. For information, call: 858-467-4201.

Although Buena Vista Lagoon is visible from roads surrounding and crossing it, there are few places to stop and get a close-up look. The Buena Vista Audubon Nature Center is one such spot; it is also possible to park on the shoulder of Carlsbad Blvd. where it crosses the lagoon. Farther east, a paved parking lot is located on Jefferson St. west of Marron Rd., but it is closed except during occasional public tours. Maxton Brown Park at the corner of Laguna Dr. and State St. on the south (Carlsbad) side of the lagoon provides a lovely distant view of Buena Vista Lagoon, along with benches, picnic tables, and barbecue grills. Call: 760-602-7513.

CARLSBAD CITY BEACH: *W. of Ocean St., between Pacific Ave. and Carlsbad Village Dr., Carlsbad.* The northernmost section of Carlsbad's long shoreline is a sandy stretch of beach popular for swimming, surf fishing, and surfing; surfing hours are restricted from May to October. Lifeguard towers are staffed during the summer. Residences line a low bluff above the sand, and access to the beach is via stairways along Ocean St.: at the north end of Ocean St. (north of the Army and Navy Academy), at the end of Cypress Ave. (push the gate open during daylight hours), and at the ends of Beech Ave., Christiansen Way, Grand Ave., and Carlsbad Village Dr. An additional beach access stair is located one-half block south of Carlsbad Village Dr. between two large palm trees; a beach shower is at the bottom of the stairway. Street parking. Beach fires are prohibited, and no dogs are allowed on Carlsbad beaches. For information, call: 760-602-7513.

CARLSBAD STATE BEACH: *W. of Carlsbad Blvd. between Pine and Tamarack Avenues, Carlsbad.* Also known as Robert C. Frazee Beach, this half-mile-long sandy beach is backed by a bluff. A paved walkway runs along the top of the bluff, next to Carlsbad Blvd., and ramps and stairs lead down to the beach. There are picnic tables, benches, and a grassy area on top of the bluff; stairways to the beach are located opposite the ends of Sycamore, Maple, Cherry, Hemlock, and Tamarack Avenues. There is a separate

Carlsbad City Beach at end of Ocean St.

paved bicycle path at the base of the bluff. Parking areas include a lot on Ocean St. south of Oak Ave., where a ramp leads down to the beach, curbside along Carlsbad Blvd., and at the end of Tamarack Ave. Lifeguard stations are staffed during the summer months. Dogs, skateboarding, bicycles, and alcohol are prohibited. Call: 760-438-3143.

South of the mouth of Agua Hedionda Lagoon, the sandy beach is part of Carlsbad State Beach. A paved path runs along Carlsbad Blvd., next to the beach, and there are short ramps down to the sand. Lifeguard towers (which are staffed seasonally) are spaced along the shore. Chemical toilets; shoulder parking.

AGUA HEDIONDA LAGOON: *E. and W. of I-5, 1.4 mi. S. of Carlsbad Civic Center, Carlsbad.*
Originally a salt marsh, Agua Hedionda Lagoon was extensively dredged and channelized in the 1950s to accommodate the Encina Power Plant, located seaward of the lagoon. The lagoon provides cooling water for the power plant, and the channel from the ocean to the lagoon is kept permanently open. The lagoon is also a popular recreation spot; unlike the other San Diego coastal lagoons, it supports motorboats and water skiing. Sailing and kayaking are also popular. In spite of alteration, Agua Hedionda provides a variety of habitat types, including mudflats, saltwater and freshwater marshes, and areas of deep water. Wading and diving birds, including western grebes, surf scoters, and ruddy ducks, can be seen in the lagoon waters. Forster's and Caspian terns frequent the lagoon.

Carlsbad State Beach

Overlooking the westernmost basin of Agua Hedionda Lagoon near the ocean is an area of informal paths off Garfield St., south of Tamarack Ave.; there are nice views, but no facilities. Carlsbad Aquafarm raises oysters and other shellfish in the west basin of the lagoon, and public tours of their facilities are offered occasionally; call: 760-438-2444. There is public access to the middle basin of Agua Hedionda Lagoon from the south end of Harbor Dr., off Chinquapin Ave.

The inner basin of Agua Hedionda Lagoon, located east of Hwy. I-5, provides separate open water areas for personal watercraft,

Carlsbad State Beach

Agua Hedionda Lagoon

powerboats, and non-motorized craft. A fee permit is required to boat in Agua Hedionda Lagoon; for an application, visit the Carlsbad Swim Complex at 3401 Monroe St.; for information, call: 760-602-4685. The only public launch area for motorboats is at the end of Harrison St., where California Watersports, a private vendor, provides a launch ramp, a loading dock, boat and motor sales, equipment rentals, snack bar, picnic area, and restrooms; fees apply. For information, call: 760-434-3089. Small craft may be hand-launched from the shore near the end of Bayshore Dr. Public lateral access along the lagoon is also available west of the end of Bayshore Dr.; the area is open between sunrise and sunset. Fishing is allowed in very limited areas of the lagoon, and no boat anchoring is allowed anywhere. No swimming or wading in the lagoon.

Several informal dirt paths offering views of the inner basin of Agua Hedionda Lagoon lead to the shoreline from Adams St. east of Hoover St. and at the end of Hoover St. From the end of Cove Dr., a paved walkway leads to the shoreline, where a public trail managed by the Agua Hedionda Lagoon Foundation continues about 500 feet west, and a separate public accessway extends a short distance to the east. From Park Dr. at the end of Kelly Dr., a dirt path leads along a thicket, part of an ecological reserve managed by the Department of Fish and Game. Good birding; bring binoculars.

AGUA HEDIONDA DISCOVERY CENTER: *1580 Cannon Rd., Carlsbad.* Open since 2006, the Agua Hedionda Lagoon Foundation Discovery Center provides a variety of programs and exhibits, including a native plant garden, talks on natural history, and demonstrations by Paa'ila Indian basket weavers. The Foundation is also working to expand the public trail network adjacent to the lagoon. The Discovery Center is open on Monday from 10 AM to 4 PM, on Wednesday and Friday from 11 AM to 4 PM, and on Saturday from 12 noon to 4 PM. Free entry; for information, call: 760-804-1969.

Legoland California Resort, a popular children's amusement park in Carlsbad, includes the Sea Life Aquarium featuring freshwater fish, sharks and other marine species, and tidepool animals that are native to California. Fee for entry; for information, call: 760-918-5346.

Eastern basin, Agua Hedionda Lagoon

STAIRWAY TO BEACH: *Carlsbad Blvd. opposite end of Cerezo Dr., Carlsbad.* A stairway next to a residential complex provides access down the bluff to a narrow beach, part of South Carlsbad State Beach. Shoulder parking; no facilities available.

SOUTH CARLSBAD STATE BEACH: *W. of Carlsbad Blvd. opposite Poinsettia Ln., Carlsbad.* Within the stretch of shoreline between Cerezo Dr. and Poinsettia Ln. are day-use and camping facilities, which are part of South Carlsbad State Beach. There is intermittent shoulder parking along the southbound lanes of Carlsbad Blvd., where the beach is right next to the road. Lifeguard towers are spaced along the sand, as are chemical toilets. The Ponto North day-use parking lot, accessible to southbound traffic only, is located three-quarters of a mile south of Palomar Airport Rd.

Farther south still is the South Carlsbad State Beach campground. The campground is located opposite Poinsettia Ln., but vehicle entry to the campground is only from northbound or southbound Carlsbad Blvd. The campground has 220 campsites, separated by trees, on a narrow bluff above the sea. Facilities include hot-water, token-operated showers, a self-service laundry, convenience and bait store, beach equipment rentals, and an RV dump station. Ten campsites are wheelchair-accessible; a beach wheel-chair is available from the ranger station. Stairways lead down the steep bluff to the beach, which is popular for swimming, surfing, surf fishing, and diving. Camping fees apply. For park information, call: 760-438-3143. For camping reservations, call: 1-800-444-7275; site-specific reservations are accepted. No day-use parking is available within the campground; some roadside parking is available along the southbound lanes of Carlsbad Blvd. adjacent to the campground; pedestrian gates allow access to the beach between 7 AM and sunset.

Agua Hedionda Lagoon Discovery Center

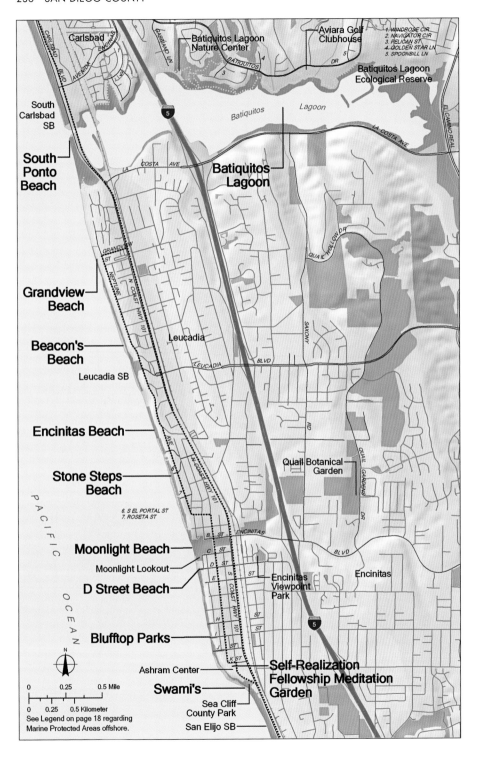

South Carlsbad and Encinitas

	Sandy Beach	Rocky Shore	Trail	Visitor Center	Campground	Wildlife Viewing	Fishing or Boating	Facilities for Disabled	Food and Drink	Restrooms	Parking	Fee
South Ponto Beach	•					•	•	•	•	•	•	•
Batiquitos Lagoon			•	•		•		•	•	•		
Grandview Beach	•						•			•		
Beacon's Beach	•						•			•		
Encinitas Beach	•						•			•		
Stone Steps Beach	•	•					•			•		
Moonlight Beach	•						•	•	•	•	•	
D Street Beach	•	•					•			•		
Blufftop Parks						•				•		
Self-Realization Fellowship Meditation Garden								•	•	•		
Swami's	•	•					•	•	•	•		

SOUTH PONTO BEACH: *W. of Carlsbad Blvd., at mouth of Batiquitos Lagoon, Carlsbad.* A wide stretch of sand, part of South Carlsbad State Beach, is located at the mouth of Batiquitos Lagoon. The lagoon mouth is stabilized by jetties and continuously kept open to the sea. The jetties are constructed of flat rocks, allowing foot access on top of them. Offshore from the lagoon mouth is a favorite surfing spot, called Ponto.

There is intermittent shoulder parking along the southbound lanes of Carlsbad Blvd., next to the sand; do not block the bicycle lane. There is also a large parking area called Ponto South, accessible to southbound traffic only. The parking lot is open from 7 AM to sunset; adjacent restrooms have running water. Lifeguard towers, staffed seasonally, are spaced along the beach. Except during very high tides, beachgoers can walk south along the narrow beach for several miles, to Moonlight Beach in Encinitas and beyond. From the Ponto South parking lot, a staircase leads up to a blufftop lookout, from which there is a panoramic view of the coast.

South Ponto Beach

BATIQUITOS LAGOON: *E. and W. of I-5, N. of La Costa Ave., Carlsbad.* The lagoon, which has been dredged to keep it from filling in with sediment, is split by bridges into three basins. The small west basin can be glimpsed from Carlsbad Blvd., but there is no formal public access. A splendid view of the middle basin can be had from a Carlsbad city blufftop park on the north side of the lagoon. From Carlsbad Blvd., take Avenida Encinas east to Windrose Circle and turn right. An unsigned dirt path, starting just west of Navigator Circle, leads 300 yards south to an observation platform and short trail above the lagoon; bring binoculars or a spotting scope to view wildlife. Shoulder parking; no facilities.

The large east basin of Batiquitos Lagoon can be viewed close-up from a two-mile-long nature trail that starts at the south end of Gabbiano Ln. At that location, there is a small parking area, as well as the Batiquitos Lagoon Nature Center, operated by the nonprofit Batiquitos Lagoon Foundation. The Nature Center is open Monday through Friday from 9 AM to 12:30 PM and Saturday and Sunday from 9 AM to 3 PM; for information, call: 760-931-0800. The Nature Center and part of the nature trail are wheelchair accessible. Additional parking lots and access points to the Batiquitos Lagoon shoreline trail are located along Batiquitos Dr. at four locations: Pelican St.; opposite the end of Golden Star Ln.; at the Aviara Golf Clubhouse; and opposite Spoonbill Ln. A more distant, high-level view of Batiquitos Lagoon is available from a parking lot located south of the east basin, off La Costa Ave. east of Hwy. I-5.

GRANDVIEW BEACH: *1700 Neptune Ave., Encinitas.* A stairway, located between residences, leads down the steep bluff to a narrow sandy beach. Opposite the stairway on Neptune Ave. north of Grandview St. is a no-fee parking lot, open from 5 AM to 10 PM. A lifeguard tower on the sand is staffed during the summer months. Grandview Beach is managed by the city of Encinitas; call: 760-633-2740. On Encinitas beaches, no glass containers or alcohol are allowed; dogs not permitted. For current surf and tide report, call: 760-633-2880.

The Leo Carrillo Ranch Historic Park, an Old California-style rancho, is located at 6200 Flying LC Lane, off Carrillo Way near Melrose Dr. in eastern Carlsbad. The adobe buildings are surrounded by gardens, and there is a four-mile-long loop trail through open space reserves. There is a visitor center, and no-fee walking tours are available. No dogs allowed, except service animals. The grounds are open daily except Monday, while the buildings have more limited open hours; for information, call: 760-476-1042.

BEACON'S BEACH: *Neptune Ave. at W. Leucadia Blvd., Leucadia.* Also known as Leucadia State Beach, but operated by the city of Encinitas and known locally as Beacon's Beach. A steep switch-backed trail with railings leads down the bluff face from an off-street parking lot on Neptune Ave. Lifeguard tower on the beach is staffed during the summer. Good surfing, swimming, surf fishing, and skin diving. For information, call: 760-633-2740.

Beacon's Beach

Moonlight Beach

ENCINITAS BEACH: *Between Beacon's Beach and Stone Steps Beach, Leucadia.* Steep cliffs and blufftop residential development limit access to this narrow beach. Walk south along the beach from the Beacon's Beach stairway or north from Stone Steps Beach.

STONE STEPS BEACH: *W. end of S. El Portal St., off Neptune Ave., Encinitas.* A long stairway, partly of stone, leads to a narrow sand and cobble beach. The city of Encinitas provides lifeguard service; the tower is staffed during the summer. Limited streetside parking along Neptune Ave., which is one way northbound. One block south of El Portal St., at the end of Roseta St., there is a blufftop viewpoint with benches but no beach access.

MOONLIGHT BEACH: *W. ends of B and C Streets, Encinitas.* Moonlight Beach is a wide, sandy spot along an otherwise narrow shoreline. At the end of C St. there is a beach parking lot and the nicely landscaped Moonlight Lookout, which has a paved path, picnic tables, and benches. At the end of B St. there is a drop-off point for pedestrians and parking for disabled visitors, but no general parking. On the beach are sand volleyball courts, equipment rentals, a snack bar, picnic tables, fire rings, outdoor showers, and restrooms.

Six blocks inland of Moonlight Beach along D St. is Encinitas Viewpoint Park, which has lawns, picnic tables, and a high-level vantage point from which to view an ocean sunset. Across the street from the park is Encinitas's striking new city hall. One mile inland of the beach, on Quail Gardens Dr. north of Encinitas Blvd., is Quail Botanical Gardens. The garden includes 35 acres of varied plantings, including native plants from southern California's coastal sage scrub and maritime chaparral plant communities and exotics from some of the world's rainforests and deserts. A colorful succulent garden mimics the appearance of an undersea coral reef, while a firescape garden offers ideas on landscaping for fire safety. Open from 9 AM to 5 PM daily, except Thanksgiving, Christmas, and New Year's Day. Admission fee is waived on the first Tuesday of each month. Call: 760-436-3036.

Year-round lifeguard service provided by the city of Encinitas; inquire at the lifeguard station for a beach wheelchair. For beach information, call: 760-633-2740. For current surf and tide report, call: 760-633-2880. No glass containers or alcohol; dogs are not allowed on the beach.

D STREET BEACH: *W. end of D St., Encinitas.* A landscaped viewing area is located on top of the bluff, and a long, wooden stairway leads down to the sand and cobble beach. Lifeguard tower is staffed seasonally. Limited on-street parking. An informal, view-only overlook is located at the end of E St.

BLUFFTOP PARKS: *W. ends of H St., I St., and J St., Encinitas.* Small grassy parks at three street ends offer views of the coast, but no beach access. Benches and on-street parking at each location, plus a picnic table at the end of I St.

SELF-REALIZATION FELLOWSHIP MEDITA-TION GARDEN: *215 K St., Encinitas.* A lovely semi-tropical garden offers a peaceful spot for meditation and views of the sea; the garden is located on the grounds of the Ashram Center, established by Paramahansa Yogananda in 1937. Open Tuesday to Saturday from 9 AM to 5 PM and on Sunday from 11 AM to 5 PM. Commercial photography and bathing attire are prohibited. For information, call: 760-753-2888.

SWAMI'S: *W. of Coast Hwy. 101, S. of K St., Encinitas.* Swami's is known for its large surf; fishing, diving, and swimming are also popular. City of Encinitas lifeguards staff the beach during the summer months. Also known as Sea Cliff County Park, the blufftop area has a pleasant garden and a shady picnic area with barbecue grills, restrooms, and a heavily used, no-fee parking lot. An outdoor shower is located near the base of the stairway. The beach extends southward for more than a mile; north of the stairway, a rocky reef extends into the surf zone. Do not disturb tidepool life. For beach information, call: 760-633-2740. For a current surf and tide report, call: 760-633-2880.

Self-Realization Fellowship Meditation Garden

Encinitas is known for the cultivation of poinsettia plants. The poinsettia is named for Joel Roberts Poinsett, who was appointed in 1825 by President John Quincy Adams as U.S. ambassador to Mexico. Diplomacy was Poinsett's vocation, but botany may have been his real love. In Mexico, he came across the plant known by the ancient Aztecs as *cuitlaxochitl* and by modern plant-lovers as the poinsettia (*Euphorbia pulcherrima*). The flamboyant red bracts, or top leaves, are more noticeable than the plant's small flowers. In its native Mexico, the poinsettia grows as a shrub or small tree in the subtropical and tropical highlands and blooms during the shortest days of the year. Poinsett propagated the plant and passed it on to friends who did the same.

One poinsettia grower was southern California's Albert Ecke, who raised the plants for sale during the winter holidays, first in Hollywood and later, starting in 1923, in Encinitas. The climate in San Diego County suited the poinsettia plants, which came from relatively cool, high-elevation areas of the tropics. Encinitas had the additional advantage of convenient rail service for distribution of the plants. For 40 years, poinsettias were field-raised at the Encinitas ranch for spring shipment to greenhouses, where they would be brought to bloom by the end of the calendar year. By the 1960s, shipment by air began to be employed for the greenhouse-grown cuttings, which included new and bushier varieties of the plant. In recent years, some steps in production have shifted offshore, but more than half of the world's flowering poinsettias still begin life at the Paul Ecke Ranch greenhouses in Encinitas. Research and breeding of new commercial varieties of poinsettias, including cultivars with pale-colored and speckled bracts, also continues in Encinitas. Visitors can see displays of the plants at the Flower Fields in nearby Carlsbad, along with 50 acres of spring-blooming ranunculus, a sweet-pea maze, and other flowers. This commercial attraction is open usually from March to May; fee applies. For information, call: 760-431-0352.

Poinsettia plants

Moving Beaches, Shifting Sands

C ALIFORNIA'S coastline is ever-changing. The changes reflect the dynamic interactions between the geologic characteristics of the land and the area off-shore, as well as land uplift, subsidence, and deformation from seismic events; environmental factors of wind, rain, and solar drying; and the coastal factors of tides, currents, and waves. Not only is the shoreline itself dynamic, but also the seemingly immovable rocks, reefs, cliffs, and rivers are subject to alteration.

Coastal bluffs may have the appearance of stability, but rain can erode the upper part of a coastal bluff, cut or enlarge gullies, and carry large volumes of sediment into streams flowing to the coast. Episodes of heavy rain are a source for much of the sand that moves along the coast, forming and reforming the beaches. Bluffs and gullies deposit sands at the back edge of the beach, where it can be sorted and carried into the littoral system by waves washing onto the beach. Besides sediments eroded from bluffs, there are sediments carried by rivers. These sediments are deposited at the mouths of streams in flood and ebb deltas, and from there the sand moves along the coast by waves and currents.

In the recent past, major floods have caused river channels to migrate, shifting the location of river mouths overnight. The Los Angeles River shifted location many times throughout the Los Angeles basin before being channelized in its current location, with its mouth at Long Beach. The San Diego River's mouth shifted between San Diego Harbor and Mission Bay until 1876, when levees were built to fix the river flow through Mission Bay and thereby minimize sedimentation of San Diego Bay.

Beaches, perhaps the most popular shoreline feature, are changeable, too. The basic concept of beach dynamics, called a sand budget, explains changes in beach width through a sand volume accounting system that says if the amount of sand entering a segment of beach is equal to or greater than the amount of sand leaving the beach area, then the beach width should stay the same or expand. If, on the other hand, the amount

Seal Beach, Orange County

of sand leaving the beach is greater than the amount of sand entering the beach, then beach erosion occurs. Variability in river sediment delivery and in bluff erosion changes the volume of sand reaching the beach and the locations where sand will deposit.

Waves and currents move beach sand up and down the coast. The dominant direction of sand transport tends to be from north to south along most of the southern California coast. Swell from southern hemisphere storms and some El Niño storms can move sand from south to north, and in some locations sand may make many trips past a given location before moving out of the littoral cell. The most significant locations where sand moves out of the cell are at submarine canyons, such as Redondo, Scripps, and La Jolla Canyons. A distinctive pattern of sand transport is found in southern San Diego County, in the Imperial Beach Littoral Cell, where the dominant direction of sediment transport is from southeast to northwest.

Beach sand tends to move not only laterally along the coast, but also onto and off shore. Wide beaches near coastal rivers and streams tend to have seasonal changes in width, reflecting the movement of sand onshore by low-energy waves and offshore to sand bars during the winter by high-energy waves. Marine development may create sand deposition areas. The offshore Santa Monica Breakwater, located parallel to the shore just north of the pier, was constructed as an anchorage for small boats, but it quickly became a beach stabilization feature. Sand accumulated in the lee of the breakwater, forming a salient that at one time almost connected the shore with the breakwater. The salient became a barrier to longshore transport of sand and caused almost a mile of the upcoast beach to widen and remain fairly stable.

Santa Monica State Beach, Los Angeles County

Along much of the southern California coast, sand transport volumes have changed significantly in the last century and a half. Clearing of vegetation and land development have mobilized large volumes of surface sediment; fires and fire suppression have changed the volumes of mobile sediment; flood control channels, dams, and reservoirs have reduced the carrying capacity of coastal streams and trapped sediments that would otherwise reach the coast. The net result of all these human activities has been the reduction of beach sand supplies.

The expectation from the sand budget concept is that beaches will erode or retreat landward if supplies of sediment from streams and other sources decrease. However, as researchers have focused on sediment supplies and losses and on volumes of sand on the beach, the enormous losses of available sediment that have occurred in southern California have not caused the magnitude of beach erosion that would be expected. One hypothesis for the differences between changes in available sand volume and beach width is that significant volumes of beach sand are coming to shore from offshore sand deposits; however, these offshore contributions have never been well-quantified. There is still much to be learned about the dynamic coast.

The southern California coast has a wide variety of beach types. There are many wide sandy beaches along the shore of Santa Monica Bay, in northern Orange County, and, in San Diego County, at Oceanside, Ocean Beach, Mission Beach, and Pacific Beach. There are picturesque pocket beaches at Laguna Beach and La Jolla and around Catalina Island and the other Channel Islands. In northern San Diego County locations such as San Onofre, Encinitas, Solana Beach, and Torrey Pines, there are narrow beaches that overlie a shallow bedrock platform and are backed by steep coastal bluffs. And there are some areas of the coast where there is no dry beach at all, and the toe of the coastal bluff is beneath the surface of the ocean.

Pocket beaches are small segments of beach confined between rocky headlands or points and often have a slight crescent shape. They tend to be fairly stable, exhibit small changes from year to year, and behave differently from wide sand beaches. The main seasonal beach changes for pocket beaches are shifts of sand within the limits of the rocky points—moving on and off shore or shifting up and down coast to align with the direction of incoming wave energy. Many of these beaches, like those along the coast at Laguna Beach or La Jolla, are backed by fairly durable bedrock that is resistant to wave erosion. Seawalls that have been built at the back of pocket beaches serve mainly to protect development that is located too close to the bluff edge. Or, since many pocket beaches form where the bedrock is jointed and fractured, shore protection at these beaches is intended to prevent joints and fractures from further enlarging and threatening development.

Narrow beaches backed by coastal bluffs have a different dynamic from both wide sand beaches and pocket beaches and tend to be greatly influenced by water level and wave energy. The beach and back shore often interact as a coordinated system. When the beach is wide, it can protect the back shore from wave attack. As the beach narrows, the bluff backing the beach will be hit more frequently by waves, and the bluff will erode inland. The bluffs often erode through a process of notch undercutting. As the notch deepens, the rest of the upper bluff has less support and stability. The undercut erosion is usually very gradual, and the erosion or retreat of the main portion of the bluff is normally episodic and extensive, as slabs of bluff measuring five to ten feet thick collapse suddenly onto the beach. This bluff failure supplies some sediment to the beach, moves the bluff face farther from the wave attack, and, if not subject to human intervention, leads to a beach bluff system where the beach is wider and the bluff is again protected from frequent wave attack. This process repeats up and down the beach and bluff system. The narrow-beach-and-bluff system often takes a fairly linear shape, indicating that the beach and bluff retreat dynamic has tended to be fairly consistent for long segments of the coast.

The linear shoreline characterized by a narrow beach and gradually retreating bluff has been interrupted in many locations by seawalls, which attempt to protect development on the upper bluff by halting the notch undercut and lower bluff erosion. One style of bluff protection wall consists of massive I-beam and soldier pile structures that dominate the visual character of the shoreline. These walls have many visual and environmental drawbacks, and the bluff protection wall designs have changed over time to a system of smaller tieback walls with a visual coating that allows the walls to blend into the surrounding natural bluffs. The main purpose of the walls, either large I-beam walls or smaller tieback walls, is to halt erosion and prevent retreat of the back beach.

It is often said that seawalls protect the land or development inland of the walls but do nothing to protect the beach seaward of the wall. On narrow beaches backed by bluffs, walls that protect the bluffs will interrupt the beach and bluff retreat system, and as the beach continues to erode, there will be no further bluff retreat to contribute sand and put the beach and bluff system back into balance. Over time the beach will tend to disappear. As more seawalls are built along narrow-beach-and-bluff sections of the coast, this imbalance will increase, and beach areas will narrow more and more, unless steps are taken to augment the available beach with nourishment sand. It can be important to pay attention to tides before starting a long beach walk along a narrow beach backed by a high bluff, because some areas that can be passable during a low tide may have no available dry beach during a high tide.

Tieback seawalls in San Diego County; wall is colored to blend with bluff

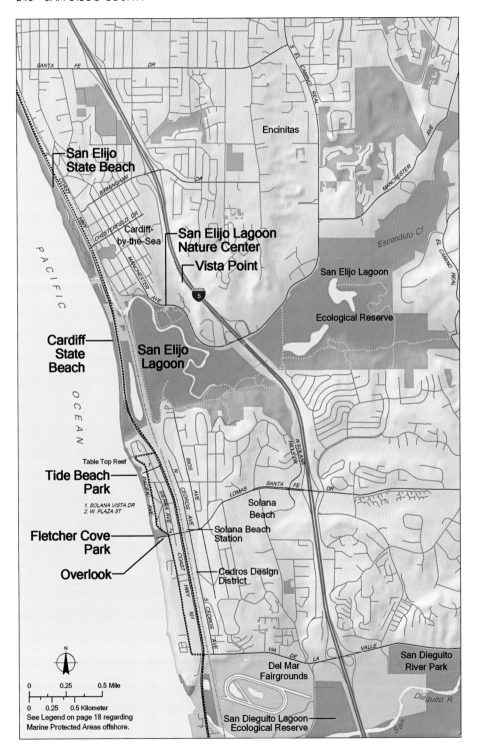

San Elijo State Beach

Encinitas

San Elijo Lagoon Nature Center

Cardiff-by-the-Sea

Vista Point

San Elijo Lagoon

San Elijo Lagoon

Ecological Reserve

PACIFIC

Cardiff State Beach

San Elijo Lagoon

OCEAN

Escondido Cr

Table Top Reef

Tide Beach Park

1. SOLANA VISTA DR
2. W. PLAZA ST

Solana Beach

Fletcher Cove Park

Solana Beach Station

Overlook

Cedros Design District

San Dieguito River Park

Del Mar Fairgrounds

San Dieguito Lagoon Ecological Reserve

Dieguito R

N

0   0.25   0.5 Mile

0   0.25   0.5 Kilometer
See Legend on page 18 regarding
Marine Protected Areas offshore.

Cardiff-by-the-Sea and Solana Beach

	Sandy Beach	Rocky Shore	Trail	Visitor Center	Campground	Wildlife Viewing	Fishing or Boating	Facilities for Disabled	Food and Drink	Restrooms	Parking	Fee
San Elijo State Beach	•	•			•	•	•	•	•	•	•	•
San Elijo Lagoon Nature Center			•	•		•		•		•	•	
Vista Point										•		
San Elijo Lagoon			•			•				•		
Cardiff State Beach	•	•				•	•		•	•	•	
Tide Beach Park	•					•	•			•		
Fletcher Cove Park	•					•	•			•	•	
Overlook						•						

SAN ELIJO STATE BEACH: *Coast Hwy. 101, .2 mi. N. of Chesterfield Dr., Cardiff-by-the-Sea.* All of the shoreline of Cardiff-by-the-Sea is within one of two state beaches: San Elijo State Beach, which offers camping and day use, and Cardiff State Beach, for day use only. The campground includes 171 sites on a narrow bluff above the beach. Campsites can accommodate trailers up to 35 feet long; sites with hookups can accommodate RVs with a wheelbase of up to 24 feet. Campground facilities include coin-operated hot showers, laundry, a grocery store, bait shop, ATM, surfboard rentals, and restrooms. The campfire center offers weekly nighttime film screenings, and there is a junior ranger program. Stairways lead down to a partly sandy, partly cobble beach, which is popular for surf fishing, swimming, diving, and surfing; beach showers available. Fee for camping. For reservations, call: 1-800-444-7275. For park information, call: 760-753-5091.

Vehicle entry to the San Elijo State Beach campground from Coast Hwy. 101 is from the southbound lanes only (that is, a right turn). Pedestrian entry to the park is at the end of Chesterfield Dr., where there are signalized pedestrian crossings of Coast Hwy. 101 and the adjacent railroad tracks. On the inland side of Coast Hwy., there is a landscaped footpath that runs north and south along the east side of the railroad tracks.

A separate day-use parking area is located 300 yards north of the San Elijo State Beach

San Elijo State Beach

San Elijo Lagoon Nature Trail

campground entry; approach from either northbound or southbound Coast Hwy. 101. A paved ramp runs down the bluff face to the beach. Restrooms available. Day-use parking is open sunrise to sunset; fee applies for parking within the state beach; some parking is also available along the highway shoulder. A paved path runs north along the top of the bluff seaward of Coast Hwy. 101.

SAN ELIJO LAGOON NATURE CENTER: *2710 Manchester Ave., .7 mi. W. of Hwy. I-5, Encinitas.* The old nature center is planned by 2009 to be replaced by a new, larger facility, containing exhibits about the San Elijo Lagoon Ecological Reserve. Already in place is a fully wheelchair-accessible, raised boardwalk loop that leads from the parking area through a thicket of arroyo willows and along the edge of the salt marsh. The parking area is open from 9:30 AM to 5:30 PM. For information, call the nonprofit San Elijo Lagoon Conservancy: 760-436-3944.

VISTA POINT: *San Diego Fwy. (Hwy. I-5), S. of Birmingham Dr., Cardiff-by-the-Sea.* Accessible only from the southbound lanes of Hwy. I-5; the vista point overlooks San Elijo Lagoon and the Pacific Ocean.

SAN ELIJO LAGOON: *E. and W. of I-5, S. of Manchester Ave., Encinitas.* San Elijo Lagoon offers a wide range of habitats and good locations to view birds and other wildlife. Rising tides bring ocean water into the west basin of the lagoon, which is dominated by salt marsh vegetation such as pickleweed, saltgrass, alkali heath, and other salt-tolerant species. Farther east in the lagoon, brackish to freshwater species of marsh vegetation predominate. Eight miles of public trails are located along the south side of San Elijo Lagoon, both west and east of Hwy. I-5, off Lomas Santa Fe Dr. From a trailhead at the north end of Rios Ave in Solana Beach, trails lead in several directions. One short fork leads northwest into the marsh. Another trail, part of it marked with plant identification signs, leads eastward to N. Solana Hills Dr. Along the way look for arroyo willow, lemonadeberry, and coast prickly pear.

A second major trailhead is located near the east basin of San Elijo Lagoon, in Rancho Santa Fe, on El Camino Real south of La Orilla. From that point, the trail heads west for over three miles, past riparian woodland, marsh, and coastal sage scrub plant communities. Look here for the endangered coastal

California gnatcatcher. The same trail can also be reached from the north ends of Santa Inez Dr., Santa Carina Dr., and Santa Helena Dr. The lagoon is jointly managed as an ecological reserve by the San Diego County Dept. of Parks and Recreation and the California Dept. of Fish and Game; for information, call: 858-467-4201.

CARDIFF STATE BEACH: *Coast Hwy. 101, directly W. of San Elijo Lagoon, Cardiff-by-the-Sea.* This day-use park offers swimming, surfing, and surf fishing. The proximity of kelp beds and sandy beach provide shore anglers with the opportunity to catch sandy-shore species, such as croakers, perch, sharks, and rays, as well as the occasional reef species, such as calico bass and sand bass. Facilities include restrooms, outdoor showers, picnic tables on the sand, and racks for waxing surfboards. The parking lot is at beach level, and there is a landing and launch zone for hand-carried and soft-bottom boats; the launch area is closed in summer. The beach is patrolled by lifeguards year-round, and lifeguards staff the towers in summer. For information, call: 760-753-5091. Fee for parking; parking lot hours are 7 AM to sunset. No parking on the adjacent highway shoulder, but some shoulder parking is permitted south of the strip of seaside restaurants. There is public pedestrian access along the shoreline seaward of the restaurants.

The large Seaside day-use parking area is located three-quarters of a mile south of the Cardiff State Beach parking area. Facilities include lifeguard towers, restrooms, and beach showers. Fee for parking. Table Top Reef and its tidepools are inhabited by marine life south of the parking area.

TIDE BEACH PARK: *Pacific Ave. at Solana Vista Dr., Solana Beach.* A stairway leads down the bluff, opposite the end of Solana Vista Dr., to a sandy pocket beach. Street parking; there are beach showers, but no restrooms. Tidepools are at the north end of the beach. Lifeguards are on site from 10 AM to 6 PM, during summer months only.

FLETCHER COVE PARK: *End of W. Plaza St. (west extension of Lomas Santa Fe Dr.), Solana Beach.* A paved ramp leads to a sandy beach in an indentation in the high bluffs. The beach is also known as Pillbox from its World War II-era role as a gunnery installation. There is a paved viewing platform at the base of the bluff, reachable by a ramp. For recorded surf and tide information, call: 858-755-2971.

The beautifully designed park above the beach includes rock retaining walls with mosaic artwork and colorful succulent plants. Facilities include picnic tables, a children's play area, a half-court basketball area, amphitheater, outdoor showers, and restrooms.

Cardiff State Beach

Fletcher Cove Park

There is a small, no-fee parking lot, and an additional no-fee lot is located one-half block farther south on Sierra Ave. In Solana Beach, glass containers and smoking are prohibited on all beaches. Dogs, other than guide animals, are not allowed on beaches or beach accessways or in beach parking lots; leashed dogs are allowed in Fletcher Cove Park from sunrise to 9 AM and from 4 PM to sunset.

Solana Beach Department of Marine Safety headquarters are located in Fletcher Cove Park; lifeguards at the cove are on duty daily, from 8 AM to 6 PM in winter, and from 8 AM to 8 PM in summer. The city of Solana Beach offers a popular junior lifeguard program for boys and girls from 9 to 17 years in age. Participants learn water safety, lifesaving techniques, physical fitness, and respect for the marine environment. For information, call: 858-720-4445. The Community Center Building, located at 133 Pacific Ave. overlooking Fletcher Cove Park, can be rented for private functions; call: 760-793-2564.

Amtrak and Coaster trains stop at the Solana Beach station, at 105 N. Cedros Ave., three blocks east of Fletcher Cove Park. The train tracks have been placed below grade in this area, and there is easy pedestrian access across the rail line. A nearly-two-mile-long paved path, landscaped with exceptionally colorful flowering plants, runs along the west side of the railroad tracks. Fanciful mosaic-tiled arches adorn the route. This segment is Solana Beach's share of the planned Coastal Rail Trail, a multi-use path alignment that runs from Oceanside all the way to the old Santa Fe depot in downtown San Diego. To the south of Lomas Santa Fe Dr. along Cedros Ave. is the Cedros Design District, with art galleries, home design shops, and a Sunday afternoon farmer's market.

OVERLOOK: *S. of Fletcher Cove parking lot, Solana Beach.* A stairway leads up from the south side of the Fletcher Cove parking lot to blufftop viewpoints among residential structures. There are panoramic views of the ocean and coastline.

"Biodiversity," or biological diversity, refers to the variety of plants, animals, and other living things in a particular place or region. Biodiversity can also be used to describe the diversity of genes within a species, or the diversity of biological communities, ecosystems, or landscapes in a larger area. Biodiversity measures are sometimes used as indicators of the health of biological systems. San Diego County is very rich in biodiversity. Along with the rest of California, San Diego County is among the top ten "biodiversity hotspots" on earth. Biodiversity hotspots harbor the greatest concentrations of living species, especially endemic species, which are those that are found nowhere else on earth. San Diego County, which has a greater variety of native plant species than any other county in the continental US (more, even, than many states) aptly bears the label of biodiversity hotspot.

San Diego County's Mediterranean climate (hot, dry summers and cool, wet winters), varied topography and soils, and physiographic regions that include not only the coast, but also foothills, mountains, and Sonoran Desert, together create a number of distinct habitats. Habitat types include beaches, salt marshes and lagoons, coastal sage scrub, grasslands, chaparral, oak woodlands, riparian areas, mixed conifer forests, freshwater marshes and meadows, and desert. This incredible habitat diversity in turn supports the huge variety of native plants, as well as animals and micro-organisms, that are found here.

In addition to the vast number of native plant species in San Diego, the county is a "conservation hotspot" because of the large numbers and variety of rare, threatened, and endangered species

that it supports. Plant species listed in those categories include the Torrey pine, San Diego thornmint, Encinitas baccharis, thread-leaved brodiaea, coastal dunes milk-vetch, and salt-marsh bird's beak. A few of the listed animal species are the San Diego fairy shrimp, Quino checkerspot butterfly, tidewater goby, arroyo toad, red-legged frog, least Bell's vireo, coastal California gnatcatcher, coastal cactus wren, light-footed clapper rail, and the Pacific pocket mouse.

Quino checkerspot butterfly

San Diego thornmint

San Dieguito and San Onofre

L IKE MANY COASTAL ESTUARIES in San Diego County, the San Dieguito wetlands located north of the city of Del Mar have been artificially divided by the construction of old Hwy. 101, the coastal railroad, and Hwy. I-5. These barriers have had profound negative effects on water movement. The extensive wetland fill, urban construction, and coastal bridges have constrained the location of the mouth of the estuary, which often fills with sand. As a result, the estuary frequently has been isolated from the renewing effects of the ebb and flow of the tides.

As part of the power company's habitat restoration activities, the Southern California Edison Company will maintain an open inlet at San Dieguito Lagoon in perpetuity. In return for ensuring the beneficial effects of tidal flushing on the whole estuary, the company will receive from regulatory agencies a restoration "credit" of 35 acres. Also at San Dieguito Lagoon, Edison began in 2006 the massive grading necessary to restore 115 acres of degraded wetland to salt marsh, mud flats, shallow open water habitats, and nesting sites for California least terns. The excavation of some two million cubic yards of earth will be accomplished over a period of two to three years. After completion of the restoration project, the public will be able to visit this wonderful wetland world and hike along miles of trails that are being constructed by the San Dieguito River Park, the interagency parks authority that is one of the principal backers of this major wetland restoration.

Why is an electric utility company that is responsible for supplying electricity to some 13 million California residents improving coastal habitats at San Dieguito Lagoon? The reason is to offset the enormous environmental impacts of the San Onofre Nuclear Generating Station, of which Southern California Edison is the major owner. The San Onofre Nuclear Generating Station (SONGS) is located in northern San Diego County adjacent to the Marine Corps Base Camp Pendleton. The large domes of Units 2 and 3

San Dieguito Lagoon restoration in progress

View seaward of San Dieguito Lagoon restoration in progress

are visible from Hwy. I-5, and the multiple lines of transmission cables that cross the freeway carry enough power to supply 2.75 million households. Unit 1 was shut down in 1992 after 25 years of power generation. Units 2 and 3 are expected to operate at least until 2022.

As with conventional power plants, the power source (in this case nuclear fission) is used to boil water to create the steam that turns the turbines to generate electricity. However, a great deal of excess heat is created, and the steam has to be cooled and condensed back into water before flowing once again to the steam generator. The necessary cooling is accomplished by pumping cold ocean water into the plant through 18-foot diameter pipes buried in the sea floor. The cooling water takes up the excess heat and carries it back to the shallow coastal sea.

The cooling process has a number of environmental impacts. All the small planktonic organisms and fish larvae that are in the water are killed when they pass through the cooling condensers, and larger animals, like fish (and occasionally turtles and seals), that are sucked in end up on a screen that is designed to prevent kelp and animals from clogging the system. Most of the fish are able to escape through a fish return system, but one or two hundred pounds of fish and other animals are killed each day. These sources of mortality, called "entrainment" and "impingement," are common to all coastal power plants that use ocean waters for cooling in once-through systems. Because of the huge volumes of water required for cooling, the death of larvae and adult fish can have significant impacts on coastal populations of these organisms.

The San Onofre power plant withdraws and discharges about 1.6 million gallons of water every minute. The cold ocean water is heated up about 19 degrees Fahrenheit before it is returned to the sea. This increase in temperature has been observed at other power plants to have serious environmental effects, especially at those plants that discharge into enclosed water bodies. The San Onofre plant was specially designed to

Marine biologist examines kelp on reef constructed to mitigate impacts of turbid water

avoid those problems by very rapidly cooling the water when it is discharged. This is accomplished by discharging the heated water through a series of 126 individual ports arrayed in a line for nearly a mile across the shallow sea floor. Each port is about a yard across and oriented at an angle toward the surface and pointed either upcoast or downcoast. The force of the discharged water pulls in cold ocean waters 10 to 20 times the volume of the discharge. The turbulent mixing of the large volume of heated water with the truly enormous volumes of ambient sea water cools the discharged waters very rapidly, and there is very little temperature change at the sea surface as close as a few hundred feet to the line of discharge ports. Good engineering design, therefore, has negated the potential temperature impacts of the cooling system.

Unfortunately, there is no free lunch. The displaced water that cools the discharge, much of it from close to shore, is often turbid. As a result, the cooling system frequently creates a large surface plume of murky water that is carried by currents over the nearby San Onofre kelp forest and that reduces the light that reaches the ocean floor. This murky water interferes with the recruitment and growth of young kelp and has decreased the average size of the kelp forest. As so often happens, by solving one problem, humans have created another.

Southern California Edison was required to fund intensive studies of the environmental impacts of the San Onofre plant. These studies were overseen by the Marine Review Committee, which was comprised of three scientists—one appointed by the Edison Company, one appointed by a consortium of environmental groups, and a chairman who was an independent scientist from the University of California. After over ten years of intensive study, the Marine Review Committee reported that the San Onofre Nuclear Generating Station kills large numbers of organisms in its intake cooling waters, substantially reduces the mid-water fish populations in the Southern California Bight, kills at least 20 tons of fish per year in its intake system, moves turbid water into the San Onofre kelp bed, and has substantial adverse effects on the kelp community, including giant kelp, fish, and large benthic, or bottom-dwelling, invertebrates.

The California Coastal Commission has required mitigation for these impacts, meaning that the Southern California Edison Company must undertake projects to offset the negative consequences of operating the San Onofre plant. As mitigation, Southern California Edison has committed to restore a total of 150 acres of degraded wetlands at San Dieguito Lagoon, as described above, to mitigate impacts to marine fish populations caused by mortality to fish eggs and larvae.

The company has also committed to construct an artificial reef to mitigate impacts to the San Onofre Kelp Bed marine community. The mitigation reef must be large enough to sustain 150 acres of medium to high density giant kelp and its associated natural community, including other algae, invertebrates, and fish. Creation of such a large and complex marine environment is a huge undertaking, and it was decided first to test different design concepts with much smaller experimental reefs totaling about 22 acres. Fifty-six square modules, each about 130 feet on a side, were constructed of quarry rock or scrap concrete, with eight modules clustered in each of seven locations scattered along the coast between the San Mateo Kelp Forest off Trestles Beach north to the San Clemente Municipal Pier. Construction of the experimental reef was completed in the fall of 1999, and the five-year monitoring period was completed in December of 2004. The results of the experiment were very promising, and the full-scale reef was constructed in 2008. Prior to completion of the large mitigation reef, one could often see floating on the ocean's surface uncannily square patches of kelp canopy, which marked the location of the experimental modules.

Sea star on kelp holdfast

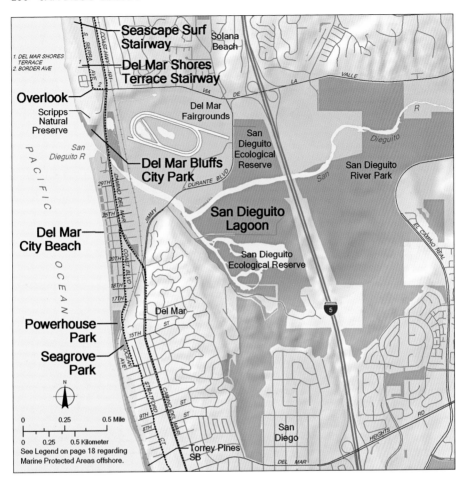

Seascape Surf Stairway

Solana Beach

1. DEL MAR SHORES TERRACE
2. BORDER AVE

Del Mar Shores Terrace Stairway

Overlook

Scripps Natural Preserve

San Dieguito R

Del Mar Fairgrounds

Del Mar Bluffs City Park

San Dieguito Ecological Reserve

DURANTE BLVD

San Dieguito River Park

San Dieguito Lagoon

Del Mar City Beach

San Dieguito Ecological Reserve

PACIFIC OCEAN

Del Mar

Powerhouse Park

Seagrove Park

N

0   0.25   0.5 Mile
0   0.25   0.5 Kilometer
See Legend on page 18 regarding Marine Protected Areas offshore.

Torrey Pines SB

San Diego

Del Mar Bluffs City Park

Solana Beach to Del Mar

	Sandy Beach	Rocky Shore	Trail	Visitor Center	Campground	Wildlife Viewing	Fishing or Boating	Facilities for Disabled	Food and Drink	Restrooms	Parking	Fee
Seascape Surf Stairway	•					•					•	
Del Mar Shores Terrace Stairway	•					•					•	
Overlook				•								
Del Mar Bluffs City Park	•					•	•		•	•	•	
San Dieguito Lagoon		•				•						
Del Mar City Beach	•					•	•	•	•	•	•	
Powerhouse Park								•	•	•		
Seagrove Park										•		

SEASCAPE SURF STAIRWAY: *501 S. Sierra Ave., Solana Beach.* The sandy beach is popular for swimming, surfing, snorkeling, and surf fishing. A stairway down the steep bluff is on the north side of a large residential complex; no-fee parking is located 50 yards south of the accessway, on the inland side of Sierra Ave. Beach shower available, but no restrooms. Stairway open from 6 AM to 10 PM. City of Solana Beach lifeguards are on-site daily during the summer months, from 10 AM to 6 PM.

DEL MAR SHORES TERRACE STAIRWAY: *180 Del Mar Shores Terrace, Solana Beach.* Walk seaward along Del Mar Shores Terrace and turn right near the end to reach a paved path between residential buildings and a stairway to the sandy beach. On-street parking along South Sierra Ave., plus two small, no-fee parking lots at 721 and 733 South Sierra Ave., open from 6 AM to 10 PM. No other facilities are available.

OVERLOOK: *End of Border Ave., Del Mar.* The ocean can be glimpsed from a fenced spot at the terminus of Border Ave.

DEL MAR BLUFFS CITY PARK: *W. of Camino del Mar, just N. of the San Dieguito River mouth, Del Mar.* At the mouth of the San Dieguito River is a broad, sandy beach. There is pay-and-display parking along the southbound shoulder of Camino del Mar. Summer lifeguard service and non-wheelchair-accessible chemical toilet; no other facilities.

The Scripps Natural Preserve, located on the bluff at the north end of the beach, offers nice views of the San Dieguito River mouth.

SAN DIEGUITO LAGOON: *E. of Camino del Mar at the San Dieguito River mouth, Del Mar.* San Dieguito Lagoon is an Ecological Reserve managed by the Department of Fish and Game and part of the much larger San Dieguito River Park that extends inland within the river's watershed. A 55-mile-long, multi-use Coast to Crest Trail is planned along the San Dieguito River, to link the sea at Del Mar with the inland mountains of the Peninsular Range. Segments of the Coast to Crest Trail are open already, including a 1,400-foot-long boardwalk extending east from Jimmy Durante Blvd. on the north side of the river. On the south side of the river from Jimmy Durante Blvd. westward is a quarter-mile-long path with benches and river views. For information, call: 858-259-1955. In and around the lagoon are found salt marsh and coastal sage scrub plant communities, and chaparral and oak woodland are found farther inland in the river valley.

DEL MAR CITY BEACH: *W. of Camino del Mar, from 29th St. to Torrey Pines State Beach, Del Mar.* Del Mar has a wide, sandy beach, with good swimming and surfing. Surf fishing and grunion catching are popular. Beach access is available at residential street ends from 29th St. south to 18th Streets, but parking is very limited. City of Del Mar lifeguard stations are located at 25th St., where there

Powerhouse Park

are restrooms and a beach shower, and at 20th St., where there is a beach shower only.

Public metered parking for beach-goers is located along the north edge of the Poseidon Restaurant parking lot, west of Coast Blvd. Next to the parking lot is the city of Del Mar's 17th St. lifeguard station, where lifeguards are on duty year-round and a surf rescue boat is stationed. Restrooms and an outdoor shower are at the same location. For information about beach facilities or the Del Mar Junior Lifeguard program, call: 858-755-1556. Additional off-street, fee parking is located inland of Coast Blvd. near the Amtrak station, and there is metered parking along Coast Blvd.

On Del Mar beaches, blue flags designate safe swimming areas; a yellow sign with a black ball means no surfing allowed. Glass containers are prohibited on the beach. Dogs are allowed on Del Mar beaches, subject to

seasonal restrictions: north of 29th St., dogs are allowed on leash from June 16 through Labor Day and off leash under voice control the rest of the year; from 29th St. to Powerhouse Park, dogs are allowed on leash from the day after Labor Day through June 15th only; south of Powerhouse Park, leashed dogs are allowed year-round.

POWERHOUSE PARK: *Coast Blvd. between 17th and 15th Streets, Del Mar.* A grassy park overlooking Del Mar City Beach has picnic areas, a playground, and short, paved paths to the sand. Outdoor shower and restrooms are located in the main park building. Fee parking lot across Coast Blvd.

SEAGROVE PARK: *Ocean Ave. at 15th St., Del Mar.* Seaward of the coastal highway, but inland of the railroad tracks, is a grassy area with paved, wheelchair-accessible path and benches on the bluffs overlooking the ocean. Metered, on-street parking.

Jacob Shell Taylor, who established the resort town of Del Mar in 1885, built a dance pavilion on the beach and a large swimming pool that extended out into the ocean called a "Natatorium." It had low wooden walls and a set of viewing decks above and provided a bathing area protected from waves and from the dreaded "stingaree" (stingray). The remnant pilings from the bathing pool can still be seen offshore at low tide from atop the coastal bluffs west of the railroad tracks, near the ends of 8th and 9th Streets.

The concept of an annual agricultural fair in San Diego County dates back to the 1880s, but the event had no permanent home for the first 50 years. During that time there were also intermittent years with no fair at all, particularly during World War I and the Great Depression. In 1936, the 22nd District Agricultural Association purchased the property known today as the Del Mar Fairgrounds and began construction of permanent facilities. In the meantime, California voters approved pari-mutuel racetrack betting as a way to help support the various agricultural fairs statewide, which were floundering financially. The Del Mar Turf Club, with help from Bing Crosby, began leasing the racetrack at the new fairgrounds in the 1930s to run an annual horse meet, beginning with harness racing in 1936.

The earliest county fairs provided a venue for farmers to exchange ideas; judge livestock; test the cooking, baking and preserving skills of the farm wives; and race horses, although the horse racing is now a separate event with its own season. While continuing its agricultural events and exhibits, the modern fair has expanded significantly and now has something for everyone. There are exhibits of hand-made furniture, hobbies, sewing, and quilting; commercial sales and demonstrations; a flower show; a variety of entertainment; and the always-popular midway. Some folks just come to the fair for the food; full meals are offered, but many prefer finger foods, including almost anything "on a stick."

Over the years, various events have been added to the fairground's annual calendar. Satellite wagering has become a daily event, except when the live horse meet is happening. Equestrian events have always been part of fairground activities, with a dozen or more classic horse shows and dressage events held annually. The National Horse Show, which was once part of the fair, is now held here each spring for about three weeks during April and May. Another summertime event is professional bull riding, which occurs in July or August and features riders from the U.S., Canada, Brazil, and Australia.

However, the annual San Diego County Fair, running from mid-June to the Fourth of July, and the thoroughbred racing season that runs from mid-July into September, remain the two events that draw the largest crowds to the fairgrounds, with the fair alone attracting well over a million visitors. The District also runs several smaller annual events, including the "Holiday of Lights," outdoor decoration displays, the "Scream Zone" Halloween haunted house, and the annual Flower Show. The facilities are also rented for trade and consumer shows, gun shows, antique fairs, concerts, and annual pumpkin patches and Christmas tree sales.

San Diego County Fair

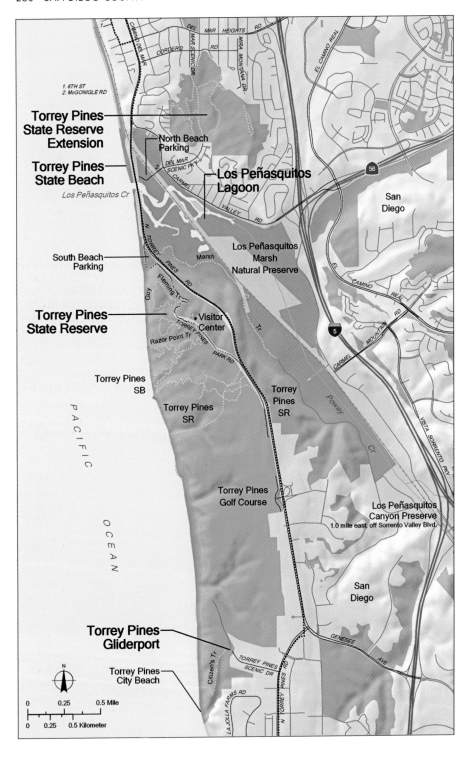

1. 6TH ST
2. McGONIGLE RD

Torrey Pines State Reserve Extension

North Beach Parking

Torrey Pines State Beach

Los Peñasquitos Cr

Los Peñasquitos Lagoon

San Diego

South Beach Parking

Los Peñasquitos Marsh Natural Preserve

Marsh

Torrey Pines State Reserve

Fleming Tr

Guy

Visitor Center

Razor Point Tr

PARK RD

Torrey Pines SB

Torrey Pines SR

Torrey Pines SR

PACIFIC

Torrey Pines Golf Course

Los Peñasquitos Canyon Preserve
1.0 mile east, off Sorrento Valley Blvd.

OCEAN

San Diego

GENESEE

Torrey Pines Gliderport

Torrey Pines City Beach

Citizen's Tr

TORREY PINES SCENIC DR

LA JOLLA FARMS RD

N

0   0.25   0.5 Mile

0   0.25   0.5 Kilometer

Torrey Pines

	Sandy Beach	Rocky Shore	Trail	Visitor Center	Campground	Wildlife Viewing	Fishing or Boating	Facilities for Disabled	Food and Drink	Restrooms	Parking	Fee
Torrey Pines State Beach	•					•	•	•		•	•	•
Torrey Pines State Reserve Extension			•			•					•	
Los Peñasquitos Lagoon			•			•						
Torrey Pines State Reserve			•	•		•		•		•	•	•
Torrey Pines Gliderport			•						•	•	•	

TORREY PINES STATE BEACH: *McGonigle Rd., off Carmel Valley Rd., San Diego.* The state beach is popular for swimming, surfing, and fishing. The North Beach parking lot is located next to Los Peñasquitos Lagoon and is open from 8 AM to sunset; fee for parking. Facilities are wheelchair accessible with assistance; a beach wheelchair is available. Lifeguards are on duty at Torrey Pines State Beach year-round; lifeguard towers are staffed during the summer months.

Additional beach parking is located south of the Los Peñasquitos Lagoon mouth along the southbound shoulder of Torrey Pines Rd., as well as at the South Beach parking lot next to the entrance to Torrey Pines State Reserve. The beach can also be reached on trails that start within Torrey Pines State Reserve. Dogs are prohibited on the beach and at Torrey Pines State Reserve, including inside vehicles. Call: 858-755-2063.

Torrey Pines State Beach extends over four miles from 6th St. in Del Mar past extremely high, reddish sandstone bluffs to Torrey Pines City Beach. Carbonaceous beds of the Del Mar Formation are exposed in the cliffs, revealing fossils of shallow water mollusks from the middle Eocene period. An assortment of oysters, burrowing clams, petrified wood, and leaf imprints can be seen. Look offshore for dolphins, porpoises, sea lions, and, during their annual migration in winter and spring, California gray whales.

TORREY PINES STATE RESERVE EXTENSION: *E. of Camino del Mar, off Del Mar Heights Rd., San Diego.* Separated geographically from the main Torrey Pines State Reserve is a small forest of Torrey pine trees, set among buff colored sandstone ravines. The park has no facilities other than several trails that lead among the trees, offering views of Los Peñasquitos Lagoon, the ocean, and coastal sage scrub vegetation. One trailhead is located south of Del Mar Heights Rd., at the end of Mar Scenic Dr.; the trail leads south down a canyon and connects to the end of Del Mar Scenic Parkway. Another trailhead is at the end of Mira Montana Dr.; head east from Mar Scenic Dr. on Cordero Rd. and turn south to the trailhead, where there is parking and a nice ocean view.

LOS PEÑASQUITOS LAGOON: *Between N. Torrey Pines Rd. and I-5, S. of Carmel Valley Rd., San Diego.* Los Peñasquitos Lagoon is an important nursery ground for fish, including halibut and staghorn sculpin. These fish breed in the inshore ocean waters and enter the lagoon as fingerlings, usually returning to the ocean as juveniles. Dabbling and diving ducks feed and rest in the lagoon. Willets, dowitchers, and other migratory shorebirds use the lagoon in the fall and spring. The adjoining salt marsh provides nesting sites for the California least tern, Belding's savannah sparrow, and light-footed clapper rail, all endangered species.

Los Peñasquitos Lagoon can be viewed from the Marsh Trail, which is part of Torrey Pines State Reserve. The mile-and-a-half-long trail starts on the inland side of N. Torrey Pines Rd., across from the Torrey Pines State Reserve vehicle entrance. The lagoon can also be viewed from the shoulder of Carmel Valley Rd., although there is no entry to the marsh.

Upstream along Los Peñasquitos Canyon Creek, the 4,000-acre Los Peñasquitos Canyon Preserve features a perennial stream with a waterfall, adobe structures dating from California's early days, and miles of hiking, biking, and equestrian trails. The western trailhead is located on the south side of Sorrento Valley Blvd., one mile east of Vista Sorrento Parkway. For information, call: 858-538-8066.

TORREY PINES STATE RESERVE: *W. of N. Torrey Pines Rd., 1.5 mi. S. of Del Mar Heights Rd., San Diego.* Torrey Pines State Reserve contains the only natural habitat on the North American continent for one of the world's rarest pine trees, the Torrey pine. The reserve is situated on a series of steep bluffs interspersed with deep ravines. West of N. Torrey Pines Rd., trails lead along several ridges to the beach and to several viewpoints, providing opportunities for observing plant and animal life and viewing the adjacent coastline. The Razor Point Trail offers visitors a good look at windblown trees, eroded sandstone forms, and yucca flowers in spring. The Guy Fleming Trail winds through Torrey pine trees, ferns, and seasonal wildflowers. Stay on the trails; all features in the reserve are protected, including rocks, flowers, and pine cones.

The Torrey Pines State Reserve visitor center, which is generally wheelchair accessible, offers exhibits on local geology and the flowers and trees of the area, along with a native plant garden. Trail maps and species lists are available; guided walks are given on weekends and holidays between 10 AM and 2 PM; call ahead to confirm. The reserve accommodates a limited number of people in order to protect the natural resources; visitors may be asked to come back at a later time or date if the reserve is full. It is full most weekend afternoons. Day-use fee. The reserve entrance is shared with the South Beach entrance to Torrey Pines State Beach. The gate is open from 8 AM to sunset; the visitor center opens daily at 9 AM. For information, call: 858-755-2063.

The reserve also encompasses land on the east side of N. Torrey Pines Rd. The Los Peñasquitos Marsh Natural Preserve is the habitat of a number of rare and endangered bird species, such as the least tern and the light-footed clapper rail, and is an important feeding and nesting place for migratory waterfowl and shorebirds.

TORREY PINES GLIDERPORT: *W. of Torrey Pines Rd. at the end of Torrey Pines Scenic Dr., San Diego.* Next to a 350-foot-high coastal

Torrey Pines State Beach and Los Peñasquitos Lagoon, east of the highway

bluff is the Torrey Pines Gliderport, a center for motorless aviation and a San Diego city park. Hang gliders (supported by a frame with wings), paragliders (suspended from a parachute-like strip of fabric), radio-controlled model sailplanes, and full-scale sailplanes are operated here. The gliderport is the only one of its kind adjacent to America's West Coast; a similar facility is at Kitty Hawk, North Carolina.

Beginning in 1930, gliders were car-towed off the beach, parallel to the coastal bluff, so that they could fly in the lift created by the prevailing westerly wind. The nearly flat land of the mesa east of the cliff was used for launching and landing, providing a natural emergency runway. Aviation pioneers who flew here include Charles A. Lindbergh, who on Febuary 24, 1930 flew in a glider along the coast from Mt. Soledad in La Jolla to Del Mar, establishing a claimed distance record. The historic Torrey Pines Gliderport was dedicated as a National Soaring Landmark in 1991 by the National Soaring Museum in Elmira, New York. The San Diego City Council later declared the city-owned portion of the gliderport as a San Diego City Historical Landmark, and the entire gliderport was listed on the National Register of Historic Places in 1993.

Several unimproved paths lead from near the gliderport down to the beach. Use of these extremely steep routes is not recommended, but the trails are commonly used. The so-called Citizen's Trail is at the south end of the parking lot, and other very steep, unimproved foot trails are at the far north end of the parking lot. Signs warn visitors to stay back from coastal bluffs. Chemical toilets are near the parking area.

Torrey Pines Gliderport

Torrey Pines State Reserve overlooking Los Peñasquitos Lagoon

Torrey pine, *Pinus torreyana*

Torrey Pine Forest

T HE TORREY PINE (*Pinus torreyana*) is the rarest pine, with the most restricted distribution, of any pine species in North America. Its natural distribution consists of two disjunct populations: a mainland and an island population. The mainland population, consisting of approximately 7,000 trees, occurs in and near Torrey Pines State Reserve in San Diego County. The island population of approximately 2,000 trees is on Santa Rosa Island, 175 miles northwest of the mainland population. The fossil record reveals that during the Pleistocene Epoch, when the climate was cooler and moister, Torrey pines enjoyed a much wider coastal distribution. The range of Torrey pines started to shrink during the drying period of the last ten thousand years, remaining only on sandstone bluffs and ravines at Torrey Pines State Reserve and on Santa Rosa Island. Such a population status is labeled "relictual."

There are two recognized subspecies, *Pinus torreyana* ssp. *torreyana* on the mainland and *Pinus torreyana* ssp. *insularis* on Santa Rosa Island. The pines growing on the island are shorter, broader, and bushier than their mainland counterparts. The Torrey pines on Santa Rosa Island also have thicker and scalier bark and rounder cones.

The Torrey pine forest is the only southern California coastal pine forest. Torrey pines occupy zones of maritime climate close to the ocean and exposed to fog for a significant portion of the year. They are also restricted to nutrient-poor, acidic, sandy soils. The vegetation communities found associated with Torrey pines include coastal sage scrub, chaparral, dune scrub, and coastal salt marsh. Some species commonly associated with Torrey pines are chamise, California sagebrush, toyon, lemonadeberry, California scrub oak, and many species of manzanita, ceanothus, buckwheat, and native wildflowers.

Torrey pines are slow growing and are usually no taller than 40 feet, although they can attain heights of up to 60 feet. The needles are in fascicles, or bunches, of five and are eight to twelve inches long. Torrey pines have large cones, up to four inches by six inches in size. The cones are harder and heavier than most other pine cones. Amazingly, Torrey pine taproots may reach 25 feet into sandstone, and their lateral roots can extend up to 225 feet from the trunk. The oldest Torrey pines are about 150 years old.

Torrey pines are monoecious, which means that each individual tree has both male and female cones. Cones are pollinated from January to March and reach maturity in the summer, two and one-half years later. The Torrey pine cone drops most of its seeds during the autumn three years after it appears; however, a few of the seeds will stay in the cone until the cone eventually falls in two, three, or even ten years. There are two seeds under each scale of a cone, and an average cone will have about 100 seeds. The seeds of the Torrey pine are edible and are some of the largest of all pine seeds. However, you could break a tooth trying to eat them, because they are much harder than most pine seeds. Nevertheless, the seeds are eaten by birds, rodents, and other mammals. At Torrey Pines State Reserve, the dusky-footed and desert wood rats consume large quantities of Torrey pine seeds and may greatly reduce the seed stock. Torrey pine seeds are nearly wingless, and therefore wind dispersal is negligible, making birds such as scrub jays important seed disseminators.

The Torrey pine population in Torrey Pines State Reserve consists of large, mature individuals; seedlings and saplings are infrequent. A serious concern at the reserve is the low rate of seedling establishment and survival in the recent past. If past trends continue, the age of the stand of Torrey pines will continue to increase. Unless seedlings are encouraged to establish, the stand will eventually go extinct.

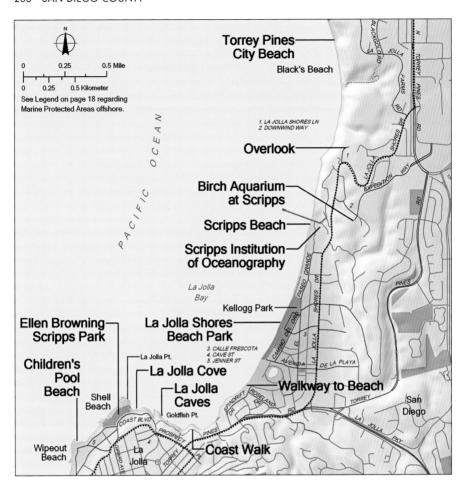

Torrey Pines City Beach

Black's Beach

1. LA JOLLA SHORES LN
2. DOWNWIND WAY

Overlook

Birch Aquarium at Scripps

Scripps Beach

Scripps Institution of Oceanography

La Jolla Bay

Kellogg Park

Ellen Browning Scripps Park

La Jolla Shores Beach Park

3. CALLE FRESCOTA
4. CAVE ST
5. JENNER ST

La Jolla Pt.

Children's Pool Beach

La Jolla Cove

Shell Beach

La Jolla Caves

Goldfish Pt.

Walkway to Beach

San Diego

Wipeout Beach

La Jolla

Coast Walk

See Legend on page 18 regarding Marine Protected Areas offshore.

PACIFIC OCEAN

La Jolla Cove

Torrey Pines City Beach to La Jolla

	Sandy Beach	Rocky Shore	Trail	Visitor Center	Campground	Wildlife Viewing	Fishing or Boating	Facilities for Disabled	Food and Drink	Restrooms	Parking	Fee
Torrey Pines City Beach	•											
Overlook						•						
Birch Aquarium at Scripps				•		•	•		•	•	•	
Scripps Beach	•	•								•		
Scripps Institution of Oceanography						•				•		
La Jolla Shores Beach Park	•					•	•		•	•		
Walkway to Beach	•											
Coast Walk		•	•			•						
La Jolla Caves						•						•
La Jolla Cove	•	•				•			•			
Ellen Browning Scripps Park		•	•			•			•			
Children's Pool Beach	•	•				•			•			

TORREY PINES CITY BEACH: *W. of La Jolla Farms Rd., San Diego.* Also known as Black's Beach, this three-mile stretch of sand is backed by high, erodible cliffs that make the beach hard to get to. If high tides and surf allow, beach goers can approach from Torrey Pines State Beach, one mile to the north, or La Jolla Shores Beach, one mile to the south. Be careful of informal paths leading down the bluffs, which are unstable.

A steep but paved pedestrian path to the beach is located at the south end of Black Gold Rd., at La Jolla Farms Rd. The beach path is on property owned by the University of California; permission to use it is revocable by the owner. Although a long walk from anywhere, Black's Beach offers good surfing, especially at the south end of the beach. Swimmers should use care due to rip currents. City of San Diego lifeguards are on duty from spring break through October, but there is no permanent lifeguard station. Without official sanction, Black's Beach is known as a clothing-optional beach. Dogs must be leashed and are permitted only between 6 PM and 9 AM. No restrooms. For information, call: 619-235-1169. Limited on-street parking is available in the vicinity.

OVERLOOK: *N. end of La Jolla Shores Ln., La Jolla.* A short path leads between residences to a blufftop overlook that provides views of the coast and offshore marine reserve. On-street parking only. Do not trespass on private property.

BIRCH AQUARIUM AT SCRIPPS: *2300 Expedition Way, off N. Torrey Pines Rd., La Jolla.* The aquarium has nearly 400 species of creatures and features living coral displays, an outdoor tidepool with touchable animals, a variety of sharks and other fishes, and a kelp forest tank showing marine life off San Diego. Ctenophores, or sea gooseberries, are sometimes on display. The aquarium organizes outdoor excursions, including kayaking, whale watching, and tidepooling. Ocean views from the Aquarium are outstanding. Open 9 AM to 5 PM daily, except Thanksgiving, Christmas, and New Year's Day; fee for entry. Metropolitan Transit System bus No. 30 stops at Downwind Way near Expedition Way; Downwind Way is off La Jolla Shores Dr.

SCRIPPS BEACH: *W. of La Jolla Shores Dr. at the Scripps Institution of Oceanography, La Jolla.* Sandy beach near the 1,090-foot-long Ellen Browning Scripps Memorial Pier, a research facility of the Scripps Institution of Oceanography. There are tidepools north of the pier that are popular for observing intertidal marine life; tidelands and ocean waters off Scripps Beach are part of the marine protected areas designated by the Department of Fish and Game. Do not touch or disturb the marine life. Limited on-street parking along El Paseo Grande; metered public parking available on weekends and holidays in Lots P002 and P003 on El Paseo Grande west of La Jolla Shores Dr.

SCRIPPS INSTITUTION OF OCEANOGRAPHY: *8602 La Jolla Shores Dr., La Jolla.* The Scripps Institution of Oceanography is a leading research and education institution affiliated with the University of California. Access to the Ellen Browning Scripps Memorial Research Pier is usually limited to researchers, but public, guided, full-moon tours are held seasonally, offering a chance to learn about the nocturnal habits of marine creatures; call: 858-534-3474. Public walking tour maps of the campus are available at Birch Aquarium.

LA JOLLA SHORES BEACH PARK: *Camino del Oro at Calle Frescota, La Jolla.* Often-gentle waves make this spacious beach one of San Diego's best for swimming; however, be alert for rip currents. Surfers and divers also use the beach. The nearby waters, including

the La Jolla Submarine Canyon, are part of a marine protected area; removal of marine life or objects is prohibited. City of San Diego lifeguards are on duty daily from 9 AM, year-round. A manually operated beach wheelchair is available; contact the lifeguard station or call: 619-221-8899. For recorded weather and surf conditions, call: 619-221-8824. For other information about the beach, call: 619-235-1169. Small boat launching in the gentle surf is possible at the foot of Avenida de la Playa, south of La Jolla Shores Beach Park. Four-wheel-drive vehicles are allowed to drive on the sand to deposit hand-launchable craft. Kayakers should use caution where swimmers are present.

Grassy Kellogg Park lies to the north and south of the large beach-level parking lot at the foot of Calle Frescota. The park has picnic tables, barbecue grills, and lawns for lounging or play. Restrooms and beach showers available. No glass beverage containers or alcohol allowed at La Jolla Shores Beach and Kellogg Park. Beach fires are allowed only in provided containers. Leashed dogs permitted from 6 PM to 9 AM only; clean up after your pet.

WALKWAY TO BEACH: *W. of Spindrift Dr., near Roseland Dr., La Jolla.* A narrow concrete walkway and steps lead to a wide sandy beach at La Jolla Bay. Sunbathing and swim-

La Jolla Shores Beach Park

Terrestrial and oceanic forces and land-forms meet at the shoreline. At La Jolla Bay, two small canyons on the land are associated with two extensive submarine canyons immediately offshore. The Scripps Submarine Canyon is the seaward extension of the unnamed valley located just north of Scripps Institution. This submarine canyon extends from the nearshore in a southerly direction. The La Jolla Submarine Canyon begins off La Jolla Shores beach, joins with the Scripps Canyon about a mile offshore, and then extends another 32 miles seaward to a junction with the San Diego Trough at a depth of 3,600 feet. The walls of the Scripps and La Jolla submarine canyons are eroding gradually, and the canyons are moving slowly landward. Both canyons actively trap long-shore sediment and carry this material offshore into deep water sinks. The canyons thus act as a terminus to the littoral cell, leaving less sand available for transport to beaches farther south.

The submarine canyons in La Jolla Bay also influence the size and energy of waves that reach the shore. As waves move landward through shallow water, they lose much of their energy, but waves moving up the relatively deep submarine canyons can focus wave energy and form large breakers. Generally the south end of La Jolla Shores beach is more suited to swimming, while the northern end features large surfing waves. Rip currents are a danger here; be aware of the water conditions, and swim near a lifeguard.

ming only; no surfing allowed at this location. On-street parking.

COAST WALK: *Seaward of Prospect Pl. and Torrey Pines Rd., La Jolla.* A dirt path with benches along the La Jolla bluffs provides a panoramic view of the ocean and beach and glimpses of sea caves. At the east end, the walk can be entered at Torrey Pines Rd. just east of the Prospect Pl. intersection; from the west end at Goldfish Point, enter the walk adjacent to the Cave Store. Limited street parking nearby.

LA JOLLA CAVES: *Along the shoreline near Coast Walk, La Jolla.* The name La Jolla, derived from the Mexican geographical term referring to a hollow on the coast worn by waves, is exemplified by the caves worn into the sandstone cliffs east of Point La Jolla. Most of the caves are accessible only from the sea, via kayak. The Sunny Jim Cave can be reached by a constructed tunnel from the Cave Store, an old-time curio shop at 1325 Cave St. (the building faces Coast Blvd.) Open on weekdays from 10 AM to 6 PM and on weekends from 9 AM to 7 PM; fee for entry. Call: 858-459-0746.

LA JOLLA COVE: *E. of Point La Jolla and N. of Coast Blvd., La Jolla.* Facing northeast, a somewhat unusual orientation among California's ocean beaches, sandy La Jolla Cove is blessed with clear water and striking sandstone rock formations. An early beach resort, La Jolla Cove was the site of a popular dance pavilion built in 1894. In those days, on the Fourth of July, divers were paid $25 by a railroad company for each dive made "flambé"; a springboard was placed on the blufftop over the ocean and the diver would pour oil on his body and set himself afire before leaping. In 1905, a building was erected in the area with hot saltwater baths and a bowling alley.

La Jolla Cove is an especially fine place for snorkeling in the clear waters; bright orange Garibaldi fish are abundant. The cove is part of a marine protected area administered by the Department of Fish and Game. Removal of fish, shells, or any other materials is prohibited. No flotation devices or bodyboards are allowed. Lifeguards are on duty daily, starting at 9 AM in summer and sometimes later during the rest of the year. The beach is highly popular, and nearby street parking is

Shell Beach, north of Children's Pool Beach

often at a premium. Restrooms and showers are located at adjacent Ellen Scripps Park. No fires allowed on the beach. For information, call: 619-235-1169.

ELLEN BROWNING SCRIPPS PARK: *Coast Blvd. at Girard Ave., La Jolla.* The landscaped blufftop park overlooking La Jolla Cove is named for Ellen Browning Scripps, one of the most generous and influential La Jollans. Ellen Scripps emigrated from England in 1844 with five siblings and her widowed father. After a career that included starting several successful newspapers and acquiring a substantial fortune, she settled in 1896 in La Jolla, where she lived for 35 years. She made generous contributions to hospitals, schools, libraries, museums, and more, much of it anonymously. Miss Scripps, as she preferred to be called, failed in her intention to give away all her wealth, and a foundation bearing her name continues her tradition of philanthropy. The park has lawns, picnic tables, barbecue grills, restrooms with showers, and a paved path along the bluff edge. For information, call: 619-235-1169.

CHILDREN'S POOL BEACH: *Coast Blvd. at Jenner St., La Jolla.* Children's Pool Beach is partially enclosed by a seawall, which has trapped sand within it. Harbor seals haul out on the beach and use the waters nearby during much of the year. The public can view the seals from the seawall. During the pupping season, swimming is strongly discouraged, due to water contamination from the seals. The Marine Mammal Protection Act prohibits harassing or disturbing the seals at any time. Wipeout Beach is another tiny pocket beach, located nearby to the south; Shell Beach is located 300 yards to the north. On-street parking; non-wheelchair-accessible restrooms. Call: 619-235-1169.

Harbor seal

Children's Pool Beach

Children's Pool Beach in La Jolla has splashed local newspaper headlines since the early 1990s. Long before then, philanthropist Ellen Browning Scripps had funded the construction of a breakwater seaward of the shoreline (and subsequently granted the lands to the city of San Diego) to create a "safe bathing pool for children, sheltered from the ocean surf and winds." This project was initiated as a result of two children having drowned in the area. For many years this safe haven was a pleasant and inviting place to swim, free from the waves that typically jostle even adult swimmers.

Around 1992, a few harbor seals began to haul out on Seal Rock, a nearby offshore formation. Harbor seals must come out of the water about eight hours a day to rest, dry off, and regulate their body temperature. By 1993 so many harbor seals were hauled out on the rock that they began to attract large crowds of people, who would often try to get as close to the seals as possible to take their picture or even pet them. Action that causes the seals to stampede into the water is regarded as harassment and is a violation of the federal Marine Mammal Protection Act. In order to protect the seals, the city of San Diego made Seal Rock a temporary marine reserve.

Once the seals had their rock free from human disturbance, they began to haul out at Children's Pool Beach, instead. Biologists and marine mammal experts are not sure why this change occurred; apparently lying on a warm, soft, sandy beach was more appealing than a hard rock formation. Children's Pool Beach is the only regularly used haul-out site on the California mainland south of Point Mugu. Drawing large crowds of spectators, the popular pinnipeds that have colonized this sheltered cove have turned the area into a large tourist attraction, where people can view them at a close distance in their natural habitat.

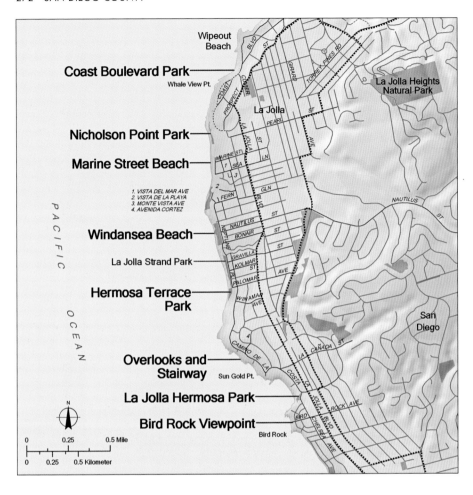

Wipeout Beach

Coast Boulevard Park

Whale View Pt.

La Jolla Heights Natural Park

La Jolla

PEARL

Nicholson Point Park

Marine Street Beach

MARINE ST
1 SEA
3

1. VISTA DEL MAR AVE
2. VISTA DE LA PLAYA
3. MONTE VISTA AVE
4. AVENIDA CORTEZ

2

FERN

GLN

NAUTILUS

P A C I F I C

Windansea Beach

NAUTILUS
BONAIR

ST

La Jolla Strand Park

GRAVILLA
KOLMAR
ST
PALOMAR

AVE

ST

Hermosa Terrace Park

WINAMAR
AVE

O C E A N

San Diego

4

CAMINO DE LA

LA CAÑADA ST

Overlooks and Stairway

Sun Gold Pt.

COSTA

La Jolla Hermosa Park

ROCK AVE

Bird Rock Viewpoint

BIRD

CHELSEA AVE

Bird Rock

N

0   0.25   0.5 Mile

0   0.25   0.5 Kilometer

Coast Boulevard Park

La Jolla

	Sandy Beach	Rocky Shore	Trail	Visitor Center	Campground	Wildlife Viewing	Fishing or Boating	Facilities for Disabled	Food and Drink	Restrooms	Parking	Fee
Coast Boulevard Park	•	•	•			•	•				•	
Nicholson Point Park	•	•				•						
Marine Street Beach	•	•				•	•					
Windansea Beach	•	•				•				•		
Hermosa Terrace Park	•	•				•						
Overlooks and Stairway		•				•					•	
La Jolla Hermosa Park		•				•						
Bird Rock Viewpoint		•				•	•				•	

COAST BOULEVARD PARK: *W. of Coast Blvd. at Cuvier St., La Jolla.* A grassy shoreline park overlooks the sparkling, blue-green waters of the Pacific Ocean. There are benches and picnic tables set in a green lawn, a paved path, and a handicapped-accessible parking space. At the northern end of the park, there is a nice view of the beach below, where skim-boarders play in the surf. At the southern end of the park, there is a short city-owned dirt path and a separate stairway to the rocky shelf located above the water's edge; look for tidepools, but do not disturb the marine life. On-street parking. For information, call: 619-235-1169.

NICHOLSON POINT PARK: *S. end of Coast Blvd., La Jolla.* An easy-to-miss paved path leads between adjacent residential buildings, numbered as 100 and 202 Coast Blvd., to a short stairway leading to a small sandy beach; check tide tables before visiting. The sandy beach extends south to Marine Street Beach, some 300 yards distant.

MARINE STREET BEACH: *W. of La Jolla Blvd., at the end of Marine St., La Jolla.* A quarter-mile-long beach of fine sand with scattered rocky areas can be reached via three pedestrian accessways: at the north end of Vista del Mar Ave., at the west end of Marine St. via a short stairway, and at the west end of Sea Lane. Swimming, surfing, bodyboarding, and diving are popular. Halibut, Pacific bonito, and white croaker are common fish

caught offshore. The rocky reefs and sandy coves that fringe the La Jolla coastline give shore anglers a chance to catch various reef species, including halfmoon, calico bass, halibut, and various perch and croaker species, as well as the occasional white seabass. The opaleye is a common nearshore fish that uses kelp beds for food and shelter and is named for its blue opalescent eyes. Horseshoe Reef, a popular surfing spot, is just north of Marine St. Lifeguards are stationed on the beach in summer only. Dogs, which must be leashed, are allowed from 6 PM to 9 AM only. There is limited, on-street parking only; no facilities.

WINDANSEA BEACH: *W. of Neptune Pl., from Vista de la Playa to Palomar Ave., La Jolla.* The shoreline at this park is made up of huge, flat sandstone slabs that shelter pockets of soft sand. The rocky reef offshore produces big waves, and this is one of the most popular surfing spots on the coast. Waves are sometimes too large for inexperienced surfers and swimmers; the submerged rocks, in particular, demand caution. Due to the steepness of the beach, this is not a good diving spot.

Bonair St. leads to Windansea Beach, and there is a no-fee 18-space parking lot, including a disabled parking spot, at the end of Bonair St. On-street parking can be hard to find. From Neptune Pl. north and south of Bonair St., several short stairways lead to the beach, where the rocks form nooks popular with sunbathers. A paved walkway located at the end of the cul-de-sac named Vista de la Playa, off Monte Vista Ave., leads to the northern end of Windansea Beach. An additional shoreline accessway is located near the west end of Fern Glen, where it curves south and becomes Neptune Place. Near the curve, a pedestrian-only paved path leads from Fern Glen to the shoreline; walk around the vehicle barrier on the right-hand side.

At the south end of Windansea Beach, also known as La Jolla Strand Park, a paved sidewalk runs along Neptune Pl., overlooking the sea, and there are stairs down to the beach opposite Gravilla St. and near Kolmar St. There is a chemical toilet located seaward of Neptune Pl. at the end of Gravilla St.; there are no beach showers at this location. Lifeguards are on Windansea Beach daily during summer and on weekends during spring months and also in September. For recorded weather and surf conditions, call: 619-221-8824.

HERMOSA TERRACE PARK: *W. of Camino de la Costa, S. of Palomar Ave., La Jolla.* Between Palomar Ave. and Winamar Ave., a hard-to-

Windansea Beach

find paved path leads from Camino de la Costa between two houses to the shoreline. Or, when the tide is not too high, approach from the north along the rocky shoreline; there is a stairway at the end of Palomar Ave. The small, seasonally sandy beach is backed by sandstone formations. On-street parking only; no facilities.

OVERLOOKS AND STAIRWAY: *W. of Camino de la Costa, La Jolla.* Along Camino de la Costa there are two overlooks between residences, one less than 100 yards north of Avenida Cortez and a second 100 yards south of Avenida Cortez. A stairway to the rocky reef and sandy pocket beach is located on Camino de la Costa, 200 yards west of La Cañada St.; a handful of parking spaces are available at that location. Coastal views extend to the south past Bird Rock to Pacific, Mission, and Ocean Beaches.

LA JOLLA HERMOSA PARK: *W. of Camino de la Costa, at the intersection with Chelsea Ave., La Jolla.* A quiet neighborhood spot, La Jolla Hermosa Park offers visitors picnic tables, a barbecue grill, and benches from which to enjoy the expansive view of the sea. A steep path equipped with a guide rope provides rough access down to a rocky cove. On-street parking only; no facilities.

BIRD ROCK VIEWPOINT: *End of Bird Rock Ave., La Jolla.* A large guano-covered rock located 120 feet offshore, Bird Rock is actually named not for its avian visitors, but after Mr. Bird, who was one of the first developers of the shoreline community. In 1907, this subdivision was known as "Bird Rock, City by the Sea." At the foot of Bird Rock Ave. was the Bird Rock Inn, built from stone taken from the beach. Charles Lindbergh was said to have eaten at the Inn before his historic flight in the *Spirit of St. Louis* to New York and Paris.

Limited parking is available at the end of Bird Rock Ave., where there is a paved wheelchair-accessible lookout. Birds, including pelicans and cormorants, do indeed roost on the rock. There is a stairway to the rocks below, where tidepools are exposed at low tide. No facilities.

Windansea Beach is a beautiful, white sandy beach with aqua-blue waters. The beach ranks alongside Malibu, San Onofre, and Huntington Beach as having a significant impact on surf culture, as well as the overall development of the sport of surfing. Windansea is known as one of the best reef breaks in the area. During the summer months, when other beaches may have two or three feet of surf, it is not unusual for Windansea to have significantly larger surf, perhaps up to six or eight feet high.

A prominent feature of this beach is the historic palm-frond-covered surf shack, first constructed on the sandstone shelf next to the beach in 1946 and rebuilt later. In the 1950s, annual summer luaus took place at the beach until police be-gan to curb the wild crowd. Many notable surfers have frequented this beach throughout the years. In 1963, using cement, iron, a mop, a light bulb, and a beer can, two local residents built a six-foot, 400-pound version of their "Hot Curl" cartoon character gazing out to sea, symbolizing a surfer's desire to find the "perfect wave." This surf and cultural icon helped inspire Hollywood to film a string of "Beach Party" movies in the 1960s, which included stars Frankie Avalon and Annette Funicello, among others; one movie even featured the statue itself. The surf culture at this beach was further memorialized by author Tom Wolfe in his 1968 novel, *The Pump House Gang*, which was about a group of surfers from Windansea Beach.

Windansea Beach

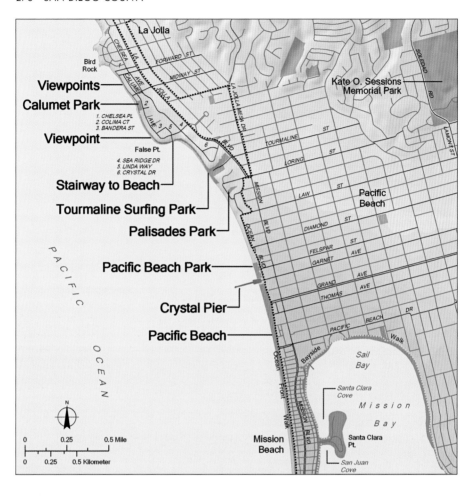

Tourmaline Surfing Park

La Jolla to Pacific Beach

	Sandy Beach	Rocky Shore	Trail	Visitor Center	Campground	Wildlife Viewing	Fishing or Boating	Facilities for Disabled	Food and Drink	Restrooms	Parking	Fee
Viewpoints		•										
Calumet Park		•	•									
Viewpoint		•										
Stairway to Beach	•	•					•					
Tourmaline Surfing Park	•	•					•			•	•	
Palisades Park	•		•				•			•		
Pacific Beach Park	•		•				•		•	•		
Crystal Pier							•					
Pacific Beach	•		•				•	•	•	•	•	

VIEWPOINTS: *W. of Chelsea Ave., La Jolla.* At the end of Chelsea Place there is an ocean overlook, and a steep, informal path leads down the hazardous bluff face to a narrow, rocky beach below. There are also blufftop viewpoints at the ends of Forward and Midway Streets.

CALUMET PARK: *W. of Calumet Ave., between Midway St. and Colima Ct., La Jolla.* An unsigned, landscaped picnic area is located on the bluff above the sea. There are benches and a paved perimeter path. At the north end of the park, a steep, unimproved path can be used to scramble down to the cobble beach. On-street parking; no facilities.

VIEWPOINT: *W. of Calumet Ave., opposite end of Bandera St., La Jolla.* A short dirt path near False Point leads to an ocean overlook. There is no access to the beach. On-street parking; no facilities.

STAIRWAY TO BEACH: *Seaward of Sea Ridge Dr., opposite Linda Way, La Jolla.* A somewhat eroded stairway leads to a cobble cove beach, popular for fishing and surfing. A somewhat wider, sandy beach lies downcoast of the stairway. There is a bench on the bluff, overlooking the sea. On-street parking only; no facilities.

TOURMALINE SURFING PARK: *W. of La Jolla Blvd., at the end of Tourmaline St., La Jolla.* This beach park, managed by the city of San Diego, is deservedly well-known for surfing and windsurfing. The park offers a wide expanse of sand, along with picnic tables, restrooms, and outdoor showers. The beach-level, no-fee parking lot has 103 spaces; street parking in the surrounding neighborhood can be hard to find. Lifeguards are on duty daily, year-round. For beach information, call: 619-235-1169.

PALISADES PARK: *W. of Ocean Blvd., between Loring St. and Law St., Pacific Beach.* Palisades Park is a grassy blufftop strip, from which several paths and stairways lead from Ocean Blvd. down to the sand. A pleasant picnic area with restrooms and an outdoor shower overlooks the beach near the intersection of Ocean Blvd. and Law St. The wide sandy beach below the bluff extends in both directions from Palisades Park, a total of three miles from Tourmaline Surfing Park south past Pacific Beach to Mission Beach. On-street parking.

PACIFIC BEACH PARK: *W. of Ocean Blvd., from Diamond St. to Thomas Ave., Pacific Beach.* Landscaped Pacific Beach Park, incorporating a paved path, benches, palm trees, and other amenities, runs parallel to the beach. At the north end of the park the path is located atop a low bluff, while at the south end the path slopes down to beach level. At the end of Diamond St. there are public restrooms and a beach shower, and a stair-

The palmy appearance of San Diego reflects the early efforts of pioneer horticulturalist Kate O. Sessions. When Sessions arrived in San Diego in 1884, a young woman 27 years of age, the town had no more than about 10,000 residents. Within a few years, the rapidly growing population and the marvelous climate helped her career to blossom. She raised and sold cut flowers (at the corner of 5th Ave. and B St. in downtown San Diego), landscaped the new Hotel Del Coronado (which opened in 1888), and propagated trees for San Diego's parks and streets.

As city gardener, Sessions favored eucalyptus, camphor, and pepper trees, along with the queen palm, also called Cocos plumosa. Sixth Ave. from Date to Upas Streets, next to Balboa Park, is lined with these graceful palms, which are now extraordinarily tall. Perhaps due to an early visit to Hawaii, her taste leaned toward exotic flowering plants, including bougainvillea, bird-of-paradise, and cape honeysuckle. But Sessions also promoted the use of colorful California natives, including white-blooming Matilja poppy, golden-flowered flannel bush, and blue-blossomed ceanothus. Kate Sessions exchanged plants and information with noted botanist Luther Burbank in northern California and plant experts elsewhere. She became known as "the Mother of Balboa Park," which she planted extensively, well before the park became the site of the Panama-California Exposition in 1915. Balboa Park is the home of the world-famous San Diego Zoo, as well as many museums and other attractions.

After 1914 Kate Sessions settled in Pacific Beach near the park that now bears her name. She encouraged the city of San Diego to build a road up Mount Soledad, where there is a spectacular 360-degree view of La Jolla, the city of San Diego, and the coastline (take Soledad Mountain Rd. north from Pacific Beach to La Jolla Scenic Dr. South and turn right). In her later years, Sessions received numerous honors for her work with plants and landscaping. At awards ceremonies she wore her usual garb of a grey tweed suit with a long skirt, high black shoes, and a firmly placed black felt hat. Sessions was forthright in her opinions, but modest about her own accomplishments. Upon receiving a noteworthy award when she was past 80 years of age, she was said to have remarked that her "bad ears" had prevented her from hearing what was said, but added, "I hope they were talking about the flowers and not about me."

way leads down to the sand; limited street parking nearby. There is also a stairway to the beach at the end of Felspar St. The paved shoreline path, accommodating pedestrians, skaters, and bicyclists, continues south along Pacific Beach.

CRYSTAL PIER: *End of Garnet Ave., Pacific Beach.* The 1,000-foot-long wooden Crystal Pier was opened at Pacific Beach in 1926 to attract land buyers to what was then a rural area. The pier contained an amusement midway lined with shops and arcades.

The major attraction was a stucco ballroom claimed to be "the only dance floor in the nation cushioned with cork where couples 70 and 80 years old can dance all night without getting tired." The ballroom was later demolished because of faulty construction.

In 1936, the pier was remodeled and a motel with cottages replaced the amusement midway. Today, Crystal Pier is the only pier in California that provides lodging over the ocean. Seaward of the cottages, the pier is open from 8 AM to sunset for public fishing.

Species of perch and croaker are frequent catches, and the pier also attracts numerous shark species and halibut. A fishing license is required; frozen bait is available for sale, but no other supplies, so bring your own. No dogs are allowed; there are no public restrooms located on the pier. For information, call: 1-800-748-5894.

PACIFIC BEACH: *W. of Mission Blvd., from La Jolla to Mission Beach.* The long, sandy stretch of Pacific Beach, one of San Diego's most popular beaches, is located south of Crystal Pier. There are separate swimming and surfing sections on the beach. Lifeguards are on duty daily, year-round. Lifeguard headquarters is located at the end of Grand Ave., and lifeguard towers on the beach are staffed seasonally. A beach wheelchair is available at the lifeguard headquarters; for information, call: 619-221-8899. For recorded weather and surf conditions, call: 619-221-8824. San Diego's lifeguards not only patrol the beaches, but also carry out cliff rescues, underwater search and rescue efforts, and river rescues during floods. Lifeguards receive training in first aid and cardiopulmonary recuscitation.

Dogs are allowed on Pacific Beach and in adjacent parks only if on leash and only from

Queen palms, 6th Ave. at Upas St. near Balboa Park

6 PM to 9 AM. Beach fires are allowed only in provided containers; burn only wood, charcoal, or paper, and put the fire out thoroughly before leaving. Restrooms and showers are located at the end of Grand Ave. and in the median of Pacific Beach Dr., a block inland from the beach. For beach information, call: 619-235-1169. A paved promenade shared by pedestrians, skaters, and bicyclists parallels the beach. Many recreational outfitters and other shops are located near the beach, mainly north of Pacific Beach Dr.

Pacific Beach

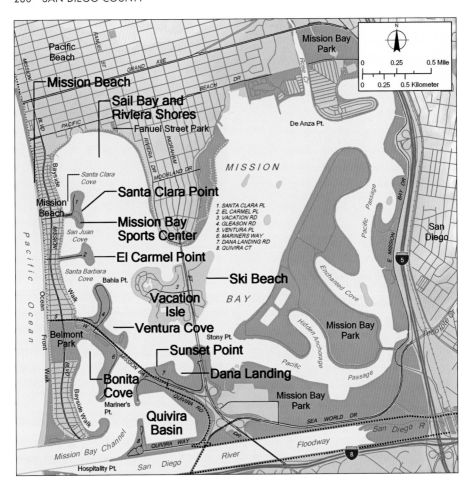

El Carmel Point

Mission Beach and Mission Bay West

	Sandy Beach	Rocky Shore	Trail	Visitor Center	Campground	Wildlife Viewing	Fishing or Boating	Facilities for Disabled	Food and Drink	Restrooms	Parking	Fee
Mission Beach	•	•					•	•	•	•	•	
Sail Bay and Riviera Shores	•	•					•		•	•		
Santa Clara Point	•						•		•	•		
Mission Bay Sports Center							•		•	•	•	
El Carmel Point	•	•					•		•	•		
Ventura Cove	•			•			•		•	•		
Bonita Cove	•								•	•		
Sunset Point							•		•	•		
Quivira Basin							•		•	•	•	
Dana Landing							•		•	•	•	•
Vacation Isle	•						•		•	•		
Ski Beach							•		•	•		

MISSION BEACH: *W. of Mission Blvd., S. of Pacific Beach Dr., San Diego.* Mission Beach, also known as the Strand, is perhaps San Diego's most popular beach. A paved, wheelchair-accessible promenade runs its entire length, and there is access to the beach from street ends along the peninsula. Free public parking is available north and south of Belmont Park, on both sides of Mission Blvd.; the lots fill up quickly on summer days.

Restrooms and showers are located north of Belmont Park at the lifeguard station at Ventura Pl., and south of Belmont Park on Ocean Front Walk. Lifeguards are on duty daily, generally from 9 AM to dusk; beach lifeguard towers are staffed seasonally. Dogs are allowed on the beach only if leashed and only before 9 AM or after 6 PM (after 4 PM from November 1 to March 31). Beach fires are allowed only in provided containers; burn only wood, charcoal, or paper, and be sure to put the fire out thoroughly before leaving. For recorded weather and surf conditions, call: 619-221-8824.

A manually operated beach wheelchair is available at the lifeguard station at Ventura Pl.; call: 619-980-0275. At the same location, two motorized wheelchairs are available during the summer from San Diego Park and Recreation Dept. staff, between 11:30 AM and 5:30 PM on weekends and between 11:30 AM and 4:30 PM on Monday, Wednesday, Thursday, and Friday; for information, call: 619-525-8247.

SAIL BAY AND RIVIERA SHORES: *S. of Pacific Beach Dr. between Mission Blvd. and Riviera Dr., Mission Bay.* The blue-green waters of Sail Bay and the adjacent sandy beach are accessible from several points around its perimeter. Paved Bayside Walk follows the inland edge of the beach, starting at W. Mission Bay Dr. and continuing around Sail Bay past Ingraham St. Pedestrian access to Bayside Walk is from Santa Clara Pl. and El Carmel Pl., as well as from adjacent street ends. At the end of Fanuel St. is grassy Fanuel Street Park, which is equipped with picnic tables, a children's play area, restrooms, outdoor shower, and parking. Access to the Riviera Shores beach is available via ramps or stairs at 3862 and 3750 Riviera Dr. and from Riviera Dr. south of Moorland Dr.; on-street parking only.

SANTA CLARA POINT: *E. of Mission Blvd. at Santa Clara Pl., Mission Bay.* Public boating facilities on the south side of Santa Clara

Point include a boathouse, a one-lane concrete boat launch, a dock, and a water-ski landing and takeoff area. On the north end of the point are tennis courts, a baseball field, and a recreation center. Picnic tables with barbecue grills overlook the bay.

MISSION BAY SPORTS CENTER: *1010 Santa Clara Pl., Mission Bay.* Rentals of kayaks, sailboats, catamarans, motor boats, and other recreational gear are available. Summer youth camps offer lessons in sailing, surfing, waterskiing, and other sports. Open daily from 7 AM to 7 PM; call: 858-488-1004.

EL CARMEL POINT: *E. of Mission Blvd. at El Carmel Pl., Mission Bay.* The Mission Bay Yacht Club, founded in 1927 and active in sailing races, occupies the tip of El Carmel Point. The public is welcome to use the sandy beaches and parking areas west of the yacht club, on both sides of El Carmel Pl.; small boats can be launched here. Restrooms are located north of the yacht club entrance. The public beach extends around San Juan Cove to Santa Clara Point; paved Bayside Walk runs along the back of the beach.

VENTURA COVE: *W. Mission Bay Dr. at Gleason Rd., Mission Bay.* This sandy swimming beach has lifeguard service during the summer. Picnic tables, fire rings, and restrooms. Another small picnic area is located to the north, at Bahia Point.

BONITA COVE: *W. Mission Bay Dr. at Mariners Way, Mission Bay.* Facilities at Bonita Cove include a sandy swimming beach with summer lifeguard service, a grassy picnic area with a children's play area, and restrooms with outdoor shower. The tip of Mariner's Point, south of Bonita Cove, is a nesting area for the endangered California least tern.

SUNSET POINT: *N. of Mission Bay Dr., end of Dana Landing Rd., Mission Bay.* This popular fishing spot has picnic facilities, fire rings, restrooms, and a paved path.

QUIVIRA BASIN: *S. of Mission Bay Dr. at Quivira Rd., Mission Bay.* Quivira Basin is the site of several privately operated marinas, where guest boat slips and other boating services are available. The Hyatt Regency

Ventura Cove

Mission Bay Hotel at 1441 Quivira Rd. has a full-service marina, with sport fishing charters and seasonal whale-watching trips; call: 619-221-4858. The Seaforth Marina is located at 1677 Quivira Rd.; for information, call: 619-224-6807. The Marina Village Marina at 1936 Quivira Way has 634 boat slips with pumpout station, fuel sales, restaurant, laundry, and showers; call: 619-224-3125. The Driscoll Mission Bay Marina at 1500 Quivira Way provides 220 slips, showers, a laundry, a boat hoist, yacht sales, dive boat charters, and a deli; call: 619-221-8456.

At Hospitality Point at the west end of Quivira Way there is a public park with excellent bay views, sheltered picnic tables, and fire rings. Mission Bay Park Headquarters is nearby at 2581 Quivira Ct.; call: 619-221-8800. A paved path leads from the jetty south of the Mission Bay entrance channel inland along the San Diego River, continuing east along Friars Rd. past Hwy. I-5.

DANA LANDING: *N. of Mission Bay Dr., at Dana Landing Rd., Mission Bay.* A hotel and marina facilities are located at the horseshoe-shaped cove at Dana Landing. The Dana Hotel includes marina facilities; call: 619-222-6440. The Dana Landing Launch Ramp is a 24-hour, five-lane concrete boat ramp. The Dana Landing Market and Fuel Dock is open daily from 6 AM to 7 PM; call: 619-226-2929. The 90-slip Dana Landing Marina is located on the west side of the basin; call: 619-224-2513.

VACATION ISLE: *W. of Ingraham St. at Vacation Rd., Mission Bay.* Turn west off Ingraham St. onto Vacation Rd. and then immediately right to a small public beach with parking and restrooms; lifeguard not stationed at this site. Turn left off Vacation Rd. to reach a picnic area on the south side of the island. Nearby is the Model Yacht Pond where enthusiasts operate model sailboats and powerboats. Shady trees surround the pond, and there are picnic tables and restrooms.

SKI BEACH: *E. of Ingraham St. at Vacation Rd., Mission Bay.* Ski beach is a popular water-skiing and boating spot, with a water-ski take-off and landing area, a four-lane concrete boat launch, a dock, picnic areas set among lawns, volleyball courts, and restrooms with outdoor showers. No swimming allowed.

The Giant Dipper roller coaster is one of Belmont Park's signature attractions. The roller coaster opened on the Fourth of July, 1925 as part of the 33-acre seaside amusement park that was originally known as the Mission Beach Amusement Center. Developer of the project was John D. Spreckels, a leading developer in San Diego. Belmont Park was extremely popular through the 1930s and 1940s, but by the 1960s it had entered a period of decline, as people sought other types of attractions. The Giant Dipper closed in 1976.

By that time, the city of San Diego owned the land on which the coaster stood, while the deteriorating structure itself remained privately owned and threatened with demolition. A citizens' group that included Toni Ciani, a preservationist and architect, formed as the "Save the Coaster Committee" and took over ownership of the roller coaster. The group also raised funds for restoration and successfully sought designation as a National Historic Landmark.

The renovated Giant Dipper was reopened to the public on August 11, 1990, operated by the San Diego Coaster Company. Riders once again flocked to the coaster. Today Belmont Park is one of California's few remaining seaside amusement parks. In addition to the Giant Dipper, There are bumper cars, a wave-riding machine, restaurants, and retail shops, and at the Plunge there is swimming in southern California's largest indoor heated pool.

Colors of the Coast

B EYOND the brightly hued beach umbrellas and bathing attire of southern California is a rainbow of colors in the natural world. The native plants and animals of southern California's coast and ocean display colors that are sometimes striking, sometimes subtle. Each color of the coast has a story to tell.

Manzanita

Red

There are approximately 60 species of **manzanita** within the genus *Arctostaphylos*. They are evergreen shrubs or small trees characterized by smooth, orange-to-red bark and stiff, twisting branches. Hikers find it hard to resist caressing the smooth, cool, silky red bark of manzanitas lining the trail. According to Sherwin Carlquist, an expert on California native plants, the rich, reddish coloration of manzanitas comes from tannins in the cells of the exterior bark. Tannins are bitter compounds that are toxic to organisms such as insects, birds, and bacteria, and, when present in the bark, most likely deter predation.

Strawberry anemone

The **strawberry anemone** (*Corynactis californica*) is often referred to as the club-tipped anemone. The strawberry anemone is not a true anemone but is actually more closely related to stony corals, although it lacks its relatives' hard exoskeleton. Individuals of this species are small, averaging one inch in diameter, and they display whitish tentacles extending from a pink-to-red colored body. The strawberry anemone reproduces by fission, a process in which the parent organism divides into two identical clones. Strawberry anemones sting and capture their prey by shooting out nematocysts, or stinging cells, from the tips of their tentacles.

Starry rockfish

Orange

The **starry rockfish** (*Sebastes constellatus*) derives its name from the tiny white and yellow spots that are distributed across the body of this bright orange-colored species. Typically, three to five larger white blotches also adorn the sides of this striking fish. The starry rockfish is a sedentary, deepwater species typically found associated with rocky reefs in depths ranging from 80 to 900 feet. Juveniles of this species are distributed along the shallower depths within this range. Starry rockfish may reach a total length of 18 inches and may live up to 28 years.

Dodder (*Cuscuta salina*) is a holoparasitic plant, completely dependent upon a host for water and nutrients. Dodder taps in on its host's nutrient supply by using a modified root system that penetrates the stem tissue of the host. Dodder, also known as witches hair, resembles a tangled mass of orange, spaghetti-like strands with tiny, white, morning glory-like flowers that bloom from May to September. The orange stems of dodder lack chlorophyll and are non-photosynthetic, and dodder leaves consist simply of minute scales. The total length of twining branches produced by a single dodder plant may exceed half a mile. Dodder seeds sprout at or near the soil surface, and while germination can occur without a host, dodder's roots have to reach a green plant quickly; dodder seedlings use airborne chemical cues to locate their host plants. The species called *Cuscuta salina* is found in the middle and upper zone of California salt marshes. Dodder's most common host plant is pickleweed (*Salicornia* sp.)

Dodder

Yellow

The **sea lemon nudibranch** (*Anisodoris nobilis*) is a brightly colored slug that inhabits the rocky reefs of the California coast. The sea lemon is deep yellow in color with small black spots and protruding bumps along its dorsal surface. Two antennae, called rhinophores, extend from the anterior, or front, end of this nudibranch and are used for sensory detection. This nudibranch emits a fruit-like odor when threatened and has an acidic taste, which deters potential predators. This species preys exclusively on specific sponge species, scraping off bites of food with a file-like radula.

Sea lemon nudibranch

Coast goldenbush (*Isocoma menziesii*) is an erect, shrubby perennial in the sunflower family. Coast goldenbush has slender, leafy, branching stems, and it grows up to four feet tall. It is common on exposed, dry sandy slopes and flats among coastal sage scrub and coastal strand plants, from central California to San Diego County. Coast goldenbush is an opportunistic species and is often one of the first plants to colonize disturbed areas. Coast goldenbush has bright yellow flowers and blooms longer than many plants, starting as early as April and often continuing into December.

Coast goldenbush

Greenbark ceanothus

Green

Often referred to as "California lilacs," ceanothus species are some of the most fragrant and colorful shrubs among California's native plants. They are also evergreen and very drought tolerant. "Soap bush" is another common name for ceanothus, because when the flowers are rubbed, they lather up. **Greenbark ceanothus** (*Ceanothus spinosus*) is large, attaining heights of 6 to 18 feet, and it is easily distinguished from other ceanothus species by its smooth, olive-green bark. The Greek word *ceanothus* means "spiny plant," and this species is especially spiny. Greenbark ceanothus has small pale-blue flowers that grow in showy clusters and bloom from February to May.

Two walking sticks

The walking stick insect is a master at the art of camouflage. This insect has evolved not only to look like a stem or leaf of the plant it inhabits, but also to match the color. Walking sticks in the genus *Timema* are wingless, plant-eating insects that inhabit the chaparral of California, other areas of the western US, and northern Mexico. The species name (*Timema cristinae*) for the **walking stick** refers to Cristina Sandoval, a University of California at Santa Barbara researcher who discovered the insect. *Timema cristinae* feeds on greenbark ceanothus and is the same light green as the leaves of its favored plant. The walking stick is preyed upon by birds and lizards, and matching its host plant is an adaptation to avoid being eaten, especially since birds have excellent vision.

Blue rockfish

Blue

Blue rockfish (*Sebastes mystinus*) can be found from California north to Vancouver Island at depths extending from tidepools to 1,800 feet, although these fish are most abundant at depths of 15 to 200 feet. Schools of thousands of individuals are often found associated with kelp forests. Blue rockfish prey on smaller fishes and invertebrates and can reach 21 inches in length and live up to 24 years. North of Point Conception along the California coast this is the most frequently caught rockfish in the recreational fishery, in southern California waters blue rockfish are also important members of the bottom fish community.

Dragonflies are in the order Odontata, a Greek word for "toothed" that refers to the flies' feeding apparatus. Adult dragonflies have two-part wings of equal length, with large compound eyes and reduced antennae. Dragonflies are predators, eating anything they can catch including other odontates. Their gray, green, or brown nymphs (immature forms) are abundant on the bottom of slow-moving waters, where they spend the first four years of their lives. The nymphs emerge from the water, shedding their skin to become adult, winged dragonflies for their last few months of life, during which they mate and lay eggs, and then die. Damselflies are very similar to dragonflies, except they are generally smaller and more fragile. When a damselfly perches, its wings are closed, whereas a dragonfly spreads its wings when it perches.

Blue-eyed darner dragonfly

Violet

Purple sage (*Salvia leucophylla*), a member of the Laminaceae, or mint, family, is a three-to-five-foot shrub commonly found in coastal sage scrub plant communities. All plants in the mint family have square stems and opposite leaves, and the native California mints, like purple sage, are very aromatic. Beautiful silvery-white foliage and rose-to-lavender-colored flowers, stacked in clusters, distinguish this sage. The species name *leucophylla* means "white-leaved." Purple sage blooms from May to July, and hummingbirds, butterflies, bees, and other insects collect nectar from the flowers. Quails love the seeds. Songbirds, lizards, and other forms of wildlife use it for cover.

Purple sage

The **Spanish shawl nudibranch** (*Flabellina iodinea*) can be found in waters extending from the intertidal zone to depths of 40 feet. This nudibranch has a dark purple body covered with brilliant orange cerata, which are structures used in respiration, blood storage, and defense. The Spanish shawl nudibranch preys primarily on an invertebrate animal called a hydroid, specifically on the species *Eudendrium ramosum*. It derives several benefits from this prey, including getting its vivid coloration from a pigment within the hydroid that then serves to warn off predators with its bright hue and foul taste. In addition, the nudibranch is able to store nematocysts (stinging cells) from the hydroid in structures called cnidosacs housed in the cerata. When a predator attempts to eat the nudibranch, it is often dissuaded by a mouthful of stinging nematocysts.

Spanish shawl nudibranch

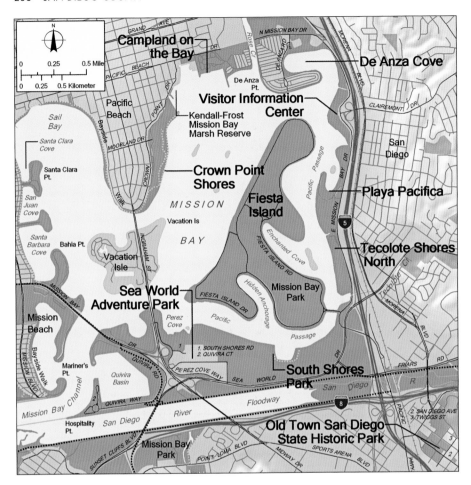

Playa Pacifica, Mission Bay

Mission Bay East and Old Town San Diego

	Sandy Beach	Rocky Shore	Trail	Visitor Center	Campground	Wildlife Viewing	Fishing or Boating	Facilities for Disabled	Food and Drink	Restrooms	Parking	Fee
Crown Point Shores	•	•		•		•				•	•	
Campland on the Bay					•		•		•	•	•	•
De Anza Cove	•				•	•				•	•	
Visitor Information Center				•					•	•	•	
Playa Pacifica	•	•					•			•	•	
Tecolote Shores North		•					•			•	•	
Fiesta Island	•		•			•	•			•	•	
South Shores Park							•			•	•	
Sea World Adventure Park				•		•	•		•	•	•	•
Old Town San Diego State Historic Park				•			•		•	•	•	

CROWN POINT SHORES: *E. of Crown Point Dr., Mission Bay.* Paved Bayside Walk follows a wide sandy beach along the shoreline east of Crown Point Dr. At the east end of Moorland Dr. there is a grassy park next to the bay with three large parking areas; facilities include picnic tables, barbecue grills, basketball courts, tot lot, restrooms, and outdoor showers. Lifeguards on duty during the summer. Parking lots close at 10 PM.

North of Crown Point Shores is the Kendall-Frost Marsh Reserve, a University of California research area, and the city of San Diego's Northern Wildlife Preserve. The two areas contain salt marsh habitat, which was much more extensive before creation of Mission Bay Park; the light-footed clapper rail and Belding's savannah sparrow depend upon the salt marsh. An interpretive kiosk is located on Crown Point Dr. just south of Pacific Beach Dr. No public access to the marsh.

CAMPLAND ON THE BAY: *2211 Pacific Beach Dr., Mission Bay.* This well-equipped private facility offers RV and tent camping. Facilities include a store, game room, playground, several swimming pools, and laundry. There is a marina, with recreational equipment for rent, and an RV dump station. Some restrooms and showers are wheelchair accessible. Leashed dogs allowed in limited areas. Call: 1-800-422-9386.

DE ANZA COVE: *3000 E. Mission Bay Dr., Mission Bay.* De Anza Cove has a swimming beach with summer lifeguard service and a boat launch ramp. Also available are picnic tables, a playground and volleyball area, and restrooms with showers.

The privately operated Mission Bay RV Resort on De Anza Rd. near N. Mission Bay Dr. offers RV camping with full hookups and a swimming beach; pets welcome. For information, call: 877-219-6900.

VISITOR INFORMATION CENTER: *2688 E. Mission Bay Dr., Mission Bay.* Take the Clairemont Dr. exit from Hwy. I-5 to the San Diego Visitor Information Center overlooking Mission Bay. The center offers lodging information and tickets to area attractions; gift shop and snack bar. Call: 619-276-8200.

PLAYA PACIFICA: *Off E. Mission Bay Dr., S. of the Visitor Information Center, Mission Bay.* A swimming beach with summer lifeguard service, picnic tables, restrooms, and basketball courts are at sandy Leisure Lagoon. A paved path follows the shoreline.

TECOLOTE SHORES NORTH: *Off E. Mission Bay Dr., S. of the Hilton Hotel, Mission Bay.* Spacious lawns, children's playgrounds (including one designed for children with physical disabilities), picnic areas, restrooms with showers, and several moderate-sized parking lots are located at this unit of Mission Bay Park.

FIESTA ISLAND: *Fiesta Island Rd. off E. Mission Bay Dr., Mission Bay.* Not landscaped like most of Mission Bay Park, Fiesta Island features grassland and dune habitat and is a good spot to look for shorebirds, grebes, and bay ducks. The only permanent facility is an aquatic youth camp run by the Boy Scouts. A permitted water ski area is located in Hidden Anchorage, and personal watercraft are allowed in the eastern part of Pacific Passage; go to Mission Bay Park headquarters at 2581 Quivira Ct. for a permit and information. Fire rings are located around the shore; dogs are allowed off-leash.

SOUTH SHORES PARK: *Sea World Dr. between Sea World and Hwy. I-5, Mission Bay.* The turnoff to this small boating area is east of the entrance to Sea World. Boat launch ramp and parking area, where boat owners may leave vehicles for up to 72 hours while out on their boats. Restrooms and an RV dump station; very limited parking for vehicles without boat trailers. No camping.

SEA WORLD ADVENTURE PARK: *Sea World Dr., Mission Bay.* This well-known theme park offers shows by dolphins and orcas and a close-up look at sharks, rays, tidepool creatures, and other marine animals. There are also amusement park rides, snack bars, gift shops, and fireworks displays. Sea World hosts school field trips and adventure camps for kids. Sea World has participated in a program that includes captive breeding of the endangered light-footed clapper rail, and through its Hubbs Research arm operates a rehabilitation facility for injured marine wildlife. Fee for entry and parking. Most facilities are wheelchair-accessible; wheelchairs and strollers available for rent. Open daily, but hours vary seasonally; call: 1-800-257-4268.

On Perez Cove at 1660 South Shores Rd. is the Sea World Marina, which has 190 slips and boat pumpout system. For information, call: 619-226-3910.

OLD TOWN SAN DIEGO STATE HISTORIC PARK: San Diego Ave. at Twiggs St., San Diego. In 1769, the first Spanish settlement in California was founded at the foot of Presidio Hill. In the early 1820s a plaza was laid out, and a small adobe town developed around it. This area was considered the center of town until the early 1870s when Alonzo Horton established a "new town" to the west, closer to the harbor. Old Town today recreates the lifestyle of California in the Mexican and early American periods from 1821 to 1872. Original adobe homes, including the Casa de Estudillo, are part of the park, which also features restaurants, shops, and a visitor center in the Robinson-Rose House. The park is open from 10 AM to 5 PM daily; call: 619-220-5422.

Old Town San Diego State Historic Park

What is now Mission Bay was explored in 1542 by Juan Rodríguez Cabrillo, who named it "False Bay" after mistaking it for the entrance to San Diego Bay. Historically, the San Diego River alternately flowed into one or the other of these bays until 1852, when the U.S. government built the first of several levees to make the river flow only into False Bay. Additional levees built in 1949-50 channelized the river so that it now flows directly to the Pacific Ocean.

False Bay was a vast marsh until the mid-1940s when a Chamber of Commerce committee recommended developing the area as a recreational attraction for tourists, to add to San Diego's mostly military economy. Creation of Mission Bay Park involved the dredging of 25,000,000 cubic yards of sand and silt and the subsequent use of the dredged materials to create the islands and peninsulas of the park. By the early 1960s, the park had achieved its current configuration; remnant marsh areas now exist in only a couple of places, although some additional marsh restoration is planned at the mouths of Rose and Tecolote Creeks.

Today, Mission Bay Park is the world's largest urban water-recreation park, measuring 4,600 acres in area, of which 2,100 acres are land and the remainder is open water. Public recreational facilities include picnic areas, restrooms, pedestrian and bicycle paths, tot lots, boating facilities, and miles of sandy beach. Commercial interests in the park include the Sea World theme park, several major hotels, marinas, restaurants, and aquatic-oriented businesses.

The scenic qualities and ease of access of Mission Bay Park make it a popular location for gatherings and special events. Group picnic areas are available for use by groups as small as a family or as large as a major corporation. Because the park is sometimes crowded during the summer months, most local organizations stage their company events during the spring and fall, when the southern California weather is ideal.

In early spring, the waters off Crown Point Shores are the site of the Crew Classic Regatta, a rowing competition that draws teams from across the country and some foreign countries. It includes junior, collegiate, and master rowers racing approximately 270 eight-oared shells in nearly 100 races. The Crew Classic draws anywhere from 15,000 to 20,000 spectators. In the fall, thunder rolls across Mission Bay when approximately 1,200 participants assemble for the annual San Diego Thunderboat Regatta. This high-powered racing event takes place over three days and draws crowds of close to 50,000 spectators. Finally, although neither the start nor finish lines are in Mission Bay Park, the Rock and Roll Marathon race, which draws approximately 20,000 runners every June, wraps around the eastern portion of the park.

Tecolote Shores North, Mission Bay

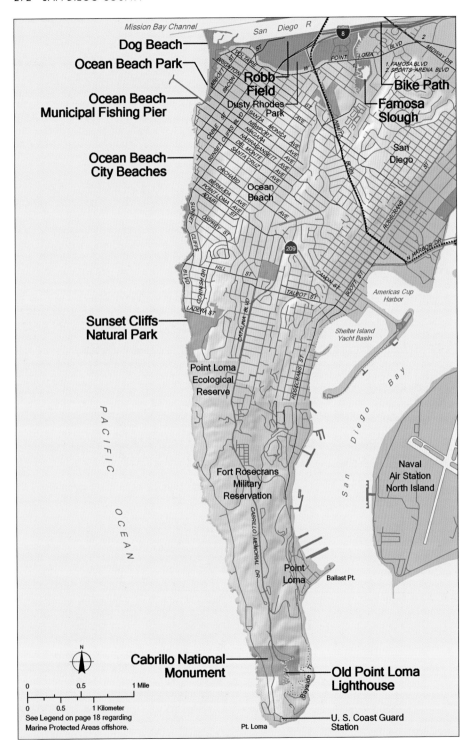

Mission Bay Channel

San Diego R

Dog Beach
Ocean Beach Park
Robb Field
Bike Path
Ocean Beach
Municipal Fishing Pier
Dusty Rhodes Park
Famosa Slough
San Diego

Ocean Beach
City Beaches
Ocean Beach

Sunset Cliffs
Natural Park

Point Loma
Ecological
Reserve

Americas Cup
Harbor

Shelter Island
Yacht Basin

PACIFIC

San Diego Bay

Fort Rosecrans
Military
Reservation

Naval
Air Station
North Island

OCEAN

Point
Loma
Ballast Pt.

Cabrillo National
Monument

Old Point Loma
Lighthouse

0   0.5   1 Mile
0   0.5   1 Kilometer
See Legend on page 18 regarding
Marine Protected Areas offshore.

Pt. Loma

U. S. Coast Guard
Station

1. FAMOSA BLVD
2. SPORTS ARENA BLVD

Ocean Beach to Point Loma

	Sandy Beach	Rocky Shore	Trail	Visitor Center	Campground	Wildlife Viewing	Fishing or Boating	Facilities for Disabled	Food and Drink	Restrooms	Parking	Fee
Bike Path			•			•						
Famosa Slough			•			•				•		
Robb Field									•	•		
Dog Beach	•		•			•			•	•		
Ocean Beach Park	•	•				•	•		•	•		
Ocean Beach Municipal Fishing Pier						•	•	•	•	•	•	
Ocean Beach City Beaches	•	•				•	•			•		
Sunset Cliffs Natural Park	•	•	•			•			•	•		
Cabrillo National Monument		•	•	•		•	•		•	•	•	•
Old Point Loma Lighthouse				•						•	•	

BIKE PATH: *S. side of San Diego River channel, San Diego.* A paved bicycle path extends from the parking lot at Dog Beach easterly along the south bank of the San Diego River to Pacific Hwy. Wintering ducks gather in the river channel, and shorebirds feed along the margins of the stream. The best bird viewing is in the stretch where the main river channel runs close to the path, between the W. Mission Bay Dr. bridge and Hwy. I-5.

Bicyclists and pedestrians cross over the San Diego River on Sunset Cliffs Blvd. (use the wide lanes on the west side of the bridge) to gain access to Mission Bay Park. There is a paved route along the north bank of the river that carries bicyclists east along Friars Rd., past Hwy. I-5 and into Mission Valley.

FAMOSA SLOUGH: *Off W. Pt. Loma Blvd. at Famosa Blvd., San Diego.* Famosa Slough, a saltmarsh and freshwater marsh, is a remnant of the once extensive Mission Bay wetland complex known as False Bay. The marsh has undergone restoration by the city of San Diego, assisted by the nonprofit organization, Friends of Famosa Slough. The marsh is a significant feeding and resting site for birds using the Pacific Flyway. Dabbling ducks, including mallards, northern pintails, blue-winged teals, and northern shovelers, rest and feed in the shallow area of the slough in the fall and winter. California least terns and shorebirds that include avocets, black-necked stilts, and killdeer forage and nest in sheltered areas of the wetland. The endangered Belding's savannah sparrow feeds on pickleweed in the slough.

Short trails both north and south of W. Pt. Loma Blvd. provide opportunities to view birds as well as native plants; look for arroyo willow and witches dodder. Monthly nature walks are held on the third Saturday of each month at 1 PM; meet at the kiosk at Famosa Blvd. and W. Pt. Loma Blvd. On-street parking.

ROBB FIELD: *End of Bacon St., off W. Point Loma Blvd., San Diego.* This park has fields for baseball and rugby, courts for tennis and basketball, and a skateboard park. In wintertime, burrowing owls have been spotted along the adjacent riverbank. Opposite Robb Field, on the south side of Sunset Cliffs Blvd., is Dusty Rhodes Park with lawns, children's play equipment, and restrooms.

DOG BEACH: *W. end of Voltaire St., off W. Point Loma Blvd, Ocean Beach.* Dog Beach is a wide stretch of sand at the mouth of the San Diego River that is used as an off-leash dog-exercise area. There is a large parking lot; non-wheelchair-accessible restrooms are nearby, at the end of Brighton Ave. Lifeguards staff the towers during the summer months.

On most San Diego city beaches, not including Dog Beach, dogs other than service animals are allowed only if leashed and only during early-morning and evening hours, that is, before 9 AM and after 4 PM from November 1 to March 31, and before 9 AM and after 6 PM during the rest of the year. For beach information, call: 619-235-1169.

OCEAN BEACH PARK: *Abbott St. at Santa Monica Ave., Ocean Beach.* This wide sandy beach has separate areas for swimming and surfing; there are also scattered tidepools. Anglers catch rockfish, lingcod, kelp bass, and Pacific bonito. For recorded weather and surf conditions, call: 619-221-8824. Ocean Beach is sometimes subject to very strong rip currents; use care in the water and swim near a lifeguard. Lifeguards are on duty daily, year-round, at the main station at 1950 Abbott St.; seasonal towers on Ocean Beach are staffed during the summer, generally beginning at 9 AM. A manual beach wheelchair is available at the lifeguard station; call: 619-221-8899. A temporary rubber walkway is often installed for wheelchair users.

Grassy picnic areas face the beach, and parking is at the ends of Santa Monica Ave.

and Newport Ave. Restrooms and beach showers are located at the lifeguard station at the end of Santa Monica Ave. Beach fires are allowed only in provided containers; burn only wood, charcoal, or paper, and extinguish fires before leaving the beach. For beach information, call: 619-235-1169.

Ocean Beach, originally named Mussel Beds for the mussel-covered rocks near the Ocean Beach Pier, began in the early 1900s as a summer cottage and resort community. In 1913, the Wonderland Amusement Park was developed on eight acres on the bay side of Voltaire St. from Abbott St. to the ocean. Attractions included a casino, dance hall, rides, a zoo, and a restaurant; the park was later demolished. In 1916 during Ocean Beach's "Hawaiian Days," Olympic gold-medal-winning swimmer Duke Kahanamoku held surfing exhibitions here.

Kelp washed to shore at Ocean Beach

OCEAN BEACH MUNICIPAL FISHING PIER: *End of Niagara Ave., Ocean Beach.* The concrete Ocean Beach Municipal Fishing Pier is the West Coast's longest, at 1,971 feet long. Fishing from the pier close to shore typically produces catches of perch and croakers. The far end of the pier extends into nearshore kelp beds, where anglers catch calico bass and sculpin. No fishing license is required to fish from the pier, although catch limits apply. Restrooms, a restaurant, fish cleaning stations, and a bait shop are available. Open 24 hours a day; wheelchair-accessible. Parking is at the foot of the pier.

OCEAN BEACH CITY BEACHES: *Between Ocean Beach Pier and the end of Bermuda Ave., Ocean Beach.* A series of small pocket beaches and a rocky reef with tidepools are located along the coast south of the Ocean Beach Pier. Stairways are at the ends of Narragansett Ave., Santa Cruz Ave., Orchard Ave., and Bermuda Ave., and a steep paved ramp is at the end of Cable St. There is a small parking lot at the end of Del Monte Ave.; no facilities. Anglers fish in the surf for perch, corbina, croakers, and occasional shark species; grunion spawn on the beach in summer. Found in rocky habitat in the area is the spiny lobster, a native species that lacks the pinching claw of the East Coast lobsters. The spiny lobster is most active at night, scavenging along the ocean floor for a variety of food such as mollusks, sea worms, small fish, and plants.

SUNSET CLIFFS NATURAL PARK: *Along Sunset Cliffs Blvd., from Adair St. to .3 mi. S. of Ladera St., Ocean Beach.* This park includes a mile-long shoreline strip where generally inaccessible rocky coves alternate with sandy pocket beaches. A dirt path leads along the high sandstone cliffs, providing spectacular views. From December to March, watch for migrating California gray whales. There are four small parking lots, two north and two south of the end of Osprey St., all good spots to watch a sunset; no facilities. A sea cave with a circular opening to the sky is located south of Hill St.

At the end of Sunset Cliffs Blvd., a stairway leads to a very narrow rocky beach; check tide tables before visiting. At Ladera St. and Cornish Dr. there is a sloping, unimproved parking lot and a chemical toilet. Steep, eroded trails, which can be hazardous, lead down the cliff face to pocket beaches used by experienced divers and surfers. Fifty acres of upland slopes south of Ladera St. are within Sunset Cliffs Natural Park.

Ocean Beach city beach at end of Bermuda Ave.

Cabrillo National Monument

CABRILLO NATIONAL MONUMENT: *S. end of Cabrillo Memorial Dr., Point Loma.* The Cabrillo National Monument Visitor Center houses exhibits about area history. The self-guided, two-mile-long Bayside Trail leads through coastal sage scrub habitat overlooking San Diego Bay. Guided bird walks start at the visitor center at 9:30 AM on the third Saturday of each month. The whale overlook affords ocean views and a vista of the working New Point Loma Lighthouse, which is not publicly accessible. Many paved walkways and some other facilities are wheelchair accessible; a wheelchair is available for loan at the visitor center. Dogs, other than service animals, are not allowed on park trails. The monument is open daily, including holidays, from 9 AM to 5 PM. Fee for entry. Call: 619-557-5450. West of the visitor center the rocky coastline and its excellent tidepools are accessible only to visitors who arrive by vehicle.

Adjacent to Cabrillo National Monument is Fort Rosecrans Military Reservation, the site of Fort Rosecrans National Cemetery. Interred there are veterans of the Mexican War of 1846–1848 and later conflicts, including 22 recipients of the Medal of Honor, the nation's highest military award.

OLD POINT LOMA LIGHTHOUSE: *Within Cabrillo National Monument, Point Loma.* The old Point Loma Lighthouse, built in 1854 with sandstone from Monterey and bricks from Ballast Point and Point Loma, is one of the eight original New England-style lighthouses on the West Coast. The lighthouse site is 462 feet above sea level. Heavy fogs obscured the beacon of the lighthouse, and it was abandoned in 1891 for a more suitable site closer to the water's edge. The old lighthouse has been restored to its 1880s appearance and is open to visitors; not wheelchair accessible.

Old Point Loma Lighthouse

Off Point Loma is an area internationally recognized as one of the best sites for diving within a kelp forest and undersea reef environment, in water depths of 30 to 80 feet. Kelp fronds reach toward the surface from boulder fields interspersed with unique pinnacles and overhanging rocky shelves. In deeper water, divers can investigate the ancient sea cliffs, now submerged, that once stood along the mainland shoreline.

As divers swim through the kelp forest, large schools of blacksmith and sardines shimmer through the upper canopy. The middle levels of the canopy host several species of large predators that hunt these small fish. Calico bass, white seabass, yellowtail, and the occasional giant sea bass glide through the kelp strands in search of their next meal. Divers may encounter hovering Pacific electric rays (also called torpedo rays), so named because they stun their prey using electric discharges of as much as 50 volts. Along the seafloor, sea urchins graze and sea cucumbers vacuum the bottom. Spiny lobsters scavenge along the reef, and bottom-dwelling fish, such as the California sheephead and various rockfish species, swim about.

Northwest of Point Loma is a 600-acre dive preserve known as Wreck Alley, where divers can investigate several sunken ships. In the year 2000, the HMS *Yukon*, a 366-foot-long Canadian destroyer escort ship, was intentionally sunk as an artificial dive reef. The ship descended to the seafloor on its own the day before its planned sinking, and it rests on its side, rather than upright as originally intrnded, in water 100 feet deep. The hull of the ship is covered with large white *Metridium*, or ostrich plume, anemones. Numerous reef-related fishes call the ship home. Sitting upright in 80 feet of water is the U.S. Coast Guard cutter *Ruby E*. The 165-foot-long ship was intentionally sunk in 1987. Colonies of strawberry anemones carpet the ship's exterior.

Blacksmith swimming through kelp canopy

Giant Kelp Forest

J UST AS redwood trees are dominant in their habitat, giant kelp in the giant kelp forest is at once the keystone species, the main structural element of the forest, a major nutrient source, and a habitat for other plants and animals. The kelp forest is a three-dimensional ecosystem, with a canopy community, an understory, and a bottom community, called the benthos. In this respect, the kelp forest can be likened to a terrestrial rainforest, with its structural complexity and its great diversity of species. Benthic species in the kelp forest include algae, sea stars, urchins, and flatfish, to name a few. The understory is comprised of algae that rise several feet off the seafloor and provide habitat for several invertebrates and many species of fish. The canopy of the kelp forest includes the fronds of the kelp, where many "yoy," or "young of the year," fish hide as they grow. Each kelp forest zone supports a unique suite of species

Giant kelp forests are found from southern Alaska to Baja California near the coast, generally where the ocean floor is rocky rather than sandy. Giant kelp thrives in cool, nutrient-laden ocean water that moves and surges, and in depths between 30 and 60 feet. A general observation is that giant kelp does not grow well above 68 degrees Fahrenheit. The annual ocean temperature off southern California averages 63 degrees Fahrenheit (as opposed to 54 degrees off northern California), and in summertime, aided by the Southern California Countercurrent that brings water north from Baja California, the ocean temperature often tops 70 degrees. As a result, kelp forests in southern California tend to be less dense; more vulnerable to grazing by snails, fish, and other herbivores; slower-growing; and less persistent than central and northern California kelp forests. Episodes of warmer-than-normal ocean water known as El Niños, or ENSOs (El Niño Southern Oscillation), when water temperatures may rise well above what kelp can tolerate, are extremely hard on southern California kelp forests. Kelp forests off Los Angeles, Orange, and San Diego Counties were virtually wiped out during the El Niño events of 1982-83 and 1998.

Giant kelp forest

The subtidal zone off southern California is dominated by sandy substrate, just as sandy beaches characterize much of the southern California coastline. Pockets of hard substrate on the ocean floor off southern California (comprised of sandstone, mudstone, and shale, in contrast to the hard volcanic and granitic substrates found farther north) are surrounded by plains of sand, thus exposing the kelp forests that colonize these areas to the erosive force of sand scour. Southern California kelp forests are also vulnerable to large swells caused by winter storms. During especially strong storms, the holdfasts of kelp are ripped from the sea floor, sometimes carrying large quantities of sand and shale with them. A mass of kelp is often washed up on the beach, where it forms large piles of wrack, which itself is an important beach ecosystem resource. The combined effect on southern California kelp forests of an El Niño event, with its warm ocean water, along with strong winter storms and the forces of sand scour is formidable. Fortunately for the kelp forests and for the species that thrive within and around them, giant kelp readily re-establishes.

Giant kelp (*Macrocystis pyrifera*) is a brown alga, or seaweed, that is more widely distributed in the southern hemisphere than in the northern hemisphere. It is found along the coasts of Peru, Chile, and Argentina in South America, along the tip of South Africa, and along most of the coast of New Zealand, as well as along the coasts of numerous southern hemisphere archipelagos. On the west coast of North America, giant kelp occurs mostly from Santa Cruz to Punta San Hipólito, which is midway down the Baja California peninsula, and in isolated patches beyond both of these boundaries.

Giant kelp

Giant kelp provides the structural component of the giant kelp forest, and it is what gives divers the impression of being in an amazing underwater grove of lofty trees. On average, an individual kelp organism lives from one to four years. Remarkably, under ideal conditions, a giant kelp stipe can grow up to two feet in one day. It can attain lengths of 120 feet and spreads out on the surface forming a thick canopy. Giant kelp has a two-part life history with both macroscopic (sporophyte) and microscopic (gametophyte) stages. Sporophylls that produce and release spores grow off the sporophyte near the top of the holdfast. The spores settle out to become either male or female gametophytes that produce sperm or eggs that, when fertilized, become the sporophyte completing the cycle. Giant kelp is harvested for the chemical called alginate, which is used in many commercial products, such as ice cream, tooth paste, and paint, to create a creamy finish.

Elk kelp

Elk kelp (*Pelagophycus porra*) is also called "elkhorn" or "bull" kelp, because its single stem, known as a stipe, bifurcates into two parts that resemble antlers or horns. Another kelp, *Nereocystis luetkeana*, shares the same common names and also has a single stipe leading from the holdfast that is anchored to the ocean floor to a single float bulb (pneumatocyst). However, while *Pelagophycus porra* has two stipes that each support one huge blade, numerous blades grow directly off the float bulb in *N. luetkeana*. *P. porra* grows in relatively deep water (60 to 100 feet), and its enormous blades may be an adaptation for gathering as much light as possible for photosynthesis. *P. porra* never reaches the ocean surface because its blades, which are 20 to 60 feet long, weigh it down. The blades hang in the water like giant curtains, and the ends drape along the bottom. Since *P. porra* lives in deep water and is less affected by storms, its holdfasts are about a tenth the size of the massive holdfasts found on giant kelp.

Blue-banded goby

The **blue-banded goby** (*Lythrypnus dalli*) is one of the most vibrantly colored species inhabiting California's coastal waters. This diminutive fish is characterized by a brilliantly red body marked by intensely blue bands, from four to nine in number. Blue-banded gobies rarely grow to more than two inches in length, and they live, on average, only 18 months. The blue-banded goby is a very territorial species often found on rocky reefs not far from a crevice or the safe haven offered by the spines of a sea urchin. The rounded shape of the pectoral and caudal fins of this fish is an adaptation that favors perching rather than swimming.

Blacksmith

Blacksmith (*Chromis punctipinnis*) are small, perch-shaped denizens of the California kelp forest. Adult blacksmith reach a total length of 12 inches and have a grayish blue coloration highlighted by several dark spots along the dorsal surface. Juvenile blacksmith display a bicolor pattern with a blue anterior and a yellow posterior. This abundant local species can be found in schools of hundreds of individuals all facing into the current, where they capture plankton for food. At night the fish retreat into the rocky crevices of the reef, where they can be found "sleeping" in large numbers, often piled on top of each other.

The **California moray** (*Gymnothorax mordax*) is easily identifiable as the only eel in California that does not have pectoral fins. Several rows of sharp canine-like teeth in a mouth that is often open, due to the need for the fish to pump water over its gills, create a menacing countenance. Morays live in rocky reefs, and their depth range extends from very shallow, in tidepools, to 130 feet. This species reaches five feet in total length, and may live more than 20 years. Morays are nocturnal predators with poor vision that rely on their sense of smell to locate the invertebrates that compose the majority of their diet. This eel species forms a symbiotic relationship with the red rock shrimp; in exchange for protection from predators, a small shrimp removes parasites and dead skin from its host eel.

California moray

The **tree fish** (*Sebastes serriceps*) is one of the many varied species of the rockfish family (*Scorpaenidae*) that is associated with reefs along the California coast. The tree fish has a compact body, reaching a maximum length of 16 inches, with large spines along its head and dorsal fin. The yellowish-olive-colored body bears several distinct dark bands. Tree fish have bright orange or red lips that they flare to ward off other tree fish competing for space on the reef. Juveniles do not possess the brightly colored lips and are not harassed by adult fish. The tree fish is a solitary species and a nocturnal feeder, preying opportunistically upon small fish, mollusks, and crustaceans. Like other rockfish species, the tree fish is slow-growing and long-lived.

Juvenile tree fish

The **California sea cucumber** (*Parastichopus californicus*) is the largest sea cucumber species found along the U.S. Pacific coast, reaching lengths of over two feet. The California sea cucumber has a soft, cylindrical, orange-to-reddish-brown body, covered with wart-like protrusions. Sea cucumbers are detritivores and use a system of oral tentacles to probe for detritus, bacteria, and fungi located within the seafloor sediment. Sea cucumbers are members of the animal phylum Echinodermata, and, like their sea star relatives, they are adept at regeneration, which can serve as an escape mechanism. When threatened, a sea cucumber may expel its internal organs and then crawl away from the confused predator. The lost organs are later regrown.

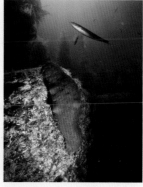
California sea cucumber

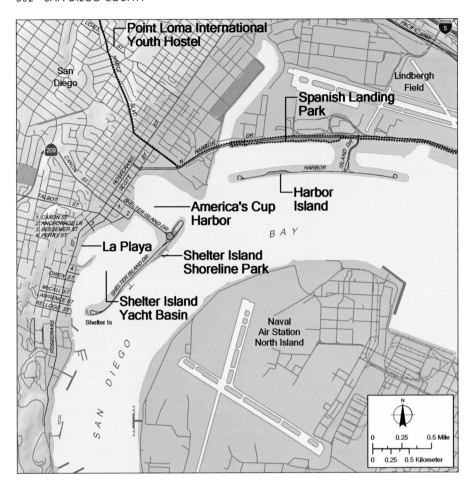

Spanish Landing Park

San Diego Harbor

	Sandy Beach	Rocky Shore	Trail	Visitor Center	Campground	Wildlife Viewing	Fishing or Boating	Facilities for Disabled	Food and Drink	Restrooms	Parking	Fee
La Playa	•		•				•					
Shelter Island Yacht Basin							•		•	•		
Shelter Island Shoreline Park	•	•	•			•	•	•		•	•	
America's Cup Harbor							•				•	
Point Loma International Youth Hostel									•	•	•	•
Spanish Landing Park	•		•				•			•	•	
Harbor Island		•	•			•	•			•	•	

LA PLAYA: *W. shoreline of Shelter Island Yacht Basin, San Diego.* A narrow strip of sandy beach is located along the yacht basin margin, with a narrow trail along it. From Rosecrans St., access to the shoreline path is available at the ends of Talbot St. and Bessemer St. Between 1824 and 1846, this was the site of a thriving cattle hide tanning operation. South of the Southwestern Yacht Club, access to the bay's edge is available at the ends of Perry St., Owen St., McCall St., Lawrence St., and Kellogg St. Street parking; no facilities. Swimming is prohibited within the marked yacht channel.

SHELTER ISLAND YACHT BASIN: *E. of Rosecrans St. and S. of Shelter Island Dr., San Diego.* Shelter Island was a submerged shoal until the city of San Diego began dredging San Diego Bay in the 1930s and 1940s, dumping the surplus onto the shoal. In 1950, the city added a causeway to connect the island to the mainland. Today, Shelter Island is developed with yacht clubs, hotels, and restaurants; the basin can accommodate almost 2,000 small craft. Boating facilities include transient berthing and mooring areas, marine supplies, and boat sales and services.

SHELTER ISLAND SHORELINE PARK: *Along Shelter Island Dr., San Diego.* There is public access to the edge of San Diego Bay on a paved, mile-long wheelchair-accessible path. Much of the shoreline facing out toward the bay is rocky, but there is a small sandy beach south of the traffic circle. Picnic tables and restrooms are spaced along the shore. Southwest of the boat launch ramp is a public fishing pier. The pier's location close to the harbor entrance offers anglers the best opportunity to catch several bay species, including sand bass, calico bass, jacksmelt, croakers, halibut, and several species of sharks and rays.

Facing the bay is a 24-hour, ten-lane boat launch ramp, the closest one in San Diego Bay to the ocean. Fuel is available at High Seas Fuel Dock, 2540 Shelter Island Dr.; call: 619-523-2980. Boat repairs and services are available at several locations on Shelter Island Dr. A public viewing area is at the corner of Shelter Island Dr. and Anchorage Ln. The Port of San Diego offers a 28-slip visitor dock, available on a first-come, first-served basis, at the southern end of Shelter Island; for information, call: 619-686-6227. A pumpout station is at the same location. For general information about Port of San Diego facilities, call: 619-686-6200.

AMERICA'S CUP HARBOR: *E. of Rosecrans St., N. of Shelter Island Dr., San Diego.* Formerly known as the Commercial Basin and home to a commercial fishing fleet, the basin offers public views of the boating activity from the west side of Shelter Island Dr., 200 feet north of the traffic circle. Fuel is available at High Seas Fuel Dock, 2540 Shelter Island Dr.; call: 619-523-2980. Sport-fishing and whale-watching trips are offered by a number of vendors, including Pt. Loma Sport Fishing at 1403 Scott St., 619-223-1627; Fishermen's Landing at 2838 Garrison St., 619-221-8500;

and H&M Landing at 2803 Emerson St., 619-222-0784. Classic wooden boats are on view at the annual Wooden Boat Festival, held on Father's Day weekend at Koehler Kraft Boatyard; call: 619-222-9051.

POINT LOMA INTERNATIONAL YOUTH HOSTEL: *3790 Udall St., San Diego.* Located midway between Mission Bay and San Diego Bay and near the Ocean Beach district, this Hostelling International facility has 28 beds for individuals or groups; family rooms available. Breakfast and linens included; community kitchen, laundry, garden, barbecue on site. Internet access available. Neighborhood shopping is nearby. Open daily from 8 AM to 10 PM, year-round. Call: 619-223-4778.

SPANISH LANDING PARK: *On the San Diego Bay side of N. Harbor Dr., W. of Harbor Island Dr., San Diego.* A sandy bay beach and paved shoreline path are located right across from Lindbergh Field, San Diego's International Airport. Picnic areas, restrooms, and parking lots are located at intervals. The park is named for the arrival in mid-1769 in San Diego Bay of a Spanish exploratory expedition commanded by Gaspar de Portolá and accompanied by Padre Junipero Serra. The band of soldiers, sailors, and potential settlers came from La Paz in Baja California, some by sea and some by land, all suffering great privation. One ship was lost at sea with all aboard. Upon arrival, Portolá soon set out overland to find Monterey Bay, while Serra remained behind to found Alta California's first Franciscan mission.

HARBOR ISLAND: *Along Harbor Island Dr., San Diego.* The south side of Harbor Island has a two-mile-long wheelchair-accessible path with benches and landscaping. A small grassy park with restrooms and off-street parking is located near the west end of Harbor Island Dr. There are fine views of San Diego Bay from Harbor Island; due south is Naval Air Station North Island.

The north side of Harbor Island, facing the airport, is lined with marinas that can accommodate a total of about 1,000 vessels; some marinas have guest berths or moorings. A fuel dock and a sanitary pumpout station are located at Harbor Island West, 2040 Harbor Island Dr.; call: 619-291-6443. Other facilities include hotels, restaurants, shops, and boating services.

Harbor Island

The San Diego Unified Port District was created by the California state legislature in 1962 to manage the harbor and maintain for statewide benefit the public tidelands and submerged lands surrounding San Diego Bay. The port is governed by a seven-member Board of Port Commissioners; one commissioner each is appointed by the city councils of Chula Vista, Coronado, Imperial Beach, and National City, and three commissioners are appointed by the San Diego City Council.

The approximately 5,480 acres under port jurisdiction include both water area and upland historic tidelands around San Diego Bay and the Imperial Beach coastline. The port is one of the largest naval ports in the country and draws a mix of commercial, recreational, and military traffic. The port has an active commercial maritime program, and operates two cargo facilities at the Tenth Avenue Marine Terminal and National City Marine Terminal. Each year there are 375 cargo ship visits to San Diego, and cargo tonnage topped 2,887,540 metric tons in 2006.

But perhaps more than any other California port, the Port of San Diego encourages and promotes the tourist and recreational use of public tidelands. On the tidelands there are sixteen public parks, ten miles of scenic bike and walking paths, six fishing piers, ten playgrounds, six public boat docks, four boat launch ramps, seven public beaches, and a wide variety of public art. There are also public marinas, private yacht clubs, boatyards, restaurant docks, and anchorages within San Diego Bay that, in total, provide approximately 6,000 boat slips.

More than 60 restaurants and 14 hotels operate on port lands, and San Diego's Convention Center is located on the bay front. The port also owns and operates the B Street Cruise Ship Terminal, and there are more than 200 cruise-ship visits to San Diego each year. Three museums—the Maritime Museum of San Diego, the San Diego Aircraft Carrier Museum, and the Railcar Museum in National City—are located on the bay. The port also provides sponsorship funding for numerous community events held in and around the San Diego Bay tidelands throughout the year, such as the Holiday Bowl Big Bay Balloon Parade held annually in December. For more information about the Port of San Diego, see: www.thebigbay.com.

Maritime Museum of San Diego

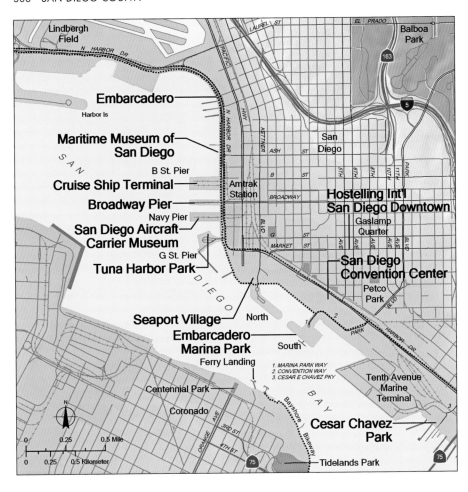

Embarcadero

San Diego Downtown

	Sandy Beach	Rocky Shore	Trail	Visitor Center	Campground	Wildlife Viewing	Fishing or Boating	Facilities for Disabled	Food and Drink	Restrooms	Parking	Fee
Embarcadero			•			•	•		•		•	
Maritime Museum of San Diego				•		•			•	•	•	
Cruise Ship Terminal						•						
Broadway Pier					•	•						
San Diego Aircraft Carrier Museum				•			•		•	•		•
Tuna Harbor Park						•						
Seaport Village							•		•	•	•	
Embarcadero Marina Park–North and South	•					•	•		•	•	•	
San Diego Convention Center							•			•	•	
Hostelling International San Diego Downtown							•		•			•
Cesar Chavez Park							•		•	•		

EMBARCADERO: *Along Harbor Dr., W. of downtown San Diego.* Views, restaurants, shops, and harbor excursion tours are available along the waterfront. There is a paved pedestrian/bicycle path with benches; the path is wheelchair accessible. Pedicabs ply the streets, offering rides to visitors; agree on a price first. San Diego's passenger rail station is near the Embarcadero, on Kettner Blvd. at Broadway.

MARITIME MUSEUM OF SAN DIEGO: *1492 N. Harbor Dr., San Diego.* At the end of Ash St. is a museum without walls, comprising a collection of historic ships. The collection includes the steamship *Berkeley*, the steam yacht *Medea*, and other vessels. The *Star of India* is the world's oldest ship still sailing. Since 1863, it has been around the world 21 times. Onboard the Maritime Museum's collection of ships are permanent and changing exhibits on maritime history, sailing ships, steamships, and pirates. For students there are history and science programs, some of them offered at sea. The MacMullen Library and Research Archives aboard the *Berkeley* houses materials about naval history and ships of the Pacific. Open daily, year-round, from 9 AM to 8 PM, and until 9 PM, from Memorial Day to Labor Day. Admission fee. Call: 619-234-9153.

CRUISE SHIP TERMINAL: *B St. Pier, San Diego.* Many cruise ship lines call San Diego home or visit the city regularly, tying up at the B St. Pier. Cruise ship itineraries include Mexico, the Caribbean, Hawaii, and the South Pacific. Passengers only are allowed in the terminal, due to security restrictions.

BROADWAY PIER: *Foot of Broadway, San Diego.* Boating services and fine bay views are available from the vicinity of the Broadway

San Diego Harbor Excursion boats depart from 1050 N. Harbor Dr. near the Broadway Pier for bay tours and nature cruises outside San Diego Bay; call 619-234-4111.

Hornblower Cruises offers trips around the harbor and whale or dolphin watching tours, departing from 1066 N. Harbor Dr.; for information, call: 1-888-467-6256.

The San Diego Water Taxi provides on-call service from Tuna Harbor Park to hotels on Shelter Island, Coronado, the South Bay and other points; call: 619-235-8294.

Pier, and cruise ships sometimes tie up here. The 26-mile, mainly flat, Bayshore Bikeway begins at the Broadway Pier and follows the perimeter of San Diego Bay. Start by taking your bicycle on the pedestrian ferry to Coronado and then follow the signed route south. There are nice views of the bay and beaches; parts of the route pass through industrial areas. Call the San Diego Association of Governments at 619-595-5324.

SAN DIEGO AIRCRAFT CARRIER MUSEUM: *Navy Pier, 910 N. Harbor Dr., San Diego.* The aircraft carrier *Midway* is open for self-guided tours, while docents, many of them U.S. Navy veterans, are available to give first-hand accounts of experiences aboard the ship. Restored aircraft are on view, along with flight simulators. The flight deck, restrooms, and some exhibits are wheelchair accessible. Gift shop and café. Fee for entry, but upon request, escorted visitors may go without charge to the flight deck only; call: 619-544-9600.

TUNA HARBOR PARK: *Foot of W. G St., San Diego.* A landscaped park provides views of San Diego Bay. A striking piece of public sculpture, entitled *Unconditional Surrender*, depicts a post-war homecoming, with the aircraft carrier *Midway* as a suitable backdrop. Metered parking. At the far end of the park, the G Street Pier contains facilities for the commercial fishing fleet.

SEAPORT VILLAGE: *849 W. Harbor Dr. at Kettner Blvd., San Diego.* Shops and restaurants overlook the water, with attractions that include a vintage, hand-carved wooden carousel. Open daily; call: 619-235-4014.

EMBARCADERO MARINA PARK – NORTH AND SOUTH: *End of Marina Park Way, San Diego.* The northern arm of the park is at the foot of Kettner Blvd., next to Seaport Village. The southern arm of the park is on the bayward side of the Convention Center, out of sight of Harbor Dr. To reach that area, turn off Harbor Dr. at the signalized intersection with Park Blvd. and head toward the bay. Both north and south parts of the park have lawns, picnic tables, restrooms, parking, and a paved perimeter path; the southern part also has basketball courts, a covered pavilion, a fishing pier, and a snack bar. This is a Port of San Diego park; call: 619-686-6200. San Diego Symphony summer pops concerts are held at Embarcadero Marina Park South; call: 619-235-0804.

SAN DIEGO CONVENTION CENTER: *Harbor Dr. at 8th Ave., San Diego.* The waterfront convention center has a striking, nautical appearance. From Harbor Dr. near the foot of 5th Ave., pedestrians can climb a stairway up and over the Convention Center, or ride the unique glass funicular elevator, to reach Embarcadero Marina Park. There are fine city and bay views from the top of the Convention Center.

HOSTELLING INTERNATIONAL SAN DIEGO DOWNTOWN: *521 Market St., San Diego.* Located in the popular, historic Gaslamp Quarter, the hostel has 74 beds and accommodates individuals or groups; family rooms are also available. Breakfast and linens included; community kitchen, laundry, game room, Internet access, and lockers available. Wheelchair accessible; non-smoking areas. Open 24 hours, year-round. For information, call: 619-525-1531.

CESAR CHAVEZ PARK: *Foot of Cesar E. Chavez Parkway, San Diego.* The landscaped park, maintained by the Port of San Diego, has picnic tables, restrooms, parking, and an observation pier; call: 619-686-6200.

Star of India, Maritime Museum of San Diego

"I had left him quietly seated in the chair of Botany and Ornithology in Harvard University, and the next I saw of him, he was strolling about San Diego beach, in a sailor's pea-jacket, with a wide straw hat, and barefooted, with his trousers rolled up to his knees, picking up stones and shells." So wrote Richard Henry Dana, Jr., author of *Two Years Before the Mast*, after encountering his acquaintance Thomas Nuttall in 1836 in a setting far from home. Dana, a former Harvard student, wrote the famous book about his experiences in the California hide-and-tallow trade in the 1830s. At the time of their meeting, Nuttall, curator of the Harvard College botanic garden, was near the end of a journey that brought him to the Pacific Coast via the Columbia River and then to the Hawaiian Islands, Monterey, Santa Barbara, and finally San Diego, where he prepared to sail home on the same ship as Dana, the *Alert*. Along the way, Nuttall picked up "flowers and shells and such truck, and had a dozen boxes and barrels full of them."

Thomas Nuttall, a self-taught naturalist, had an uncanny ability to recognize similarities and differences among plants, birds, animals, and minerals. After he arrived in the young United States in 1809 from England, he often ventured on foot and alone beyond the frontier, collecting specimens that were unknown to science. Back home, he organized and named his finds. Now, as then, scientists name an organism with two Latin words, the first for the genus and the second for the species. Names often illustrate a characteristic of the plant or animal or recall a related place or person. The one who first publishes a description is known as the "author" of a species.

Thomas Nuttall is the author of thousands of species of American plants and animals. He is also recalled in the names that others have chosen; Nuttall's sunflower (*Helianthus nuttallii*) was named in 1842 by Nuttall's colleagues, John Torrey and Asa Gray. The intertidal invertebrate of the California coast called Nuttall's chiton (*Nuttallina californica*) was named in 1847 by Lovell Augustus Reeve, an English shell fancier. John Torrey, incidentally, is well-known in southern California because of the Torrey pine (*Pinus torreyana*), named in his honor in 1855 by explorer Charles Parry.

Years before Darwin published *The Origin of Species* in 1859, Nuttall grasped the concept that organisms display adaptations to their environment. He sometimes predicted accurately where he would encounter certain plants, before he got there, based on characteristics of the environment. He authored an early guide to ornithology, provided bird specimens to John James Audubon, and contributed to books by other authors, who often lacked his extensive field experience.

Thomas Nuttall (1786–1859)

San Diego's Military History

I T WOULD BE difficult to overstate the significance of the military's role in shaping the history and the social and economic structure of San Diego. The statistics alone are impressive; there are approximately 95,000 uniformed military personnel assigned to various commands and units in the San Diego area. Dependents and families bring the total military population to about 175,000, with another 57,900 retired military personnel residing in San Diego County.

The bulk of the military presence in San Diego comes from the Navy and the Marines, whose facilities in San Diego County include Marine Corps Air Station Miramar, Marine Corps Recruit Depot (MCRD) adjacent to Lindbergh Field, Marine Corps Base Camp Pendleton, Naval Station San Diego (known locally as the 32nd Street Naval Station), Naval Base Coronado, and Naval Base Point Loma. San Diego is the site of the largest naval fleet in the world; 69 Navy ships call San Diego Bay home—nearly one-sixth of the Navy's entire fleet and about one-third of the U.S. Pacific Fleet. The city's naval complex is the Navy's second largest, behind only that in Norfolk, Virginia.

There are approximately 148,616 military jobs in the San Diego region, and studies estimate that $11.7 billion in direct defense spending supports an additional 145,660 San Diego jobs. This represents 20 percent of the total employment in San Diego. The multiplier effect of military base operations, defense contracts, payrolls, and other spending accounts for up to one-fourth of the region's total economic output.

San Diego was not always the military powerhouse that it is today, but it has been the site of at least one military facility since 1769, when it was settled by Spanish-speaking colonists. The Presidio of San Diego, now a park and historical landmark, was a fort established on May 14, 1769 by Commandant Pedro Fages under the authority of the King of Spain, Charles III. The Presidio was the first permanent European settlement on the Pacific Coast of what is now the United States and was the base of operations for the Spanish colonization of California. It remained the seat of military power in California through its Mexican period.

San Diego Aircraft Carrier Museum, San Diego Harbor

View from Cabrillo National Monument, Naval submarine facilities near Ballast Point, at left

But it was during the pre-World War I era that the San Diego transformation into a military town began in earnest. The special relationship between San Diego and the military did not arise by happenstance, but was the result of a deliberate effort by city leaders at the turn of the 20th century to cultivate a means of job and wealth creation that would be an alternative to the traditional smokestack industries that might have damaged the city's quality of life and famous tourist appeal.

Much of the credit for the grand strategy to make San Diego the "Gibraltar of the Pacific" goes to William Kettner, a local insurance businessman and civic booster. In 1908, President Theodore Roosevelt dispatched the Navy's Great White Fleet—an armada of 27 naval warships—on a record-setting, round-the-world cruise to announce the newly established "360-degree" defense capacity of the United States, based on sea power. When they learned the fleet was not planning on stopping at San Diego, a group of San Diego civic leaders, headed by Kettner, pleaded their case to the Navy, which reluctantly agreed to a brief three-day stay. The fleet had to anchor off Coronado, since San Diego Bay at that time was too shallow to accommodate battleships.

The fleet was greeted at San Diego, its first U.S. port of call, on April 14, 1908 by thousands of exuberant residents. The following days were filled with parades, speeches, and banquets, as the sailors were given the royal treatment by the citizenry. Practically the entire population came out to celebrate.

The event proved pivotal in San Diego's development. Inspired by the outpouring of public support for the fleet, Kettner and other city leaders began a campaign to promote San Diego's visibility and strategic importance in Washington, D.C. To do that, the city needed a local representative. In 1912, William Kettner ran for and was elected to Congress with a mandate to bring home federal defense dollars.

Through his position on the Naval Affairs Committee, Kettner befriended Franklin D. Roosevelt, then President Wilson's Assistant Secretary of the Navy. Roosevelt visited San Diego during its 1915 Panama-California Exposition, which Kettner used to successfully promote San Diego as the ideal location to provide security for the soon-to-be-completed Panama Canal and as a place to train naval recruits. Over the eight years of his congressional term Kettner successfully obtained federal money to dredge San Diego Bay to accommodate modern deep-draft warships, build the Naval Fuel Station on Point Loma and the Naval Radio Station near College Grove, and to add facilities at the Naval Station at 32nd Street, Naval Base Coronado, and the Naval Hospital next to Balboa Park. In each case, there was considerable competition from San Francisco and Los Angeles to attract the federal money and prestige associated with these facilities, and their presence in San Diego is a credit to Kettner's shrewd, aggressive politics and unflagging local boosterism. While not yet a major base, by the end of World War I, San Diego was the only West Coast city in a position to offer the efficiencies of concentrated naval services. After he died in 1930 at age 65, Kettner was honored by the city's renaming of Arctic Street as Kettner Boulevard.

After the end of World War I, San Diego's growing military infrastructure began to attract commercial interests. On May 9, 1927 Charles Lindbergh departed from the naval base at North Island, Coronado in the *Spirit of St. Louis*, an airplane custom-built in San Diego by Ryan Airlines, on his way toward completing the world's first solo trans-Atlantic flight, from New York to Paris.

As World War II approached, Reuben H. Fleet relocated Consolidated Aircraft from Buffalo, New York to San Diego and began the production of seaplanes and Liberator bombers for sale to the U.S. government and its allies. World War II transformed the San Diego economy and landscape. The war mobilization effort in San Diego attracted tens of thousands of defense workers from around the nation. In 1940 alone, 50,000 workers and their families moved to San Diego in search of employment in the defense industry. Between 1940 and 1950, San Diego's population more than doubled.

With its huge defense plants and proliferating military bases, a greater percentage of San Diegans were involved in the war effort than almost anywhere else in the country. Working in three eight-hour shifts around the clock, Consolidated Aircraft produced 33,000 airplanes during the war years, including B-24 Liberator bombers and PBY Catalina flying boats. Ryan Aeronautical Company built 1,300 trainer planes for the Army and Navy. Consolidated Aircraft later acquired Vulcee Aircraft and became Convair—for decades the largest private employer in the county.

Following the end of World War II, the arms race between the United States and the Soviet Union poured tens of billions of dollars into San Diego defense industries. In the 1980s, defense spending was largely responsible for making San Diego the leader in California in employment and population gains, and one of the fastest-growing metropolitan areas in the United States.

With the end of the Cold War, cutbacks in U.S. defense spending and resulting impacts to the aerospace industry were a jolt to San Diego's economy. Just as they did before World War I, San Diego's leaders turned to investment in environmentally and tourist-friendly industries, this time including computer technology, biotechnology, and international trade.

Historically, the military presence has impacted the natural environment and public recreation in a number of ways. The Navy holds deed to about one-third of the total shoreline around San Diego Bay, most of which is off-limits to the public for security reasons. Sediments and fish in the bay are often contaminated by a range of toxic compounds associated with military and industrial operations. Fuel storage tanks beneath parts of the Point Loma Naval Base have leaked about 1.5 million gallons of fuel.

With considerable encouragement from environmentalists, the military itself has increasingly taken on a stewardship role in preserving and improving the environment. Clean-up and restoration activities are being undertaken at numerous sites around San Diego Bay and also at the north end of San Diego County's coast, at Camp Pendleton. Camp Pendleton represents one of the last significant major open spaces in coastal southern California, and is home to 17 threatened or endangered species. The Marine Corps base occupies approximately 125,000 acres of largely undeveloped land, with more than 17 miles of coastline. An annual bird survey determined that one-third of the estimated 3,000 least Bell's vireos in existence make their home at Camp Pendleton, as do almost all of the 2,000-or-fewer remaining Pacific pocket mice. Southern steelhead trout swim in the base's San Mateo Creek, brown pelicans skim the coastline, and rare plant species, such as San Diego button celery, sprout around seasonal pools. Formerly available to the public for hiking and recreation, Camp Pendleton has been largely closed after the events of September 11, 2001. However, hunting and fishing permits are available to all Marines and former Marines and a public bicycle route crosses the base.

While no longer a "sleepy little Navy town," the City of San Diego and the surrounding area still contain the largest military and defense complex in the nation, if not the world. On the waterfront of San Diego Bay, near downtown San Diego, is the USS *Midway*, the longest-serving aircraft carrier in the history of the U.S. Navy, now part of the San Diego Aircraft Carrier Museum. Each year in early summer, a group of survivors of the Battle of Midway, involving the aircraft carriers USS *Enterprise*, USS *Yorktown*, and USS *Hornet*, gather for a photograph on the flight deck of the USS *Midway* Museum to pay tribute to those sailors and marines who fought at that crucial battle. The 1942 carrier battle of Midway Island is considered to be the turning point of World War II and proved conclusively the potential of naval aviation. The selection of San Diego as the site for the USS *Midway* Museum reflects both the city's long history with the military and the ongoing close relationship between the two.

USS *Midway*, San Diego Aircraft Carrier Museum

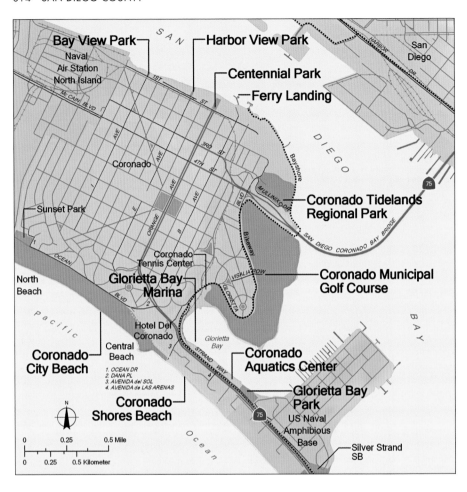

Coronado Tidelands Regional Park

Coronado

	Sandy Beach	Rocky Shore	Trail	Visitor Center	Campground	Wildlife Viewing	Fishing or Boating	Facilities for Disabled	Food and Drink	Restrooms	Parking	Fee
Bay View Park						•		•				
Harbor View Park						•						
Centennial Park								•				
Ferry Landing						•	•		•	•	•	
Coronado Tidelands Regional Park	•		•			•	•	•		•	•	
Coronado Municipal Golf Course									•	•	•	•
Coronado City Beach	•					•	•			•		
Coronado Shores Beach	•					•	•				•	
Glorietta Bay Marina							•				•	•
Coronado Aquatics Center							•		•	•	•	•
Glorietta Bay Park	•					•	•			•	•	

BAY VIEW PARK: *End of "I" Ave. at 1st St., Coronado.* A small, nicely landscaped park with benches and a paved, wheelchair-accessible viewpoint faces the San Diego skyline. At low tide, look for shorebirds feeding on the nearby flats. A city of Coronado park. Call: 619-522-7300.

HARBOR VIEW PARK: *End of E Ave. at 1st St., Coronado.* A short landscaped path leads to a bay overlook. No facilities.

CENTENNIAL PARK: *End of Orange Ave. at 1st St., Coronado.* A lovely, landscaped park with a paved promenade along the water and especially nice views of San Diego and the bay. Leashed dogs allowed on sidewalks only. Call: 619-522-7300.

FERRY LANDING: *End of B Ave. at 1st St., Coronado.* The ferry pier, where pedestrians and bicyclists embark for the Broadway Pier in San Diego, doubles as a fishing pier. A small sandy beach is next to the pier. The adjacent shopping area has food services and restrooms. Coronado's Visitor Center is at 1100 Orange Ave. and is open daily from 9 AM to 5 PM on weekdays and from 10 AM to 5 PM on weekends; call: 619-437-8788. For San Diego Padres games at PETCO Park, park free at the ferry landing in Coronado and ride across the harbor; call: 619-234-4111.

CORONADO TIDELANDS REGIONAL PARK: *End of Mullinix Dr., off Glorietta Blvd., Coronado.* This large bayfront park is maintained by the Port of San Diego. There are ball fields, picnic areas, children's play equipment, and ample lawns. There is also a sandy beach, a good place to launch a kayak. The elaborate Coronado Skatepark has concrete bowls, ramps, and jumps; for hours, fees, and rules, call: 619-708-8341. Leashed dogs allowed in Tidelands Park on paved areas only. The paved Bayshore Bikeway passes through the park along the bay's edge and continues south under the San Diego-Coronado Bridge, skirting inland around the Coronado Municipal Golf Course.

CORONADO MUNICIPAL GOLF COURSE: *2000 Visalia Row, off Glorietta Blvd., Coronado.* An 18-hole, par-72 public course overlooks Glorietta Bay. Pro shop, driving range and practice bunker, affordable green fees, club and cart rentals. Dress code requires collared shirts and no cut-offs. Call: 619-435-9485. South of the golf course at 1501 Glorietta Blvd., the Coronado Tennis Center offers eight public courts, instruction, and a pro shop; call: 619-435-1616.

CORONADO CITY BEACH: *W. of Ocean Blvd., Coronado.* A very wide sandy public beach extends almost two miles along the oceanfront of Coronado between two military facilities, Naval Air Station North Island and the U.S. Naval Amphibious Base. Coronado City Beach is popular for swimming, surfing, and surf fishing. Anglers catch shallow sandy bottom fish, including surfperch, corbina, queenfish, and croaker. Mexico's Coronado Islands are often visible offshore, some 13 miles away. The Coronado Surfing Academy offers surfing lessons at Coronado and at Silver Strand State Beach; call: 619-293-3883.

Just north of the Hotel Del Coronado, on the stretch of sand known as Central Beach, there are volleyball courts, restrooms, and the main Coronado lifeguard station. Beach wheelchairs available from a lifeguard include a manual chair that can be used without assistance and a powered chair; call: 619-435-1867. Lifeguards are on duty from 9 AM to dusk. No glass or alcohol allowed on the beach.

Near the intersection of Ocean Blvd. and Ocean Dr. is North Beach, which has fire rings, restrooms, and a dog exercise area and dog wash; pets must be under voice command. A lifeguard tower on North Beach is staffed seasonally. On the inland side of Ocean Blvd. is grassy Sunset Park.

CORONADO SHORES BEACH: *Seaward of Coronado Shores Condominiums on Hwy. 75, Coronado.* Downcoast from the Hotel Del Coronado is another stretch of Coronado's City Beach. A seasonal lifeguard tower on the beach is staffed during the summer. California barracuda and white seabass spawn near shore. Anglers catch corbina and surfperch from the beach. A wheelchair-accessible concrete promenade runs along the top of a seawall; a paved ramp to the promenade leads to a no-fee parking area at the end of Avenida de las Arenas. Fee parking is located between the Hotel Del Coronado and Avenida del Sol.

GLORIETTA BAY MARINA: *1715 Strand Way, Coronado.* The cozy Glorietta Bay Marina accommodates 100 boats and has pumpout facilities; for use of a guest slip, call: 619-435-5203. Adjacent to the marina is the Hotel Del Coronado's historic Coronado Boathouse, now renovated as a bay-view restaurant.

CORONADO AQUATICS CENTER: *1845 Strand Way, Coronado.* The Coronado Aquatics Center is a municipal swimming facility, open to the public, with a 50-meter lap pool and a 25-yard instructional pool, both outdoors and heated. Showers, locker rooms, and snack bar. Facilities are wheelchair accessible. Open year-round; fee for entry. For hours and information, call: 619-522-2464. A gymnasium with courts for basketball, volleyball, and badminton, a climbing wall, and a fitness center is located adjacent to the Aquatics Center, which is part of the Coronado Community Center.

GLORIETTA BAY PARK: *1875 Strand Way, Coronado.* This small city park, adjacent to the Aquatics Center, faces Glorietta Bay. There is a sandy beach next to a lawn with picnic sites, some wheelchair-accessible, as well as a children's play area and restrooms. The park shares an entrance from Strand Way with the Coronado Community Center, opposite Avenida de las Arenas.

A small boat launch ramp with a pier, funded by the City of Coronado and the California Dept. of Boating and Waterways, is located between the Coronado Community Center and Glorietta Bay Park. A 72-hour anchorage area is located nearby. For permits and information, contact the Harbor Police; call: 619-686-6272.

Coronado Shores Beach

The legendary Hotel Del Coronado, located on 28 oceanfront acres, opened for business in 1888 and has been a favorite destination of dignitaries, the affluent, and families ever since. With its tall cupolas, red turrets, and gingerbread trim, the "Hotel Del," as it is referred to by the locals, is one of the few surviving examples of a wooden Victorian beach resort. The Hotel Del was designated a National Historic Landmark in 1977.

The Del's colorful history dates back to 1885, when businessmen Elisha S. Babcock, H.L. Story, and Jacob Gruendike bought all of Coronado and North Island for $110,000. After individual lots were subdivided and auctioned off, the money generated was used to begin construction of the hotel in 1886. The Hotel Del Coronado was the first hotel in the world to have electric lighting throughout. Every room in the main building of the hotel was unique and extravagantly furnished. The magnificent Crown Room dining area has a 33-foot-high, rib-vaulted ceiling constructed without nails. Tennis, swimming in the pools, and rabbit hunts were some of the activities offered to travelers seeking luxurious accommodations and health benefits from the salt air.

Famous guests over the years include Thomas Edison, L. Frank Baum (who wrote *The Wizard of Oz*), Charlie Chaplin, Babe Ruth, and Charles Lindbergh. In 1920, the future King Edward VIII of England was a guest at the hotel. Rumor has it he may have met his future wife, Wallis Simpson, at the hotel. Every president since Lyndon Johnson has stayed at the Del. In 1958, the Del was the backdrop for the comedy classic *Some Like It Hot*, starring Marilyn Monroe, Tony Curtis, and Jack Lemmon. The Del is even reported to have its own ghost—Kate Morgan, a young woman who checked into the hotel in November 1892 and was found dead on the beach four days later, a victim of suicide or possibly murder.

Today the Del has been both restored and expanded, and it now has nearly 800 rooms, including those in towers and private cottages adjacent to the original structure. A public promenade runs along the beach. During the winter holidays, the hotel sets up a public outdoor beachfront ice-skating rink.

Hotel Del Coronado

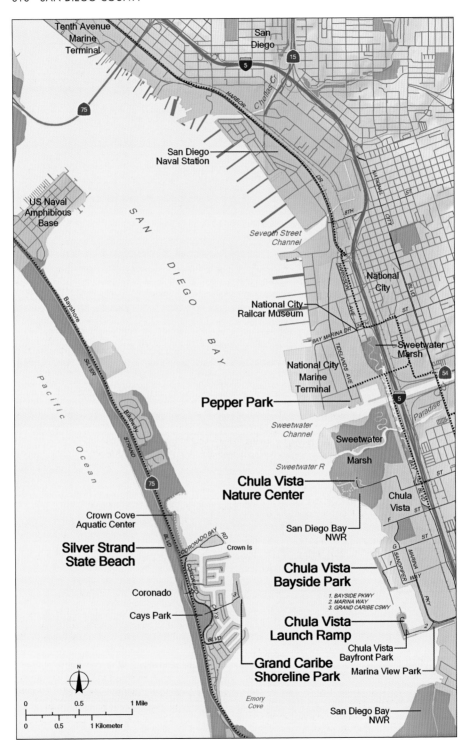

South San Diego Bay

	Sandy Beach	Rocky Shore	Trail	Visitor Center	Campground	Wildlife Viewing	Fishing or Boating	Facilities for Disabled	Food and Drink	Restrooms	Parking	Fee
Pepper Park						•	•		•	•	•	
Chula Vista Nature Center			•	•		•		•	•	•	•	•
Chula Vista Bayside Park			•			•	•	•		•	•	
Chula Vista Launch Ramp							•	•		•	•	
Grand Caribe Shoreline Park							•	•		•		
Silver Strand State Beach	•		•	•	•	•	•		•	•	•	

PEPPER PARK: *S. end of Tidelands, Ave., National City.* Among busy port facilities is an eight-lane boat launching ramp and landing dock with a sanitary pumpout station. The park includes a landscaped picnic area with barbecue grills, children's play equipment, restrooms, and a fishing pier lighted for night use. The parking area is open from 6:30 AM to 9:00 PM. Use the Bay Marina Dr. exit from Hwy. I-5 to reach Tidelands Ave. For information, call: 619-686-6200. The 244-slip Pier 32 Marina, opened in 2008 next to Pepper Park, includes 244 slips, showers, laundry, and a delicatessen. Call: 1-800-729-7547. The National City Railcar Museum is near Pepper Park, at the intersection of Bay Marina Dr. and Harrison Ave.

CHULA VISTA NATURE CENTER: *Foot of E St., within Sweetwater Marsh, Chula Vista.* The Chula Vista Nature Center contains exhibits depicting Southern California's coastal habitats, including bay waters, salt and freshwater marshes, and upland habitats. An aquarium displays fish and moon jellies, and a shallow touch tank houses sharks and rays for close-up inspection. Walk-through aviaries typically contain shorebirds and ducks, and hawks and owls are on display, too; birds are rescue animals that cannot be released into their native habitats. Endangered light-footed clapper rails have been raised here in a captive breeding program. A native plant garden adjoins the Nature Center, and there is a mile-and-a-half-long loop trail with views of Sweetwater Marsh; guided nature walks are offered.

Sweetwater Marsh and the south end of San Diego Bay together make up the 2,620-acre San Diego Bay National Wildlife Refuge complex, which protects most of the remaining coastal salt marsh and intertidal mudflat habitat found in San Diego Bay. The Belding's savannah sparrow, light-footed clapper rail, and western snowy plover, all threatened or endangered species, may be found at Sweetwater Marsh.

To minimize impacts on the marsh, visitors park off-site in the free lot at E St. and Bay Blvd. in Chula Vista; a free shuttle to the Nature Center runs every 10 to 15 minutes. The shuttle accommodates strollers and wheelchairs. Alternatively, take the San Diego Trolley to the nearby E Street Station and ask the Visitor Information Center staff to call for a shuttle pickup, or call the Nature Center direct. The Nature Center is open Tuesday through Sunday, except major holidays, from 10 AM to 5 PM (last shuttle to the center is at 4 PM). Fee for entry. Gift shop and picnic areas available; OK to bring food. Call: 619-409-5900.

CHULA VISTA BAYSIDE PARK: *End of Bayside Pkwy., Chula Vista.* From Marina Pkwy., take Sandpiper Way to Bayside Pkwy. Chula Vista Bayside Park includes a quarter-mile of shoreline with shady lawns and picnic facilities, restrooms, and parking. A paved pedestrian and bicycle path runs along the shore. For park information, call: 619-686-6200. The Chula Vista Marina, at Sandpiper Way and Marina Parkway, has 553 slips, a guest dock, and two restaurants, and the adjacent RV park has 237 sites with full hook-ups; call: 619-422-0111.

CHULA VISTA LAUNCH RAMP: *W. end of Marina Way, off Marina Parkway, Chula Vista.*
A public boat launch ramp, operated by the Port of San Diego, has ample parking for boat trailers and a sanitary pumpout station. The launch ramp is open from 6:00 AM to 10:30 PM. Boaters should check navigational charts carefully; shoals abound. This ramp is some 12 miles distant from the ocean. Swimming, fishing, and water-skiing are popular in the area, although swimming and skiing are prohibited within the launch basin. Call: 619-686-6200. Landscaped Chula Vista Bayfront Park, adjacent to the launch ramp, has barbecue grills, children's play equipment, and restrooms.

GRAND CARIBE SHORELINE PARK: *End of Grand Caribe Causeway, off Coronado Cays Blvd., Coronado.* Turn east off Hwy. 75 opposite the entrance to Silver Strand State Beach, then bear right on Coronado Cays Blvd. and left on Grand Caribe Causeway. This small bayfront park maintained by the Port of San Diego has colorful native plants, a sculpture entitled "Sheltering Wings," and spacious views. Kayaks can be launched here. On-street parking; park hours are 6 AM to 10:30 PM. Non-waterfront Cays Park at the intersection of Coronado Cays Blvd. and Grand

Caribe Causeway has large lawns, picnic tables, tennis courts, and restrooms.

SILVER STRAND STATE BEACH: *5000 Hwy. 75, Coronado.* Silver Strand State Beach offers access to both ocean waves and quiet bay waters. The sandy ocean beach is noted for its tiny silver-toned seashells. Three pedestrian underpasses beneath Hwy. 75 provide easy access from the ocean side, where there is parking, to the bay side. The northern end of the gently curving beach has up to 1,000 parking spaces and is popular for swimming, surfing, clamming, surf fishing, and beachcombing. Prevailing breezes make Silver Strand a great spot for kiteboarding, which is limited to the southern part of the beach; surfing and swimming also have designated areas. Surf fishing for perch, corbina, and yellowfin croaker is popular; grunion are caught on the sand during the summer. Sheltered picnic areas are located on the beach, and fire rings are available in the summer. Up to 134 camping spaces are available in the northernmost ocean-side parking area for self-contained RVs only; no tent camping allowed. Restrooms and beach showers are for day-use visitors only. For camping reservations, call: 1-800-444-7275.

The lifeguard headquarters is in the middle of the beach, near the second underpass, and additional stations are staffed in sum-

Sweetwater Marsh, Chula Vista

San Diego Bay is a 17-square-mile harbor surrounded by the cities of San Diego, Coronado, National City, Chula Vista, and Imperial Beach. What is now California was discovered for Spain by Juan Rodríguez Cabrillo when he entered this harbor—which he found to be "closed and very good"—on September 28, 1542. Although a natural embayment, much of the bay's current shoreline contours are the result of filling mud flats with dredge spoils to create new developable land, including most of North Island, Shelter Island, Harbor Island, and Lindbergh Field, which is San Diego's international airport. U.S. Navy land makes up approximately one-third of the shoreline.

Historically used as a dump and sewage outfall, San Diego Bay has benefited from clean-up efforts that began in the 1960s and 1970s and have helped restore environmental diversity and productivity to the bay's ecosystems. Today, the bay is home to 280 species of marine and coastal birds, over 100 species of fish, and numerous marine invertebrates, algae, and plants, including the endangered California least tern and the Eastern Pacific green sea turtle. Bay habitats include salt marsh, tidal mud flats, and eelgrass beds.

The southern end of the bay is the site of the South Bay Power Plant, an electrical generation facility, and the South Bay Salt Works, which for over 100 years has produced solar-evaporated salt in artificially created ponds. The bay is also a popular recreational resource, used for sailing, motor boating, jet skiing, water-skiing, windsurfing, kayaking, and sport fishing.

mer. Both manually operated and motorized beach wheelchairs are available at the lifeguard station; shaded picnic areas and most restrooms are wheelchair accessible. Dogs are allowed only on a six-foot leash and not on the beach, in the underpasses, or on the bay side of the park. Fees for camping and day use. Park gates open at 8 AM; closing time varies seasonally from 7 PM to 9 PM. For park information, call: 619-435-5184.

The southern end of the state beach, over a mile long, is the undeveloped Silver Strand Natural Preserve. The coastal strand plant community found along the back beach includes sand verbena and saltbush. Gulls, terns, plovers, sandpipers, godwits, curlews, herons, grebes, and loons frequent the shallow water adjacent to the beach.

On the bay side of the park there are picnic areas, restrooms, and the three-quarter-mile-long paved Crown Cove Trail, bordering the quiet waters of the cove. The Crown Cove Aquatic Center, part of Southwestern College, offers lifeguard training and classes in water and boating skills to at-risk youth and school groups; for information, call: 619-575-6176. Crown Isle Marina, at the nearby Loews Coronado Bay Resort, 4000 Coronado Bay Rd., offers rental kayaks, sailboats, powerboats, bicycles, and more. Gondola tours of the bay are also available; for information, call: 619-424-4466.

Pepper Park, National City

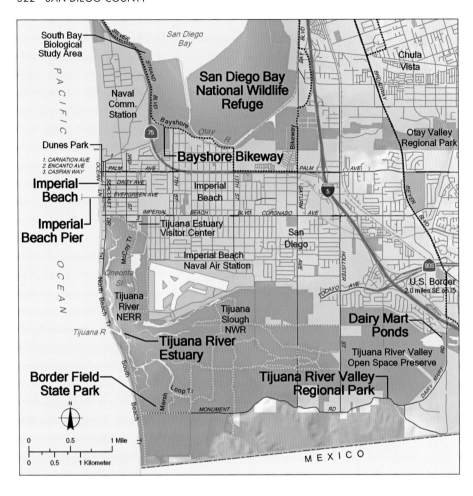

Imperial Beach and Pier

Imperial Beach to Mexico

	Sandy Beach	Rocky Shore	Trail	Visitor Center	Campground	Wildlife Viewing	Fishing or Boating	Facilities for Disabled	Food and Drink	Restrooms	Parking	Fee
San Diego Bay National Wildlife Refuge						•	•					
Bayshore Bikeway			•			•						
Imperial Beach	•					•	•		•	•	•	
Imperial Beach Pier						•	•		•	•	•	
Tijuana River Estuary		•	•	•		•		•		•	•	
Dairy Mart Ponds			•			•						
Tijuana River Valley Regional Park			•	•		•		•		•	•	
Border Field State Park	•		•			•				•	•	

SAN DIEGO BAY NATIONAL WILDLIFE REFUGE: *S. end of San Diego Bay.* The South Bay unit of the San Diego Bay National Wildlife Refuge includes wetlands, salt ponds, and a portion of the Otay River floodplain at the south end of San Diego Bay. Black skimmers, western snowy plovers, and California least terns nest in the salt ponds at the south end of the bay. The refuge also includes eelgrass beds and other open-water areas from Emory Cove north. Eelgrass is an important food source for birds such as black brant, gadwall, and northern pintail, and the warm, shallow waters with eelgrass beds serve as a nursery for juvenile fish. Fishing and boating are allowed in the open water area of the Wildlife Refuge, however public access to the salt ponds is not allowed.

Views of the wildlife refuge are available at a northbound pullout on Hwy. 75 north of Imperial Beach. The pullout is signed as the South Bay Biological Study Area, and it is equipped with parking, benches, and interpretive panels; bring binoculars or a spotting scope to look for shorebirds. Plans for additional public facilities include a wildlife-viewing boardwalk along the edge of the wildlife refuge from 7th St. to 13th St. in Imperial Beach. For information about the San Diego Bay National Wildlife Refuge, call: 619-575-2704.

BAYSHORE BIKEWAY: *Around San Diego Bay, from downtown San Diego to Imperial Beach.* The 26-mile-long Bayshore Bikeway circles San Diego Bay and passes near beaches and other area attractions. Much of the bikeway follows a route separate from city streets. One place to gain access to the trail is at the north end of 13th St. in Imperial Beach, where there is parking. Future improvements to the bikeway are planned, including a short-cut across the flats at the southeast end of San Diego Bay. For information, call the San Diego Association of Governments at 619-595-5324.

IMPERIAL BEACH: *W. of Ocean Ln., from Carnation Ave. to S. end of Seacoast Dr., Imperial Beach.* This wide, sandy beach is popular for swimming, body surfing, and surf fishing. Access to the beach is available along Seacoast Dr. at street ends from Palm Ave. to Encanto Ave. Restrooms with beach showers are located near the pier. A motorized beach wheelchair is available Friday through Sunday, from 10 AM to 2 PM, by 48-hour-advance reservation; for information, call: 619-685-7972. Imperial Beach lifeguards are on duty year-round; lifeguard towers are staffed during the summer. For beach information, call: 619-423-8328. For a recorded surf and tide report, call: 619-595-3954.

Three blocks north of the Imperial Beach Pier at Seacoast Dr. and Daisy Ave. is pleasant Dunes Park, with a sandy beach, volleyball area, picnic tables, a playground, and a striking sculpture of three dolphins riding a wave. A block south of the pier is Portwood Pier Plaza, which has ten colorful surfboard benches inscribed with vignettes of local surfing history, a playground, picnic tables, and an outdoor performance area. At the foot of the pier itself is *Surfhenge*, a public art piece by Malcolm Jones consisting of four giant, glowing surfboard-shaped arches, weighing three-quarters of a ton each and believed to be the largest colored acrylic moldings ever cast. Big-wave surfing has a long history in the Imperial Beach area, including at the spot known as the Slough, off the mouth of the Tijuana River.

IMPERIAL BEACH PIER: *End of Evergreen Ave., Imperial Beach.* The wooden Imperial Beach Municipal Pier, 1,853 feet long, marks the approximate center of the beach. Anglers fish from the pier for halibut, mackerel, and species of perch and croaker. Facilities on the pier include a restaurant, fish-cleaning area, and restrooms. A small parking lot is located a block north of the pier, at the end of Elm Ave.; additional parking is on the street.

TIJUANA RIVER ESTUARY: *W. of Hwy. I-5, between Imperial Beach and the International Border.* The Tijuana River is an ephemeral stream that originates in Mexico and flows north into the U.S., forming a huge, 2,500-acre wetland complex. Public beach accessways and trails north and south of the mouth of the estuary are separated by the river, and there is no bridge near the mouth. Unlike many southern California streams, the Tijuana River ordinarily remains open to the sea all year. Beaches and sand dunes, salt marshes, freshwater marshes, and riparian habitat are found in the lower channel of the river. The tidal channels of the river serve as a nursery for fish species that include California halibut, topsmelt, and northern anchovy. Crabs, clams, and mud worms are common invertebrates in the marsh.

The best place to start a visit is at the Tijuana Estuary Visitor Center at 301 Caspian Way, near the south end of 3rd St., in Imperial Beach. The visitor center contains exhibits about the resources of the estuary and adjoins a native plant garden that is ablaze in spring with bright yellow bush sunflowers and other flowering plants. Several foot trails start at the visitor center, some accommodating bicycles and leashed dogs; check signs for restrictions. Guided nature walks are available. The visitor center is open Wednesday through Sunday from 10 AM to 5 PM, and the trails are open daily from 10 AM to 5 PM. For information, call: 619-575-2704. The Tijuana River National Estuarine Research Reserve is a federal-state-local partnership that manages the estuary, provides educational programs to the public, and conducts research. For information, call: 619-575-3613.

The three-quarter-mile-long North Beach Trail, which provides views of the ocean and estuary, starts at the south end of Seacoast Dr., the southwestern-most residential

Surfhenge, a public art piece by Malcolm Jones

street in the continental US. The trail leads along a narrow sandbar between the ocean and Oneonta Slough to the mouth of the Tijuana River. The northern part of the Tijuana River Estuary is within the Tijuana Slough National Wildlife Refuge; all wildlife and plants are protected. The southern part of the Tijuana River Estuary, south of the Tijuana River mouth, lies within Border Field State Park. To reach the park, exit Hwy. I-5 at Dairy Mart Rd. and head west four miles on Monument Rd.

DAIRY MART PONDS: *S. of Hwy. I-5, both sides of Dairy Mart Rd., San Diego.* Hiking and equestrian trails around the freshwater ponds provide opportunities to view wildlife, particularly migratory birds. Dairy Mart Ponds are managed by San Diego County as part of the Tijuana River Valley Open Space Preserve. For information, call: 619-428-2946.

TIJUANA RIVER VALLEY REGIONAL PARK: *2721 Monument Rd., San Diego.* This relatively wild park includes miles of hiking and equestrian trails and is a good spot for birders. There is an equestrian staging area and community garden located at 2310 Hollister St., three-quarters of a mile north of Monument Rd.; equestrian trails lead to the ocean. Guided bird walks also start here. Maps and information, restrooms, and a picnic table

are available at park headquarters at 2721 Monument Rd.; call: 619-428-2946.

BORDER FIELD STATE PARK: *W. end of Monument Rd., San Diego.* Border Field State Park is the site of the International Boundary Markers that were established as a result of the Treaty of Guadalupe Hidalgo of February 2, 1848, officially ending war with Mexico. Horseback riding, hiking, and wildlife observation are popular activities in the state park. The park has a very remote and undeveloped appearance, although part of it is actually within the boundaries of the city of San Diego, and urban neighborhoods of Tijuana are located just across the border fence. Given Border Field State Park's low-lying location, access roads are often flooded. Check conditions before planning a visit; call: 619-575-3613.

From the end of Monument Rd., a hiking and equestrian trail leads to the beach, where a mile-and-a-half stretch of sand extends from the mouth of the Tijuana River to the International Border. Anglers catch perch, corbina, and halibut in the surf. Most trails are open to both hikers and equestrians, but the Marsh Loop Trail is for foot traffic only; dogs and bicycles are not allowed on trails in the state park. Visit the Tijuana River Estuary Visitor Center for trail maps and more information.

Tijuana Estuary Visitor Center

Protecting Coastal Resources

IN THE 21st CENTURY, the challenge of protecting California's coast is greater than ever. Some threats to coastal resources are of long standing, while others have come to be recognized only recently. On the positive side, California continues to be at the forefront of coastal research and innovation.

Invasive Species Threaten California's Native Habitats

California is characterized by a remarkable range of plant and animal habitats, supporting an enormous biodiversity of native organisms. The state is home to 830 species of native mammals, birds, freshwater fish, amphibians, and reptiles, and over 6,000 species of native plants. The continued survival of California's native ecosystems and species is threatened by the presence of certain non-native species. While many new non-native species arrive in California each year, only a small percentage of them end up flourishing and negatively affecting native species, thus earning the label "invasive." The effects of invasive plants on natives include competing for water, sunlight, and nutrients; interbreeding with native populations; and introducing disease. Moreover, invasive plants can cause physical or chemical changes to the invaded habitat. Without local competitors, predators, or diseases invasive plants can spread unchecked across a landscape, often resulting in an area being dominated by a single species. Similarly, native ecosystems are threatened by invasive animals preying on, or parasitizing, native animals.

Non-native species have been identified in habitats throughout California. The means of entry are myriad, including ships, trains, cars, and airplanes. Even individual tourists who travel abroad may inadvertently introduce organisms when they return. Some examples of the many invasive species challenging southern California are *Didemnum*, a fast-growing colonial tunicate; the encrusting bryozoan named *Watersipora subtorquata*; Argentine ants; yellow starthistle; pampas grass; giant reed; French broom; and Scottish broom.

An especially troublesome invasive species of algae, *Caulerpa taxifolia*, was discovered in June of 2000 at Agua Hedionda Lagoon in San Diego County. Caulerpa is native to the Indian Ocean and has been used commonly as ornamentation in aquaria. Release from public and home aquaria is believed to be the source of the invasion of Caulerpa into natural habitats.

The aquarium strain of Caulerpa is a speedy invader. It reproduces vegetatively and via fragmentation, meaning a broken-off piece can readily grow and take over a new area. Caulerpa produces a chemical that is toxic to fish and other would-be predators. Finally, it is what is called a "habitat-generalist," meaning it can become established in a variety of places, including rocky reefs, sand flats, and sea grass beds.

Caulerpa thrives in enclosed or semi-enclosed seas and bays. It achieved infamy in the Mediterranean Sea where native plants were replaced with huge carpets of Caulerpa. In 1999 the species was placed on the U.S. Federal Noxious Weed list. Because awareness of this potential invasive was high, a number of government and private groups were poised for action when Caulerpa was subsequently found in Agua Hedionda Lagoon in San Diego County. An interagency group known as the Southern California Caulerpa Action Team responded just 17 days after the invader was identified. The quick response led to successful containment. Treatment involved covering Caulerpa patches with sealed tents inoculated with herbicide to kill the algae and prevent re-

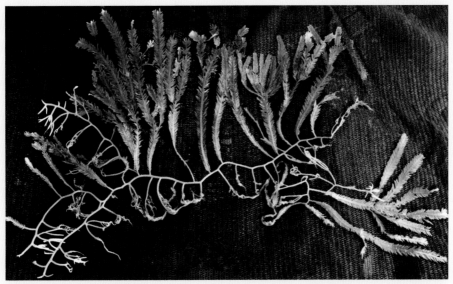

Caulerpa taxifolia, fronds and runners

growth. The lagoon continues to be monitored for Caulerpa outbreaks. Similar responses in Huntington Harbour and other bays and harbors in southern California have been successful at preventing the establishment of Caulerpa. However, continued vigilance and rapid response to new introductions of Caulerpa must continue in order to avoid the magnitude of infestation seen in the Mediterranean.

Marine Debris: An Enormous Threat to the World's Oceans

The quantity of debris in the world's oceans is steadily increasing. In some locations, studies show a ten-fold increase every few years. Most of this debris is made of plastic, and about 80 percent of it comes from land—the trash you see on the street that gets washed down storm drains to the ocean. The problem is growing because our reliance on disposable consumer goods is increasing. In 2001, each American used an average of 223 pounds of plastic, and by the end of the century's first decade, according to the plastics industry, we will use 326 pounds per capita.

Another reason the problem is growing is that plastic persists in the marine environment for centuries and may never fully biodegrade. The plastic just keeps accumulating. Scientists have designated two portions of the Pacific Ocean as the "Garbage Patches" due to the high concentration of debris. These are large areas—the Eastern Garbage Patch is estimated to be twice the size of Texas. Debris accumulates there due to ocean currents. Debris studies in these areas have found that floating plastic fragments outweigh surface zooplankton, on which many marine organisms feed, by a factor of six. Off the coast of Los Angeles and Orange Counties, studies have found eight million plastic fragments per square kilometer.

When exposed to sunlight, plastic photodegrades, meaning it breaks into smaller pieces. These pieces, as well as plastic resin pellets (the feedstock used in the plastics manufacturing process) and small consumer items, such as bottle caps, are ingested by marine mammals, fish, seabirds, and turtles, which often mistake the plastic bits for food. Large items are also ingested by animals. Plastic bags and balloons floating

Ocean-feeding seabirds mistake plastic marine debris for food. This Laysan albatross chick's stomachful of plastic most likely caused or contributed to its death.

in the ocean, for instance, resemble the jellyfish that are food for some animals. Plastic ingestion can have deadly consequences for wildlife, by creating a false sense of being full, so that the animal stops eating, or by blocking the intestines or causing suffocation. Large seabirds, such as albatross, that feed by skimming the surface of the open ocean ingest debris items such as bottle caps, cigarette lighters, and party balloons, which they then feed to their young. One study of Laysan albatross chick carcasses found that 90 percent contained plastic.

Marine animals can also be harmed by becoming entangled in debris, which can lead to infection, suffocation, reduction of feeding efficiency, and drowning. Researchers have estimated that more than 100,000 marine mammals and sea turtles die in the North Pacific each year due to entanglement in plastic nets and fishing lines.

Plastic in the sea can serve as a sponge for oily toxic chemicals that do not easily dissolve in water (such as DDT, DDE, and PCBs). Studies in Japan found that plastic pellets absorbed and concentrated these hormone-disrupting chemicals, so that the pellets contained one million times the level of chemicals found in surrounding seawater. The chemical components of plastic itself are another potential source of toxins for the animals that ingest plastic and for others in the food chain, including humans. For more information, visit www.plasticdebris.org.

The problem of invasive species in marine waters is made worse by marine debris. A wide range of species, including barnacles, polycheate worms, and mollusks, attach to ocean debris, which serves as a "raft" for the organism. Species transported by drifting debris move slowly on ocean currents, giving them time to acclimate themselves to new environments. As on land, the introduction of an invasive, alien species into the marine environment can be devastating for the ecosystem, because the invaders compete with and can crowd out the native species.

Combating the problem of marine debris, like that of climate change and invasive species, is going to require change on the part of individuals, as well as institutions and society as a whole. There is no easy fix. We must reduce our reliance on disposable products in general and plastic disposables in particular, reduce fossil fuel use and seek alternative sources, and, in general, take proper care of our ocean and coast.

Southern California's Scripps Institution of Oceanography

The more we learn about the coastal environment, it seems, the more there is to know. To effectively meet challenges facing the coast and ocean requires understanding the problems and their potential solutions. Scripps Institution of Oceanography at the University of California at San Diego, commonly called "Scripps" is one of the world's oldest, largest, and most important centers for global science research and graduate student training. Since its founding in 1903, the institution has grown in scientific scope from a focus on the ocean to a broad agenda that includes the earth's biological, physical, chemical, geological, geophysical, and atmospheric characteristics. Hundreds of research programs, covering a wide range of scientific interest areas, are under way in 65 countries. The institution has a staff of some 1,300 persons and annual expenditures of approximately $140 million from federal, state, and private sources. Scripps Institution operates a fleet of vessels, including a research platform and four oceanographic research ships for exploration worldwide.

One research program carried out by Scripps is the Southern California Coastal Ocean Observing System (SCCOOS), which is an observational network that records data on a range of physical processes in the ocean off the southern California coast. Ocean surface currents are mapped using high-frequency radar, meteorological readings are taken from a network of stations along the coast, and records of ocean temperature, salinity, and other characteristics are collected.

Scripps Institution graduate student conducting research on Scripps Beach

The Coastal Data Information Program (CDIP), in existence since 1976, includes the collection and analysis of wave data. CDIP operates a network of wave-measuring sites along the entire West Coast of the US, in Hawaii, and at a station at Kings Bay in Georgia. Wave information is updated hourly and supplied in real time to National Weather Service computers and to the public over the Internet (see: www.cdip.ucsd.edu). In addition, forecasts of the waves are provided up to three days in advance, helping to predict storm intensity and landfall.

In 2005, scientists at Scripps and their colleagues at Lawrence Livermore National Laboratory's Program for Climate Model Diagnosis and Intercomparison produced the first clear evidence of human-caused warming in the world's oceans. Using a combination of computer models and real-world data, they captured signals of the penetration of greenhouse gas-influenced warming in the oceans, concluding that ocean warming is produced anthropogenically (that is, by human activities).

Climate Change and Rising Seas

A rise in the level of the sea is one of the most direct consequences of global warming. Over thousands of years, the changing level of the sea has been a major factor, along with seismic events, in altering the shape of the California coast. In the future, as the global climate changes, rising sea levels will inundate more areas of the coast, potentially reducing the size of beaches, flooding wetlands, and altering the areas subject to tidal action.

While many of the consequences of climate change can be anticipated, a particular challenge lies in predicting how large those consequences may be and when they might occur. Global trends in sea level mimic trends in global temperature, and a key input for temperature change is the emission of greenhouse gases. A significant source of greenhouse gases is energy use. Future sea level, therefore, is closely related to future global energy use. By the end of the 21st century, sea level rise might vary by almost a factor of four between a future that relies strongly upon fossil fuels and an alternative future that reflects aggressive efforts to reduce fossil fuel use. Planning for the consequences of rising sea level is complicated by the need to anticipate future energy demand and thus what magnitude of sea level rise is most appropriate to use for current and future coastal planning efforts. The consensus of scientists is that sea level is likely to rise be-

Beacon's Beach, Leucadia

Destructive waves at Cardiff State Beach, 1998

tween one and three feet by the year 2100, although some researchers have concluded that a major meltdown of the Greenland ice sheet could cause a much greater rise, of as much as 20 feet.

Rising sea level will move waves and water closer to existing structures. Seawalls and revetments that might protect such structures could also block public access to the beach. An effective method of protecting a coastal development without the need for "shoreline armoring" is the use of an adequate building setback between the new structure and the water's edge. Another method is constructing the building above the level of the sea. Utilizing setbacks and elevating a structure are also good ways to protect new structures located in floodplains. If fixed development setbacks are not adequate to protect structures and shoreline access, then new planning tools might be needed. Dynamic, or "rolling," setbacks or buffers could enable development to adapt to changing sea level without subsequent loss of public access.

Not only structures, but also wetlands and their resources can be protected through use of building setbacks. A setback between a wetland and a new structure can allow for some inland migration, over time, of a wetland. But, in order to be effective, establishing an appropriate coastal setback, building elevation, or wetland buffer requires information on the magnitude of future sea level rise. Beaches, wetlands, and buildings can be protected from sea level rise by using existing management tools, but using those tools depends upon predictions about California's future shoreline.

The future may be uncertain, but many governments, communities, and individuals are taking steps to reduce greenhouse gases and thus avoid or slow a rise in sea level. At the federal level, the Environmental Protection Agency has increased fuel efficiency standards, while in California, the state law known as AB 32 sets forth an aggressive program to reduce greenhouse gas emissions in the state. The multitude of steps being taken to mitigate the future consequences of global warming are positive and could help to avoid some of the worst future scenarios of global warming. At the same time that these productive efforts are being made, coastal planners who make coastal management decisions would do well to anticipate the largest possible sea level rise and develop adaptive management tools to address this rise. Relying on conservative decision-making, or the "precautionary principle," would help ensure that coastal development will not be adversely impacted by future coastal hazards.

The California Coastal Trail is planned as a continuous public right-of-way along the 1,100-mile-long California coastline, from Oregon to Mexico. The trail route is located as close to the shoreline as possible, and it is intended to accommodate various uses, as allowed by local terrain and applicable rules. Paved, urban trail segments accommodate walkers, bicyclists, skaters, and wheelchair users. Rural or sandy beach segments accommodate hikers and equestrians. An important objective of the Coastal Trail project is to provide a route entirely separate from coastal roads such as Pacific Coast Highway. Because of steep topography and limited public right-of-way in some locations, however, for the foreseeable future parts of the trail may require that users share the alignment with vehicles.

Work continues on completing links in the California Coastal Trail, more than half of which is now available for use.

The State Coastal Conservancy, the California Department of Parks and Recreation, the California Department of Transportation, and local governments are working together to make the trail a continuous one, connecting communities, beaches, parks, schools, trailheads, bus stops, visitor attractions, and campgrounds along California's magnificent coastline. For more information on the Coastal Trail, including maps for hikers and other trail users, see the California Coastal Commission's webpage at www.coastal.ca.gov and follow the link to the Coastal Access Program.

Trails mapped in this book, including segments of the California Coastal Trail, are approximate and are not intended to indicate legally established property boundaries. Use caution on trails along bluffs, railroads, and busy thoroughfares, and use good judgment where private property abuts a trail. Above all, enjoy your visit to California's coast.

Afterword

Wave   © Tom Killion

In preparing this guide, we visited and researched all beaches, parks, and coastal accessways that are described here. We have incorporated comments and corrections supplied by various agencies and members of the public, who wrote to us regarding the information in previous California Coastal Commission publications. We also sought review of draft material by staff of parks departments, local governments, land trusts, and others. The book is accurate, to the best of our knowledge. Nevertheless, conditions on the coast are constantly changing, and there may be inaccuracies in this book. If you think something is incorrect or has been omitted, please let us know. The Coastal Commission intends to continue publishing revised guides in the future and would appreciate any additional information you can provide. Please remember, however, that this book includes only those beaches and accessways that are managed for public use.

Address all comments to:

Coastal Access Program
California Coastal Commission
45 Fremont Street, Suite 2000
San Francisco, CA 94105

or e-mail to: coast4U@coastal.ca.gov.

Acknowledgments

Preparation of this book was made possible with funding provided to the California Coastal Commission from the Coastal Impact Assistance Program, a grant program for coastal states and political subdivisions which are impacted by oil and gas activities on the Outer Continental Shelf. The funding was administered by the National Oceanic and Atmospheric Administration (NOAA), through the California Resources Agency.

Additional writing and research:

Tracy Duffey

Ben Hansch

Christy Norris

Technical assistance:

Doug Macmillan

Darryl Rance

Principal Contributors, *California Coastal Access Guide* and *California Coastal Resource Guide*, from which selected material has been incorporated in this book:

Trevor Kenner Cralle

Linda Goff Evans

Stephen J. Furney-Howe

Jo Ginsberg

Christopher Kroll

Trish Mihalek

Don Neuwirth

S. Briggs Nisbet

Victoria Randlett

Sabrina S. Simpson

Pat Stebbins

Mary Travis

Jeffrey D. Zimmerman

Our sincere thanks to the following individuals and organizations for their invaluable assistance and support:

Jack Ainsworth

California Resources Agency

Gary Cannon

Barbara Carey

Deanna Christensen

Laura Davick

Gregory Dean

Scott Dennis

Barbara Dye

Karren Elsbernd

Pam Emerson

Denise Estrada

Liz Fuchs

Stephanie George

Rasa Gustaitis

Adrienne Harrison

Teresa Henry

Steve Hudson

Susan Jordan

Tom Killion

Paul Lawrence

Deborah Lee

Joan Lentz

Bonnie Lewkowicz

Karen McClune

Lee McEachern

Rob McGowan

Anne McMahon

Darlene E. Nicandro

National Oceanic and Atmospheric Administration

Office of Ocean and Coastal Resource Management

Orange County Coastkeeper

Al Padilla

Jim Peugh

Chris Potter

Leslie Ray

Redondo Beach Historical Commission

Bob Rhein

Liliana Roman

Toni Ross

Rebecca Roth

Sherilyn Sarb

Karl Schwing

Larry Simon

Gail Skidmore

Joel Smith

Becky Smythe

State Coastal Conservancy

Fernie Sy

Charles Taylor

Gary Timm

Victoria Touchstone

Amber Tysor

Meg Vaughn

Pat Veesart

Marsha Venegas

Arthur Verge

Robert Veria

Kai Weisser

Greg Woodell

Matt Yurko

Photo and Illustration Credits

© 2002–2009 Kenneth & Gabrielle Adelman, California Coastal Records Project, www.Californiacoastline.org, 58, 118, 218, 219, 226, 227, 249

© AP Images, 68

© AP Images/Chris Carlson, 191

© AP Images/Ben Margot, 143b

© AP Images/ Dan Steinberg, 59

© Peter Batson/Image Quest Marine, 33c

© Hal Beral, 93b, 152, 159a

© Andrew Borcher, 251b

Margo Bors, 54b

Cheryl Brehme, 183a

© Melody Bridge-McLane, 149

John Brew, 142b

© Peter Bryant, D. Phil., 92a, 159b, 194c, 195a

Steve Byland, 143a

California Historical Society Collection at the Univ. of Southern California, Los Angeles Area Chamber of Commerce Collection, 48, 76

California Historical Society Collection at the Univ. of Southern California, Title Insurance and Trust/C.C. Pierce Photography Collection, 63a

Mark Chappell, Ph.D., 287a

© Christopher Christie, 287b

© Phillip Colla, 183b, 183c, 229a

© Phillip Colla/SeaPics.com, 55b, 284b, 286c, 299, 300c, 301b, 301c

© Brandon Cole, 194a, 194b

© Mark Conlin/SeaPics.com, 32c, 33b, 298, 300b

Jenifer Dugan, 92b

© Steve Elgar, 221

Lesley Ewing, 25, 245, 330, 331

© William Flaxington, 55c

Erik Funk, 182a

© Mark Goodkin, 234, 235a

© Daniel Gotshall, 284c

Allen Greenwood, 216

© Tom Griffithe, 150

© Richard Herrmann, 14, 141, 182c

© Richard Herrmann/Southern California Edison, 254, 255

Hotel Del Coronado, 317

Mark Johnsson, Ph.D., 209, 210, 217

Wayne Johnson, 182b

© Tom Killion, 10, 42, 333

Bill Kloetzer, 235b

© Neal Kramer, 285c

© Peter LaTourrette, 55a, 93a, 93c, 144a, 228b

© Deborah Leonard, 251a

Ron LeValley, 144b

Steve Matson, 285a

Vanessa Metz, 328

Vanessa Metz/North Coast Stormwater Coalition, 77, 78

Thomas H. Mikkelsen, front cover, 66, 69, 70, 71, 72, 75a, 75b, 120, 122, 123, 220, 224, 225a, 233a, 233b, 239, 247, 250, 258, 262, 263b, 266, 270a, 271, 290, 296a, 296b, 302, 305, 310, 311, 322, 324, 325

© Jeff Mondragon, 300a

© Randy Morse/SeaPics.com, 32b

National Oceanic and Atmospheric Admin., 297

© Gregory Ochocki/SeaPics.com, 285b

© Steven Perkins, 284a

© Doug Perrine/SeaPics.com, 228c

© Todd Pusser/SeaPics.com, 32a, 33a

Redondo Beach Historical Commission, 64

Dan Richards/Channel Islands National Marine Sanctuary, 297

San Diego County Fair, 259

Cristina Sandoval, Ph.D., 286b

Dan Scanderbeg, 287c

© Kevin Schafer/SeaPics.com, 229b

Steve Scholl, 15, 16a, 19, 22, 23, 24, 26, 27, 29, 30, 34, 35, 36, 37, 38, 40, 41, 44, 45, 46, 47, 49, 51a, 51b, 52, 54a, 54c, 56, 57, 62, 63b, 65, 67, 74, 82, 83, 84, 85, 86, 88, 89, 90, 94, 95, 96, 99, 100, 101, 102, 104, 105, 106, 107, 108, 109, 112, 113, 114, 115, 117, 125, 126, 128, 129, 130, 131, 132, 134, 135, 136, 138, 139, 142a, 145, 148, 151, 153, 154, 156, 158a, 158b, 158c, 160, 162, 163, 164, 166, 167, 168, 170, 171, 172, 173, 174, 176, 179, 180, 184, 186, 187, 188, 190, 197, 198, 199, 200, 202, 203, 204, 206, 207, 211, 214, 222, 228a, 231, 232, 237, 238, 240, 241, 242, 243, 248, 256, 263a, 264, 268, 272, 274, 275, 276, 279a, 279b, 280, 282, 286a, 288, 291, 294, 295, 304, 306, 308, 313, 314, 316, 320, 321

© Anne Schwing, 13

© Karl Schwing, 16b, 178

© John G. Shedd Aquarium/Brenna/SeaPics.com, 301a

© Abigail Smigel/Southern California Edison, 252, 253

© Carol Ann Stanley, 192

© Julianne E. Steers, 92c

© Nick Steers, 270b

Evie Templeton/Cabrillo Marine Aquarium, 103

Tara Lee Torburn, 225b

Marc Tule, 329

Washington State Water Quality Consortium, 79

Rachel Woodfield/Merkel and Associates, 327

Alison Young, 195b, 195c

Glossary

anadromous. Migrating from salt water to fresh water in order to reproduce.

annual. A plant that germinates, flowers, sets seed, and dies within one year or less.

basalt. A dark igneous rock of volcanic origin. Basalt is the bedrock of most of the world ocean.

bay. A partially enclosed inlet of the ocean.

beach. The shore of a body of water, usually covered by sand or pebbles.

bluff. A high bank or bold headland with a broad, precipitous, sometimes rounded cliff face overlooking a plain or a body of water.

brackish. Used to describe water that contains some salt, but less than sea water (from 0.5 to 30 parts per thousand).

coastal scrub. A plant association characterized by low, drought-resistant, woody shrubs; includes coastal sage scrub.

coastal strand community. A plant association endemic to bluffs, dunes, and sandy beaches, and adapted to saline conditions; includes coast goldenbush and sand verbena.

coastal terrace. A flat plain edging the ocean; uplifted sea floor that was cut and eroded by wave action. Synonymous with marine terrace.

cobble. A rock fragment larger than a pebble and smaller than a boulder, having a diameter in the range of 2.5 to 10 inches and being somewhat rounded or otherwise modified by abrasion in the course of transport.

conifer. A cone-bearing tree of the pine family, usually evergreen.

continental borderland. An area of the continental margin located between the shoreline and the continental slope that is topographically more complex than the continental shelf.

continental shelf. The shallow, gradually sloping area of the sea floor adjacent to the shoreline, terminating seaward at the continental slope.

crustaceans. A group of mostly marine arthropods; e.g., barnacles, shrimp, and crabs.

current. Local or large-scale water movements that result in the flow of water in a particular direction, e.g., alongshore, or offshore.

delta. A fan-shaped alluvial deposit at the mouth of a river.

dorsal. Pertaining to the upper surface or the back of an organism. A dorsal fin is a vertical fin arising from the back of a fish or cetacean (whales, dolphins, and porpoises). *Compare* ventral.

El Niño. A warming of the ocean current along the coasts of Peru and Ecuador that is generally associated with dramatic changes in the weather patterns around the world.

endangered. Refers specifically to those species designated by the California Dept. of Fish and Game or the U.S. Fish and Wildlife Service as "endangered" because of severe population declines.

endemic. A plant or animal native to a well-defined geographic area and restricted to that area.

erosion. The gradual breakdown of land by weathering, solution, corrosion, abrasion, or transportation, caused by action of the wind, water, or ice; opposite of accretion.

estivate. To pass the summer in a state of dormancy.

estuary. A semi-enclosed coastal body of water that is connected with the open ocean and within which seawater mixes with freshwater from a river or stream.

exotic. Any species, especially a plant, not native to the area where it occurs; introduced.

fault. A fracture or fracture zone along which displacement of the earth occurs resulting from seismic activity.

groin. A low, narrow jetty, constructed at right angles to the shoreline, that projects out into the water to trap sand or to retard shoreline erosion; a shoreline protective device.

habitat. The sum total of all the living and nonliving factors that surround and potentially influence an organism; a particular organism's environment.

halophyte. A plant that is adapted to grow in salty soils.

haul-out. A place where pinnipeds emerge from the water onto land to rest or breed.

herb. Botanically, a plant that lacks a woody stem and whose above-ground parts last only a growing season. Medicinal and culinary herbs include plants of many growth forms, including shrubs and trees, whereas most botanical herbs are never found in the kitchen or in the pharmacy.

igneous rock. A rock that solidified from molten or partially molten material.

intertidal. Pertaining to the shoreline area between the highest high tide mark and the lowest low tide mark.

intrusion. In geology, the process of emplacement of molten rock in pre-existing rock.

invasive species. Weedy, generally non-native plants or wildlife species that invade and/or proliferate following disturbance or continued overuse.

invertebrate. An animal with no backbone or spinal column; 95 percent of the species in the animal kingdom are invertebrates.

jetty. An engineered structure constructed at right angles to the coast at the mouth of a river or harbor to help stabilize the entrance; usually constructed in pairs on each side of a channel.

krill. Any of numerous species of shrimp-like crustaceans. Krill occur in all the world's oceans, but are particularly abundant in polar waters where they form enormous swarms that are a critical food source for many large animals, including many whales.

La Niña. A periodic cooling of surface ocean waters in the eastern tropical Pacific along with a shift in convection in the western Pacific, affecting weather patterns around the world.

lagoon. A body of fresh or brackish water separated from the sea by a sandbar or reef.

longshore current. A current flowing parallel to and near shore that is the result of waves hitting the beach at an oblique angle.

magma. Naturally occurring molten or partially molten rock material, generated within the Earth and capable of intrusion and extrusion, from which igneous rocks are derived through solidification and related processes.

marsh. General term for a semi-aquatic area with relatively still, shallow water, such as the shore of a pond, lake, or protected bay or estuary, and characterized by mineral soils that support herbaceous vegetation.

metamorphic rock. A rock formed by changes in the mineralogical, chemical, and structural character of a pre-existing rock resulting from changes in physical and chemical conditions imposed at depth, generally through burial.

mollusks. Soft-bodied, generally shelled invertebrates; for example, chitons, snails, limpets, bivalves, and squid.

Monterey Formation. A group of sedimentary rocks consisting of cherts, siltstones, sandstones, and shales deposited during the Miocene Epoch and exposed extensively in coastal California.

nearshore. The area extending seaward an indefinite distance from the shoreline, well beyond the breaker zone.

pectoral. Pertaining to the front side of an organism toward the head (the chest in humans). The pectoral fins are the paired fins on the lower front of fishes and correspond to the forelimbs of four-legged vertebrates.

pelagic. Pertaining to open ocean rather than inland waters or waters adjacent to land.

perennial. A plant that lives longer than a year.

pinnipeds. Marine mammals that have fin-like flippers, including seals, sea lions, and walruses.

plankton. Free-floating algae (phytoplankton) or animals (zooplankton) that drift in the water, ranging from microscopic organisms to larger species such as jellyfish.

water, ranging from microscopic organisms to larger species such as jellyfish.

predator. An animal that eats other animals; a carnivore.

raptors. Birds of prey, such as falcons, eagles, and owls.

reef. A submerged ridge of rock or coral near the surface of the water.

relict. In ecology, a genus or species from a previous era that has survived radical environmental changes resulting from climatic shifts.

revetment. A sloped retaining wall built of riprap or concrete blocks to prevent coastal erosion and other damage by wave action; similar to a seawall.

rip current. A narrow, swift-flowing current that flows seaward through the breaker zone at nearly right angles to the shoreline and returns water to the sea after being piled up on the shore by waves and wind.

riparian. Pertaining to the habitat along the bank of a stream, river, pond, or lake.

riprap. Boulders or quarry stone used to construct a groin, jetty, or revetment.

schist. Medium- to coarse-grained metamorphic rocks composed of laminated, often flaky, parallel layers of chiefly micaceous minerals.

seawall. A structure, usually a vertical wood or concrete wall, designed to prevent erosion inland or damage due to wave action.

sedimentary rock. Rocks resulting from the consolidation of loose sediment.

shale. A fine-grained sedimentary rock formed by the consolidation of clay, silt, or mud.

slough. A small marshland or tidal waterway that usually connects with other tidal areas.

species. A taxonomic classification ranking below a genus, and consisting of a group of closely related organisms that are capable of interbreeding and producing viable offspring.

subduction zone. A long narrow belt in which one lithospheric plate descends beneath another.

substrate. The surface on which an organism grows or is attached.

surf zone. The area affected by wave action, from the shoreline high-water mark seaward to where the waves start to break.

take. As defined by the Endangered Species Act, "to harass, harm, pursue, hunt, shoot, wound, kill, capture, or collect, or attempt to engage in any such conduct."

tectonic. Pertaining to the forces involved in the regional assembling of structural or deformational features of the Earth.

terrestrial. Living or growing on land, as opposed to living in water or air.

threatened. Refers specifically to those species designated by the California Dept. of Fish and Game or the U.S. Fish and Wildlife Service as "threatened" because of severe population declines.

tidal wave. The regular rise and fall of the tides; often misused for tsunami.

tide. The periodic rising and falling of the ocean resulting from the gravitational forces of the moon and sun acting upon the rotating earth.

tidepool. Habitat in the rocky intertidal zone that retains some water at low tide.

tsunami. A sometimes destructive ocean wave caused by an underwater earthquake, submarine landslide, or volcanic eruption; inaccurately called a tidal wave.

uplifted. Pertaining to a segment of the earth's surface that has been elevated relative to the surrounding surface as a result of tectonic activity.

upwelling. A process by which deep, cold, nutrient-rich waters rise to the sea surface.

ventral. Pertaining to the lower surface, front, or belly of an organism. *Compare* dorsal.

waterfowl. Ducks, geese, and swans.

wetland. General term referring to shallow water (less than six feet deep) and land that is tidally or seasonally inundated, including marshes, mudflats, lagoons, sloughs, bogs, swamps, and fens.

Selected State and Federal Agencies

California State Agencies:

California Coastal Commission
89 South California St., Suite 200
Ventura, CA 93001
805-585-1800

California Coastal Commission
200 Oceangate, 10th floor
Long Beach, CA 90802
562-590-5084

California Coastal Commission
7575 Metropolitan Dr., Suite 103
San Diego, CA 92108
619-767-2370

California Department of Fish and Game
Marine Region Main Office
20 Lower Ragsdale Dr., Suite 100
Monterey, CA 93940
831-649-2870

California Department of Fish and Game
Marine Region Field Office
4665 Lampson Ave., Suite C
Los Alamitos, CA 90720
562-342-7100

California Department of Fish and Game
Marine Region Field Office
8604 La Jolla Shores Dr.
La Jolla, CA 92037
858-546-7170

California Department of Fish and Game
Marine Region Field Office
4949 Viewridge Ave.
San Diego, CA 92123
858-467-4201

California Department of Parks and Recreation
1416 Ninth St.
Sacramento, CA 95814
1-800-777-0369
info@parks.ca.gov

State Coastal Conservancy
1330 Broadway, Suite 1100
Oakland, CA 94612
510-286-1015

California State Lands Commission
100 Howe Ave., Suite 100 South
Sacramento, CA 95825
916-574-1900

Federal Agencies:

Channel Islands National Marine Sanctuary
3600 South Harbor Blvd., Suite 111
Oxnard, CA 93935
805-382-6149

Santa Monica Mountains National
Recreation Area
401 West Hillcrest Dr.
Thousand Oaks, CA 91360
805-370-2301

U.S. Fish and Wildlife Service
2800 Cottage Way
Sacramento, CA 95825
916-414-6464

Tijuana River National Estuarine
Research Reserve
(Cooperative state-federal project)
301 Caspian Way
Imperial Beach, CA 91932
619-575-3613

Bibliography

Albert, Ken. *Fishing in Southern California: The Complete Guide*. Huntington Beach, CA: Marketscope, 2003.

Banks, Homer. *The Story of San Clemente: the Spanish Village*. San Clemente: publisher unknown, 1930.

California Coastal Commission. *California Coastal Access Guide*. 6th ed. Berkeley: University of California Press, 2003.

_____. *California Coastal Resource Guide*. Berkeley: University of California Press, 1987.

Crump, Spencer. *Ride the Big Red Cars: How the Trolleys Helped Build Southern California*. Corona del Mar, CA: Trans-Anglo Books, 1970.

Dana, Richard Henry, with introduction by Gary Kinder and notes by Duncan Hasell. *Two Years before the Mast: a Personal Narrative of Life at Sea*. New York: Modern Library, 2001.

Dye, Barbara, and Mary Ellen Richardson. *Best Hikes on the Palos Verdes Peninsula: A Palos Verdes Peninsula Land Conservancy Guide*. Ashland, OR: Bookmasters, Inc., 2007.

Flamming, Douglas. *Bound for Freedom: Black Los Angeles in Jim Crow America*. Berkeley: University of California Press, 2005.

Goodson, Gar. *Fishes of the Pacific Coast*. Stanford, CA: Stanford University Press, 1988.

Griggs, Gary, Kiki Patsch, and Lauret Savoy. *Living with the Changing California Coast*. Berkeley: University of California Press, 2005.

Hoover, Mildred Brooke, Hero Eugene Rensch, and Ethel Grace Rensch. *Historic Spots in California*. 3rd ed. Stanford, CA: Stanford University Press, 1966.

Kampion, Drew, ed. *The Stormrider Guide: North America*. Bude, Cornwall, UK: Low Pressure Ltd., 2002.

Kuhn, Gerald G., and Francis P. Shepard. *Sea Cliffs, Beaches, and Coastal Valleys of San Diego County: Some Amazing Histories and Some Horrifying Implications*. Berkeley: University of California Press, 1984.

Linder, Bruce. *San Diego's Navy: An Illustrated History*. Annapolis: Naval Institute Press, 2001.

MacPhail, Elizabeth C. *Kate Sessions: Pioneer Horticulturalist*. San Diego: San Diego Historical Society, 1976.

Morris, William, ed. *The American Heritage Dictionary of the English Language*. Boston: Houghton Mifflin Co., 1976.

Munz, Philip A. *Introduction to Shore Wildflowers of California, Oregon, and Washington*. Berkeley: University of California Press, 2003.

Robinson, Ray. *American Original: A Life of Will Rogers*. New York: Oxford Univ. Press, 1996.

Starr, Kevin. *The Dream Endures: California Enters the 1940s*. New York: Oxford University Press, 1997.

Stuart, John D., and John O. Sawyer. *Trees and Shrubs of California*. Berkeley: University of California Press, 2001.

U. S. Army Corps of Engineers. *Report of the District Engineer on Cooperative Beach Erosion Investigation, Malibu-Santa Monica Area, California. Feasibility Study of Proposed Marine Locations for State Highway Route 60 and their Shoreline Effects*. Prepared for California Dept. of Water Resources and California Dept. of Public Works, Division of Highways. Los Angeles District, U. S. Army Corps of Engineers: Los Angeles, 1963.

Verge, Arthur C. *Los Angeles County Lifeguards*. San Francisco: Arcadia Publishing, 2005.

Suggestions for Further Reading

Bascom, Willard. *Waves and Beaches: the Dynamics of the Ocean Surface*. Garden City, NY: Anchor Press, 1980.

California Coast & Ocean, a quarterly magazine covering trends, issues, and controversies shaping the California coast; see www.coastandocean.org.

Cox, Lynne. *Grayson*. New York: Alfred A. Knopf, 2006.

Cralle, Trevor. *Surfin'ary: A Dictionary of Surfing Terms and Surfspeak*. Rev. ed. Berkeley: Ten Speed Press, 2001.

Deverell, William, and Greg Hise, ed. *Land of Sunshine: An Environmental History of Metropolitan Los Angeles*. Pittsburgh, PA: University of Pittsburgh Press, 2005.

Gale, Robert L. *Richard Henry Dana, Jr.* New York: Twayne Publishers, Inc., 1969.

Harding, D. R. *California Geology*. Upper Saddle River, NJ: Prentice Hall, 1998.

Jones, Ken. *Pier Fishing in California: The Complete Coast and Bay Guide*. 2nd ed. Roseville, CA: Publishers Design Group, 2004.

Lentz, Joan. *Introduction to Birds of the Southern California Coast*. Berkeley: University of California Press, 2005.

Lemm, Jeff. *Field Guide to Amphibians and Reptiles of the San Diego Region*. Berkeley: University of California Press, 2006.

McPeak, Ronald H., Dale A. Glantz, and Carole Shaw. *The Amber Forest: Beauty and Biology of California's Submarine Forests*. San Diego: Watersport Publications, 1988.

Mondragon, Jennifer, and Jeff Mondragon. *Seaweeds of the Pacific Coast: Common Marine Algae from Alaska to Baja California*. Monterey, CA: Sea Challengers, 2003.

Ricketts, Edward F., Jack Calvin, and Joel Hedgpeth. *Between Pacific Tides*. Rev. ed. Stanford, CA: Stanford University Press, 1992.

Schoenherr, Allan A., C. Robert Feldmeth, and Michael J. Emerson. *Natural History of the Islands of California*. Berkeley: University of California Press, 1999.

Sharp, R. P., and A. F. Glazner. *Geology Underfoot in Southern California*. Missoula, MT: Mountain Press, 1993.

Yeats, R.S. *Living with Earthquakes in California: A Survivor's Guide*. Corvallis, OR: Oregon University Press, 2001.

Index

Bold numeral indicates photograph.

EXPERIENCE THE CALIFORNIA COAST

These guides are the authoritative resource for exploring our magnificent coastline. Each lavishly illustrated volume prepared by the California Coastal Commission describes all publicly accessible beaches and accessways, along with sites of geological and historical interest. Topographical maps show beach access routes, hiking trails, and major bicycle routes. Easy-to-use charts list key facilities and amenities for all sites.

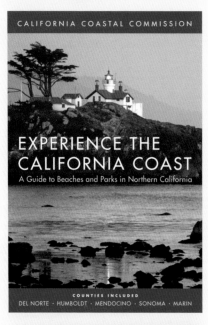

- Humboldt County's Lost Coast, Mendocino, Bodega Bay

- Redwood National Park, Sonoma State Beach, Point Reyes National Seashore

- Shipwrecks, the San Andreas Fault, waves and tides, and more

320 pp., 51 maps, published 2005, ISBN 978-0-520-24540-2

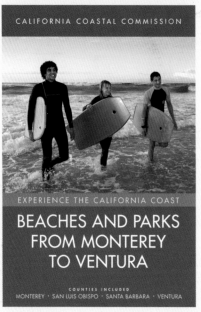

- Monterey Bay Aquarium, Big Sur, Hearst Castle, Santa Barbara

- Point Lobos State Reserve, Channel Islands National Park, Point Mugu State Park

- Northern elephant seals, Guadalupe-Nipomo Dunes, ocean currents and sand transport, and more

320 pp., 46 maps, published 2007, ISBN 978-0-520-24949-3

Also from **UNIVERSITY OF CALIFORNIA PRESS**